Rabinal Achi

MESOAMERICAN WORLDS

FROM THE OLMECS TO THE DANZANTES

GENERAL EDITORS: DAVÍD CARRASCO AND EDUARDO MATOS MOCTEZUMA

After Monte Albán: Transformation and Negotiation in Oaxaca, Mexico, JEFFREY P. BLOMSTER, EDITOR

The Apotheosis of Janaab' Pakal: Science, History, and Religion at Classic Maya Palenque, GERARDO ALDANA

Commoner Ritual and Ideology in Ancient Mesoamerica, NANCY GONLIN AND JON C. LOHSE, EDITORS

Eating Landscape: Aztec and European Occupation of Tlalocan, PHILIP P. ARNOLD

Empires of Time: Calendars, Clocks, and Cultures, Revised Edition, ANTHONY AVENI

Encounter with the Plumed Serpent: Drama and Power in the Heart of Mesoamerica, MAARTEN JANSEN AND GABINA AURORA PÉREZ JIMÉNEZ

In the Realm of Nachan Kan: Postclassic Maya Archaeology at Laguna de On, Belize, MARILYN A. MASSON

Invasion and Transformation: Interdisciplinary Perspectives on the Conquest of Mexico, REBECCA P. BRIENEN AND MARGARET A. JACKSON, EDITORS

Life and Death in the Templo Mayor, EDUARDO MATOS MOCTEZUMA

The Madrid Codex: New Approaches to Understanding an Ancient Maya Manuscript, GABRIELLE VAIL AND ANTHONY AVENI, EDITORS

Mesoamerican Ritual Economy: Archaeological and Ethnological Perspectives, E. CHRISTIAN WELLS AND KARLA L. DAVIS-SALAZAR, EDITORS

Mesoamerica's Classic Heritage: Teotihuacan to the Aztecs, DAVÍD CARRASCO, LINDSAY JONES, AND SCOTT SESSIONS, EDITORS

Mockeries and Metamorphoses of an Aztec God: Tezcatlipoca, "Lord of the Smoking Mirror," GUILHEM OLIVIER, TRANSLATED BY MICHEL BESSON

Rabinal Achi: A Fifteenth-Century Maya Dynastic Drama, ALAIN BRETON, EDITOR; TRANSLATED BY TERESA LAVENDER FAGAN AND ROBERT SCHNEIDER

Representing Aztec Ritual: Performance, Text, and Image in the Work of Sahagún, ELOISE QUIÑONES KEBER, EDITOR

Ruins of the Past: The Use and Perception of Abandoned Structures in the Maya Lowlands, TRAVIS W. STANTON AND ALINE MAGNONI, EDITORS

Skywatching in the Ancient World: New Perspectives in Cultural Astronomy – Studies in Honor of Anthony F. Aveni, CLIVE RUGGLES AND GARY URTON, EDITORS

The Social Experience of Childhood in Mesoamerica, TRACI ARDREN AND SCOTT R. HUTSON, EDITORS

Stone Houses and Earth Lords: Maya Religion in the Cave Context, KEITH M. PRUFER AND JAMES E. BRADY, EDITORS

Tamoanchan, Tlalocan: Places of Mist, ALFREDO LÓPEZ AUSTIN

Thunder Doesn't Live Here Anymore: Self-Deprecation and the Theory of Otherness Among the Teenek Indians of Mexico, ANATH ARIEL DE VIDAS; TRANSLATED BY TERESA LAVENDER FAGAN

Topiltzin Quetzalcoatl: The Once and Future Lord of the Toltecs, H. B. NICHOLSON

The World Below: Body and Cosmos in Otomi Indian Ritual, JACQUES GALINIER

Rabinal Achi

A Fifteenth-Century Maya Dynastic Drama

EDITED BY Alain Breton

TRANSLATED FROM THE FRENCH BY
Teresa Lavender Fagan and Robert Schneider

FOREWORD BY Robert M. Carmack

UNIVERSITY PRESS *of* COLORADO

Originally published as *Rabinal Achi: Un drame dynastique maya du quinzième siècle,*

Published by the University Press of Colorado
5589 Arapahoe Avenue, Suite 206C
Boulder, Colorado 80303

The University Press of Colorado is a proud member of
the Association of American University Presses.

The University Press of Colorado is a cooperative publishing enterprise supported, in part, by Adams State College, Colorado State University, Fort Lewis College, Mesa State College, Metropolitan State College of Denver, University of Colorado, University of Northern Colorado, and Western State College of Colorado.

Library of Congress Cataloging-in-Publication Data

Breton, Alain.
[Rabinal-Achí. English]
Rabinal achi : a fifteenth-century Maya dynastic drama / Alain Breton ; translated by Teresa Lavender Fagan and Robert Schneider.
p. cm. — (Mesoamerican worlds)
Includes bibliographical references and index.
ISBN 978-0-87081-873-8 (pbk. : alk. paper) — ISBN 978-0-87081-875-2 (hardcover : alk. paper) 1. Rabinal-Achí. 2. Quiché drama. I. Title. II. Series.
PM4231.Z77R3313 2007
897'.4152—dc22

2007025468

Design by Daniel Pratt

Publication of this work is made possible by the generous support of the Laboratoire d'ethnologie et de sociologie comparative (CNRS–Paris X University).

To María and José-León
to whom this book owes so much.

To Sylvie, Marion, Camille and Gabrielle,
for their patience.

Contents

Foreword by Robert M. Carmack *ix*

Preface *xiii*

Acknowledgments *xvii*

Introduction 1

- A Unique Text 2
- An Exceptional Destiny 7
  - History of a Discovery 7
  - Earlier Editions and Publications 11
  - The *Pérez Manuscript* 13
- Conflicts between the Rabinaleb and the Quiché 19
  - The Historical Context 19
  - The Trial 26
  - The Protagonists 27
- An Agonistic Joust 42
- The Current State of the Text 47
- The Present Edition 48
  - Regarding the Transcription 51
  - Regarding the Translation 53
  - Regarding the Presentation 53

Part I: The *Pérez Manuscript* 55

Part II: The Text: Transcription and Translation 123

Part III: Analysis: An Exemplary History 279

Return to the Places: Spaces and Journeys 280
Spatial Perspective 281
Temporal Perspective 286
Historical Perspective 290

Return to the Actors: Figures of the Warrior and the King 292
The Figure of the Warrior 293
The Figure of the King 297
Supremacy of One Figure over the Other 300

Return to Events 302
A Disputed Territory 302
An Impossible Alliance 306
The War: A Metaphor for the Hunt 308

Return to the Text: Epilogue 314

Glossary 319

References 373

Index 387

Foreword

I write this foreword to Alain Breton's majestic translation and interpretation of the *Rabinal Achi* as a scholar who has spent a good part of his career working with manuscripts and Maya documents generically similar to the one presented here. I understand the tremendous challenge and skills that such undertakings entail: one must possess knowledge of paleography, philology, relevant Quichean languages, pre-Hispanic and colonial Maya history, local geography and archaeology, and ethnography of the descendants of those who originally transcribed the documents.

Breton states that he spent five years in preparing this work, which is admirable and understandable given the aforementioned required skills and knowledge. His five-year endeavor, of course, was only part of his preparation for this volume. To his highly focused work on the *Rabinal Achi* must be added Breton's academic lifetime of ethnographic research among the Maya Indians of Mexico and Guatemala. His considerable ethnographic skills and knowledge of anthropology were essential to the successful completion of this brilliant study, and they insinuate themselves in every page of this monograph.

A few years ago, as part of a lecture given to a group of university scholars and students, I outlined an ideal methodological strategy for carrying out ethnohistorical research on the Maya and other Mesoamerican peoples. I realized after summarizing the strategy that it was not only demanding in the extreme but also perhaps over-idealistic. I argued that the first step must attempt to work out the most accurate empirically based reconstruction of the historical events possible; that is, to employ stringent historiographic evaluation of the sources, to produce accurate and linguistically correct translations of the texts, and to use knowledge already available on the subject from other sources and analyses in order to contextualize the facts. This step also must include a thorough investigation of the specific material and social contexts within which the historical events took place and an attempt to determine the relationship between these contexts and the events themselves.

The second step must be a reanalysis of the sources for alternative interpretations, including the search for contradictory, complementary, and deeper levels of meaning. These more critical interpretations—reading between the lines, going beyond the empirical evidence per se—must then be set alongside the primary findings not as alternative hypothetical findings (these were already determined in the first step) but as enriching and amplifying understandings. This is a reflexive step, and it insulates the researcher against overly naïve positivism.

I mention these idealistic strategic goals of ethnohistory because a reading of Breton's book reveals that he indeed has met the challenge of such an approach. It is not possible—nor appropriate—in this foreword to document point by point this claim, but readers of the book should keep them in mind as they study this complex historical document. It will not be a difficult task to carry out since Breton himself draws attention to these strategic goals, especially in the final section, Analysis: An Exemplary History. It is obvious that he is well aware of both the challenges and possibilities of ethnohistorical research.

Beyond the methodological and theoretical issues just mentioned, I draw the readers' attention to comparisons between Breton's contribution in this study and cognate recent ethnohistorical studies of the Maya peoples of highland Guatemala.

The Dutch ethnohistorian Ruud van Akkeren, for example, recently restudied many of the important Maya documents related to highland Maya history, among these the *Rabinal Achi* (see his *Place of the Lord's Daughter: Rab'inal, Its History, Its Dance-Drama*, 2000). Van Akkeren attempts to reconstruct a new pre-Hispanic history of virtually all the highland Maya peoples, and he claims to be able to connect this history to Classic period Maya developments. Breton is much more careful than van Akkeren in dealing with his text, with respect not only to translation but also to understanding the nature of the text itself. He never strays far from the Rabinal text at hand to make speculative linkages with Classic period histories or with contemporary highland Maya myth and folklore. Most importantly, Breton meticulously documents the possible alternate choices in making translations by including entries from the various Maya "dictionaries."

Dennis Tedlock's recently published book on the *Rabinal Achi* (*Rabinal Achi: A Mayan Drama of War and Sacrifice*, 2003) is far less historically oriented than van Akkeren's study. Tedlock does attempt, however, a brief reconstruction in broad terms of the late Postclassic political history of the highland Mayas, and his reconstruction is generally consistent with that of Breton. Less successfully, Tedlock attempts to establish a relationship between the cultural features represented in the *Rabinal Achi* and the Classic lowland Maya features found in mural paintings and carved monuments. Tedlock's historical speculations in this regard seem less convincing than Breton's elaborate and more focused reconstruction of late Postclassic highland Maya history and culture.

It should be noted that Tedlock does not include the Quiché text in his monograph on the *Rabinal Achi*, although he attempts to explain the reasons for his translations through endnotes. Nevertheless, Tedlock is far less exhaustive in this regard than is Breton, who makes available to the reader the extensive Maya dictionary support for his translations.

Tedlock pays considerable attention to the text itself as a discursive expression, especially its literary and poetic features. But he provides a less detailed account of the history of the text than does Breton. Furthermore, Breton provides a fuller coverage of the dance-drama as celebrated in the town of Rabinal. In fact, Breton has an established relationship with the present director of the dance-drama (José-León Coloch) and only Breton has carried out serious ethnographic research in the area. Breton's ethnographic experience shows up clearly in his impressive account of the Rabinal geography and cultural setting within which the events described in the text originally took place.

Perhaps I might be permitted a few brief comments comparing Breton's Rabinal study and my own efforts at translation and analysis of early colonial Maya documents (especially *El Título de Totonicapán*, 1983). One of the most impressive facts about Breton's *Rabinal Achi* is that he personally did all of his translations, whereas I relied on collaboration from James Mondloch, an expert linguistic specialist on the Quiché language. It is humbling to compare our translations and exegetical notes with their equivalents in Breton's *Rabinal Achi*. His translations are far more elegant and perhaps more accurate. Furthermore, his notes cover a wider set of topics and issues and are certainly more copious. His analysis of the text itself is especially praiseworthy, particularly in comparison with our relatively light treatment of the topic.

Our sources, of course, are far more historically oriented than is the *Rabinal Achi*, but it is particularly gratifying to find general consistency between them. Breton's account of broad Quiché Postclassic history as recounted in the *Rabinal Achi* fits well with our reconstructions, although there are minor differences. More importantly from my own vantage point, Breton's reconstruction of history in the *Rabinal Achi* adds a crucial new understanding of developments in the area that was not clear in other Maya documents from the early colonial period.

In particular, the historical relationships between the Rabinal and Poq'omab peoples are clarified beyond what was known from past studies. We gain new insights into the dialectical relations that existed between the Rabinaleb and Quiché. Breton's brilliant exegesis of terms applied in the *Rabinal Achi* to the Quiché capital of Q'umarkaj (Utatlán) offers a perspective on that important political center not found in the much more abundant Quiché documents. Equally informative are a series of pre-Hispanic Maya cultural features that Breton is able to identify and describe based on the text. Among these Maya features we learn about are elements of aboriginal judicial process and their view of the differences between kings and warriors, key metaphors for warfare and human sacrifice.

It is not necessary to draw out in greater detail the significance of Breton's translation and exegesis of the *Rabinal Achi* for Maya history and culture. As the reader will discover, Breton clarifies the document's significance in rich detail through notes and summaries. Most importantly, his brilliant study communicates with grace and erudition a profound sense of understanding of and appreciation for the highland native Maya world encountered by the first Spanish invaders in the sixteenth century.

– ROBERT M. CARMACK

Preface

The text of the *Rabinal Achi* ("The Man of Rabinal"), the subject of this work, is already a classic. At least five centuries old, it has experienced an exceptional destiny that has turned it into a unique jewel—a "solitaire," as it was called by Georges Raynaud, who was the last to translate it into French in 1928.

Yet, regardless of its value within a larger universal literary context, it is above all a sacred object for a distant Mayan community from the highlands of Guatemala—San Pablo Rabinal. The text of a ritual dance, the "dance of the *tun*," the *Rabinal Achi* is considered there to be a founding text, an edifying and exemplary tale that even today constitutes an essential reference, defining the historical and geographical identity of the heirs of those who composed, protected, and transmitted it from generation to generation—the Rabinaleb.

The Rabinaleb speak the language Achi (or Quiché-Achi), which belongs to the linguistic family of Quichean. This family also includes pure Quiché, Cakchiquel, Tzutujil, and other less commonly spoken languages (such as Sacapultec and Uspantec). Although Quiché-Achi is more closely related to Quiché than to any other language, some Rabinaleb consider it closer to Cakchiquel, a sign of the complex historical processes of populating and the strategies put into place by the region's different groups to recognize each other as similar while standing out individually. These strategies are expressed in the text as they are today profoundly anchored in memory and dictate behaviors.

The *Rabinal Achi* tells the story of the trial of a Quiché warrior who, just captured, appears before the royal court of Rabinal. Through the recitation of the multiple charges that are brought against him, the tale brings us into the labyrinth of an obscure past as well as into the land being fought over by the two principal protagonists, the Rabinaleb and the Quiché peoples.

We will attempt to rediscover these realms, while evoking the long road the text traveled to reach us, as well as the interior paths of its construction. Finally, and most important, we will attempt to reveal how an indigenous invention of history endowed the present with an illustrious past.

This study does not claim to supplant the analyses of historians and ethnohistorians. By presenting this edition of the *Rabinal Achi*—which is based on a new indigenous manuscript, the *Pérez Manuscript*—I hope to advance certain ideas and interpretations inferred from knowledge acquired while doing fieldwork in the region where the manuscript was born, from my own reading of the text, and from discussions held with those who currently possess it. My primary goal is to bring this remarkable yet difficult work out of the shadows in which it has been placed; but I also hope that these ideas and hypotheses may be sources of new debates and criticism out of which other interpretations or other documents may emerge.

The text of the *Rabinal Achi* is at the heart of this work. The challenge consists of drawing the maximum amount of instruction from it without distancing oneself too much from what it says. Notwithstanding, we are limited by the text itself. The numerous implicit, even hidden (esoteric) aspects—such as those relating to symbolism—deserve attention, but their in-depth examination requires that they be put back into a vast comparative perspective. For example, the *Rabinal Achi* evokes a certain number of questions connected to the local political organization, to the calendar, to cosmology, to sacrifice, but the text alone does not resolve them. In order to answer these questions, I have primarily favored what is customarily called the "literal exegesis" but I have also used "allegorical exegesis." In the current state of research on Mayan texts, and considering the ethnohistorical implications of these documentary sources, priority must necessarily be given to an internal analysis that reconciles a philological approach (which clarifies the meaning of the words) and an overall critical approach (which clarifies the meaning and the coherence of the text).

This study distinguishes the two types of exegeses in order to respect the natural and logical progression of a reader who is not fully informed on the subject. After the introduction, which presents the different contexts within which both the document itself as well as the contents and form of the tale belong, the first part begins with a reproduction of the *Pérez Manuscript* and then presents the transcribed text (the transcription of the Quiché-Achi text and the translation are placed side-by-side). The analysis of the text is separated into a third part so as not to inhibit the reading with any previous judgment. The glossary, which was conceived as a collection of glosses relative to the terms of the Quiché-Achi language, may be consulted at any time at the back of the book.

The interpretation I propose does not exhaust the substance of the *Rabinal Achi*; there is still much to be learned and more to say if one looks at it from other angles, if one analyzes it further. Guided by the goals of various projects in the works at the time I began studying the text, I decided to be less concerned with the text's subject matter (a judicial ritual) and instead focus on its meaning (regarding representations of authority and power, and indigenous conceptions of history). This choice justifies the work's title and the perhaps more literary approach to untangling the threads of the drama.

Acknowledgments

Among the many people who have contributed to the inception, the advancement, or the completion of this work, of primary importance are María Xolop and José-León Coloch Garniga, without whom my work would not have been possible.

I wish also to thank, in Rabinal, Esteban Xolop, Matías Jerónimo, José-Manuel Coloch, Juan Alvarado, Julián Sic, Francisco Mendoza, Mateo Ismalej, Santiago Canawi, Andrés García, Félix Gómez, Celso Sesam, Justo Baley, Esteban Cortés; in Cubulco and in Tres Cruces, Juan Camajá, Tomás Teletor, Sebastián Raimundo; in Guatemala City and in La Antigua, Isabel Rodas, Hugo Fidel Sacor Quiché (Instituto de Antropología e Historia), as well as Martín Chacach Cutzal, Antonio López and María Juliana Sis Iboy (then-director and linguists of the Proyecto Lingüístico Francisco Marroquín).

The support of several colleagues has proven to be essential: Carroll Edward Mace, Ruud Van Akkeren, Joanna Kozinska Frybes, and René Acuña, with whom I had the pleasure of exchanging correspondence and points of view; Nancy Farriss, Anne D. Williams, Danielle Dupiech Cavaleri, Silvia Sayavedra Olavarría, Laurence Crémière, and William F. Hanks, for the kind help they provided with documentation; Shun Ijom, Bernard Gibassier, and Esther Katz, for information concerning traditional methods of apiculture.

I am particularly indebted to Marie-France Fauvet-Berthelot, Alain Ichon, François Lartigue, and Yvon Le Bot, with whom I have had the good fortune of sharing a long professional relationship and the same passion for Guatemala;

to Alfred Adler, Pierre Becquelin, Claude-François Baudez, Victoria R. Bricker, Raymond Jamous, Mario Humberto Ruz, and Nathaniel Tarn, who were among the first readers and critics of this new translation; and above all to Marie-Charlotte Arnauld and Aurore Becquelin Monod, who have followed step-by-step the development of the manuscript.

In the course of its different stages, this work has benefited from the financial support of the Centre national de la recherche scientifique (within the framework of the Mission franco-guatémaltèque and the Laboratoire d'ethnologie et de sociologie comparative at Paris X University) and the Ministère des Affaires étrangères (Centre français d'études mexicaines et centraméricaines, Mexico and Guatemala).

Fieldwork was supported by the Instituto de Antropología e Historia of Guatemala, by the departmental authorities of Baja Verapaz and municipal of Rabinal and Cubulco, as well as their auxiliaries. While doing this fieldwork, the warm welcome of fathers Juan Valls, Melchior Fraj, and Fernando Suazo never failed.

Finally, I owe the completion of this book to the goodwill of Darrin Pratt and his entire staff, as well as to the combined talents of Robert Schneider, who has rendered into very elegant English the French text of the *Rabinal Achi,* and Teresa Lavender Fagan, who has translated and improved my own prose.

Rabinal Achi

Introduction

The *Rabinal Achi* is undeniably one of the major works of Mesoamerican literature. Yet, paradoxically, although the title has achieved relative notoriety, the text itself remains largely unknown.

The *Rabinal Achi* became famous in 1862, when the priest Charles Étienne Brasseur de Bourbourg, the man who discovered it, published it for the first time in the second volume of his *Collection de documents dans les langues indigènes.* Transcribed from the Quiché[1] and translated into French, the text is preceded by a *Grammaire de la langue quiché.* It took more than sixty years for another scholar, Georges Raynaud, to revise the translation. Despite the pioneering role played by these two Frenchmen in its discovery and dissemination, this text is today unavailable in the French language. Brasseur's editio princeps (1862b) can only be consulted at the Bibliothèque nationale in Paris; as for Raynaud's

1. In general, in the introduction, as well as in the notes and commentaries, I have retained the official (Hispanicized) or common spelling of the onomastic terms of Indian origin. The names of villages, languages, and groups of Guatemala in fact include several spellings depending on the system of transcription used. According to the phonetical norms adopted to transcribe the text of the *Rabinal Achi* into the native language, "Quiché" should be written as /k'iche'/, "Cakchiquel" as /kaqchikel/, "K'ekchi" as /q'eqchi'/, and so forth. Only the names of specific characters and places cited in the text will be rendered in their original forms.

French edition (the basis for the first Spanish edition in 1928), it was never published and the manuscript to this day has not been found. Unlike other notable works of Mayan literature, such as the books of the Yucatecan *Chilam Balam* (Péret 1955; Le Clézio 1976) or the no less famous *Popol Vuh* (Raynaud 1980; DesRuisseaux and Amaya 1987; Chávez 1990; Faurie 1991), the *Rabinal Achi* has rarely inspired new readings or analyses in France and, since 1862, has not been published.

The founding work of Brasseur and Raynaud, however, experienced a wider expansion abroad. The various existing editions or reprints—in Spanish for the most part (in several countries of Latin America) but also in English, German, and Serbo-Croatian—were published from them. Whether direct translations from the French or more or less free-form adaptations, they have inherited the defects inherent in Brasseur's and Raynaud's volumes and, without a new examination of the original text, really do not present anything new of value. One must not, however, criticize the various authors of these attempts, including Brasseur, all of whom were confronted with an obscure and complex text whose form is particularly perplexing. The nonlinearity of the story, its formal rhetoric, its extreme formalization marked by the systematic use of parallelism, the use of repetition and reported speech, the overlapping superposition of the various dialogues, and the archaism of the language make it difficult to read and immediately understand. This opaqueness probably constitutes one of the reasons why the *Rabinal Achi* has remained a text apart, largely unexplored and relatively ignored compared to others, like the *Popol Vuh, Anales de los Cakchiqueles,* and *Título de los Señores de Totonicapán.* These other texts have been widely translated[2] and are the objects of numerous studies aiming to interpret and analyze their content—both mythological and historical—making available a knowledge of the past and of ancient representations of the peoples of Guatemala.

A UNIQUE TEXT

Another reason the *Rabinal Achi* may be considered unique is related to its originality within this documentary corpus. The explicit objective of most known old indigenous texts was indeed to assert territorial rights or political legitimacies before the new colonial administration (Edmonson 1971b). They were instruments intended to defend ancestral rights and arguments for a legal recognition of those rights by the Crown of Spain. Going back, for some of them, to the most distant past, to the primordial time of myths and genesis, they all worked in various degrees toward the restitution of dynastic lineages, toward the restitution of a precise succession of events relating to the populating of the region, the demarcation of lands, the justification of facts illustrating the weight of each

---

2. For the record, throughout the world there are close to fifty editions of the *Popol Vuh,* not counting the many studies (including historical, linguistic, and literary) related to it.

group and its situation at the time when the documents were written. The conditions and the context that gave birth to them are no doubt largely responsible for the heterogeneity characterizing the composition of these texts, which for many appear to be compilations of various materials created by narrators concerned with adapting the relevance of their writings to the objective of the moment.

All of these documents manifest more or less this preoccupation of the narrators (whether or not they are identified) to include the facts of their respective eras in the course of events, to integrate into their tales the episode of contact, indeed even to connect their autochthonous history to Biblical genesis. Consequently, all of these tales, major and minor alike, are marked by syncretism and are the fruit of a colonial rewriting. In the study by Robert M. Carmack (1973), and notably in the second chapter devoted to the primary sources of indigenous history, one finds details concerning each document and the known or assumed dates of their composition. These dates range from 1542 for the *Título Nijaib III* to 1583 for the *Título de los Indios de Santa Clara La Laguna,* with a large majority composed in 1550–1560 or 1580, including *Popol Vuh, Título de los Señores de Totonicapán, Anales de los Cakchiqueles, Historia Quiché de don Juan de Torres, Título C'oyoi, Relación de Zapotitlán, Títulos Xpantzay, Título Chajoma, Relación Tzutujil,* and *Título Cajcoj.*

Nothing leads us to assume that the composition of the *Rabinal Achi* was meant to respond to such a goal or that it was written to satisfy similar needs. The text is not presented a priori either as a genesis tale or as a historical tale, even less as a genealogical chart or a title of possession of land. Even if, as we will see, some of these themes can be discerned in it, and ultimately prove to be significant, its true intent is quite different. We must therefore admit that this text, the libretto of a dance called *Xajoj Tun,* belongs to another literary genre.

As much through its form as in its content, this "dance of the *tun*"[3] is in fact related to a larger family of warrior dances, of "gladiatorial" rituals, of sacrificial representations, which have disappeared today. Listed under different names—such as *Quiché Vinak, Tum Teleche, Loj Tum, Lotz Tum, Ox Tun, Trompetas Tum,* and *Uleutum*—such dances, whose pre-Hispanic origins are undeniable, still held an important place in the indigenous ceremonies at the beginning of the colonial period.[4] Repressed by the Spanish Catholic authorities, who saw in them the expression of condemnable practices, these representations were all gradually abandoned, destined for oblivion. All, that is, except the *Rabinal Achi,* which, for reasons that remain to be established, escaped various elimination attempts and survived, almost intact, that long period of clandestine existence.

---

3. I have decided not to translate the term *tun* here. Although today that word designates the large drum with vibrating blades that accompanies two large "trumpets" in certain evolutions of the dance, all the ancient dictionaries I consulted list this term under wind instruments: "trumpet," "clarion," "flute," or "horn" (see Glossary).

4. See in particular Chinchilla Aguilar 1951; Toledo Palomo 1965; Acuña 1975 (chapters 16–18); Mace 1981; Edmonson 1985.

Unfortunately, we have little information concerning those other "warrior dances." The surviving information is summed up in a handful of deprecatory descriptions left by the few rare chroniclers who observed them (see Fuentes y Guzmán 1932–1933) or is found in legendary tales from an oral tradition cut off from any written reference, basically the same, but whose content is considerably diluted. What Father Francisco Ximénez reported (1929–1931, 1:78) about the dance of the *Quiché Vinak* already at the beginning of the 1700s evidently appears to have been the reconstitution of an oral version, both abbreviated and updated; moreover, his version shares many comparable traits with certain indigenous tales of today (e.g., the *Yew Achi* from Cubulco and the *Yegua Achi* from Momostenango).[5] Although we do not have any formal proof, it is not impossible that such tales might in fact have had written texts as support and that they might once have constituted works comparable to the *Rabinal Achi,* each serving as a local (in some way ethnocentric) version expressing a specific point of view (complementary? antagonistic?) on events and the relationships that the various communities maintained with each other. Thus, the *Quiché Vinak* dealt with the conflicting relationships between the Quiché and the Cakchiquel, whereas the *Yew Achi* portrays Cubuleros and Quiché, and the *Yegua Achi* opposes Momostecos and Quiché.

One must, nonetheless, wonder about the assumed similarity between these ancient indigenous choreographies whose diverse names hide, perhaps, their unique forms, content, and functions. The text of the *Rabinal Achi* itself evokes two of those dances to which it attributes a more limited role: those that accompanied the prophylactic rituals of bleeding before battles, called *Lotzo Tun Lotzo Q'ojom* (see lines 430–431 in this edition), and those that were performed during the return from expeditions to welcome the warriors and their prisoners of war (possibly called *Tum Teleche*) (lines 2281–2283).

In fact, the absence of any text equivalent to the *Rabinal Achi* considerably reduces comparative perspectives and limits any discussion relative to the problematics of the genre with which it would be appropriate to associate it. What do hypothetical considerations relative to the origin of the text possibly bring to this discussion?

We know nothing about the origin of the *Rabinal Achi*—not the author's identity or the date of composition—thus, anything we might say about them is only personal opinion. Two assertions, however, can be made: the first is that the substance of the tale goes back to the pre-Hispanic period; the second is that the text, even though it was transcribed into Latin characters during the colonial period, suffers from no European influence. Not one word, not one phrase, not the slightest allusion betrays the presence of an intervention on the path of Hispanization or conversion. Unlike other texts that have reached us, all similarly written down after the Conquest by a few literate Indians who adopted the spelling of the Spanish missionaries, the *Rabinal Achi* bears no trace

5. One finds tales from Cubulco in Shaw (1972: 62–63), as well as in Arnauld and Breton (1993); those from Momostenango are in Cook (1983).

of any attempt, deliberate or not, at updating. All evidence suggests that it was already (and definitively), at the moment of its passing into alphabetical writing, a contained tale, closed onto itself. This a posteriori statement, however, does not enable us to clarify the way in which the text (or the story) was composed; or to understand how it survived the final decades of the pre-Hispanic era, then the brutal hiatus of the Conquest, without losing anything of its homogeneity; or, consequently, to infer its original form. Did the *Rabinal Achi* exist only as an oral tale, or did it already lean, in whole or in part, on a "text"? Is such a narrative form compatible with what is known of indigenous codices? We probably will never know the answers to these questions, any more than we will know who composed it. Given its great unity but also its complexity, I am inclined to believe that it is a personal and unique creation, the work of an author who may have been a king or a crown prince of the time or maybe an inspired dignitary laboring in the tradition of Aztec poets. As to the question of knowing why and how this text conserved such unity, the response comes perhaps from the conversational form of the tale, which reflects the genre. Indeed, the text is an uninterrupted succession of dialogues in which each character in turn holds the role of narrator. Lacking the external point of view of a third-person omniscient narrator, the story is not told but lived and played out by each character in the first person. This absence of a narrator, whether an agent or a witness, probably contributed to the preservation of the text's homogeneity, because when it was transcribed or recopied, this format scarcely offered any possibility of narrative extension and eluded any ulterior attempt at intervention or corruption of what was stated—the deixis is fixed there once and for all.

Furthermore, we do not know anything about the primitive conditions of the *Rabinal Achi*'s production, that is, how it was produced as a "discourse" given by actors and intended for an audience. We are lacking information concerning its ceremonial contexts: what were the associated rituals, and how was the dance integrated into them? At what moment(s) and in what period(s) was this text performed and in what specific situations? What were the modalities of the actors' craft at the time, the significance connected to those performances, the functions expected from such performances? This spectacular ("theatrical," choreographed, ritual) dimension in itself begs lengthy research and cannot be broached here.[6]

That the written text was preserved in itself constitutes a remarkable fact; that it is still performed today is unique.[7] The dance of the *Rabinal Achi* is performed

6. On this subject, see the study by Kozinska Frybes (1985), which attempts a preliminary response to these questions.

7. This fact is unique only with regard to the category of dances to which the *Rabinal Achi* is connected. Many other dances accompanied by dialogues in an Indian language and whose origins go back to the pre-Hispanic period also have survived and continue to be performed in Guatemala; for example, in Rabinal notably, the *Patzka, Charamiyex,* and *Balam Kej*. But these plays cannot be compared with the *Rabinal Achi* because they are related to what the Spanish call *farsas,* that is, short comic, even clownesque, comedies using derision and ritual humor (see the study that C. E. Mace [1970] has devoted to them).

on the occasion of the patronal feast of Rabinal, which occurs during the week that precedes and includes January 25, the commemoration of the conversion of St. Paul, the tutelary saint and eponym of the community. If we are to believe him, it was Brasseur who, demanding to see the play after he had assembled the text, convinced the Indians to perform it on that precise date, which he had imposed on them. It is not impossible that he was telling the truth on the first point—perhaps he was indeed the initiator of the public renewal of the dance[8] and no doubt the dance owes the French priest for being known and recognized as it is today. It is less certain, however, that the choice of the date was the result of his authority alone. Indeed, the date is less arbitrary than it appears when one associates the performance of this dance with the feast of St. Sebastian, whose celebration on January 19 overlaps with that of the patron saint. It, therefore, would not be surprising if the Rabinaleb for a very long time already, and well before Brasseur's intervention, had fixed on a date that syncretically connected the carrying out of an autochthonous sacrificial ritual to the commemoration of a Christian figure of sacrifice. This example was not isolated.

The dance does not belong to any fixed period. According to various accounts (including Termer 1957, for the 1920s; Teletor 1945, Yurchenco 1986, for the 1940s; and more recently, Rodríguez Rouanet 1962 and Acuña 1975; to which one can add the personal communications of Henri Lehmann, Marie-France Fauvet-Berthelot and Marie-Charlotte Arnauld, as well as my own information), it has not been performed more than some fifteen times since the time of Brasseur. It was only after working on the text and investigating preparatory rituals, the speeches and prayers devoted to it, and the places of worship that house them that I had the opportunity to observe the *Rabinal Achi,* in late 1992, and to follow its various evolutions, both public and private, throughout the feasts of St. Sebastian and St. Paul. But observations relating to the dance, its choreography, its costumes, its accessories, and its music,[9] as well as those relating to the ritual context in which today are inserted representations and preparations, do not have a place here[10] (we occasionally will refer to them to the extent that they illustrate a point). Insofar as I can judge, the text's contribution to an understanding of the dance cannot be compared with what the dance might contribute to the text, and such a digression would distance us unnecessarily from the primary objective of this introduction: to present the text and its history.

---

8. We cannot claim, however, that the dance was completely forgotten. Like the text, the dance could have survived within the framework of secret rituals.

9. The addenda to Sacor Quiché et al. 1991 provides summary but useful descriptions of the choreography and music. A musical transcription also appeared as an addendum to Brasseur 1862b and is reproduced in Raynaud and Cardoza y Aragón 1929–1930, 1953, and 1972, as well as in Ballantine 1985. There is also a recording originally produced in the 1940s by Yurchenco (1978).

10. See Álvarez Aguilar 1986.

AN EXCEPTIONAL DESTINY

Many questions arise upon examining the ways in which the *Rabinal Achi* has been transmitted. We will begin with these modes of transmission, knowing that other scholars—notably René Acuña (1975) and Carroll Edward Mace (1967a, 1967b, 1981)—have already devoted lengthy studies to them, as impassioned as they are passionate. These two historians, eminent specialists of Indian literature, have often been at odds concerning this text, and their divergent opinions have sustained many controversies.[11] They both, however, share the same unshakable distrust with regard to Brasseur de Bourbourg (known, it is true, for the fantasy of some of his attempts at historical reconstruction and for linguistic theories that are unacceptable today). Within the limits of this study, I will qualify these critical judgments that are sometimes the result of assumptions and deal more with the character of the person than with the intrinsic value of his writing or—in the specific case that concerns us here—with the quality of his translation.[12]

History of a Discovery

During his third trip to America, Charles Étienne Brasseur, from the village of Bourbourg (near Dunkerque), decided to devote closer study to some documents relating to indigenous history. Having arrived in Guatemala on February 1, 1855, he was granted by Bishop Francisco de Paula García Peláez the post of overseeing the parish of Rabinal (see Figure 1). He settled there on May 18, 1855. Fifteen days later, in a letter to José Mariano Padilla,[13] he wrote:

> Rabinal, 3 de junio de 1855. . . . Aquí trabajo mucho . . . en traducir el Códice Padilla, mucho ya se ha hecho y casi todo comprendo: es manuscrito sumamente interesante. . . . *He descubierto aquí, entre las manos de un tío de un criadito mío, otro manuscrito;* es el texto del diálogo y historia del bayle antiguo de Rabinal Achi, los héroes de Rabinal. . . . It is a wonderful find. (1940: 302; emphasis mine)

That excerpt, which indicates the enthusiasm with which he began his year-long stay in Rabinal, constitutes the single and only explicit mention left by Brasseur

11. The question of the origins and the modes of transmission of the *Rabinal Achi* has raised arguments close to those that surround the genesis of the Incan *Apu Ollantay*. These are, moreover, two texts that certain commentators like to compare.

12. On the life and controversial work of Brasseur de Bourbourg, see the article by Mace (1973) and the work by Escalante Arce (1989), both of which include large bibliographies. The positive aspects of the priest's work and the relevance of some of his intuitions have been rightly stressed by Brunhouse (1973: 134) and, more recently, by Kubler (1989: 1119–1120).

13. Padilla was a collector of Guatemalan objects and a friend of Brasseur's, in whose honor Brasseur named the Codex Padilla, the text known since then by the Spanish names of *Memorial de Tecpán-Atitlán, Anales de los Xahil,* or *Anales de los Cakchiqueles* (see Recinos and Goetz 1974: 3–10).

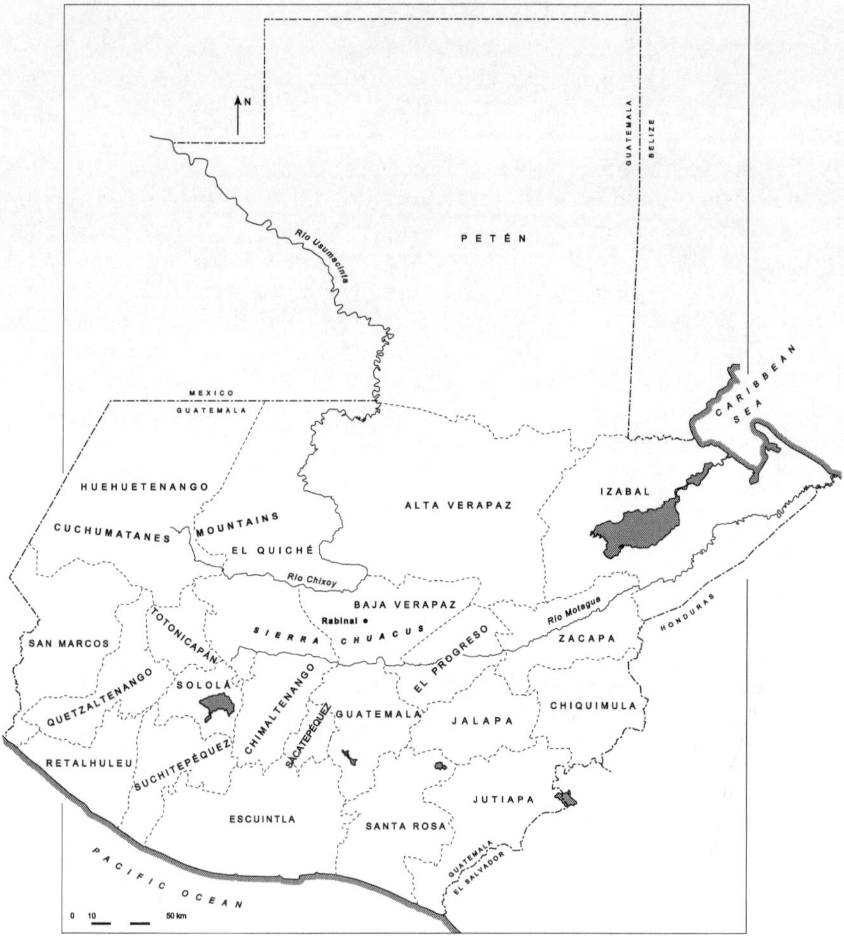

1. Guatemala: Current Political Borders and Administrative Divisions

concerning the possible existence of a local manuscript of the *Rabinal Achi* and, consequently, of a text different from the one he put down in writing more than a month later, taking dictation from Bartolo Sis. His later writings never make any other allusion to it, leading one to believe that upon his arrival in the village—and no doubt through the voice of his servant, the young "Colash" (Nicolás) López, the nephew of Bartolo Sis—Brasseur was indeed informed of the existence of a manuscript, but, contrary to that premature announcement, he never saw or read it.

All the same, his legendary curiosity and the interest and perseverance he showed toward finding the text of that "ancient ballet" were soon repaid. Lacking a manuscript, Brasseur was unsuccessful until he encountered Bartolo

Sis. Later he wrote—in English—to Ephraïm Squier: "Knowing that I had vainly endeavoured to obtain an idea of that bayle from the other Indians, [Bartolo Sis] proposed that I should write it down from his dictation, which I eagerly undertook to do, notwithstanding that it was to be in the Quiché dialect of Rabinal" (1855: 1435).

This version of the facts is reproduced on several occasions,[14] but the one that provides the most details appears in the introduction of his 1862 edition:

> One evening, while I was dreaming of these things while watching a formidable downpour, an Indian woman entered my dwelling. She was an old woman with a respectable demeanor. . . . My young servant, Colash López, brought her to me, telling me she was the wife of his uncle, Bartolo Ziz. Since she didn't speak a word of Spanish, Colash told me, on her behalf, that her husband was sick with an illness that he described to me, and asked me for a remedy for him. In Rabinal there was neither a doctor nor an apothecary; consequently, I was equipped with a small travel pharmacy which already gave me a great reputation as a doctor. Luckily for Ziz and for me, I was able to prescribe a rather simple remedy for him with the help of which he was much better in a few days. He came to see me as soon as he was better. He was about fifty years old: although he was poor compared to many of the other inhabitants of the area, his manners and language were such that I was quite surprised. After thanking me in very good Castillian, he told me that having learned through his nephew that I was curious to know about the play of Rabinal-Achí, he had come to put himself at my disposal to give me all the details about it that I wanted. I assured him that nothing would please me more. He added that he had learned it traditionally from his father and his grandfather; that he had played the role of one of the main characters in the performance that had taken place before a Dominican priest whom he named, around thirty years earlier. Since then, he continued, it had been abandoned under various pretexts, although the old people continued to talk about it; seeing that, he began to think about, for several years, putting it all together in writing, in order to transmit it as a legacy to his children. He ended by proposing that I *in turn* transcribe it under his dictation. (1862b: 17–19; emphasis mine)

We will probably never know the exact reasons that pushed Brasseur to say nothing more about another text after he had hastily announced it to his friend Padilla. All the same, the words "in turn transcribe it"[15] in the last sentence

14. See Brasseur 1945: 8 ("Poco tiempo después de mi llegada a Rabinal, obtuve de un indio viejo, perfectamente instruido en las cosas del país, que *me dictase*, en la lengua quiché, que es la de este pueblo, las palabras de un drama-baile que se usa todavía aquí, y se llama xahohtun, el baile del tun"); see also Brasseur 1946: 163–164.

15. Brasseur's specification—*lapsus calami*?—up to now has escaped the vigilance of his detractors. Indeed, some accuse him of having deliberately schemed the entire story to make credible, through a "discovery," the authenticity of a text that he had actually written. On this subject, see Goubaud Carrera in Gillin 1952: 219; and Englekirk 1957.

of this excerpt suggests that another transcription had preceded his own: the one, as we shall see, that Bartolo Sis himself had undertaken five years earlier and the very one no doubt that the young Nicolás López had mentioned to the priest when he first arrived.

Brasseur does not explain anywhere the divergences in his different accounts, and he further adds to the mystery surrounding the origin of his transcription by reproducing in it *both* the preliminary list of characters—which I will call the "epigraph"—and what it is commonly called the "prologue by Bartolo Sis," which he also inserts in his 1862 edition: "Chi huvinak vahxakib gih, chi iq ri octubre chupam ri hunab de *1830* [*sic*], mi-x-chi-v'elezah-vi *original* rech vae Xahoh-Tun, rech vae ka tinamit *San Pablo* Rabinal-vi, quxtubal-ta ve cumal v'al nu qahol, chuxe-gih-zak chi ca va apanoc" (Brasseur 1862b: 15–16; emphasis mine). [On the twenty-eighth day of the month of October of the year 1850, I transcribed the *original* of this Ballet of the Tun, the property of our town of *St. Paul* of Rabinal, to leave as a remembrance to my children and so that it remains forever after with them.]

The object of the controversy—the fact that this interpolated clause, signed by Bartolo Sis and dated October 1850, is found attached to Brasseur's text, which was assembled in July 1855—has been interpreted in different ways. Mace (1967a: 13–14; 1981: 105) proposes the argument that Brasseur's version is only a simple copy of Sis's manuscript, contradicting what the priest says concerning the alleged dictation.[16] Arguing that this concern with transmission is "too European, too romantic" and that such a formulation is not at all indigenous, Acuña (1975: 57, 73–74), on the contrary, sees the inclusion of this text as Brasseur's personal seal—a later addition, in some way a joke similar to the one Brasseur played when he translated his Parisian publisher's address into Quiché.[17]

Acuña, in other respects attentive to spotting European influences in indigenous texts (see Acuña 1983a), does not question the authenticity of the *Rabinal Achi* and recognizes, more than a century after Pruner-Bey (1863: 16), that the work was no doubt "written down in Hispano-Roman characters during the early years of the Conquest."[18] Why, then, does he suspect the authenticity of Sis's prologue when Sis is only paraphrasing a formulation that is already contained in the very body of the text? Indeed, it is in identical terms that the character portraying the Quiché warrior, the one who is to be sacrificed, expresses a comparable concern in it: "'Are u holom ca ka mam, ka cahau.' Que cha ta v'al, que cha ta ri nu qahol quxtubal-ta ve cumal v'al, nu qahol chuxe gih-zak" (Brasseur 1862b: 104–105). ["This is the skull of our grandfather, of our father." This my sons and vassals will repeat in remembrance of me, for as long as the sun will shine.]

---

16. This theory echoes an opinion already expressed by Monterde (1955: xiii).

17. "Paris, Arthus Bertrand, Editeur, 21, Rue Hautefeuille" is thus rendered as "Paris, Arthus Bertrand, *Ahvuh,* 21, *chi amag* Hautefeuille *u bi*" (Brasseur 1862b: 2–3).

18. Cited by Acuña 1975: 37.

Mace's and Acuña's theses, to which I will return when we look at the question of the different copies of the *Rabinal Achi,* do not stand up to a reasonable interpretation of the facts. One might fault Brasseur for his inconsistent explanation of the stages that led to the text, or reproach him for having precipitously and imprudently bragged of an empty discovery[19] only to ignore it completely later, or possibly criticize him for his mediocre ethnography and for his naivete about what Bartolo Sis told him regarding the purely oral retention of the work, but one cannot agree with those who attribute some Machiavelian intention to him (accusing him of such things as a pure and simple invention of the text, writing and adding of the prologue, or pirating and diverting to his benefit a source he would have destroyed). Evidently, it seems that in this case Brasseur did not make anything up: not the information that a manuscript already existed—the one that Bartolo Sis had transcribed and for which he wrote a preface in 1850—nor the fact that five years later he had assembled the entire text, including the epigraph and the prologue, under the dictation of Bartolo Sis.[20]

Earlier Editions and Publications

Thus, in July 1855, Brasseur de Bourbourg transcribed the text of the *Rabinal Achi* as it was dictated to him by Bartolo Sis. Later he wrote:

> This proposition was all that I could have wished for. . . . At that time I was still not very well versed in the Quiché language, and it was no small task for me to undertake such a work. I was able to complete it, nevertheless, by using the spelling adopted for that language by my predecessors. During the span of twelve days, I shut myself up regularly all morning long with Bartolo Ziz, Colash López, and another young man from Rabinal named Tecú, no less intelligent than Colash. They both proved capable of the role that I conferred upon them: they didn't know a bit of grammar; but it was incredible the lucidity with which they explained to me the forms and the composition of the phrases of this indigenous play; for, after each page, I translated it word for word into Spanish, for which they provided me all possible help.

19. Brasseur should not be so harshly criticized for having announced "the discovery of a manuscript" rather than "the discovery *of the existence* of a manuscript," as was most probably the case. It is plausible, moreover, that some of his hosts (e.g., Nicolás López) in fact had informed him in that direction, whereas others might have refused to show him the manuscript, going so far as to deny its existence. One can understand Bartolo Sis's reluctance to share his manuscript with a foreigner (a priest, moreover) who, barely settled, inquired with such insistence about a text that Sis knew was condemned by the Church. By asserting that he knew it by heart, Sis thus protected himself from any possibility of someone taking the document or from any risk of losing it.

20. Pedro Henríquez Ureña (cited in Mace 1967b: 33n17) reached a similar conclusion in 1936.

> This work was extremely useful to me, moreover: I became fluent in the whole of the language more quickly than with all my reading. Once I was the master of my subject, I undertook to make a clean copy of the play, by translating it gradually into French. (1862b: 19–20)

He was helped in this "cleaning up" of the French translation by a certain number of colonial grammar texts and dictionaries that he says he also used for the control of his final transcription (Brasseur 1855). These volumes, which guided his work, are those he acquired or assembled during his stay in Guatemala and incorporated into his *Bibliothèque mexico-guatémalienne* (1871), the same ones that after his death in 1874 went into the collection of Alphonse-Louis Pinart (1883) and later joined the collection of American manuscripts in the Bibliothèque nationale in Paris (Omont 1925).

They probably were also the same grammatical and lexicographical sources that Georges Raynaud used in 1928 to develop a new version of the *Rabinal Achi* from the Quiché text transcribed by Brasseur. On the whole, Raynaud's corrections are relatively minor, refining the text so that it is more faithful to the rhythm of the indigenous verse, and his more literal translation aims above all to erase the literary flights of his predecessor. But Raynaud worked in camera, and his only sources were a few linguistic texts whose original languages, although close to the Quiché-Achi of Rabinal, did not necessarily take into account distinctions unique to local usage. This concern with translating more closely but without any other source of control often led him to neglect many rhetorical figures, favoring only the lexical meanings in dictionaries, and to correct—wrongly—certain metaphorical formulations rendered correctly by Brasseur on the word of his Indian informants.[21] Several passages in Raynaud's version thus are translated erroneously, rendering them even more obscure.[22] Paradoxically, it is this version—or, more exactly, its Spanish translation first established by Luis Cardoza y Aragón (1929–1930), since the original study (in French) by Raynaud has remained unpublished—that has become the benchmark.

Most of the existing editions of the *Rabinal Achi*—such as those by Raynaud and Cardoza y Aragón (1953, 1972), Monterde (1955, 1963, 1980), Palm (1961), and Leinaweaver (1968)[23]—only borrowed from this version, adapting it or translating it into other languages. Other revisions are inspired directly from Brasseur's translation, such as those by Villacorta (1942), Padial Guerchoux and Vázquez-Bigi (1991), and an abbreviated English version by Ballantine Irving

---

21. In the present case, the recommendations Raynaud (1953: 16n6) addresses to his readers regarding "exaggerated metaphors: excellent in a village, idiotic in another, and vice versa" no doubt might be applied to him.

22. A similar criticism of the limitations of Raynaud's translation of the *Popol Vuh* was expressed by Recinos (Recinos, Goetz, and Morley 1977: 57).

23. These last two authors offer German and English translations, respectively, of the Monterde version (1955).

(1985). Finally, we must add the editions published in Spanish by Baudissonne (1944) and Montalbán (1929, 1945) and in Serbo-Croatian by Acuña (1982).[24]

THE *PÉREZ MANUSCRIPT* (1913)

Returning to our source, Bartolo Sis, responsible at that time for the *Rabinal Achi*,[25] transcribed the text of the dance himself. This work, which probably took a long time to complete, was begun on October 28, 1850, as he mentions in his prologue.

Was Sis's transcript the first written form of an oral tradition or a copy of a more ancient manuscript? Arguing in favor of the first hypothesis, Brasseur reports that the *Rabinal Achi* "was a matter of tradition and of memory" and that Bartolo Sis "had learned it traditionally from his father and his grandfather" (1862b: 287–288).

One might, however, wonder what these arguments alone are truly worth when, even today, and in spite of the incontestable existence of a written text in his possession, José-León Coloch recites the some 3,000 verses by heart, just as his father-in-law, Esteban Xolop, from whom he inherited the play, did. It is clear that the text is passed on simultaneously both in written and oral form, passed on by the memory of those who know it, and that these two paths of transmission are neither exclusive nor incompatible. So Brasseur's assertions, reported in isolation, appear to be circumstantial responses, stereotypical formulas inevitably provoked by any direct question dealing with tradition and

24. Certain parts of these various versions also were included in anthologies (such as Alcina Franch 1957, 1968; Arias-Larretta 1968; Cid Pérez and Martí de Cid 1964; and Sodi Morales 1964). French readers were able to read short excerpts from the *Rabinal Achi* that were reproduced among other texts in Péret 1989: 208–220 (based on Montalbán), Baudot 1976: 205–210 (based on Brasseur), and Garavito 1968 (based on Raynaud). Some were even able to hear it in a radiophonic adaptation dating to 1959, last broadcasted on September 23, 1990 (France-Culture). This reenactment, titled *The Warrior of Rabinal*, adapted by Nadine Lefébure, and directed by Bronislav Horowitz, is inspired by the writings of Brasseur and makes us relive through his voice his arrival in the village, his encounter with Bartolo Sis and the *Rabinal Achi*, and up to the famous presentation on January 20, 1856, which the priest would have sponsored. Eminent actors, including Pierre Vaneck, François Maistre, and Serge Reggiani, performed large excerpts from the text to music by André Jolivet. I thank Laurence Crémière, producer at France-Culture, for having exhumed this document from the archives of the Institut national de l'audiovisuel, where it is located under the reference number LR 24.951.

25. It was, presumably, by virtue of this responsibility that Brasseur (1862a: 127) granted Bartolo Sis the title of *holpop*. The unjustified use of this title, not recognized among the Quiché, comes without a doubt from an association with the corresponding function in Yucatecan society at the time of the Conquest—that of a director of dance. Brasseur, to whom we also owe the first publication of the *Relation des choses de Yucatan* by the bishop Diego de Landa (see Brasseur 1864), arbitrarily transposes the title here.

the origin of specific practices or beliefs. Consequently, they cannot be taken literally and do not definitively discard the possibility that Sis transcribed an earlier text.

An initial clue to the source for Sis's manuscript might be found in the short prologue he wrote as a declaration of intent when he began this long work. He announces, "[u nabe-bibal rech Bartolo Ziz . . .] mi-x-chi-v'elezah-vi original rech vae Xahoh-Tun," which Brasseur translates into French as "[Prologue de B. S. . . .] j'ai transcrit l'original de ce Ballet du Tun" ([Prologue of B. S. . . .] I have transcribed the original of this dance of the Tun) (1862b: 16). Besides the syntax error committed by Brasseur, who changed the verb tense from immediate future to recent past and thus transformed the date of October 18, 1850, from a start date to a date of completion, Brasseur's interpretation can be disputed. Indeed, the active form—*elezah* (*elesaj*), literally "to bring out"—associated with the locative *vi* (*wi*) suggests the following alternate translation: "[First narration of B. S. . . .] which I am excerpting from the original . . ." Because we cannot decide or definitively render this phrase as unambiguous,[26] the choice between translating Sis's words as "extracting the original" (i.e., to produce it) and translating them as "excerpting *from* the original" (i.e., to reproduce it) remains. Thus, the idea that Sis might have had a more ancient "original" in his possession cannot be ruled out.

My preference for the second interpretation would only be derived from a personal conviction if another indication, more consistent, did not lead me to believe that Bartolo Sis in reality was doing the work of a copyist rather than that of a writer. Once again it is Acuña (1975: 73), who discovered and possesses an old notebook found in Rabinal, certain fragments of which were written by Bartolo Sis and signed in his hand, who intuited this. His examination of a few notes written in this notebook provoked the following statement:

> [E]ste indio sabía leer y escribir y, por lo tanto . . . fue perfectamente capaz de efectuar la transcripción del R[abinal] A[chi] que le atribuye indirectamente Brasseur. Lo único que, en realidad, nos sorprende es que ninguna de sus anotaciones, ni siquiera aquellas que evidentemente estaban destinadas a su uso personal, aparezca redactada en la lengua de Rabinal. Nosotros no queremos poner en duda que Bartolo pudiera hablar su lengua nativa; pero el hecho de que todas, absolutamente todas sus anotaciones aparezcan en español hace sospechar que el citado Sis no escribía o, por lo menos, no solía escribir en la lengua de sus mayores. (Ibid.)

If Acuña's assessment of Sis's abilities is accurate, it is clearly improbable that Bartolo Sis, by himself, managed to put down on paper the memorized text of the *Rabinal Achi*. What is more, it seems unthinkable that he was able to undertake and accomplish such a task on his own initiative. His limited abili-

26. This formulation has left all the Quiché-Achi speakers to whom it was submitted perplexed. Thus, this question, raised originally by Robert Carmack (1973: 46n22), remains unanswered.

ties in reading and writing, however, made him capable—at the cost of many attempts and no doubt infinite patience—of undertaking the transcription of a preexisting manuscript.

Yet, only the discovery, still likely, of earlier versions of the *Rabinal Achi,* sleeping at the bottom of some indigenous chest, forgotten in a bundle of anonymous archives, will definitively erase any doubt about the issue. As it stands, Bartolo Sis remains our only point of departure, even though his original text has never been found.

Carroll E. Mace had the good fortune in 1957 to discover another copy of the *Rabinal Achi* distinct from the two printed copies of Brasseur's edition that Brasseur had sent to Rabinal in 1862. This new copy, a manuscript discreetly signed "Pérez" and dated June 12, 1913, was in the possession of Esteban Xolop, who at that time was responsible for the dance. Because Xolop was particularly attached to the traditions of his village and probably aware of the manuscript's value, he had had a copy of the Pérez manuscript made by his son Eugenio Xolop in 1952, which Acuña acquired a few years later (Mace 1981: 106).

Just as they disagreed about Brasseur's manuscript, Mace and Acuña disagree on the question of the genesis and the origin of the text Mace found in 1957, which I henceforth will call the *Pérez Manuscript.*

Mace, as we have seen, always suspected that Brasseur purely and simply copied Bartolo Sis's manuscript, then removed (indeed, even destroyed) Sis's original so that his hoax would not be discovered. Continuing logically with this thesis, he later argued that the *Pérez Manuscript* was only a copy of Brasseur's edition. To support his theory, he considerably minimized the differences that separate the two texts: "[Pérez] ignoró el silabeo de Brasseur, cambió la ortografía, añadió y omitió palabras e introdujo dísticos que no aparecen en la versión brasseuriana. Otro aspecto interesante de esta transcripción es el uso de cuatro símbolos fonéticos inventados en el siglo XVI por el padre La Parra" (1981: 105).

With the same evidence, Acuña arrives at completely opposite conclusions. The magnitude of the manuscripts' differences, whether they are related to spelling or to punctuation (and I would add to disposition), as well as the transformation of certain elements of the text, enable him to assert that

> [l]a *Grammaire* no ha sido el modelo de la copia [de Pérez] . . . hay que postular una fuente textual distinta al R[abinal] A[chi] de Brasseur: si no el manuscrito mismo de Sis, una copia emparentada estrechamente con él. El manuscrito de los Xolop es un fuerte indicio de que el de Sis jamás abandonó el pueblo; aunque, desde luego, no es una garantía de que exista todavía. Es posible, por el contrario, que la copia intermedia—de Pérez, o de alguien que no conocemos—se haya sacado porque la de Bartolo amenazaba deteriorarse. (1975: 53)

I agree with Acuña's statement that the differences between the two texts are too great to support Mace's thesis. It is completely unlikely that a copyist at the beginning of the twentieth century could have changed the printed text of Brasseur in that way and, above all, reestablished by himself the ancient phonetic signs, notably, the tresillo (/ɛ/), which for a long time had not been in use. The following two excerpts, one taken from Brasseur, the other from Pérez, illustrate this point.[27]

Brasseur (1862b: 30)
u camul ca chau
QUECHE-ACHI

Eha! ahcarroc cah, ahcarroc uleu! Qui, pa tzih ca
biih La? togobvachinak u vach tzih chi bixtah La chuvach
cah, chuvach uleu, chi nu chi, chi nu vach. "In oyeu, in
»achi, ca cha curi tzih La. La apare at anomahinak-vi
»uloc chuvach chay, chuvach labal? ca cha ri tzih La.»
La! in qo oyeu, la! in qo achi, xatalari alaui in anoma-
hinak uloc chuvach chay, chuvach labal! Xavi ca cha na-
curi tzih La: «Ch'a hiquiba na u vach a huyubal, a
»tagahal, ca cha ri tzih La.» La! in qo oyeu, la! in qo
achi! curi-ta x-ch'in hiquibi tacut u vach nu huyubal, nu
tagahal! Mana calah in bozinak-vi tzala huyu, tzala
tagah, xa in r'al zutz, xa in r'al mayul? Hulacha x-ch'in
hiquiba nu huyubal, nu tagahal! ca-rah xa x-ch'iqo
can cah, x-ch'iqo can uleu! Ca cha curi nu tzih chuvach
cah, chuvach uleu. Quehe mavi quïa tzih koh tzihoyah. . . .

Pérez Manuscript (1913: fols. 3–4)
camul.. cachau. qiché. achi

ehá: ahcaroƐ: cah. ahcaroƐ. uleu
qipa: tzih cabi ih. lá. to.ƐobaxinaƐ
uvach: tzih: chibixtah. lá. chuvach
cah. chuvach. uleú. chinuchi.
chinuvach: lain oyéu.. áchi. curi. cacha
curitzih. lá. la at pari atanimahi-
naƐ. ulóƐ. chuvach. chá. chuvach-
labal: cacha. ritzih. lá. la inqo yeú
la in qó achi. curi. xatalari.. a la vi
in nanimahinaƐ. viuloƐ. chuvach. chá
chuvach. labál. xavi cachanacu ritzih-
lá: chinhiqiba. novach. nuhuyubal
nutaƐahal. cachá. ritzih..lá. lain
qoyeu. lain. qo achi. curi. taxchin. hiqiba

27. I have chosen to present here the fragment of text corresponding to the single known excerpt of the copy made by Eugenio Xolop in 1952 as it appears in Acuña (Acuña 1975: 53, 181–182). A comparison of the *Pérez Manuscript* (1913) with the copy made by Xolop (1952) demonstrates how a copy and its model can be in every way identical. The scrupulous faithfulness of the copyist toward the source-text and the absolute respect for the writing and original layout in this case prove the almost sacred character of this document as well as of the act of reproducing it. Xolop's manuscript is an exact replica of the *Pérez Manuscript,* itself most likely recopied from the text of Bartolo Sis, which was taken almost certainly in turn from an earlier copy that probably came out of an uninterrupted series of transcriptions going back to the sixteenth century.

tacut.. uvach. nuhuyubal. nutaƐahal
maná. calah. inbozinaƐ. vi. tzala
huyub. tzala taƐah xain. ral. tzuz
xain. ral. mayul. lahulachá. ix chinhiqi-
~~nuhu~~ba. nuhubal. nutaƐahal. carah
xax chiqoƐon. cáh. xaxchiqoƐon uleu
cachá. curi. nutzih. chuvach. cah:
chuvach. uleu.. qehé: mavi. qiatzih
qoh.tzihoyah. . . .

Although, as this comparison shows, the *Pérez Manuscript* is independent from the text published by Brasseur,[28] we must agree with Acuña regarding the existence of at least two distinct channels of transmission. At the current stage of the research, Bartolo Sis indeed appears to be the single point from which these two paths separated and were developed.

The following diagram enables us to follow this dual pathway by presenting the relationships that exist between the various manuscript versions and the principal editions mentioned.

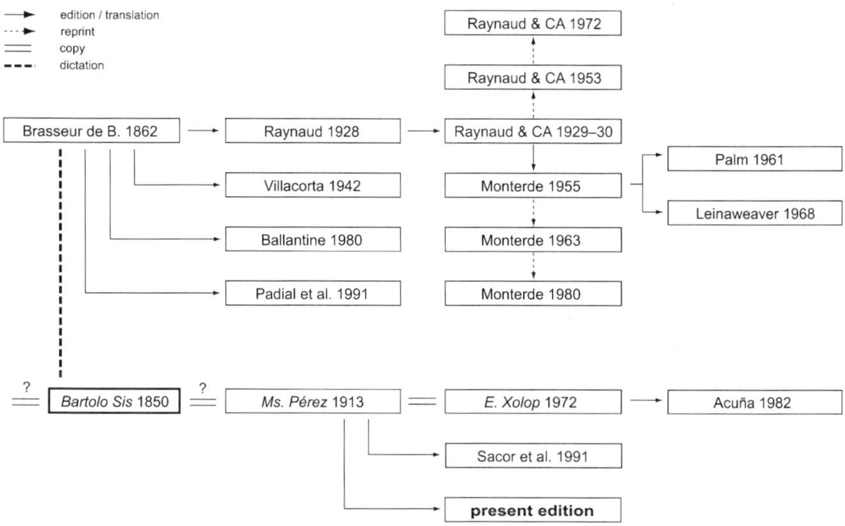

The *Pérez Manuscript* looks like a school notebook, measuring 21.2 x 16 cm, and is covered with a leather binding. It has a total of 76 pages, 65 of which are carefully calligraphied text in a tight but readable hand. Because this document

28. Henceforth, the criticism against Brasseur regarding the presentation of the text—specifically, criticism that attributes to him the origin of the epigraph and the prologue, the initiative of dividing the work into four acts, and the addition of short narrative descriptions that introduce the final three acts—loses all relevance.

is the foundation for the present edition and has remained unpublished up to now outside of Guatemala,[29] it seemed indispensable to me to reproduce it in extenso. Two essential reasons motivated this choice. The first relates to the text's exceptional nature and to the uncertainty that weighs on the future of this indigenous manuscript; as a potential object of greed, its possession is already a source of conflict. The second responds to a justification of a critical nature, since it is precisely from the analysis of the original paleography that the transcription, updated according to phonetic norms currently in use, emerges along with, quite obviously, the new translation.

It is this document that for at least a half-century has been the source of reference for those who have been successively responsible for the dance, functioning as a guide to which they refer for learning and rehearsals. Manuel Pérez's notebook was acquired around 1940 by Esteban Xolop, who kept it throughout his life and passed it on to his children, along with the musical instruments and certain accessories of the dance. Since 1987, the date of Esteban Xolop's death, possession of these objects and of the *Pérez Manuscript* is at the heart of a conflict that pits one of his grandsons[30] against one of his daughters, María Xolop. Despite this family dispute, María and her husband, José-León Coloch Garniga, who is sometimes called José-León "Tun," are and to this day remain, as far as most people are concerned, the only legitimate owners of the manuscript.[31]

Before going into the details of transcription and translation of this edition, let us look at the context in which the *Rabinal Achi* takes place and the story it relates, the initial information we can extract from it, and what commentaries it evokes. Then we will look at issues of form.

---

29. San Carlos University of Guatemala was the first to publish a photocopied reproduction of the *Pérez Manuscript,* including two short descriptions of the choreography and the music (Sacor Quiché et al. 1991). Although it is important that this text was finally made available and recognized in its country of origin, one can only regret the offhand manner in which it was translated. In the meantime, a Spanish edition of the present work has been made available (Breton 1999).

30. This grandson is the son of Eugenio Xolop, who died prematurely scarcely three months after his father's death.

31. However, the strong economic and psychological pressure exerted year after year on the Coloch family by certain members of its entourage, the municipality of Rabinal, or the Ministry of Culture (which under the pretext of a one-time subvention granted in 1988 is in a position to demand the performance of the dance during folkloric festivals) arouses the fear that the family may one day lose possession of the manuscript or that they will attempt to get rid of it. Nevertheless, this pressure has been increasing ever since the *Rabinal Achi* was officially declared part of the cultural heritage of Guatemala in July 2004 and recognized as a "masterpiece of the oral and intangible heritage of humanity" by UNESCO in November 2005.

CONFLICTS BETWEEN THE RABINALEB AND THE QUICHÉ

The Historical Context

The *Rabinal Achi* portrays the trial of a Quiché warrior, named K'iche'Achi, before the royal court of Rabinal. The trial was instigated by a rival warrior—Rabinal Achi, the eponymous character of the play—and his father, King Job Toj.

The story, constructed retrospectively through the dialogues between these three characters, leads us into the region of Guatemala's highlands located between the two pre-Hispanic capitals of Kajyub, the seat of Rabinal royalty to the east, and Utatlán (or Q'umarkaj), the center of the Quiché kingdom to the west (see Figure 2). Both were established rather late, the results of a long process during which the Rabinaleb and the Quiché shared with other groups the adventures of a complex history, the understanding and interpretation of which remain hypothetical and incomplete despite the increase over the last twenty-five years in studies devoted to it. We will look only at the broad lines of that process here, which lends itself to a four-phase periodization.

The first phase corresponds to a primitive phase of "migration," marked by a series of movements that spread out between the tenth and twelfth centuries, through which different Toltec or epi-Toltec groups,[32] originally from the Atlantic coast of the gulf (Chontalpa region) or from the Yucatán peninsula, might have penetrated in successive waves the highlands of Guatemala. According to Carmack (particularly 1968, 1979, 1981), followed by most researchers, whose theses have been widely developed by John W. Fox (1978, 1987), it was in the last of these waves that there occurred the ancestral voyage of the Quiché and the Rabinaleb, who, alongside other groups (Cakchiquel, Tzutujil), might have gone back up the valley of Usumacinta, then that of Chixoy, coming in contact with local populations there. Although particularly significant in the *Popol Vuh,* the *Título de los Señores de Totonicapán,* and the *Anales de los Cakchiqueles,* this obscure migratory episode has never been clearly established through archaeology—hence the use of "might have"—and raises a major unresolved historical question: does the emergence of a Quiché entity in the highlands result from a real displacement of populations or does it reflect the continuation of a cultural movement in the name of which the local elite, claiming a Toltec origin, sought to legitimize their power at the source in the form of migration tales?[33]

Regardless of their historical or mythical tenor, these texts describe at length the difficulties encountered during that migration, the precariousness of those

---

32. Migration tales connect the legendary name of Tula (Tollan, Tulan-Zuywa) to the places of origin of these "Toltec" groups. In these examples, "Tula" no doubt refers to the historical Tula close to Mexico City (in the State of Hidalgo) but also to other cities—Chichén Itzá in the Yucatán and Xicalango on the Gulf coast—that in the course of displacements, became many new Tulas.

33. Arnauld (in Arnauld and Michelet 1991: 78ff.) has taken a preliminary look at this thorny question.

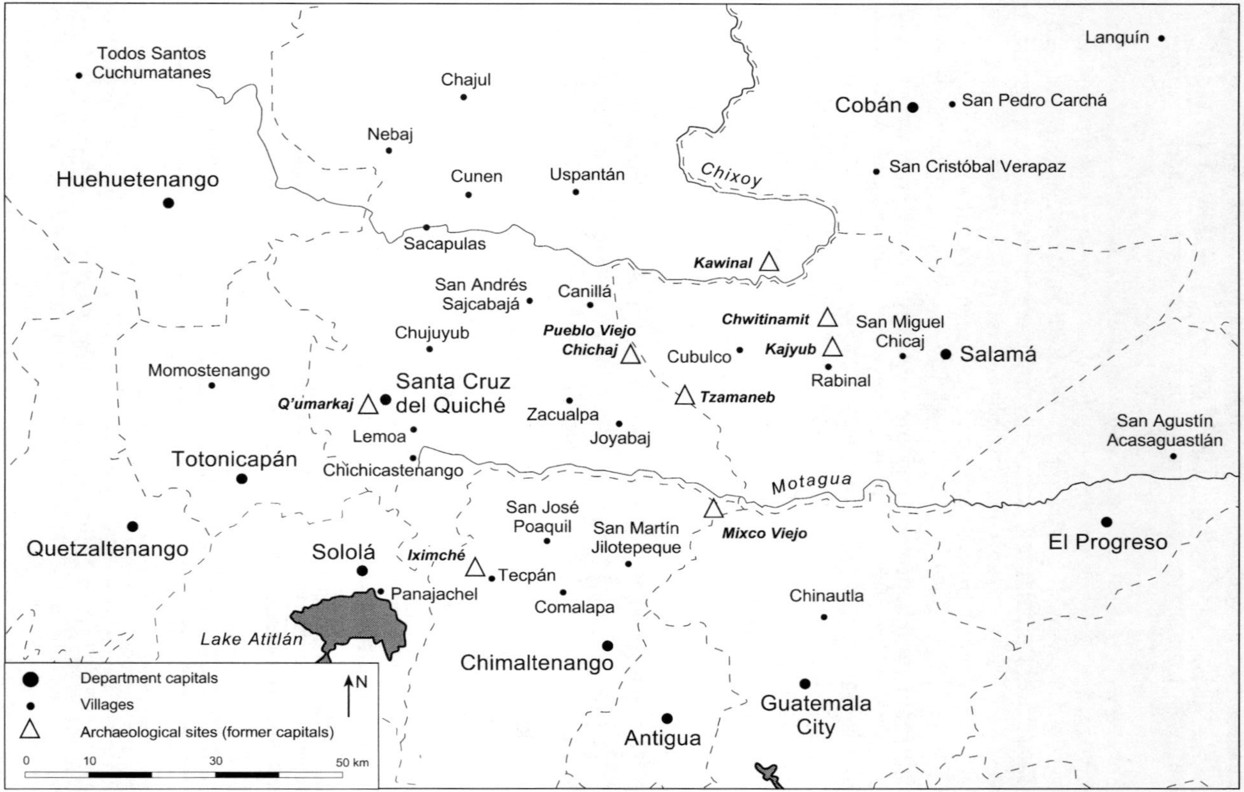

2. *The Highlands of Guatemala*

wandering ancestors' living conditions, and the events that marked their arrival in the highlands, their peaceful or bellicose encounters with the groups already settled there—generically designated by the name of Wuqamaq' (the "Seven tribes") and among whom are included the Aq'ab, Ajkejay, Rotzjayib, Uxab, K'ibaja, Bakaj, Kebatzunja, Ikomak'i, and Poq'omab. According to these documents, the migrating groups finally entered the Sierra Chuacus and reached Chi Pixab ("Place of Recommendations"). Here they held their first council, installed and exhibited their gods, received their names, and decided, after consecrating the supremacy of the Quiché lineages, each to leave in search of a place to settle.

This dispersion inaugurated the second phase, which encompassed populating the highlands of Sierra Chuacus. While the Cakchiquel and the Tzutujil were heading south, to Chuwila (Chichicastenango) and toward Lake Atitlán, respectively, the Quiché were reinforcing their local situation and establishing their first capital, Jakawitz, not far from Chi Pixab, in the mountains above the modern village of Santa Rosa Chujuyub. The Rabinaleb headed east and settled in Tzamaneb on the ridge separating the current basins of Cubulco, Rabinal, and Joyabaj. According to the *Anales de los Cakchiqueles,* it was here that they saw the dawn, the sign of a new era.

The third phase corresponds to a vast movement of expansion during which all these groups, allied within a Quiché confederation, gradually extended their control over the entire region. This movement was conveyed concretely by control of the great fluvial axes of Chixoy and Motagua and by the occupation of the fertile plateaux and basins, as well as by a transfer of capitals. Sites on the heights were abandoned in favor of new centers that overlooked interior basins and adjoining hillsides. Empowered with the new legitimacy of their ruler K'okaib (king of the fifth generation) following his voyage of investiture to the Yucatán, the Quiché then settled in Pismachi. The Rabinaleb settled in Kajyub (and probably also in Chwitinamit). These displacements and occupations marked only a first step in an ongoing process most notably for the Quiché, who extended their conquests and influence to the west (to the large basins of Totonicapán, Quetzaltenango, and Huehuetenango), to the north (into the regions of Sacapulas and the Cuchumatanes), and toward the Pacific coast. The expansion of the Quiché kingdom, begun under the reigns of K'otuja (ca. 1375–1400) and Q'uq'umatz (ca. 1400–1425), reached its heights with K'iq'ab, king of the ninth generation (ca. 1425–1474).[34]

Texts relate the numerous conflicts that peppered the course of this long history—battles opposing Quiché-related groups and local "tribes," internal struggles within the confederation, power struggles between lineages, succession conflicts—but these were never as exacerbated as at the end of the reign of K'iq'ab. From Q'umarkaj (still called Utatlán), the new capital established around 1400 by his father (Q'uq'umatz), K'iq'ab must have expended considerable

34. I am borrowing this succession of Quiché dynastic generations and the corresponding periods of the different reigns from Carmack (1981).

energy to colonize the conquered provinces and reinforce the administrative and fiscal system (collection of tributes) upon which the Quiché power mainly depended. This domination by the Quiché, most notably by the representatives of the Kaweq lineage among them, had been established to the detriment of other lineages and other allied groups. A bloody revolt directed against K'iq'ab, followed a few years later by his death, brought to light important internal schisms and led to a questioning of alliances, thereby generating a situation of permanent conflicts.

The fourth phase (ca. 1475–1524) thus witnessed the fragmentation of the political organization centered on Utatlán-Q'umarkaj. The groups there indulged in continual warfare, the purpose of which was no longer within an expansionist perspective but rather served a policy aiming to shed the burdensome previous allegiances and essentially serve local interests through political and economic emancipation, territorial defense, and the reinforcement of the control of borders. Despite the rise to power of the Cakchiquel, who had settled in Iximché, and the growing influence of the Mexicas (Aztecs) in the region during the first quarter of the sixteenth century, these conflicts continued until the Spanish Conquest.

It is no doubt within this context of repeated conflicts (common through the end of the third phase and into the beginning of the fourth) that we may situate the dispute opposing Rabinaleb and Quiché, the point of departure of the *Rabinal Achi,* and the argument for the trial opposing their respective champions.

What turning points did these historical processes, roughly summed up here, eventually take from a local point of view? How were they expressed and what was their impact on the regional scale with which a large part of the history of the Rabinaleb, as it relates to the present study, is associated?

The broad strokes of the regional history have been drawn by Alain Ichon (1982; Ichon et al. 1988: 199–206). The valley of Chixoy and the basins of the current Baja Verapaz (Cubulco and Rabinal) underwent a very ancient populating, which is seen notably in the large archaeological site of Chiwiloy (no doubt earlier than 900 B.C.); and a few habitation sites also date from the Preclassic period (between 700 B.C. and A.D. 200). Following a relative hiatus, a slow evolution, discernible in the architecture and in the ceramics, carried out the transition toward the next phase, which saw the increase of ceremonial centers and habitation sites over most of the area—the valley of Chixoy, basins, adjacent hillsides, and higher ground. This occupation, remarkably stable and homogeneous, is noted throughout the Classic period and beyond, because it continued until the tenth or eleventh century. Ichon relates this populating to groups called Pokom (henceforth Poq'omab), the same groups that the Quiché in their tales say they encountered and with whom they had to compromise on several occasions through peaceful or bellicose means. Two texts recount most specifically these contacts with the Poq'omab from the region of Rabinal. The first is the *Papel del origen de los señores,* added to the *Relación de Zapotitlán* (Estrada and Niebla 1982). Although it is very short—listing only a terse genealogy of the various Quiché rulers—the text mentions this region on three occasions. First, at the end of the migration: "El primer rey que hubo en los otatecas [quiché] fue llamado *Balam Quitze.* Este rey vino [de] hacia la parte de oriente, y trajo consigo a otros dos hermanos suyos: uno, llamado *Balam Acap;* otro, llamado *MahuƐutah.* Estos fueron iguales en mando y los que primeros poblaron la tierra de Robonal [*sic*]" (ibid.: 59).

This "populating" appears, however, to have been a temporary one on the path leading to the region of Utatlán. The *Anales de los Cakchiqueles* (Recinos 1980), which spends more time on these initial encounters, confirms the entrance of the migrating groups in force in the Poq'om land (called Patzaktzuy, "the Place of the White Gourd") and details the contacts that the allied tribes (Quiché, Cakchiquel, Rabinaleb) had at the time with the Ajkejay of Raxchich and the Poq'omab of Nimpokom and Kaqjay. If we are to believe this tale, these tribes easily obtained the cooperation of the former group but experienced strong resistance from the latter. According to the identifications attempted by Ichon (1982), the location of Raxchich conforms with the archaeological site of Pueblo Viejo-Chixoy,[35] whereas Kaqjay (possibly Nimpokom?), the capital of the Poq'omab, corresponds to Pakaqja (a site close to the current village of Rabinal). These locations confirm the contrast between the early rallying of groups from the valley of the Chixoy—which was verified somewhat later by the Aq'ab of Kawinal[36]—and the relatively greater independence of the occupants of the basin. Whereas the allies continued on their way toward the Sierra Chuacus, the Cakchiquel in passing subjugated the natives of the region of Cubulco: the Ikomak'i and their vassals, the Kaqixajay, and the Qubulahay.[37] The Cakchiquel's route, it seems, did not cross through this region for a long time. Busy elsewhere, they only returned much later when they participated in the vast hegemonic enterprise of King K'iq'ab.

The second mention in the *Papel del origen de los señores* includes the conquest "of the land of R[a]b[i]nal[38] and of its land" under the joint reign of E' and Tz'iquin, the grandsons of Balam K'itze':

> Este *Tz[i]quin* y *E* fueron iguales en mano. Y peleaban de noche, y se iban de noche a matar la gente enemiga que hallaban despobladas y descuidadas por se hacer temer, haciéndose a la apariciencia de los hombres, por visión del demonio, tigres y leones. Y volaban de noche por los aires echando fue[go] por la boca. Y desto hacían gran daño, por lo cual les tomaron mucho miedo y se les sujetó toda la tierra de Robonal. Y les hicieron

35. The merchants who once used the valley of Chixoy, an old transportation route between Lower Verapaz and the northern section of Upper Verapaz, remember this staging place called "Yaxchich," located near the archaeological sites of Pueblo Viejo-Chixoy and Los Encuentros (M.-Ch. Arnauld, pers. comm.).

36. This episode is described in detail in several texts, including *Popol Vuh, Título C'oyoi,* and *Título de los Señores de Totonicapán.*

37. The Cakchiquel were apparently alone in this enterprise, since with the exception of their own annals, no other text mentions it.

38. This term, which one finds written as "Robonal" in the Acuña edition used here, appears in the form "Robinal" in that of Recinos (1980: 245–246).

entender que eran hijos de *Tzacol Pitol,* que es como decir que eran hijos del hacedor de todas las cosas. (Estrada and Niebla 1982: 59)

The third mention evokes a conquest and the colonization of the region. After its subjugation (military, ideological, and economic), there came the time of its political integration within the Quiché state organization, which the text attributes to the king K'okaib, grandson of E':

> Este *Co Caib* sujetó a sí once señoríos de sus antecesores y fue el primero que formó pueblo; formó e hizo casa real y fuerte en Robonal. Éste fue el primero que dio asientos y hizo capit. . . . Y hizo gobernadores y capitanes, y los repartió en cabezas de calpules. Fue el primero que puso leyes y fueros, y el que hizo que pagasen tributo cada uno de lo que tenía y cogía. (Ibid.: 59–60)

Finally, returning to the *Anales,* the region of Rabinal endured repeated attacks from the Quiché (sometimes allied with the Cakchiquel) in the time of K'iq'ab. Among the many towns conquered or reconquered on the occasion of these campaigns there were notably Uxa and Nimpokom (sworn enemies), but also Chikaqyuq' (or Kajyub, the capital of the Rabinaleb) (Recinos 1980: 97).[39]

After this reading of the documents and at the crossroads of the two historical perspectives—one general, the other regional—that we have briefly sketched, it appears that the specific history of the Rabinaleb, both in its relationship to Quiché history and in its connection to the territory that was to become their own, might be summed up in this way (the dates are purely indicative):

Phase 1 (from the tenth to the twelfth centuries). The Rabinaleb are associated, according to the texts, with the migration of epi-Toltec groups from the region of the Gulf of Mexico toward the central highlands of Guatemala. They no doubt also participated in the first attempts to control the local populations (Ajquejay and Poq'omab; see first mention of the *Papel del origen de los señores*).

Phase 2 (from the thirteenth to the early fourteenth centuries). Still within the Quiché influence, they reach the Sierra Chuacus (Chi Pixab), then leave, on their part, to settle in Tzamaneb. Settled on the heights that overlook the basin of Rabinal, they assume an active role in the defense of this border with the Poq'omab, while continuing to lead raids against them (see second mention of the *Papel del origen . . .*).

Phase 3 (from approximately 1350 to 1450). Playing an active role in the dynamics of expansion, the Rabinaleb, probably supported by the Quiché or at the very least under their high patronage, finally and definitively occupy the basin (see third mention of the *Papel del origen . . .*). In the middle of this period

---

39. The Cakchiquel returned in January 1517 to "occupy the fortress of Cakhay" (Recinos 1980: 118–119). But this episode is already situated in a more recent time, later by a few decades than the moment in which the action of the *Rabinal Achi* occurs.

they build their first capital, Kajyub, as well as many other centers of equal or lesser size.[40] Although it is probable that on this occasion or earlier they obtained the submission of a part of the local Poq'omab groups, they forced many of them to abandon these ancestral territories and to scatter, some toward the south (into the region of Chinautla), others toward the north (to Beleju and Cajcoj).[41] Notwithstanding, it is not impossible that certain sites remained in the hands of other Poq'omab who were in some way "Rabinalized."

The Rabinaleb, however, did not give up Tzamaneb, which they continued to inhabit until the early years of the colonial period during 1539–1540 (Ximénez 1929–1931: vol. 2; see also Bertrand 1991). The role of this place in fact endured beyond the occupation of the basin: once the ancient border with the Poq'omab (toward the east) was repealed, Tzamaneb henceforth played a comparable role vis-à-vis the Quiché (to the west), whose continual expansion never ceased to threaten the political and territorial integrity of the Rabinaleb. This process reached its apex under the reign of K'iq'ab. The armed incursions and the reinforcement of garrisons on the outskirts of Tzamaneb revealed the Quiché ambition to continue to impose their supremacy on the Rabinaleb but also indicated the difficulties of integrating the region into the political and tributary organization centered on Utatlán. Like other groups subjected to similar pressures, the Rabinaleb rebelled on several occasions. The death of K'iq'ab, as previously noted, inaugurated the final phase of this pre-Hispanic history, which was marked by dispersion and disruption and was dominated by the increasing confrontations between its various components.

Such is the time frame in which the *Rabinal Achi* plays out. We will see, however, that although it covers all of those periods, the text never makes them the object of its story. Furthermore, unlike (once again) the other aforementioned documents, it does not describe the course of events but projects its characters into a series of episodes without worrying explicitly about situating the context or attempting to pinpoint a chronology. These reasons are why I have not cited this text in the historical reconstruction. Yet, the text can only be interpreted in relation to that reconstruction. Thus, although it contains no mention of or reference to the migration, that migration nonetheless constitutes one of its driving themes. Similarly, although it evokes the episode of Tzamaneb and the struggles against the Poq'omab, the conquest of the basin, and the wars

40. Among the important sites comparable to Kajyub are Chwitinamit and Saqkijel. Kajyub and Chwitinamit seem to have known only a single and unique phase of construction and can be considered as exclusively Rabinaleb creations (Smith 1955: 44–53); Saqkijel, however, shows two successive phases, one of Poq'om origin, the other Rabinal (see Arnauld 1993). I will return to the relationships that join Kajyub and Saqkijel, but I will leave aside Chwitinamit, a site not mentioned in the *Rabinal Achi*.

41. Some of these displacements of the Poq'omab are described in the *Título Cajcoj* (Crespo M. 1968: 12–23). Although the *Rabinal Achi*, as we will see, also mentions a "flight" of the Uxab Poq'omab (although in another context), in the oral tradition this event remains a major theme in the interpretation of regional history.

and alliances, it does not describe the modalities or the precise circumstances of these events. A reader who does not recognize these themes and events in the recesses of the text would be legitimately tempted to see in it only a verbal duel devoid of any narrative intent, of any message of a "historical" nature. The trial that is brought against K'iche' Achi is more than a personal affair and much more than an epiphenomenon (such as the expression of a revolt); it is a trial brought against the Quiché, who in their capacity as allies and rivals, as brothers as well as enemies, represent one of the great and permanent challenges that the Rabinaleb ever had to face. Thus, the trial concentrates the essence and, in some sense, all the ambiguity of this long, shared history.

After reading the text we will return to its interpretation. It is now time to enter the text more fully.

THE TRIAL

The *Rabinal Achi* is divided into four acts and follows a linear unfolding that corresponds to the real time of the narration. During the first act, the longest (taking up half of the text), K'iche'Achi is captured, indicted, and questioned by Rabinal Achi. Specifically, the prisoner is captured while he is attempting to lure Rabinaleb subjects in order to seize and kidnap them. After his capture, he behaves in an aggressive, ironic manner and only later agrees to reveal his identity after many prevarications. Once his origins are established—he *is* indeed a Quiché warrior, the son of Balam Ajaw Balam K'iche'—then begins a long series of accusations against him that set out the reasons for the trial. In the second act, Rabinal Achi tells Job Toj, his sovereign, about the capture and questioning, and the king proposes a compromise: if the Quiché warrior performs an act of allegiance, if he proves to be respectful and willing, the king promises to welcome him among his own and provide him with weapons, clothing, and ornaments; give him food and drink; and give him a wife. Rabinal Achi immediately rejects this offer, as he considers it a personal offense, but later he accepts because of the king's insistence. The third act shows Rabinal Achi reporting his father's words and proposals to K'iche' Achi, who immediately refuses any compromise and continues to act threatening. Finally, in the fourth act, K'iche' Achi is brought before Job Toj, and the captive consents to a parody of conciliation (a formal ritual?), during which he rejects all offers and demands before finally being put to death.

These various exchanges are ordered according to a logical continuity that from the moment K'iche' Achi's appears among the Rabinaleb through his capture and his trial inevitably leads to his being sacrificed. Even if these successive phases show the two warriors outside or inside the fortress (where the king resides), these actions are set within a single unity of place explicitly named in the text: Kaqyuq' Tzilik Kakoqonik Tepekanik (line 331),[42] the

42. Henceforth, quotes taken from the *Rabinal Achi* and references to the text refer to the foliation of the *Pérez Manuscript* and to the line numbers of the present edition.

last capital of the Rabinaleb, today associated through tradition (as through toponymy) with Kajyub, the great archaeological site overlooking the current village of Rabinal.

As in all trials, the narration constantly goes back and forth between mimesis and diegesis, that is, between the action in progress (the unfolding of the trial itself) and the recalling of facts and misdeeds imputed to K'iche' Achi, his failings, his treachery, behaviors that, throughout the events, reinforce the accusation and give rise, throughout the story, to many returns to the past. This evocation of "precedents," which is broken down into different sequences (see Part 3), highlights both the importance of the litigation and the magnitude of what is at stake. Among other things, the Quiché warrior attempted to conquer and seize the territory of the Rabinaleb, take (metaphorically) the most fertile lands, seize a certain number of subjects, destroy several habitation sites, and, even more serious, capture King Job Toj. Finally, and even though the Quiché authorities had pronounced an end to hostilities, he went beyond his prerogatives by violating those dispositions and by attempting to hunt new victims at the outskirts of Kajyub, the place where he was captured. The *Rabinal Achi* denounces that transgression above all and takes the opportunity to list the series of acts that preceded it during the long period of troubles and conflicts that opposed the two groups.

A series of preliminary observations can be directly deduced from certain constitutive elements of the text, beginning with onomastic terms designating the different protagonists, whether or not they are actually represented by actors of the dance.

The Protagonists

Today there are seven characters represented by dancers, but only four of them have speaking parts: Rabinal Achi, Job Toj, and K'iche' Achi, who are responsible for most of the dialogue; and Ixoq Mun, who appears on only five short occasions. Rabinal Achi's wife and two warriors, Eagle(s) and Jaguar(s), complete the list of characters but do not speak. With the exception of the implicit presence of an eighth character—the queen (wife of Job Toj)—the text conforms to this list.

The epigraph, which like a list of credits announces and briefly introduces the various participants, immediately specifies certain of their characteristics. Various allusions found in the body of the text, however, enable one to correct or to complete this preliminary information and to see other characters appear who, although absent from the production, are no less fully protagonists in the story.

The Actors

With the exception of K'iche' Achi, the prisoner of war facing trial, everyone represented here is a member of the royal court of Rabinal—the king and his son, their respective wives, warriors, and servants (slaves)—before which the captive appears.

K'iche' Achi. Described as the son of "balam achi balam k'iche'," K'iche' Achi, in the eyes of the judicial ritual, undeniably holds the central role.[43] In the epigraph he is simply called "kaweq k'iche' achi" and in the text, "kaweq k'iche' winaq." The first of these terms refers to his lineage: Kaweq was the name of one of the "major lineages" (according to the terminology established by Carmack [1981: 163]) of the Quiché group. The second, *k'iche'*, is obviously an ethnonym. As for the terms *achi* or *winaq,* they specify, respectively, that a man is denoted (and in particular a male warrior, which he is), or an individual as a member among others in a group. These two modes of reference and address are combined to signify that the conflict opposing the Rabinaleb and the Quiché comes out of both a specific conjuncture, in which K'iche' Achi represents the enemy, and a general situation attesting to a prolonged hostility with the Kaweq, of which the present event is but a new episode. Other elements will enable us to confirm this analysis.

K'iche' Achi's primary function is that of a warrior, just as is Rabinal Achi's. Indeed, the two characters' attributions are identical: the armed extensions of their respective rulers, they are the emanation of reciprocal resentments and grudges that those rulers have nourished, the instruments of their plans. As K'iche' Achi proclaims:

> While I am the anger
> I am the strength of the sovereign of the Yaki Kunen
> of the Yaki Chajul,
> King Balam Achi
> Balam K'iche'. (lines 192–196)

Job Toj. Given this name in the epigraph (fol. i), the king of the Rabinaleb is referred to throughout the text as Ojob Toj. This name is no doubt of calendrical origin, associating in its composition a number (in a series of thirteen) and a sign (in a series of twenty)—in this case *job* or *jo'ob* ("five") and *toj* (generally translated as "storm").[44] It is possible that the name "Five-Storm" derives from a principle of divine affiliation or identification: we know through the *Popol Vuh* that the Rabinaleb honored Hun Toj ("One-Storm"), a similar or minor divinity of the Quiché god Tojil (D. Tedlock 1985: 353).

Today, these interpretations are largely rejected by the Quiché-Achi speakers of Rabinal, who categorically refuse the translations—which Brasseur and Raynaud already proposed— and suggest rather "cough" for *ojob* and "payer" for *toj.* It is not surprising that folk etymology is totally different

43. If only because he is the accused, it is logical that K'iche' Achi is at the center of the story: his presence and actions are the reason for the trial (Garapon 1985).

44. Having faith in this etymology (which appears the most probable), I have chosen to systematically correct the name of this character from Ojob Toj to Job Toj.

from the archaic sense of the terms. On the one hand, this name comes out of a system of nomenclature linked to an ancient divinatory calendar that is forgotten today.[45] On the other hand, it might borrow one of its components from a non-Mayan language that was once esoteric and is no longer in use: as Lyle Campbell has established (1983: 83), the origin of *toj* might be found in the proto-Mixe-Zoque *tu:h* (in Mixe, *toh*), which means "to dampen." The only trace of *toj* that the local language appears to have conserved is perhaps found in the term *toji,* which is used to describe places that are always green and wet, such as the banks of a permanent stream or certain wooded mountaintop areas that bathe in the clouds and usually drip with moisture.[46]

The only character whose name is consistently attached to the title of Ajaw, Job Toj is the supreme authority of the Rabinaleb. Additionally, he is often designated (and designates himself) as Mama Ajaw, an expression that adds to the royal title the privilege of age and the respect owed to elders (and to ancestors).[47] Out of all the glosses provided by the colonial dictionaries to translate the term *ajaw,* including "lord, master, possessor" (see Glossary), we will focus on the one proposed by Angel (n.d.: fol. 103v): "Gran persona, el Principal como anciano o más viejo, que entiende en los pleitos, o casamientos." Indeed, these are the two essential functions—justice and marriage—over which Job Toj exercises his authority.

Other descriptions associated with him, such as "r-ajaw-al aj-rabinal-eb" (fol. i), "ajaw chakachib tzamanib," and "kawuq rabinal" (fols. 2, 10, 13), specify both his quality and his adherence: Job Toj is the sovereign of the Rabinaleb,

45. Certain diviners-healers from Rabinal still use a system of counting days that is related to the traditional divinatory calendar (a cycle of 260 days formed through the association of 13 numbers and 20 signs) but in extremely weakened forms (often translated literally from the unfolding of the seven-day week) and reduced to a few terms (signs) whose ancient meaning is unknown. For example, Félix Gómez, one of these diviners, holds to the following series: *mej, kan, batz', kej, kamey, tz'ikin, anil, ajawaq, ik', q'ij, tzarajmaq*. As for José-León Coloch, he still has a little school notebook of some twenty pages that belonged to his father-in-law, Esteban Xolop, in which Xolop had attempted to copy a complete calendar series. The notebook contains several attempts, with errors and strike-outs, covering the periods of January 10–February 5, January 10–April 5, then January 10–October 28, all for the year 1963. Xolop wrote down these twenty day-names: *toj, tzii, bati, e, aj, ix* (or *hix*), *tziquin, ajmac* (or *hajmac*), *noj, tijax* (or *tigax*), *cahuc* (or *cabuoc*), *ajpu* (or *hajpuu*), *mox, ix* (or *ixj* or *hixj*), *aabal* (or *uabal*), *cat, can, came, quej,* and *anil.* I have since learned that this list was dictated to Esteban Xolop by one of his friends from San Miguel Chicaj.

46. This relationship connecting Job Toj with rain has not been erased from the collective memory. Buried, as the locals say today, on the acropolis of Kajyub, where requests for rain are made and where Ascension rites take place, the ancient ruler "lives" under the traits of the Santísimo Sacramento del Altar (celebrated during the Corpus Christi), whose laugh triggered the first rainfall as well as the dawn. These transformations, performed by the genesis myth of the colonial (and modern) village of Rabinal, have been analyzed in Breton 1982.

47. Grandfathers, as well as ancestors, are called *mam* (see Breton 1989).

the king of the Chakachib Tzamanib, the high representative of the Kawuq lineage of Rabinal.

We recognize in the second term of "Chakachib Tzamanib" the name used in other texts or chronicles to designate the first capital of the Rabinaleb: Tzamaneb, otherwise called Tzamanich (Ximénez 1975, 1: 54), Tzamaniel (ibid., 2: 326), Zamanib (Brasseur 1946: 166), or Semaneb (Teletor 1955: 188). The origin and the meaning of these names have not been clarified and we still cannot confirm or contradict the hypothesis of Acuña (1975: 5), who, associating Tzamaneb with Itzamna and Chakachib with Chak, connects them potentially to the complex of the ancient Mayan divinities of rain. Interestingly, Acuña, in 1964, was the first to propose, on the basis of descriptions left by his predecessors, the archaeological identification of Tzamaneb with the site of Los Cimientos–Patzaj (overlooking the current hamlet of Tres Cruces). But these points raise even more questions. Do Tzamaneb/Tzamanib and Chakachib refer to a place or to a group? And to which duality does the pairing of these two terms refer?[48]

Rabinal Achi. The son of the sovereign Job Toj, Rabinal Achi is presented with the title "ajaw u-q'alel rabinal" (in the epigraph) or most often "u-q'alel achi rabinal achi" (in the text). These titles refer explicitly to a high military function, translated in various dictionaries as "captain." In the organigram of Quiché titles, this title was for a time exclusively connected to the Nijaib lineage, which was subordinate to the Kaweq lineage. The title later became more widely distributed, in agreement with the expansionist aims and the necessities for control over the conquered regions during the reign of K'iq'ab, and thus was conferred upon the young allied lords and to the vassal warriors who had had military successes (Carmack 1981: 177). Replaced within the context of Rabinal's politico-military organization, which probably was modeled on its Quiché homologue, the title *u-q'alel* designates the war chief whose attributions are also those of a "court advisor." As Carmack (ibid.: 171) points out, "[H]is role was to explain, question, testify, denounce, and, in doing so, to help . . . make important decisions"—a definition that corresponds with surprising appropriateness to Rabinal Achi's function as the trial unfolds.

The etymology and translation of the expression *u-q'alel,* however, are not clearly established. Dennis Tedlock (1985: 349) proposes that it is a derivation of

48. On first sight, the mark of the plural (-Vb) relates these two terms to ethnonyms, that is, a collective naming in some way equivalent to that of "Rabinaleb" (which, except in the epigraph, is not used in the text). "Tzaman" and "Chakach" have disappeared from the indigenous onomastic of Rabinal, but "Chakach" is, however, a widespread patronym in the Cakchiquel groups of the San Martín Jilotepeque region, particularly in the communities of San Juan Comalapa and San José Poaquil. An interesting topic for further inquiry is the hypothesis that the Chakachib belonged to the branch called Chajoma, a formerly Poq'om group that became Cakchiquel and that early on occupied the region of Xoyabaj (Pueblo Viejo-Chichaj; see *Título Chajoma,* in Crespo 1968: 55–58).

q'alunel, "one who holds something in his arms." Yet, it may also be connected with *q'alq'ab* (the "bracelet of precious stones"), *q'al* ("adornment"), and *q'ab* ("hand").[49] Both Rabinal Achi and K'iche' Achi take pride in wearing such a bracelet as a symbol of their rank.

U Chuch Q'uq' u Chuch Raxon. The possible meanings connected to the name of this female character, whom the epigraph presents as Rabinal Achi's wife, are extremely rich and difficult to determine. Two literal translations, scarcely distinguished in dictionaries, are "Mother of the Green Birds" and "Mother of the Green Feathers." In fact, the terms *q'uq'* and *raxon,* individually or together, refer to specific species—the resplendent quetzal (*Pharomachrus mocinno*) in the first case and a "bird whose throat is the color of moss and whose wings are blue" (*Cotinga amabilis,* according to Recinos et al. 1977: 82n3) in the second—or to their feathers. Appearing throughout Mesoamerica among the most ostensible insignias of power and included among the principal articles of tribute and the most prized accessories in ritual dances, the tail feathers of these birds are symbols of wealth and their colors—green (blue)[50]—associate them with precious stones. Dictionaries explicitly note this equivalency, which is also confirmed in our text: "u-chuch q'uq' u-chuch rax-on ri yamanik xtekoq-ib ki-bi" (fol. i). In order to respect this polysemy, an acceptable translation of this complex appellation should be "Mother of the Green Paraphernalia."

Whatever the difficulties in defining the physical and material entity named, the title "mother" suggests a relationship of intimacy, protection, and affection between the character and the objects (feathers) of which she is the holder.[51] Francisco de Varea (n.d.: fol. 389) notes the use of *q'uq'* ("ƐuƐ") to designate "green, long feathers with which [the Cakchiquel] dance" and adds that this term is used "for tribute" and also "for the young girl"; as an example, he cites "nuƐuƐ, nuraxon, xtinya chave re numeal xtiqule avuqin."[52] Also called "Princess" and represented in the dance by a young girl of around ten years old, this character thus embodies a wealth of associations through her name, the most interesting of which, in my opinion, is inspired by the mention that she has "come from Tzam Q'am Karcha" (*ri pe-t-e-naq tzam q'am karcha*), which is repeated in the text (fols. 38, 42, 57, 58).[53]

---

49. Brasseur already proposed this interpretation in 1946 (165n19).

50. These two colors are not distinguished linguistically.

51. The image of parental love among the Quiché-Achi of Rabinal today is translated by the pair *ch'uq/matz,* "to shelter, envelope in one's arms, protect" and, by extension, "to possess, be responsible for."

52. Although Varea does not specify the translation or the context, this statement—perhaps formal or ritual—probably can be attributed to the young girl's father at the moment he gives her to her future husband, as Acuña has pointed out (1978: 39n35): "This precious bird, this green feather that I give you, [is] my daughter, let her marry you" (my translation).

53. Like Ixoq Mun (who is discussed later in the introduction), the princess is dressed in the manner of the K'ekchi women "of Cobán."

It is tempting to connect this place of origin with the contemporary village of San Pedro Carchá (in Alta Verapaz), one of the most important centers of K'ekchi ethnicity. Located some forty kilometers north of Rabinal, near the town of Cobán and similarly situated in the heart of a mountainous, hilly region covered with mountaintop forests fed by abundant rains—the favored habitat of the quetzal—the large town of San Pedro Carchá occupies a strategic position. With the waters of the Río Cahabón going through it and the slopes to the east and north heading off gradually into warmer lands, the region of Carchá was considered a favored landing granting access to the lowlands,[54] just as in other times it served as an obligatory point of passage between the lowlands and the highlands.[55] Thus, José-León Coloch's reading of [*u-*]*tzam q'am karcha* as "the end of the bridge [or of the ladder] of Carchá" might be in complete agreement with this interpretation.[56]

The marriage that, according to the epigraph, joins Rabinal Achi to a woman from Carchá, is apparently not purely contextual. Indeed, when Job Toj proposes that K'iche' Achi marry the "Mother of the Green Paraphernalia," it is clear that he does not mean Rabinal Achi's wife; thus, the name of the character refers to a plural entity, as certain passages of the text suggest: "some are deployed, others are not" (fols. 42, 57, 58). Thus, beyond being an emblematic figure of the alliance, the "Mother of the Green Paraphernalia" is a complex configuration

---

54. The importance of this location is pointed out in the *Popol Vuh,* which identifies this place, called *nim xob karcha,* as the location for the ballgame courts where the twins One-Hunahpu and Seven-Hunahpu, and later Hunahpu and Xbalanqué, face off before their voyage to the underworld of Xibalbá (D. Tedlock 1985: 109, 177, 338). The karstic landscape of Alta Verapaz offers many paths of natural access to the underworld and therefore many potential avenues leading to Xibalbá. Beyond the importance of the indicator *cham* (K'ekchi word for "deep") in the regional toponymy, certain places are identified as opening such "doors." For example, Semuc Champey, a place close to Lanquín where the raging waters of the Río Cahabón plunge with an impressive din into a ravine, is called Xbalbá by the K'ekchi, who still consider this location a place of torment, a door to hell (De León 1985: 53).

55. The migration of the Quiché ancestors, as described in the *Título de los Señores de Totonicapán*, borrows this same route: "Desde el Oriente [la Costa del Golfo], parece que se dirigieron al sur por el río Usumacinta. Pasaron por Verapaz, cerca de Carchá, y luego siguieron el Río Negro hacia el occidente. Bajaron por una de las ramas de ese río para llegar al valle de Sajcabajá. De allí . . . el rumbo los llevó al área de Quiché al suroeste" (Carmack and Mondloch 1983: 218).

56. The geographical and linguistic inquiry that we have carried out in the company of José-León Coloch in the region of San Pedro Carchá and in Alta Verapaz did not enable us to establish with more precision the meaning of the toponym (which might be of K'ekchi origin) or to localize it. We will retain, however, as a possible alternative to the interpretation of this name the meaning that Basseta gives (1698: fol. 225v) for the verb *tzamo,* "to play ball," which would connect this term to the mythical place where the episode described in the *Popol Vuh* occurs (see note 54).

that might symbolize an obligatory perennial link with the region of Carchá and therefore with the Maya lowlands.[57]

Let us sum up the relationships that connect these main characters:

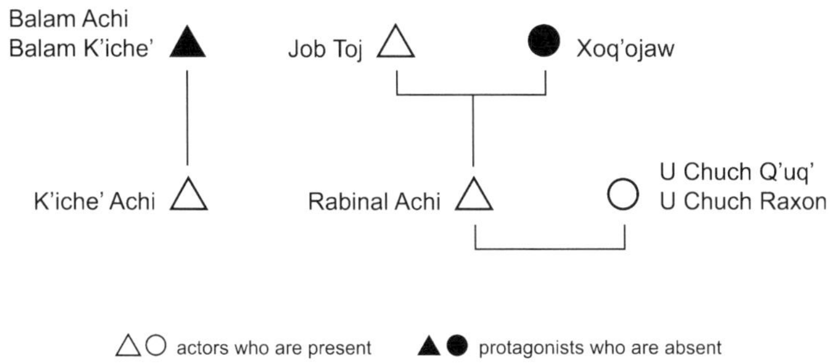

Ixoq Mun. A male or female servant in the court of Rabinal, Ixoq Mun appears in the dance wearing a *huipil*[58] "of Cobán," similar to that of the "Mother of the Green Paraphernalia."[59] This character is called "mun ixoq mun" in the epigraph[60] and "ixoq mun" or, more simply, "mun" at the time his/her appearance is announced in the text. His/her complete name—"achij mun

57. Maybe this assertion would attest to the permanence of the Quiché peoples' ideological attachment to the values of Classic Mayan civilization. If, for these peoples, Tula is the favored reference for all legitimation of power, a reference to the Classic Maya lowlands should not be overlooked as another probable horizon of historical legitimacy. Through the roles and characteristics assigned to each character, the *Rabinal Achi* might offer a specific illustration of the connection between these two references, one that borrows the paths of affiliation, the other those of alliance. This double ideological focusing—toward Tula and toward the lowlands—has been pointed out in other sources (see, e.g., Freidel 1985). Aside from the *Rabinal Achi,* the existence of favored matrimonial ties between Rabinaleb and K'ekchi of Cobán is reinforced by Ximénez (1929–1931, 1: 194) and by Carmack (1973: 180n16) and commented on by Fox (1987: 233). Even today, the K'ekchi and the Rabinaleb consider each other as *baluk,* "brothers-in-law."

58. *Huipil* is a word of Nahuatl origin designating the ample shirts worn by Indian women. The note "of Cobán," by which those concerned assert the origin of the article of clothing, designates the K'ekchi through antonomasia.

59. There is no explanation of the relationship connecting these two characters who share a common origin. At the very most, the simple hypothesis could be advanced that by virtue of servants' attachment to their masters, the "imported" wife kept her own domestic personnel with her.

60. This variation is probably a copyist's error for "achi(j) mun ixoq mun," attributable to confusion engendered by the immediate proximity of the element /achi/ of "rabinal achi" (see fol. i). This type of error is associated with what philologists call a "jump from the same to the same" (see Dain 1975: 48). Incidentally, the term *mun* is no longer used today and has been abandoned in favor of *muy* (as in "Ixoq Muy"), but neither one is understood by contemporary Quiché-Achi speakers.

ixoq mun" — is uttered on several occasions by Job Toj throughout Act IV. This name, formed by two word pairs in which the term *mun* ("slave") is successively associated with *achi-j* ("male, man") and with *ixoq* ("female, woman"), also corresponds to a single formal character, a single actor in the dance.[61] It is probable, however, that like the preceding character, Ixoq Mun incorporates a number of protagonists under the artifice of a single name.

The epigraph indeed mentions multiple "players" who are supposed to accompany the action of the principal group of actors: *k'i-a-taq aj-labal-ib r-uk' k'i-a-mun-ib . . . achi wepu ixoq* ("a multitude of soldiers and many slaves . . . both men and women"). The likelihood, defended by Acuña (1975: 91, 119), that such a crowd of participants in the past took part in the production seems credible. Yet, I disagree with Acuña's assertion that the existence of seven central characters (only four of whom have speaking parts) implies a "decadence and an abandonment on the part of the community" (ibid.: 92). Perhaps this incorporation is a response to the necessities of the genre (such as exemplarity of the story and the allegorical dimension of its interpretation) and to the specific ritual constraints linked to the status of the speech. Among the actors, some represent not specific individuals but archetypes of collective entities, as signaled by their names alone. Reducing the number of players — because of the potentially secret nature of these dances during the colonial period or now the exorbitant cost of such productions — does not fundamentally challenge the ritual's faithfulness to an ancient canon.

Kablajuj u Q'anal Kot Balam. The same phenomenon of artifice and condensation is at work in the case of the "Twelve [Yellow] Eagles, [Twelve] Yellow Jaguars," reduced to only two actors. They represent the fighters (*aj-labal-ib*) and warriors (*achi-j-ab,* "men par excellence") of Rabinal, regrouped into two military orders — Eagles and Jaguars — following an organization frequently noted in Mesoamerica in the Postclassic period, in which the eagle and the jaguar were, since the time of the Toltecs, the icons of the diurnal sun and of the nocturnal sun, respectively (Baudez and Becquelin 1984).

PROTAGONISTS WHO ARE ABSENT

Xoq'ojaw. Job Toj's wife is designated by a title formed by the association and contraction of the terms *[i]xoq* and *ajaw* and can be translated as "woman-sovereign" or, if her husband is recognized as king, "queen."

Presented at the opening as part of the actors-dancers and addressed as such on one occasion by Rabinal Achi (fol. 34), Xoq'ojaw is not included in the cast of characters. A passing reference by Celso Narciso Teletor (1945: 51) implies that

61. The multiple and ambiguous nature of the character is explicitly stressed in the dance's performance as it is played by a man who wears the *huipil* of the K'ekchi women while wearing a mask with a moustache.

she was indeed a member of the cast in the 1940s. We do not know exactly when and why this character was eliminated, but this change had already occurred in 1955 when Francisco Rodríguez Rouanet (1962: 55–56) attended one of the rare performances of the dance.

Saqil Al Saqil K'ajol. This expression, translated literally as "the White Children," designates the subjects of Job Toj and Rabinal Achi, that is, the Rabinaleb (or Chakachib Tzamanib). The related terms *al* and *k'ajol*—"child of woman" and "son of man," respectively—refer to the biological descendants of a couple. As shown by Carmack (1976: 247–248), however, the meaning of the expression *al k'ajol* was extended among the Quiché to designate generically common folk (as opposed to those whom he calls "nobles" or "aristocrats") and vassals (as opposed to "lords"). Thus, this phrase served as a contrast to the terms formed from the root *ajaw* both in these two meanings as in the terminology of kinship. This contrast between these categories still functions in Rabinal and applies to all familial, social, and political relationships (Breton 1989).

The adjective *saqil,* derived from *saq* ("white, light"), connotes the idea of excellence.[62] Thus, like its inhabitants, the territory occupied by the Rabinaleb is described as *saq-il jyub saq-il taq'aj,* literally, the "white (light) mountains, white (light) valleys." Beyond the physical aspect, the expression contrasts the characteristic landscapes of the basin of Rabinal with the wooded lands of the high mountains—wild, uninhabited places described by the generic term *chi k'achelaj,* "where trees abound." Whiteness and light bathe the civilized world and illuminate the center of that world, the "navel of the sky and of the earth," the control of which constitutes the principal reason for the conflicts described here.[63] By establishing the distinction between "vassals or macehuales" (*al 4ahol*) and "the human lineage" (*çakil al çakil 4ahol*), Domingo de Vico (n.d.a: fol. 7v) confirms this interpretation. By characterizing Jakawitz as *zaqui huyub* (the "white mountains"), in contrast with Awilix and Tojil (places belonging to the realm of the "great forests"), the *Popol Vuh* manifests the same break between the place of dawn and the places before dusk (D. Tedlock 1985: 303; see also Carmack 1981: 89–90).

Balam Achi Balam K'iche'. Referred to as Balam Achi Balam K'iche' in the epigraph, the complete name of K'iche' Achi's father—balam ajaw balam achi balam k'iche'—appears later in the text (fol. 10). This title is a direct reference to one of the four eponymous ancestors, Balam K'itze', founder of the Kaweq

62. A metaphorical translation of the expression *saqil al saqil k'ajol* might be "the true children," a term that approaches "true men," which is used in other languages and by other Mayan groups (such as the Tzeltal and Tzotzil of Chiapas).

63. Myths that currently establish Rabinal as the original place of day—*waral x-alax-ik q'ij x-alax-ik saq,* "the day (the sun), light, is born here"—largely repeat this conception (see Breton 1982).

lineage (Carmack 1981: 122). Called "sovereign of the Quiché" (*r-ajaw-al k'iche'*; fol. i) and "king of the Quiché land" (*ajaw k'iche' jyub k'iche' taq'aj*; fols. 10, 14), Jaguar King, Jaguar Man, Jaguar K'iche' does not seem to be a proper name[64] but, more probably, a title that passes from one dynastic generation to the next, connecting them to a genealogical line identified by and with that founder.

A brief mention indicates that he is *r-ajaw-al ri yaki kunen chajul* (fol. 6), "Sovereign of the Foreigners of Kunen and Chajul."[65] Without any doubt, this name is a historical point of reference, situating the reign of Balam Ajaw Balam Achi Balam K'iche' in the final fifty years of the pre-Hispanic period, the years during which the Quiché extended their control over many groups, including the Kunen (see *Título C'oyoi,* in Carmack 1973: 293, 317–318).[66]

The Sovereign Authorities (of the Quiché). Finally, there are characters who are mentioned on two occasions in the *Rabinal Achi* and whom the text describes as follows:

ajaw teken toj
ajaw teken tijax
q'umarmachi
chi taq ta sib
    taq ta simaj
k'oxoma aj
k'oxoma cho
k'oxoma siwan
k'oxoma tz'ikin ki-bi ki-chi'
ki-wach la q-ajaw-al
        la [qa-]winaq-il
(lines 1058–1069)

ajaw teken toj
ajaw teken tijax
q'umarmachi
taq ta sib
taq ta simaj
k'oxoma aj
k'oxoma siwan
k'oxoma cho
k'oxoma kab
k'oxoma tz'ikin ki-bi ki-chi'
        ki-wach
(lines 1434–1444)

---

64. If we knew this specific identity, we could date some of the events related by the *Rabinal Achi* and possibly situate the time of the trial, because we know with relative precision the names of the principal Quiché rulers and the periods of their reigns (see, notably, Carmack 1981: 122).

65. This mention also appears in the epigraph (fol. i), but there it refers to K'iche' Achi.

66. Actually, Cunen and Chajul are two villages located north of the Río Chixoy, in the Cuchumatanes mountains. Apart from the *Rabinal Achi,* no other source mentions Chajul, thus we are unable to confirm a durable supremacy of the Quiché over the Ixil region, except perhaps through the kingdom of Uspantán, which included Cunen. (The common link with Uspantán explains the association of these two villages, one Ixil and the other Uspantec.) This connection with Uspantán was pointed out by Pierre Becquelin (1969: 114; see also 1970): "It is probable that the Ixils preserved their independence in spite of raids by the Quiché of Utatlán. At the time of the Conquest, in order to resist the Spanish, the Ixil chiefs placed themselves under the hegemony of Uspantán. The struggle was brief and submission definitive." In a study devoted to the history of the Cuchumatanes, William George Lovell (1985: 51) mentions a possible Quiché conquest of the Ixil region at the beginning of the fifteenth century, although recognizing that control of Utatlán was relatively loose and probably indirect.

Their mention, first by K'iche' Achi, then by Rabinal Achi, to recall that a decision for peace between their peoples had been reached (then broken by K'iche' Achi) suggests that these characters relate to a structure of power commonly recognized by the two warring parties. The long description to which this structure lends itself raises many problems of translation and interpretation. Moreover, the fact that it appears formulated in these terms only in the *Rabinal Achi* and to my knowledge nowhere else eliminates the possibility of comparative analysis. Therefore, I will analyze one segment at a time.

First, let us consider the segment *Ajaw Teken Toj Teken Tijax*. We are already familiar with the terms *ajaw* and *toj*. The element *tijax*, like *toj*, designates a day in the ritual calendar. In his *Vocabulario*, Vico offers the following definitions:

> *toh*: nombre de un día de los indios; su significado es el aguacero o lluvia. (fol. 190v)
>
> *tihax*: nombre de un día de la semana a la cuenta de los Indios; su significado es el cuchillo de pedernal. (fol. 186)

The Toj-Tijax association, by connecting the rain and the flint knife, evokes the connection between fertility and human sacrifice. This same relationship, noted throughout Mesoamerica particularly in ceremonies to Xipe Totec, is implicitly found in an observation related to the ancient solar calendar.

According to the reconstruction of this calendar, established through various sources by Carmack (1981: 87–88), the annual cycle of the Quiché indeed began in late February / early March with the "month" called Tequexepual.[67] The return of that month thus marked the renewal of the cycle. It, moreover, was symbolically associated with the harvest and was devoted to the collection of tributes. We know that it corresponded to the "month" Tlacaxipeualiztli of the Aztec (Nahuatl) calendar, which Rémi Siméon presents as follows:

> [T]lacaxipeualiztli s.v. "Desollamiento de hombres." Segundo mes del año, considerado como el primero por Gómara y otros autores. Según Sahagún, este mes se extendía desde el 22 de febrero hasta el 13 de marzo y, según Clavijero, desde el 18 de marzo al 6 de abril. El símbolo representativo de este mes es una piel humana. El primer día se celebraba la gran fiesta del dios de los orfebres, *Xipe*, el desollado, con sacrificios de prisioneros y con ejercicios militares. R. *tlacatl, xipeua*. (1986: 562)

From a lexicographical point of view, the bringing together of these two terms—and their transformation, from Tlacaxipeualiztli (Nahuatl) to Tequexepual (Quiché)—offers perhaps an opportunity in passing to clarify the *teken* element (a possible cognate of / teque- /), which is unknown in Quiché and Cakchiquel dictionaries and might have a Nahuatl origin. As Siméon suggests,

67. Or "Tecoxepual" (Basseta 1698: fol. 160v) or "Tacaxepual" (Vico n.d.a: fol. 177v).

it might derive from *tlacatl*: "hombre, noble, señor" (ibid.: 561).[68] These meanings, basically similar to that of the Quiché term *ajaw* that preceded it, enable us for the time being to render this segment as "King(s) Master(s) of the Rain, Master(s) of the Flint Knife."

Are we dealing with a double title given to a single sovereign or with specifications tied to two figures incarnating royal power?[69] In light of the associations evoked, is this title bestowed on the bearer of high functions having to do with the calendar (and, thus, with agriculture), tributes, and sacrifices?[70] The hypothesis deserves consideration: the mediating function that the two opposing parties of the *Rabinal Achi* recognize in them and the very significance of these realms in their speech support it. We can also keep in mind that these titles and functions reveal royalty's intimate association with war.[71]

Next I will analyze the second segment: *Q'umarmachi Chi Taq ta Sib Taq ta Simaj*. To all appearances this expression refers to the capital of the Quiché state, better known by the Nahuatl name of Utatlán, whose archaeological remains are found near the contemporary Santa Cruz del Quiché, administrative seat of the department of El Quiché. This town is designated here by a blended word—/q'umar/ + /machi/—combining the names of its two primary urban components: Q'umarkaj and Pismachi (or Chismachi). That these names are mentioned together situates us in the ultimate period of the autochthonous history of the Quiché.[72] The founding of Pismachi goes back to the second half of the fourteenth century, but Q'umarkaj was founded between 1400 and 1425 and then entered into a period of major development and formidable influence under the reign of K'iq'ab, between 1425 and 1475 (Carmack 1973, 1981).

---

68. On the basis only of the formal resemblance and of meanings associated with the terms that surround *teken—ajaw* and the binomial *toj/tijax*—various possibilities can be suggested, allowing the connection of "teken" with other Nahuatl words, such as *tequitl* ("tributo, impuesto, trabajo, tarea, empleo, funciones, cargo, etc."; Siméon 1986: 511) or *tecutli* ("noble, hidalgo, señor, alto personaje, primer magistrado de una ciudad"; ibid.: 454). One might also see in this word the origin of the term *tecum* shared by several high Quiché dignitaries (see Ximénez 1929–1931: book 1, chapters 27 and 28), such as the famous Tecum Uman, who led the first Indian resistance against the armies of Pedro de Alvarado.

69. One finds such references to "double" rulers in the *Popol Vuh,* as well as in Ximénez 1929–1931: book 1, chapters 27 and 28.

70. The name Ajaw Teken Tijax might be a direct allusion to the function of "sacrificer," if we believe the chronicler Francisco Vázquez, who in 1570, close to a half-century after the Conquest, noted the clandestine persistence of certain sacrificial practices. Vázquez (1937–1944, 2: 28–29; see also Orellana 1984: 206), in his report about a certain Gonzalo Méndez's saving of a young girl in extremis about to be sacrificed by the Indians of Atitlán, specifies in fact that one of the officiants bore the name of Ajaw Jun Tijax.

71. For a discussion of war connotations linked to Tojil, see Himelblau 1989 (specifically, chapter 3).

72. Numerous sources relating to this period place the two names side by side (e.g., in the *Anales de los Cakchiqueles,* in the form "Gumarcaah-chi-Yzmachi"), but the *Rabinal Achi* is unique in the way it melds these names into one.

The segment *Chi Taq ta Sib Taq ta Simaj* can be broken down into *chi,* a locative; *taq,* a pluralizer; *sib,* "smoke"; and *simaj,* "pointed, sharp object." Assuming that the unrecognized particle *ta*[73] does not appreciably alter the reading, I propose the translation "(place) where smoke and points (blades) abound." Beyond a functional description of the city, this expression imposes a view of it as the seat of intense ceremonial activity frequented by many armed warriors.[74]

The final segment that we will analyze is *K'oxoma Aj/Cho/Siwan/Kab/Tz'ikin.* Although most of the associated terms are immediately identifiable—*aj,* "stem, rush, cane"; *cho,* "body of water, lake, lagoon"; *siwan,* "ravine"; *kab,* "honey, bee"; and *tz'ikin,* "bird"[75]—the same is not true of the term *k'oxoma,* which has never been adequately clarified by the various translators of the *Rabinal Achi.* Some have ignored it, simply reproducing it without commentary (e.g., Brasseur, Villacorta Calderón, and Padial Guerchoux and Vázquez-Bigi), whereas others have proposed direct ("racimos"; Raynaud and Cardoza 1972: 48–49) or periphrased translations ("cuando se distribuyeron"; Sacor et al. 1991: 83), all equally unconvincing.

The fact that *k'oxoma* appears in the *Pérez Manuscript* in the form *q'uxuma* (/k'uxuma/) has led José-León Coloch and myself to believe that it concerns a term derived from *k'ux,* "heart," and to propose as a primary hypothesis a symbolic interpretation of the city as the "heart" of the world. This designation could then be read as a coat of arms whose secondary terms would provide in a certain sense heraldic elements borrowed from the landscape and the fauna.[76] An examination of the dictionaries and grammars, however, proved incapable of identifying this particular derivation of *k'ux* in /k'uxuma/. Another path was also offered with the term *k'uxum,* "consistent, thick matter," including a

73. *Ta* perhaps is a doubling of *taq* to denote a great diversity or a multitude. This form is found nowhere else, except perhaps in the Cakchiquel grammar of Torresano (1754: fol. 35), which points out *bataktaon,* "a diversas partes."

74. The points (or blades) considered here as metonymic figures of weapons—Basseta (1698: fol. 178) gives *zimah* as a synonym for "arrow"—also perhaps allude to "temalacatl" (platform for gladiatorial sacrifices) and to "tzompantli" (altar used to display skulls), two structures that occupied a central position in ancient Q'umarkaj according to a drawing dating from the first years of the Colony (see, notably, Carmack and Mondloch 1983: 39, 204).

75. This series of terms, placed alongside *k'oxoma,* presents no obvious internal logic, such as that of a calendar series; *aj* and *tz'ikin* are names of days, but *cho, siwan,* and *kab* are not. Similarly, some of these terms often appear to be connected to other terms in other contexts—for example, *siwan/tinamit; cho/palow; tapich'olol/tz'ikin,* or *kuk/tz'ikin*—but they are presented here in isolation and do not form any identifiable pairs among them. We, however, can note that these terms are elements frequently encountered in Quiché toponomy.

76. This type of representation of the Quiché capital, notably through its references to the aquatic element (rushes, lakes) and to ravines, also evokes those elements that generally are attached to Mesoamerica's mythical places of origins—Tula, Tollan, and Zuywa—as well as to large historical metropolises (see Davies 1977).

particular example cited by Thomás de Coto (1983: 89)—*ru 4uxum chicop*: "la madera carcomida" (the worm-eaten wood)—eventually enabled us to connect *k'uxum* to the meaning of *q'umar* (in Q'umarkaj), a term glossed in Varea (n.d.: fol. 385) and Vico (n.d.a: fol. 237) as "madera, ropa o paja podrida o molida de vieja" and "podrirse la madera," respectively.

Without neglecting these different approaches that open onto an always possible polysemy, painstaking research into possible comparable forms has led to another and, in my opinion, more fertile interpretation based on reading /k'oxoma/ (the form definitively retained in the present transcription instead of /k'uxuma/), concerning which Coto (1983) proposes the following definitions:

> *tin 4oxomah,* espiar o acechar de lejos. (212)
>
> *tin 4oxomah,* mirar contemplando o nivelando con la vista si va derecha la obra, edificio, o otra cosa . . . mirar de lejos, como para ver o oír lo que tratan otros . . . también, cuando de lejos van con la vista puesta a alguna parte, como a árbol, peña, cerro, etc., para salir a él, como los marineros que se gobiernan por el norte . . . este verbo [*4oxomah*] se compone de *4oxom,* que es la certificación que se hace con la vista de alguna cosa, como los exploradores que van a atalayar y contemplar las tierras y fuerzas de los contrarios, la disposición y gente que tienen. (350)
>
> *tin 4oxomah,* notar de lejos lo que otros hacen. (372)

Relating to the function of the Quiché capital—the city par excellence—these various meanings considerably enrich our interpretation. Indeed, according to these translations of *k'oxoma,* the city proves to be a place of watching, a lookout, a sentinel, an observatory from which one controls and looks out over the surrounding area. This conception also corresponds to the city's privileged position in the Postclassic period, installed on a series of plateaux broken up by deep ravines, and no longer describes its symbolic dimension but its eminently military and strategic role organically connected to its defensive mission in the permanent (and hazardous) process of Quiché establishment and expansion.

We can further note that *k'oxoma* is constructed from the same root as *k'oxtun,* the "fortress," whose literal translation would be "the stone look-out" (Edmonson 1965), and that this watchout function probably extended to all major Postclassic sites established on the hillsides surrounding the basins or on the peaks overlooking them.[77] The same concern with observation and surveillance is further conveyed in the regional toponymy through the frequency of words formed from the root *muqu-* ("to see from afar," "to watch," "to espy";

---

77. The city's function as an observatory, deduced from analysis of the terms relating to the city in the *Rabinal Achi,* is supported by the archaeological study of the orientation of buildings called "long houses" (or *nim ja*) with which such sites are endowed. It confirms and illustrates the fact that the territorial control exercised from these places was above all a "control through sight" (see Arnauld 1993).

see Glossary, *muqubal*), which confer a comparable character upon these places.[78]

This digression, stemming from the characterization of Quiché's capital city, should not distract us from the list's explicit reference to men, to those "King(s) Master(s) of the Rain, Master(s) of the Flint Knife." The immediate context tells us that these men are "our masters our eminencies" and attributes to them the following initiatives: *x-e-pixab* ("they recommended"); *mi x-oj-ki-chok-o* ("they summoned us"); and *mi x-oj-ki-sik'i-j* ("they called us") (lines 1052–1057). Similarly, the terms that conclude this listing and specify its object lead us to them: *ki-bi ki-chi' ki-wach* ("[such are] the names of their mouths, of their faces").

These formulations, however, are too ambiguous to enable us to deduce a precise translation in terms of political organization. Should these expressions of plurality be connected to the double figure of a leader and/or to the probable existence of a more extended council of chiefs, in the middle of which would rule, for example, the high representatives of the nine "great houses" of the Kaweq lineage or those of the twenty-four "great houses" of the Quiché group?[79] In the context of a crisis in which such a council is expected to intervene, another type of assembly might be called for the occasion, bringing together the Quiché governors and other groups under their control—*e r-ajaw-al . . . ju-jun chi tz'aq chi k'oxtun* ("the lords . . . of each fortress, of each wall"; lines 1432–1433)—who, we are told, number twelve (lines 241–243). Whatever the case may be, it is indeed a constituted body of sovereign authorities that is evoked here; a body organically identified with Q'umarmachi, the Quiché capital, through a relationship of eponymy. The text offers other examples of this usage that designate the leaders by the names of the places over which they rule ("Lord K'amba"; line 767) or, inversely, that attribute to places the names of those who govern them ("Balam Ajaw Balam Achi Balam K'iche', name of the threshold, of the face of my fortress, of my wall"; lines 339–344).

Uxab Poq'omab. These final protagonists appear in the text only through actions and speech that are attributed to them by other characters. They represent local groups identified with the famous "tribes" that were encountered in early times by the waves of epi-Toltec migrants—Quiché, Rabinaleb, and Cakchiquel—the same ones who proved hostile to them[80] and impeded their

78. It is perhaps appropriate also to include in this category two of the urban components of ancient Utatlán (Carmack 1981: 215 *ff.*): one to the north, Chisalin, also called Mukwits Pilocab ("mountain observatory of the Ilocab"), and the other to the south, today known by the Spanish names of Resguardo ("defense," "toll house") or Atalaya ("watchtower," "belfry").

79. In the *Título de los Señores de Totonicapán* one finds the most precise indications concerning the placement and the detail of this organization into "great houses" (*nim ja*) in Q'umarkaj (Carmack and Mondloch 1983: 197).

80. Several texts (*Popol Vuh, Anales de los Cakchiqueles,* and *Título de los Señores de Totonicapán*) mention attacks carried out by the Poq'omab against Jakawitz.

expansion. In light of the story and its temporal connection with our reconstruction of the regional history, the Uxab Poq'omab certainly represent the former occupants of the basin of Rabinal whom the Rabinaleb had to confront from Tzamaneb. The *Rabinal Achi* evokes this border situation, the attacks endured and the expeditions led against the Rabinaleb, and reserves a large place for the presence of these enemies in their close entourage. I will return at greater length to these groups during the analysis of the text and notably to the important role they play as intermediaries in the relationships that unify and/or oppose Rabinaleb and Quiché.

AN AGONISTIC JOUST

Once again, the central issue of the *Rabinal Achi* resides in the resolution of a fundamental ambiguity dealing with the relationship between the Rabinaleb and the Quiché. It is an ambiguity that is exploited admirably by the rhetoric of the tale by applying and developing to their extreme conclusion the traditional forms of parallelism.

Like other great Mayan texts, the *Rabinal Achi* is strongly marked by that stylistic process that connects the uniform repetition of recurrent items and the multiform contrast of varied items in permanent combinatorial rules.[81] Unlike Western poetic tradition, which favors a play on metric and phonological forms, this parallelism operates essentially on syntactical and semantic levels. It derives its strength and its effects from the pairing of words, phrases, and groups of phrases, following rules of composition that have been abundantly described.[82]

The unity defining the principal canonical variant from which the parallelism is constructed, according to a simple description recently recalled by William Hanks (1989: 92), fundamentally consists of "two immediately adjacent lines that are identical in all respects except one. The nonidentical parts thus form a pair of terms which, in this system, acts as a single lexical unit with a single metaphorical interpretation."

This basic form is in itself extremely rich and open to all sorts of combinations and developments that work at different levels of the text. On the one hand, by setting apart a lexical pair, it puts into play associations that, while preserving for each of the parallel terms its own meaning as well as its figured meanings, contribute to the development of another meaning. The examples proposed by our text are many: the pair *juyub-taq'aj* (literally, "mountain-valley")

81. This process is also at work in every formal discourse (e.g., prayer, ritual dialogue, and sacred speech). Parallelism can be considered to be one of the criteria distinguishing literature from non-literature (Edmonson 1973).

82. For the Quiché one can refer notably to Norman 1983; Ridder 1989; and D. Tedlock 1983a, 1983b; but also, among the many studies devoted to this question in the Mayan languages of the highlands of Guatemala and Mexico, see Townsend 1980 (Ixil language); Becquelin Monod 1979, 1986 (Tzeltal); Gossen 1974 (Tzotzil); and Fought 1985 (Chorti).

designates metaphorically, depending on the context, "a place," "a land," or "the earth"; *kaj-ulew* ("sky-earth") expresses "the world"; and *tz'aq-k'oxtun* (literally, "fortress-wall"), "the citadel." These associations, or semantic pairs, subjected to strongly codified rules of composition,[83] suggest processes of conceptualization unique to the culture (Edmonson 1973), and many relate to Mayan modes of conception of the nature of things (Neuenswander 1986). Depending on the relationships that connect them (e.g., synonymy, antonymy, or complementarity), the parallel terms lend themselves, both within each pair and from one pair to another, to a play of contrastive forces, either complementary or contrasting, that contribute to what might be called a "poetry of meaning."[84]

Further, as parallel "verses," the paired lines participate in a "poetry of the word," unfolding a phrasing whose rhythm is given by (and contained in) repetition. Parallelism functions here as a prosodic process that, from the formal unity described, arranges the discourse (text) into "couplets," then into "packets," and "echoes," until it finally makes its mark on the whole of the work. The various manifestations of this gradual process deserve to be shown briefly.

The most immediate form of parallelism is seen in verses of the type:

.... A Ex.: *ma at on r-al* ***sutz'***
.... B *ma at on r-al* ***mayul*** (lines 76–78)

It is often presented in a condensed (truncated) form:

.... A Ex.: *la ka-θ-cha ri a-tzij ch-u-wach* ***kaj***
(...)* B *ch-u-wach* ***ulew***
* optional (lines 63–64)

This last variant of the couplet is, by far, the most frequently encountered one in the *Rabinal Achi,* if only because it affects the many oratory formulas marking the beginning or the end of the citations, direct or reported, which the speakers send back and forth: "What says thy word facing the sky, facing the earth?"

When the phrases become longer and more complex, there are successive connections that are linked together "in a wave" within a single unity of meaning:

---

83. The formation of pairs most often obeys the observance of stable rules, such as the law of the "heavier second" (Jakobson 1963: 218–219). Moreover, many pairs of words appear as exclusive, and certain couplings are almost automatic (e.g., *juyub-taq'aj, al-k'ajol*). For a glimpse of the Quiché rules of composition and an explanation of how they lend themselves to predictability, see Norman 1983.

84. It is no doubt in the rendering of these semantic pairs that the translator experiences the most difficulty and frustration, because he or she is constantly pulled between the observance of the binary rhythm that these pairs imprint on the text and respect for the metaphorical figures that they weave, between a rather literal or rather free translation (both of the terms and the pairs), between the option for an uncompromising coherence with regard to the various occurrences of a term (or of a pair) whatever the context and an acknowledgment of their changing meanings (although close) depending on the environment.

.... A Ex.: *a la ta k'u k'o wi ri chi* ***u-qajibej***
(...) B *a la ta k'u k'o wi ri x chi* ***r-elebej***
.... C *wa* ***tz'ij***
(...) D *wa* ***cholanik***
.... E *mi x-oj-tzijon uk' la ch-u-wach* ***kaj***
(...) F *ch-u-wach* ***ulew***

(lines 201–205)

Rarer are the forms that I call "crossed" (or "mixed"), which result from a double lexical parallelism:

.... A C Ex.: *in k-in-tajinik in kojol r-etalil ulew chi* ***u-benebal q'ij***
(...) B D *chi* ***r-okibal aq'ab***

(lines 398–400)

Finally, one can note that the speech, far from being reduced to a monotonous succession of verses obeying these few canonical forms, easily accumulates several of them:

Ex: **keje** *k'ut chi-qa-**tanaba** taj u-tijik ri saqil* ***al***
saqil ***k'ajol***
are ta *k'u chi-qa-**kam** u-tijik la qa-**ch'u' nima kinaq***
*la qa-**xtapakal***
*la qa-**xkorowach***
*la qa-**tz'uley u-ji'***

(lines 263–269)

This last excerpt is particularly remarkable insofar as it highlights three new facts: (1) the parallelism does not affect just the lexical elements but also the tools of grammatical connection (*keje-are ta*); (2) the contiguity of the verses can be differed (as in this example, by the insertion of the pair *al-k'ajol* within the co-text constructed around the pair *tanaba-kam*); and (3) the layout can include more than two parallel terms.

The work of Dennis Tedlock (1983a) rightly has highlighted the importance of the series of unity over the couplet in Quiché ritual discourse and tales. The *Rabinal Achi* provides several examples. We can cite, to illustrate such series in three, four, and more terms, the following sequences:

—Series with three terms

Ex.: *ma pa x-e-k'is la ka-ib*
ox-ib ***u-q'ab amaq'***
siwan
tinamit

(lines 1009–1012)

—Series with four terms

Ex.: *r-umal ix-**θ-jarik***
*ix-**θ-twanik***
*ix-**θ-tuxarik***
*ix-**θ-tzarajmaqirik** u-pam ju-jun chi wa'bal*
chi okibal

(lines 248–253)

—Listing

Ex.: *mi x-in-tzaq-k'amaj*
mi x-in-tzaq-kolobej chi-r-ech ***nu-saqi ka'am***
nu-saqi kolob
r-uk' ***nu-yakim wit***
nu-yakim w-ikaj
nu-chinku
nu-q'alq'ab
nu-salmet

(lines 1384–1392)

Alongside these operations of "versification" (and while continuing to include them), the process is extended to embrace entire sequences of the text, which it contrasts as so many parallel "ensembles." Two short passages illustrate the rhetorical power of this phenomenon: the first which plays on the contrast of contrary propositions (inducing a rupture and provoking an effect of surprise), the second on the apposition of successive propositions (describing a course and contributing to create there, on the contrary, an effect of accumulation, continuity, and completion).

Ex.: *ri* ***ix*** *tapich'olol*
tz'ikin
in *r-oyewelal*
in *r-achijilal ri ajaw ri yaki kunen*
ri yaki chajul
la ajaw balam achi
balam k'iche'

(lines 190–196)

Ex.: *x-i-pe chi k'u chila xa wi chiri chik x-θ-ul nu-tzaqa wi u-**ka**-mul nu-yebal*
nu-sik'ibal . . .
*x-i-pe chi k'u chila xa wi chiri chik x-θ-ul nu-tzaqa wi u-**rox**-mul nu-yebal*
nu-sik'ibal . . .
*x-i-pe chi k'u chila xa wi chiri chik x-θ-ul nu-tzaqa wi u-**kaj**-mul nu-yebal*
nu-sik'ibal . . .

(lines 413–428)

But repetition also works on higher levels. Freeing itself from the strict contiguity and the constraints of the gradual construction, it is developed in increasingly larger circles and in cycles.[85] One of the major characteristics of

---

85. The extension of the parallelism from words to phrases, then from groups of phrases to parts of the text, following a process that is so perfectly and systematically achieved in the *Rabinal Achi,* is a fact that was observed and stressed as early as 1928 by Raynaud (Raynaud and Cardoza y Aragón 1972: 12; "entre los textos publicados hasta hoy, creo que el [*Rabinal Achi*] es, podríamos decir, el modelo del paralelismo yendo de la palabra al discurso"). Fought (1985) provides a detailed study of the mechanisms that lead to such developments in the Chorti language.

the *Rabinal Achi*—which should probably be considered a rule of the genre[86]—consists precisely in this use of quasi-symmetry found in the alternated interventions of the characters. Introduced and closed by a series of protocolary formulas, almost all of the replies of the agonistic joust opposing the two warriors (Acts I and III) obey two phases of development: the first, which, while questioning it, repeats (in the form of reported discourse) the earlier speech of the adversary; the second which, covering it (in the form of direct discourse), reveals the point of view of the speaker.[87] It is by borrowing the paths (and the voices)[88] of these "overlapping" dialogues[89] that the story is gradually woven and acquires meaning, for the repetition of the declarations of the opponent is neither neutral nor gratuitous. In the same capacity as the minimal parallel unities that associate two terms to construct a single and richer figure, the repetition always proceeds through rhetorical sliding (e.g., misunderstanding, ambiguity, hyperbole, irony, insolence, and challenge), which from reply to reply opposes the narrative points of view and confers on the story both its depth and its unicity.

Finally, and here we touch on the formal structure of the work, the parallelism governs the balance of the relationships that are established over all four acts by the main characters. Thus, Act I and Act III bring together the two warriors (Rabinal Achi and K'iche' Achi), whereas in Act II and Act IV they each in turn encounter the king (Job Toj). If we confine ourselves to this formal distribution of the actants (whether one considers them as dramatis personae or classifies them according to their "functions," in Propp's sense), and if we assign them the letters A (for K'iche' Achi), B (for Rabinal Achi), and C (for Job Toj), the text is presented in its whole in the form, mutatis mutandis, as a "mega-series" of pairs.

Act I	*Act II*	*Act III*	*Act IV*
A	B	B	A
B	C	A	C

Such a construction is neither, as we can guess, fortuitous or artificial and can only have an effect on its interpretation. We will return to this later to show how it informs the contents and participates in the message. The

86. *Rabinal Achi* is, as we have said, the sole representative of this genre: no other text among all those we have had the opportunity to cite is comparable to it in this realm.

87. This description does not account for all forms of reported discourse. That discourse is in fact used on many other occasions, notably to convey the words of a third party (see Act III, when Rabinal Achi repeats to K'iche' Achi the recommendations that have just been addressed to him by Job Toj), to give voice to absent protagonists (see Act I, the episode involving the Uxab and the Poq'omab), and to recall the words or the inner thoughts of the one who is speaking.

88. It is important to remember that this text is to be spoken aloud and performed in public.

89. The reader should refer to the text to identify this process, the illustration of which would oblige us to reproduce excessively large excerpts.

rigorous balance it obeys also militates in favor of the ancientness of this four-part division.[90] Indeed, the places implicated, the definition of roles, the play of dialogues, and also the development of the plot, the dramatic progression, and the tragic nature of the tale derive their strength and cohesion from this structure. The form assuredly comes out of a literary necessity, which invites us to consider it as being contemporary with the contents; we will see that they support and clarify each other.

THE CURRENT STATE OF THE TEXT

Although it is fixed in writing, the *Rabinal Achi* has aged, and the text we read today has suffered through the years and as a result of copying, from some greater or lesser changes that have been detrimental. The two transcriptions that we now have—that of Brasseur, and the *Pérez Manuscript*—both were produced from a long series of successive copies and consequently have undergone additions, accumulated a certain number of errors, and show omissions.

The additions include some copyists' interventions that serve as reference marks without affecting or changing the text but personalize the copy and confer upon it its instrumental nature, such as the several "música" mentions in the prologue, the numbers recently inscribed opposite the various speeches of the actors by Esteban Xolop (according to Coloch), and the signature of Pérez. Other interventions by copyists are impossible to date, such as the brief scenic indications introducing Acts II, III, and IV and, above all, an epigraph that, judging it by the few divergences from the text, betrays a certain loss of information relative to the description of the characters. Errors of transcription, however, are apparently rare. The concern with establishing the translation of certain passages with the maximum of coherence vis-à-vis the local context but also, gradually, with regard to each part and also to the entire text allowed me to detect some and to suspect others. Among these errors, some are accidental, resulting from a lack of attention, whereas others are more systematic, such as when archaic forms or terms not understood by the copyist were transformed to satisfy a subsidiary interpretation. Some of these latter examples have no impact on the translation (*yamanib* for *yamanik,* line 17; *jub* for *juyub,* line 175) but others do (*kalaj* for *q'alaj,* line 116; *ixketaq* for *skataq,* line 1232). The corrections that have been judged useful have been indicated in the text and, as much as possible, explained and discussed in the form of notes.

Regarding omissions, the problem is more serious. The first among them is found only in the *Pérez Manuscript* and thus can be directly attributed to Manuel Pérez, who between folios 2 and 3 of his copy allowed part of the source-text to escape. The tenor of the fragment is luckily identifiable and can be substituted

90. This concern with structure has been completely obliterated in certain adaptations of the text. such as Villacorta's proposed division into three scenes (1942) or Monterde's two acts and three tableaux (1955). Based on the evidence I present here, these changes are hardly defendable and have no justification.

since this missing part corresponds, save one syllable, to the entire page 28 of Brasseur's transcription (1862b).[91] I took the initiative to restore this passage—inserted between lines 65 and 66—in the present edition. Unfortunately, other gaps are forever irreparable, since they date from much longer ago, even before the two above-mentioned copies and, thus, evidently earlier than the work of Bartolo Sis. Such is the case with the fifth intervention of K'iche' Achi and with the sixth intervention of Rabinal Achi, which disappeared from the accounting of replies. The loss of these dialogues, whose length and importance we cannot know, is particularly regrettable insofar as it introduces a hiatus between two important episodes—the first relating to the conflictual relationships with the Uxab Poq'omab (from Tzamaneb?) and the other where K'iche' Achi is supposed to attempt to seize the territory of the Rabinaleb (near Kajyub). Consequently, the historical interpretation of these events is considerably weakened and precious details concerning their possible chronological connection are definitively unknown.[92] Finally, a certain number of indications encountered locally in the text lead me to believe that certain parts of dialogues have gradually been blurred. Examples include snippets of reported discourse that seem inopportune and sometimes aberrant with regard to the context and also sometimes the announcement of a speaker is not followed with an effect.

THE PRESENT EDITION

This new version of the *Rabinal Achi* is the result of five years of close work on the text. However, such an undertaking would probably not have been envisioned and, a fortiori, brought to fruition without an even longer association with the place where it was born and with the people who for hundreds of years have cultivated its spirit and its form.

Early on I had the opportunity to work in Rabinal for an entire year. The object of that field research was the organization and the religious life of the

91. The fact that the missing part in the *Pérez Manuscript* corresponds closely to a page of Brasseur's printed text should not reignite the quarrel opposing those who believe in an affiliation between the two texts and those who maintain their independence. The fact that the two paginations are, in this precise place, almost identical is a matter of pure chance, and this correspondence of pages has not been verified in what follows. Furthermore, the difference of a syllable, as minimal as it might be, constitutes rather supplemental evidence to refuse the thesis that suggests that the *Pérez Manuscript* is a pure and simple copy of Brasseur's edition.

92. The age of this error leads us to recognize the equivalent age of the notes relating to the various times characters speak and to believe that such precise accounting might be the sign of a narrator. With the exception of Brasseur 1862b and of Sacor Quiché et al. 1991, the other editions consulted do not reproduce these notes. We can observe in passing that those who use Manuel Pérez's notebook (notably Eugenio Xolop) were no doubt intrigued by this apparently discontinuous accounting and thought it advisable to correct it by adding new notes in the margins in order to respect what they considered to be the logical succession of the actors' speech.

Quiché-Achi, a broad theme that led me, from July 1978 to August 1979, to follow the cycle of village festivals that were the responsibility of religious confraternities (*cofradías*); to attend a great number of public and private celebrations that give rhythm to domestic, social, and agricultural life; and to attentively observe the ritual practices, to gather myths and oral traditions, and to record long sessions of prayer and of ritual speeches held by the *tinientes,* those specialists of "the speech of the ancestors" who led the ceremonies. At the time I had only a passing interest in the *Rabinal Achi,* which I considered an abstruse and boring text after a superficial reading. My lack of knowledge of the language prevented me from undertaking a critique of the available versions, and a timid attempt to gather various competent people,[93] as Brasseur had done some 120 years earlier, quickly proved frustrating and useless. It was only eight years later, with the relative improvement of the situation in Guatemala following the terrible period of violence that had struck the Indian communities,[94] that a return to Rabinal was possible. In the meantime, using works of Quiché grammar, I had pursued the study and analysis of my ethnographic and linguistic materials. In May 1987 I met José-León Coloch Garniga and María Xolop, and there began several months of a close collaboration with a view to transcribing and translating the recordings made during my first stay, to which many other texts were added. The following year, on May 19, 1988, while we were working together on one of these recordings—a prayer said to be of the "evening of the masks," *Velación de las máscaras,* whose contents mentioned certain places cited in the *Rabinal Achi*—Coloch excused himself, disappeared for a few moments into the adjoining room of the house, then returned to our worktable, serious and without saying a word, holding the old notebook out to me. Everything came to a standstill; we then immediately undertook the transcription and the translation of the text written down in 1913 by Manuel Pérez, which kept us fully occupied from May 25 to June 4.

Coloch and I then continued to work together to attempt to resolve the countless questions that were raised by this enterprise but also to visit the places, to recognize and to follow the routes, and to identify the actions that occurred in the course of the story. These inquiries and debates, during three other stays in Rabinal (in 1989, 1990, and 1992), directed the choices that have presided over this publication.

The present edition, therefore, is in large part owed to José-León Coloch, if only for the confidence that he showed in me by offering me access to the

93. Among these people were Esteban Xolop, Matías Jerónimo, and Celso Sesam.

94. Among the many works dealing with and analyzing the serious events of 1979 to 1985, see in particular Carmack 1988; Breton and Arnauld 1994; and Le Bot 1992. Guatemala is unfortunately used to political troubles that often end up in violence directed against the indigenous communities. I have been told that, during one of these periods of extreme unrest, Esteban Xolop, fearing for himself and his family, felt compelled to leave his house, but not without having first buried the manuscript of the *Rabinal Achi* (along with the musical instruments and masks) in a place known only to him so that these treasures would not be destroyed or stolen in his absence.

document and the authorization to reproduce it. I would have liked him to be the coauthor of this work, but a certain amount of associated research led me to noticeably modify his reading of the text, to complete and enlarge our common experiences, and, finally, to propose interpretations that differed or went too far beyond his own. Thus, we agreed that I should maintain entire responsibility for these choices.

I cannot possibly list all the other irreplaceable people who either closely or from afar, directly or indirectly, have also contributed to this work carried out in the field, in contact with whom the lexicographical analysis was gradually refined and the meaning of certain passages made clear.

Last, but in an entirely other realm, the study of several colonial dictionaries (*vocabularios*) and ancient grammars (*artes de lengua*) had a decisive role in my choices, enabling me to carry out the multiple verifications necessary to understand the archaic forms frequently encountered in the text. Most of the works consulted are found in the Bibliothèque nationale in Paris—which Brasseur and Raynaud had access to—and I added works from foreign collections (notably, North American) and other sources more recently published (Coto 1983; Ximénez 1985, 1993). Although in the first analysis I favored the two dictionaries dealing exclusively with the Quiché language (Basseta 1698; Tirado 1787), I extended my examination to all languages of the same linguistic family and, notably, to Cakchiquel, which has been documented as much if not more so.

The principal sources to which I have referred are listed below in chronological order. "Q" is used to indicate a Quiché source and "C" indicates a Cakchiquel source.

Dictionaries

Vico n.d.a [16th century] (Q, C)
Varea n.d. [ca. 1620] (C)
Coto 1983 [ca. 1690] (C)
Villacañas n.d. [ca. 1692] (C)
Santo Domingo 1693 (C)
Basseta 1698 (Q)
Angel n.d. [17th century] (Q, C)
Guzmán 1984 [1704] (C)
Ximénez 1985 [ca. 1710] (Q, C)
Tirado 1787 (Q)

Grammars

Vico n.d.b [16th century] (Q)
Martínez n.d. [17th century] (Q)
Ximénez 1993 [ca. 1710–1715] (Q, C)
Torresano 1754 (C)
Anleo n.d. [18th century] (Q)

All of these works appear in the references; the linguistic and lexicographical materials taken from them have been regrouped, entry by entry, in the glossary located at the back of this book.

Regarding the Transcription

The *Pérez Manuscript,* although dating from the beginning of the twentieth century, preserves certain characteristics from the ancient script invented by Father Francisco de la Parra in the 1550s to transcribe "los carácteres proprios de estos idomas, que en ningún otro se hallan" (Torresano 1754: 140), that is, essentially the glottals, unknown in Spanish.[95] These signs, which one finds in the works of this era and later (such as those used here to establish the glossary), are the following:

Ɛ	glottalized uvular [q']
4	glottalized velar [k']
4h	affricate glottalized palatal [ch']
4,	affricate glottalized alveolar [tz']
tz	affricate alveo-fricative [tz]
tt	glottalized alveolar [t']

Although the manuscript retains the tresillo (Ɛ, or an inverted form of the number "3") and, to a lesser degree, the cuatrillo (in the form of "4"), the text shows, however, a certain indecisiveness in the transcription. That indecisiveness is manifest in the variability of the same word in different places in the text (e.g., *caroƐ/qaroƐ/ƐaroƐ*) in the assignment of a single sign to different phonemes (e.g., *z* for [s], [tz], or [tz']). Moreover, certain variations in writing are specifically linked to certain portions of the text; thus, the writing *tz* is systematic from folios 1 to 15 and then from 44 to the end but changed to *z* in folios 16 to 43, with the exception of an isolated occurrence of *tz* on folio 34. Similarly, writing *qu-* before the vowels *e* and *i* is found in the epigraph and the prologue, then disappears (replaced by *q-*) only to reappear in folio 14 and remain consistent until the end. Do these marked differences mean that Manuel Pérez is not the only artisan of this copy and that one or even two people assisted him in the task? Without paleographic expertise, which alone might assure us that this was indeed the case, one can only guess that these variations, faithfully reported, come from an older copy.

Only a new transcription effected according to recognized modern norms enabled us to resolve these inconsistencies in writing. Hoping that this version of the *Rabinal Achi* will be accessible to Guatemalan readers, I have opted to follow the guidelines of the Academia de las Lenguas Mayas, whose rules, rendered common for all the autochthonous languages of the country, are essentially practical: avoid the use of diacritical signs, respect as much as possible the characters on the keyboards, and cause the smallest difference possible vis-à-vis the writing of the national language (Spanish). I, however, have introduced two changes with respect to official orthographical norms: first, regarding the transcription of the phoneme /b/, which, in order to be a

95. On this question one can read the very thorough introduction of René Acuña to the edition of Coto 1983 (xxiii–xxvi), or Rosa Helena Chinchilla Mazariegos's introduction to the work of Ximénez (1993).

systematically voiced consonant, has been retained as such (thus we have the spelling "Rabinal," instead of "Rab'inal"); and second, regarding the spelling of the term *poq'om,* which has been used instead of *poqom* for reasons explained at the end of Part 3.

Different orthographic systems thus were solicited in the course of this work, including those of the *Pérez Manuscript,* my own transliteration, and also old dictionaries. Citations from these sources preserve the original orthography. The different systems' principles of graphic equivalence are laid out below:

Adopted signs	*Pérez Manuscript*	*Dictionaries*
t'	t	tt
tz	z / tz	tz
tz'	z / tz	4,
ch	ch	ch
ch'	ch	4h
k	c / qu / q	c / qu
k'	q	4
q	ε	k
q'	ε / g	ε
s	z / tz	ç / z
j	h	h / j
w	v	v

The other signs retained are common to the three systems except for the glottal '—which, although not noted in the dictionaries or the *Pérez Manuscript,* is suggested sometimes in the latter by an accented vowel. I have systematically restored it here.[96]

Quiché-Achi is an agglutinative language (like most Amerindian languages), thus identifying the roots (verbal and/or nominal) by isolating them from the series of affixes that are connected to them was a priority in my analysis of the text. I have chosen to give the reader the result of this breakdown morpheme by morpheme to give support to the translation.

Considering the relative orthographic indecisiveness from which the *Pérez Manuscript* suffers, but also in order to reconstruct archaic forms that apparently have been modified through time, a certain number of corrections have been made to the original spelling. Explained in the notes, these corrections are indicated in the text by the symbols listed here.

{...} omission of a letter (ex: *{o} job* should be read *job*)
[...] replacement of a letter (ex: *k'[o]x[o]ma* instead of *k'uxuma*)

Finally, and to harmonize the morpheme-by-morpheme presentation, it seemed indispensable to reestablish certain syntactical characteristics that,

---

96. It is appropriate to point out that spoken Quiché-Achi has a tendency to confuse the phonemes *q'* and *'*, a phonological trait by which it is essentially distinguished from Quiché. For obvious reasons, I have not taken this tendency into account in the transcription.

although erased from the spoken language, are components of the language's representation.[97] In particular, the following complementary notations are provided.

- *(...)* reconstitution of sandhi (e.g., *ch(i) u-xmut* instead of *chuxmut*); also used to indicate certain phenomena of apocope (e.g., *j(u)yub* instead of *jyub*)

- *θ* restitution of the absolutive mark of the third person within the verbal syntagmas (e.g., *ka-θ-ch'aw-ik*: cursive aspect–third person singular-TO SPEAK-intransitive suffix ["he speaks"])

Regarding the Translation

Aware of the constraints of form outlined above, the translation that I propose (which appears opposite the native-language text) is, by design, literal. I, in fact, deliberately set out to favor the rhythm and to respect as faithfully as possible both the "natural" meaning of the words and their ordering in the phrase.

The glossary, which contains glosses of noteworthy entries excerpted from ancient sources, provides a means to appreciate the importance of translation choices by eventually replacing them in a temporal, historicized perspective. Thus, its inclusion limits the number of notes, which are already numerous and often long.

Regarding the Presentation

The presentation of dialogue and the division of phrases obey formal considerations that, notwithstanding, are often arbitrary with regard to the enunciative reality of the speech (in a situation of reciting). Given the strength and importance of the parallelism, I have chosen a presentation that makes this process visually obvious (paired words are located above and below each other), at the risk of suggesting too strongly an appearance of versification when the discourse is perhaps only prose.

I stressed above the inherent difficulties in reading the text, notably those that are induced by the overlapping process in the succession of dialogues. I have remedied this challenge by establishing a typographical distinguo between the phases of direct discourse (« . . . ») and the phases of reported discourse (". . ."), and within reported discourse, between citations referring to the speaker's own words or inner thoughts (which appear in roman type) and those relating to the words of a third person (which are italicized).

As a final warning, it is appropriate to recall that this text, above all, is meant to be spoken (recited, performed) and heard (seen, listened to, felt) by people

---

97. Because the text consists only of dialogues, it is logical that the writing bear the marks of oral discourse.

sharing the same, common experience. Despite my efforts in this introduction and the many notes of commentary to present the text so that other people—us, editor and readers—can attempt to participate a little in this experience, this presentation remains incomplete and only delivers a small facet of the *Rabinal Achi,* merely "the words to say it," but until it is performed, it is nothing more than a written score "waiting for actors."

Perhaps, to infuse the text with a breath of life, we should read it out loud.

PART I

The Pérez Manuscript

[fol. i]

are qui vae xaholab................

ahau hoBtoh; Rahaval ah....
Rabinaleb: Rabinal; açhi. ahau...
u εalel. Rabinal. ugahd ahau.......
hobtoh,.........................
caveε quiche. achi. Rahaval: eyá....
qui ah cunen ahchahul. ugahol......
Balam; achi. Balam.. qiche. riRaha.....
val. qiché vinaε. xoεohau. rixoεil ....
ahau. hobtoh: uchuch: uεu. uchuch....
Raxon. Ri. yamanib extecoqib...........
qixbi. Rixoεil Rabinal achi. mun.......
ixoε: mun: Rech. Rabinal. ahi............
ecablahuh: uεanal: cot. Balam qibi.......
achihab. ah Rabinaleb....................
qiataε. ahlabalib. Rug: qia. munib,.......
alahil chic achi vepu ixoε...................
exahol chire xahoh tun...................

[fol. 1]

unabe... Bixbal. Rech. Bartolo ȥiȥ....

chikuvinaƐ. VahxaƐib. Ɛih chi.....
19.. rioctubre. rikunab. de 1850. año..
mixchin veleȥahvi orihinal.......
Rech. vaexahoh. tun, Rech. vae.....
Ɛatinamit S.ampablo Rabinal.....
vi.. quxtabal.. tavé. Ɛumal.. val....
nuqahol. chubeƐih chubeȥaƐ.........
chiƐavapanoƐ.. quekeƐut...........

[fol. 2]

Rabinal. achi. vepu. xahok. tun ...
unabe. Banbal..
unabe. mul. cachavic
quiche achi...............

1º Λ

q. Catelulo℥ voromahau ca℥om........
ahau xacuxere chinabe vae mavi......
Canuqitzo. uchayic. uvixal ucuta-....
mil.. ahau chacachib. tzamanib........
Cavu℥. Rabinal. cacha curinutzih....
Chuvach. cah. chuvach. uleu. qeké....
mavi. qiatzih. qinchau uqla: cah uleu...
chi. qohi, uq la. u℥alel ahi ~~Rabinal: achi~~.
..~~Chi~~... Rabinal achi

1º R unab~~e~~, mul. cachay. Rabinal. achi....

Λ

eha: oyenachi. cave℥ qiche vina℥: la....
Cacha: riatzih. chuvach: cah. chuvach......
.uleu: catelulo℥ voron ahau. ....

[fol. 3]

chupam ral nupocob. rug nuyagim.....
.vi. nuyagim vicak. nuchin:qu. nugalgab..
nuꜩakcab nuꜩalmet. cat chatacut......
aviri uhuyubal aviriatataɛabal aviri...
at boꜩinaɛ.vi..ꜩala. huyub. ꜩalataɛak..
ma.at.onral.ꜩuꜩ. ma at onral.mayul..
ma at. on.oɛotam loɛ. chuvach. chá.....
chuvach: labal: cachá. curinuꜩik.........
chuvach.cak. chuvach uleu. qeké......
..mavi. qiyá. ꜩik.cok:ꜩikon avug...
.cak: .uleu. chiqoki.avug:.............
canab. teleché..vinaɛ..............

camul.. cachau.qiché.achi

2

:chá: ahcaroɛ.cak, ahcaroɛ. uleu....
qipa: ꜩik cabiik.lá. toɛobaxinaɛ.......
uvach: lꜩik: chibixtak.lá. chuvach...
.cak. chuvach.uleú. chinuchi.
.chinuvach; lainoyeu..achi. curi.câha..
curitꜩik.lá. la at pari atanimaki:..
naɛ. uloɛ. chuvach, chá. chuvach:...

[fol. 4]

.labal: çacha ritz̧ik. la. laingoyeu......
:laingo achi. curi. xatalari. .ala vi......
.in nanimahinaƐ. viuloƐ. chuvach. chá.....
.chuvach. labál. xavi cachanacuri tz̧ik...
.la: chinkiqiba. novach. nukuyubal......
.nutaƐakal. caká. ritz̧ik. lá. lain......
.qoyeu. lain.qo achi. curi. taxchin. tiqiba....
.tacut. uvach. nukuyubal. nutaƐakal...
.maná. calak. inboz̧inaƐ. vi. tz̧ala.......
.kuyub. ŧz̧ala taƐak xain. ral. tz̧utz̧......
.xain. ŕal. mayul. lakulacha. ix chinkiqi-
[illegible]ba. nukubal. nutaƐakal. carak.....
.xax chiqoƐon. cák. xaxchiqoƐon ubeu......
.cacha. curi. nutz̧ik. chuvach. cak:
chuvach. uleu.. qeke. mavi. qiatz̧ik....
.gok. ŧz̧ikoyak: uqlá. uƐalel. achi.....
Rabinal. achi. cak. uleu. chiqohi. uqlá.....

2º R. urox mul cachau Rabinal achi........

..Ɛhá. hoyeu. achi. qanab: teleché...
.vinaƐ. laqachá. nacuri: atz̧ik....

[fol. 5]

.chuvach.cah.chuvach. uleu. lain...
.qóyeu. lain. qóachi. curi. vex.:....
.chinkiqiba.nukuyubal. nutaꜫakal....
.maná. calah. inbotz̧inaꜫ: vi. tz̧alá....
.kuyub. tz̧alatataꜫah. xain: kal.....
.tz̧ukz̧. xain. kal..mayul: mapa: cacha...
.riatz̧ik: veba.mavi. ixchakiqiba...
.uvach. riakuyubal. uvach. riata.:..
.ꜫahal. tacarah.cah. tacarah.uleú..
.xaatvahim.xaatperahim.catin.......
.voqiz̧ah. chuvach. vahaval. chuvach..
.nuvinaꜫil. chupam. unimal.tz̧aꜫ....
.chupam. unimal. qoxtun. cachá.....
.curi. nutz̧ik. chuvach: cah. chuvách..
.uleu. qehé.cah uleú chiqohi...........
.avuq..canab. teleché.vinaꜫ......

3° 9: urox.mul. cachau. qiché. achi...:.....

.ahqároꜫ; qáh.

.ahqároꜫ: uleu: .laᵉᵃcha. curi.tz̧ik...
.lá: chuvach.qah.chuvach. uleu. alá:
.taᶜᵘqovi. rixchi.roqibeh. rixchi.ketebeh.

[fol. 6]

.ri.tzik.riuchalanic. rimix coh.tzikoyah.....
.uqla·chuvach.qáh·chuvach.uleu.....
.arebax.chirelebeh.arex.chuɛahibeh....
.rumal.ixchahiqiba·ixcha.calahi....
.zah.uvach·ahubal·uvach·ataɛahal.
.vemavi ixchacalahitzah.ta^ca^rah.......
.qah·tacarah.uleu.xá.at.vahim...
.xá·at perahim(ixcatnucoh)chuvach..
.vahaval·nuvinaɛil·cacha.curi.......
.nutzih.chuvach·qah.chuvach.uleu...
carah·atqáh.carah.atuleu.ri...
.bala(ixchinhiqiba·cut.)uvach......
.nuhuyubal·uvach·nutaɛahal......
.riixtapichol·ontziqin.inroye velál...
.inrachihilal.ri·ahau.riyagi........
.cunen.riyagi.chahul.laahau.....
.Balam.achi...Balam qiche.qilá......
.huqutah.ɛahinaɛvi·ra.ɛanibal....
.tzutz.mayul chinuhi^yu^bal chiunuta...
.ɛahal.ala·taquqóvi............
.richuɛahibeh alastaqaqovi.rixchirele...
.beh.vatzih.vauchalanic.(mixoh.tzikon..)
.uqlá·chuvach·qáh.chuvách uleu.qéhe..
.cah.uleu.chiqohi:uqláuɛalel achi Rabinal achi...

[fol. 7]

3.° R. ucah mul cachau Rabinal achi........

.oyeu.achi. qaveƐ. qiche. vinaƐ. xape.....
xalal. ricanuto, xalal. vatz. xape....
.xalal. nuchaƐ. Ɛatznapux. tzach. nu-..
.qux. chi[ri]rech.ilic la. chirech tzuic la...
chirik [u]nimal tzaƐ. chirik. unimal.....
qoxtum. lal. bari. qaban la. roƐibal...
.utiu. qaban.la. roƐibal, yac. qaban.la..
.roƐibal. utiuy. Balam. chirik. unimal....
.tzaƐ. qoxtun. qaboyibeh.lage. latza-...
.Ɛil.al. qahol. ricƐeletzam bi. chuvach......
unimal tzaƐ. chuvach. unimal.qoxtun.
.etzuquy re uchicopil Ɛan[a]cab. raxa cab.....
.tzuƐbal.rech. vahaval..nuvinaƐil. mama..
.akan. okobtoh xacuxere. lahulachá. uyá..
.qic.utzilibitzaxic vaoyoval..achihilal......
.tamix yacchilalá. mapa xohqitziqih xoh-..
qichoco. ecablahuh. chiahavab. erahaval...
.huhun. chitzaƐ. huhun.[chi] qoxtun...............

.mapax, chariqitzih. chiƐe. chipe.-..
tanabalaƐ. cablahuh. chioyeu........

EOQENIOXdop

[fol. 8]

.ulaε. cablakuk. chiachikab. chul.....
.tatanabalaε. pixabaxiqilalaε. Rumal.....
.ixkaric ixtuanic. ixtuxaric. ixtꜯarak.......
.maεiric. upam, kukun. chivaibal......
.chi oqibal. xalol. xaxil chic qexilil......
.. chicanoε. chupam. qitꜯaεil. qiqoxtu......
.nal. ritꜯaεil. al qahol. Rumal. xabé......
.leheb. chic. xalakuk chic, chiqiriε. chic...
.qitꜯaεil. qiqoxtunal. qehé cut. chiεata......
.nabatah. utikic. ritꜯaεil al tꜯaεil......
.qáhol. aretacu. oxi; chiεaqam, utikic......
.laεachu.ú. nimaε. qinaε. laεá. ix......
.tapaqál. laεá ixqorovach. laεa tꜯu......
.ley. uki. mapax. chari εapixabaxi......
.qil. qumal e.ahavab. erahavál:......
.naεipe. mavi. chiqovic. rakabal. qux......
.la. chirech: vaoyoval. va. achilailal...
.mapa. Beleheb. moεoh. Beleheb. chu......
.may. ixbec. umuεic upitꜯic vaoyoval....
.va achikilal. qumal. eahavab. chila...
.chiqotom: chiticram. chuchexic. are......
.cu. catokoritꜯah. lari. varal. chux......
mut. ;qah. chuxmut. ulew. qehe cut.....

[fol. 9]

.mix pixabtacan la. chikuyubal la.......
.chitaɛahal lá.rumal.varal ꝗaɛa.......
.chayvi vixal.la. ꝗutamil.lá. varal.......
.chuxmut. ꝗak. chuxmut. uleu. mavi.....
.culo. chiɛik. chaɛab. chiɛak tachipan.....
.la. chikuyubal.la. chitaɛahal.la.......
.ɛatz̨.cu varal.lal.camel.lal.tz̨achel varal
.chuxmut. ꝗak. chuxmut.uleu. ꝗeke.....
.cut. canuyopiz̨ak. tz̨ikol.la.chuvach...
.vakaval. chuvach nuvinaɛil. chupam...
.unimal.tz̨aɛ.unimal ꝗoxtum ꝗacha......
.ꝗuri.nutz̨ik chuvach ꝗak. chuvach...,
.uleu. ꝗeke.mavi ꝗiatz̨ik. ꝗoktz̨ikonic....
.ꝗak uleu.chiꝗoki.uꝗlá.........
..ꝗaveɛ..ꝗiche..vinaɛ.........

4º 9.

uꝗak mut-ꝗachau-ꝗiche achi:

.eka: oyeu: achi-uɛalel achi-Rabinal-achi.....
.la ꝗachá. naꝗuri tz̨ik la. chuvach ꝗak.......
.chuvach. uleu. lakulachá. uyaꝗic.
.kioyoval achikilal. cacha.ritz̨ik la. ke.....
.tz̨uꝗulic. xepixab.chinabe la ɛakaval [illegible]...

[fol. 10]

.laꜫavinaꜫil. xaquxere.manaq̧ovi.chirech....:.
.vilic.nupetic. chinu huyubal. chinutaꜫahal....
.chiri.mixet...vi. huntaꜫon. tz̧amahel chux-...
.mut.qah. chuxmut. ulen. chuvach. ahavá-...
-rinaꜫ. tz̧aꜫ. qaꜫyuꜫ. tz̧ilic qaq̧oꜫonic tepe-.....
.canic. ubinchi.uvach.latz̧aꜫ. laq̧oxtun: ma-...
.pa qayutux .apanoꜫ. laq̧al peꜫ oqal qaq̧o-..
.xelapanoꜫ. chuvach. vahaval.nuvinaꜫil.....
Balam.ahau.Balam.achi.Balam qiche......
.ubi. uchi uvach lanutz̧aꜫ....................
.la nuq̧oxtun........................taz̧é chuta-:
.apanoꜫ.-ri.ahau Balam. ahau Balam.......
:qiche. rumal. tatz̧ee. qarayix. uq̧amic.ri.....
.ahau. chaq̧achib. tz̧amanib. qavuꜫ Ra-..
.binal. chuvach.uxab. chuvach.poꜫomab......
.chiꜫaban.tautz̧il.comal. chutaꜫ taviuloꜫ...,..
.royovelal.rachihilal. riahau qiche. huyub...
-qiché taꜫah. chulechabenatah. chirech.....
.tz̧aꜫil.huyub...ritz̧aꜫil.taꜫah. chipe........
.tacut. rinuchaꜫ. rinunimal. chulecha-...
.benatacut. varal chuxmut.qah. chux-...
.mut..ulen. chiroch. tz̧aꜫil.huyub.chirech...
.tz̧aꜫil taꜫah. chulticonatah chukavexa-...

[fol. 11]

.xanatak: xatac·quta·chibec. utꜩam ꜫaqum....
.utꜩam, ꜫaltꜩagil qum ꜫaltꜩagilnay. qeke....
.qut. ixcha·cu.uyebal. utꜩiqibal.·lataꜫom...
.chuvach. vakaval......................
......qeke qut. mixutꜩaꜫapanoꜫ·uy:ebal.....
.utꜩiqibal. vakaval. nuvinaꜫil...........
:eka: ek: voyevalal. vachikilal. chiok.....
.at.tokel. qat.tꜩelekabaloꜫ. tumal: xivula....
.ak. la:taꜫom. tꜩamakel. ixpe chuxmut..
.qak chuxmut. ulen. chayaqauloꜫ......
.ri agovil. riavachikilal kal achab.....
.kal. apocob. chatꜩalak. uloꜫ. raꜫan.....
.kuyub. :raꜫan·taꜫak..............

.ixcha: apanoꜫ. uyebal.. utꜩiqibal. lavakaval....
.nuvinaꜫil. inkintantak·inqin·takiniq....
.in:qotꜩol. ketalil. ulen. chubenebal. ꜫik·chi...
.kogibal. aꜫab. chimachmal·teu. mach...
mal·koxan. chila·pan. tꜩakaxaꜫ·chucke..
.xic. qekecut. mixin·yaquloꜫ. kal nuchab..
.kal. nupoqob.. mixin. tꜩalakquloꜫ. raꜫan...
.kuyub. raꜫan. taꜫak. chiri·qut. xul nu....
.tꜩaꜫavi. nabe·nuyebal. nutꜩiqibal. chuvach.

[fol. 12]

Jrama tun   12

chuchexic

.cholochic: kuyub.cholochic.chak xipe.chi.

.qu.chila.xavi.chirichic.xulnu.ꜩaɛavi....

.uqamul.nuyebal.nuꜩiqibal.chirichic.....

.chinim che.paraveno: chiqabraɛan......

.chuchexic.xipechiquchila.xavichirichic....

.xulnuꜩaɛavi.uroxmul.nuyebal.nu-...

.ꜩiqibal.xavi.chirichic panchalib.chuchexic...

.xipechiquchila.xavi.chirichic.xulnu ꜩa-...

.ɛavi.uqak mul.nuyebal.nuꜩiqibal......

.xolchaɛak: chuchexic.chiri xintavi.....

.catakinuꜩoɛ.loꜩotun.loꜩo ɛokom.cumal...

.la: cabhakuk.uɛanal.qot.Balam: taꜩe...

.nim.qalananqak.qalananulen.qima-...

.mayik: qechakakic.qimayik.qeva-...

.kakic.laqablakuk.uɛanal qot.uɛa-...

.nal.Balam: quc.achik.mun.ixoɛmun......

ℓ

....chiriqut.mixnubixtak: vi.chuvach-...

.qah: chuvach.uleu.ixchaqurinuꜩik.....

.chuvach: qah.chuvach.uleu.qatel-...

.uloɛ.vorom.akau.qaɛom.akau.....

.xaquxere.chinabe vemavi.qanuqiꜩo...

.uchayic.uvixal.uqutamil.la.akau....

[fol. 13]

.rkaqachib..tz̨amanib.qavuɛ.Rabinal...
.ixcha quri nutz̨ik laqocuchubanri.chi...
.echla..lalakau.manava.qoxinmayik...
.manaqoxin:ɛutik.xavare.uchabal tz̨ik....
.xubixtak.chuvach.qak.chuvach.uleu.......
.uɛalel, achi.Rabinal.achi, chicha.ta....
.chiqulá.kumulchic.qeke.qak.uleu.....
.chiqoki.uqlá.uɛalel achi.Rabinal.achi....

+

4ª:.u romul cachau Rabinal.achi.......

:chá:oyeu achi.qaveɛ.qiché.vinaɛ.
.laqachanaquri.atz̨ik.chuvach.qak.chu...
.vach.uleu.ɛi~~ch~~tz̨ik.aretz̨ik..rixbixtak...
.la.managaxukal.tz̨ik.mixbixtak.la.chi...
.ɛatz̨ik.varal.xelvi.kun.taɛon tz̨ama...
.kel.chiɛatz̨ik.okmixok.taɛanic.chila...
.qiché.kuyub.qiché.taɛak.xaquxere...
.maca~~ma~~mac.mana.itz̨el.rixok.taɛanvi...
,qechuta.apanoɛ.la.akau.Balam......
.akau.Balam.qiché.tatz̨é carayix..
.uqamic.utz̨achic.la.akau.chaqachib.....
.tz̨amanib..cavuɛ.Rabi~~v~~nal.~~qavuɛ~~...

[fol. 14]

.qumal.eah.uxab.ahpoƐomab. varal chux.—...
.mut..qah. chuxmut. uleu. chiƐabanta.—....
.utzil. chomal chutaƐquloƐ.riahau. qiche....
.huyub.qiche.taƐah.riroyovalal. rachi....
.hilal. chulechabenatah..chirech.tzaƐil....
.huyub.tzaƐil.taƐah. chultiqonatah.chul....
.avexanatah.xavi.taqoh.tiqonahic.,qoh—.....
.avexanic. xataqula..chibec..utzam.......
.Ɛaqum..utzam Ɛatzaqil.qum. tzaqilnay......
.ixchanabe. riƐatzih.chuvach.qah.........
. chuvach.uleu..xaquxere. rumal xaloƐ....
.xohqelebeh.laxaloƐ xoholuƐahibeh.la.....
varal chuxmut.qah.chuxmut. uleu.......

.Camó. chirech.qah.qamó. chirech uleu.....
.mixohyopitah.uloƐ..chuvach.Ɛatzaqil.....
.ƐaqoxtunalXaquxere. rumal.chiƐa.—...
.yac chá. chiƐayac.labal. ixchá.qelebeh....
.eah.uxab.eahpoƐomab. xaquxere....
.ixchinya.eƐomal.la. taƐiqilal. lá.....
.Chila tabala. chanvila chuvach.....
.nimbe. chiroqobayá. tziqin. chuvach...
Cholochic.tzaƐchun. chuchexic......

[fol. 15]

......mata. quchiyala. rahabal. qicux cah=....
.uxab. cahpoꜫomab. mayuz qupih bila.....
.chiqituyubal. chiqitaꜫahal. qema=..
yih taqulá. qeꜫutih taqulá. .varal....
chux mut. qah. chuxmut. uleu ixcha......
.nabe. rerinutꜯih. xaquxere. rumal.....
managux. chala. qilic qitꜯuic cah=....
uxab cahpoꜫomab. rumal. ixqi. ꜯol-
copih qib chiuxil chi amoloil chi-
ꜯanical chi chequenal. xanim que-
lememic. quechololic. ixquimah ra-
ꜫan. huyub équempec. xeꜫanáhal...
chuchexic. xacuxere mixnuꜯaꜫapa-
noꜫ. nuꜯubal. numuꜫubal chuvach..
cah. chuvach uleu xaqate mixnu-
vilo. cah uxab cahpoꜫomab. chiricut
mixpah nucux mixꜯocotah nucux
chirech ilic lá ꜯuic lá rumal ixya-
bila. rahabal quicux cahuxab -
cahpoꜫomab. chiricut mixinꜯaꜫapanoꜫ
nuyeꜫal nuꜯiqibal chiech lá éha éha..
oyeu uchi cauꜫ qiche vinaꜫ naꜫiꜯ
pa rumal mixeyuꜯ cupihbila cah-

[fol. 16]

uxab eahpoꜫomab chiquikuyubal
chiquitaꜫahal akꜫaroꜫ qah ah-
ꜫaroꜫ ulew xacuxere mixeCocoben-
ꜫanoꜫ. chiꜫakuyubal chiꜫataꜫahal
ꜭaꜫanapanala yebal la ꜭiquibal la
chiquech eah uxab eahpoꜫomab
hampanavi ixquechaubꜫ chiricut
mix ꜭaꜫapanꜭlá yebal la ꜭiquibal-
la. chiqueck ꜫahuxab eahpoꜫomab
chiricut mixquiꜭaꜫ uloꜫ quiyebal
quiꜭiquibal ꜫhá. ꜫha. ixahuxab ix-
ahpoꜫomab quixꜭelehanabanloꜫ
kitana ipixabaxiquil varal chux-
mut. qah chuxmut ulew............

mix chaquapanala chiricut mixe..
cha uloꜫ ꜫahuxab eahpoꜫomab..ꜫh.ꜫh...
oyew achi qaveꜫ quiche vinaꜫ arecuri
mixohyuꜭcupitahuloꜫ chiꜫahuyubal
chiꜫataꜫahal manare varal ꜫoh...
etar. vi.. quc val. quc. nuqahol covi...
xe-ꜫꜫaꜭuꜭ xeꜭaꜫ ꜫiꜭuꜭ chimaꜫch......
mal teu chimachmal horon ....

[fol. 17]

chuxe umukibal raxon chuxe: ꜫanál
peꜫ. uꜫanal qaco.o chuxe ꜫaná puvaꜫ...
chuxe ꜭaꜫipuvaꜫ xepich xeꜫ^cat^. quc...
val.. quc nu cahol arena rival arenu...
qahol mana qoqax caquiriꜫvi huper...
chaꜫap ꜭuꜫbal que xa eꜭulic qoc uloꜫ
hoqal peꜫ hoqal qácoo rumal eah...
pichi eahcot chuxe ꜫih chuxeꜭaꜫ. are..
curi. ral uqahol uꜫalel achi rabinal..
achi. xacu chiqaꜫ rail chicaxcal qaqi-
riꜫvi huperchaꜫap ꜭuꜫbal que chuxe.
ꜫih. chuxeꜭaꜫ. xaui xahunraꜫan qa-
ꜭunchirih queke kun caꜭun chiquivach.
xa eheꜭehoh xaequinrivih riquiumamah
uꜫalel achi rabinal. achi. chuxeꜫih
chuxeꜭaꜫ. mixchauloꜫ quiyebal qui-
ꜭiquibal eahuxab eahpoꜫomab rumal.
ucoꜫobal qui qux.............................

..................., mix cha chicu apanalai
chiquech...eha..eha.. ixahuxab. ixah-
poꜫomab. lacacha nacuriꜭih chuvach-
cah chuvach uleu arenah... ral ucahol....

[fol. 18]

oyeu achi rabinal achi manago..
choc chiquih chiquivach chuvi qui-
ꜯuqunic quicahalenic chicahpa·chi-
qahxuqutal chukolom·ulew·chiran-
ɛan·ulew·pahun varabal pacaib varabal
rumal coquicovil qachihilal arecuri...
ral uqahol xacu quemayixic quesɛu-
tixic. ꜯuculic quecholotic quiel chiqui -
huyubal chiquitaɛahal qarah xahun
xacaib.chic. caquiric quiꜯaɛil quiqox -
tunal. rumal xaque mayixic xaque ɛutixic
chuviqui ꜯuqunic quicahalenic............
arecuri·* ral.ucahol oyeu achi uɛalel-
achi·Rabinal achi· xacuhun xacaib
chiquelic ubi·xavi·xaɛi xahun xacaib·
chirquiric uloɛ quiꜯaɛil quiqoxtunal·
.... mixcha apanala chiquech eah
uxab eah poɛomab.............

mixcha chicuri nuꜯih.. ehá... ehá..
oyeu achi caveɛ quiché vinaɛ mix taba..
la.. ri quiyebal quiꜯiquibal. eahuxab
eahpoɛomab mixquiꜯaɛuloɛ ahqaroɛ...

[fol. 19]

cak ahcaroꜫ uleu ꜫaꜯikcucuchiꜯik mixe-
ꜫaꜫabencanoꜫ. varal chuxmut cak...
chuxmut·uleu. chiquiviꜫ al chiquiviꜫ
qakol ꜫaꜯikcuchiꜯik maxechabentak
chirech·ꜯaꜫil kuyub·ꜯaꜫil taꜫak xaculo.
xacumayik mixulquiꜯala uquiyal ꜫik..
uquiyal aꜫab varal chuxmut qak chuxmut
uleu. xavi xulquiꜯala kalchab la kal
pocob la xavi xulquiꜯala uvach cux la uvach
teleb la manacoxoponvi ꜫaꜯikcuchikik ✗
maxechabentacula varal chuxmut -
cak chuxmut uleu eta amcula apa-
covi ketal uleu la chanibekcu la ꜯalak..
cubila kaꜫankutiyub kaꜫantaꜫak ꜫaꜯik-
cuchiꜯik: inoyeu achi inuꜫalel achi in-
Rabinal achi quinetarvicanoꜫ quc val
quc nucakol varal chux mut cak chuxmut-
uleu·cachacurinuꜯik chuvach cak chu-
vach·uleu. queke cak uleu chicoki uqla
oyeu achi qaveꜫ quiche vinaꜫ.......... ·
......u vaꜫmul cachau quiche achi....

5º q

chá! chái ahcaroꜫ cak ahcaroꜫ.......

[fol. 20]

uleu ɛaȥikcuchiȥik manaxinechaben-
tak. varal chuxmut cak chuxmut uleu.
chirech ȥaɛil huyub ȥaɛil taɛak. lata=
loɛ laxamayik mixulnuqiȥá uqial: ɛik.
uqial aɛab chiri chuxmut ~~[illegible]~~ cak - x
chuxmut uleu! lamana qoxoponvi voye=
ual: vachikilal akcaroɛ qak akcaroɛ—
uleu!. kinbala chinukuyubal chinu=
taɛakal: mixchacukinuȥik chuvach=
qak chuvach uleu! mixnuȥalak cubi-
kaɛan huyub kaɛan taɛak chila cut -
mixin etaqamakavi ȥam. qamba chu-
chexic ixchacukinuȥik chuvach qak
chuvach uleu! lamana koqicam ixchin -
taqik tacubi akauqamba chirech nux=
tapiac: paqivi. kal paqivi uqakol uɛa-
lel. achi Rabinal achi mixcha ucoɛobal-
nucux. xaqu xere qarak cagoɛon qak -
gacoɛon uleu! ixchachicukinuȥik kinel
chicu. chiri chilachicut mixinetacamara-
vi. ȥamȥaɛqikel huyub ȥaɛqikel taɛak
mixnuȥaɛvi nuyebal nuȥiqibal ak=
carol. qak. akqaroɛ uleu!........................

[fol. 21]

la ꜫaꜯik chiꜯik manaxinechabentah
varal chuxmut. qak: chuxmut uleu!
chiricut mixinꜫakꜫakoꜫ chiri chiꜯabiya
xaqate mixnuvilo ruleval nabelic
xambelic ruleval ꜫanboꜯaꜫikal ꜫana-
ꜯuclic ꜯaꜫi ꜯuclic ꜫarixqac ꜯiqin ....

cacha curinnuꜯik chuvach ꜯah, chuvach
uleu! lamana roqicam mixchin loto-
teh tacubi xaꜯcaꜫin veva ruleval na-
belic xambelic chupam ralnuchab...
chupam ralnupocob chiricut mix nu nuꜫ-
teeh: rucnuxtapiyac chupam rule-
val nabelic xambelic xinel chicuchiri
chilachicut mixinetacamaravi ꜯam-
ix tincurun chuvach ximbaka chuchexic
xinel chicuchiri chilachicut mixine
tacamaravi. ꜯamqiꜯintun: chiricut
xintunakvi xoꜫnucux oxlahuvinꜫ ꜫih...
oxlahuvinaꜫ aꜫab. rumal. manaxi-
nechabentah. varal chuxmut. cak. chux-
mut uleu! chirech ꜯaꜫil kuyub ꜯaꜫil-
tuꜫah cacha curinuꜯik. chuvach. cak.

[fol. 22]

chuvach uleu! ahεaroε. cah. ahεaroε.
uleu! laεaꜯik chiꜯik manaxine chaben-
tah. varal chuxmut. cah. chuxmut......
uleu! laxaloε lă(xa)mayih mixulnuqiꜯa..
uqiyal. εih. uqiyal aεab. cacha curinu-
ꜯih.. chuvach cah. chuvach uleu! xavi.....
xulnuqiꜯa uvach nuqux. uvach nute-
leb managohoponvi voyeualal. vachi-
hilal. iXchacurinuꜯik chuvach cah..
chuvach uleu. hinbala chinuhu......
yubal. chinutaεahal. ixchacurinu-.
ꜯih: chiricut mixin ꜯalah ubi raεan..
huyub: raεantaεah ixcha curinuꜯih...
quehe. cah uleu. chiqohi uqla..........
uεaleh achi Rabinal achi!.........

uvuεmul cachan.

Rabinal achi

5° R

ehá! oyenachi qaveε qiché vinaε!.......
val nuqahol..........maεiparumal xea-
yacubi. valnuqahol managoavoqibal...
chique..............xaqueyuꜯ cupih canoε...
chiqihuyubal chiqitaεahal vemavi.......

[fol. 23]

ixqueyutꜩcupik canoꜫ tarak · qak tarak ulen-
ꜩanꜩiloh qak çanꜩilohuk mix cha nuyebal
Rumal inkintantak. inquintatinic ingotꜩol...
Retal ulew. chila ꜩaim moꜫoꜩu·um.. chu-
chexic. tamix yacbila riꜩaꜫilal ꜩaꜫil-
qakol. chupam ꜩalchab la. ralpocob la...
chiricut mana xoꜫ. cux la chirech. utayic.
nuyebal nuꜩiqibal chiricut mixinꜩalak-
culoꜫ raꜫan kuyub raꜫantaꜫak chila-
cut. mixin.. netaqamaravi chiripanaka..
che. el.- chuchexic chilacut mix nuꜩaꜫvi..
nuyebal nuꜩiqibal chiech la ate cuchiri....
mixeyutꜩcupik canla riꜩaꜫil al ꜩaꜫil-
qakol chiri chinimchée. chicabraꜫan....
paravero.- chuchexic xaꜩcaꜫinchic mana-
xeyopikic. chila qiché kuyub qiché taꜫak.
chiricut mixeꜩelvachin uloꜫ ixquimak-
uloꜫ.. raꜫan. kuyub.. raꜫantaꜫak taꜩee...
qaꜩakꜩat qoqipam. quexirxotileb.. ucoꜫ...
taxeꜩelvachin uloꜫ.. xaquxere: maxeyopi-
tak chic.. chupam quiꜩaꜫil qui qoxtunal...
xacuchirichic mixeamaꜫelabxi chiri-
pamaꜫá. chuchexic......................xavi qilal.......

[fol. 24]

mixul eꜯak la rivahaval nuvinaɛil chiri
chatinibal chuchexic mapaxavi. intin-
tantah. inquintahinvcoɛ incohol retal-
uleu. chilaꜯamtha chuvach. qula vach.
abah. chuchexic. xacuxere mixinꜯaɛuloɛ
nuꜯubal numuɛubal chuvach. cah. chu-
uleu! xanim raɛanibal. ꜯuꜯ. mayul. chic..
hichotinaɛ. chicanoɛ. chuvach uximal-
ꜯaɛ. unimal. qoxtun. chiricut mix-
nuꜯaɛuloɛ nuyebal. nuꜯiqibal. chuvach..
qah chuvach uleu! ixchacurinuꜯih.........
cha...cha... oyeu achi qaveɛ qiché. vinaɛ.
uatzanal. nuvinaɛil.......... naɛipaRumal.
xulaveꜯah. chupam. unimal. ꜯaɛ. unimal.:-
qoxtun xamana qoavoqibal chirech xa.-
chayuꜯcupih canoɛ. chupam unimal. ꜯaɛ...
unimal qoxtun. ixchacurinaꜯih xacuxe-
re. mana xoɛ quxla chirech utayic. nuyebal.
nuꜯiqibal ixchacurinuꜯih uvemavi. ixcha.:-
yuꜯcupih canoɛ. rivatzanal nuvinaɛil tacarah.
qah tacarah. uleu! canꜯiloh qah canꜯiloh uleu!
pacah. nube puleu nube ixchacurinuꜯih chiricut
mana. xoɛ. cuxla chirech utayic nuyebal nu-

[fol. 25]

ꜭiqibal mixin ꜭalahcubi raꜫanhuyub raꜫantaꜫah.
chilacut mixinetacamaravi chupan.....unimal
ꜭaꜫ. unimal.goxtum. xacuxere minuvilo xaraꜫa-
nibal. ꜭuꜭchic raꜫanibal mayutchic hichotinaꜫ-
chic chuvach unimal.ꜭaꜫ. unimal goxtum
xalol xaxilchic quexililchiqanoꜫ quetunan
chiꜫanoꜫ quexililic chupam unimal
ꜭaꜫ. unimal goxtum ~~...~~ chiricut pah.
nuqux ꜭocotah nuqux xinꜭalah chicubi
raꜫan huyub raꜫantaꜫah chilacut mi-
xinyopitah apanoꜫ quiché huyub quiché
taꜫah qatecuchiri mixnuriꜫo vahaval-
nuvinaꜫil xanim ꜭaꜫim chirih ꜭaꜫim chu-
vach: chupan aꜫam chun chiricut mixnu-
tarih. chirech. ralnuchab. ruq. ralnupo-
cob. rucnuyaquim vi. nuyaquimviꜫah ruq-
voyevelal vachihilal xacuxero mix-
nuvilo. vahaval. nuvinaꜫil xanim. lolo-
xinaꜫ.. chirih uvach chupam. aꜫam. -
chum. chiricut mix nulototeh. chupam...
ral. nuchab- ralnupoꜫob ꜫaꜭihcuchiꜭih..
vematain ꜫaꜭcuchila. qachayvi uvi-
xal. ucutamil lavahaval lanuvi........

[fol. 26]

naƐil chila qiché huyub qichétaƐah..
arecuri. Rumal. mixin yacchiviuloƐ....
Chupam ral chab ruc. ral nupocob.......
nrixulnuhetezah chivicut chupam uzaƐil.
uqoxtunal. rivahaval nuvinaƐil...........

mapá ~~mix~~eqizlá. caib. oxib. uƐab. ama....
Ɛ.. zivantinamit chiri balamvac.. chi..
tintot. vi. poƐlah. chicarcararah. chicunu..
chiƐozibal taƐah tulul. chuchexic hanicpa-
cut. mavi chigouic rahabal quxla. chirech
vaoyoual va achitilal arenäcol toho-
rizah. lari varal chuxmut. qah. chuxmut-
uleu! quehecut ixtinyopizah zihol la. chu-
vach. vahaval nuvinaƐil quehecut mix....
pixabtacanla chituyubal lá chitaƐahal lá.
rumal varal caƐachayvi vixal la cuta-
mil la. varal chuxmut qah chuxmut uleu!
qacha curinuzih. quehe mavi qiyazih qoh-
zihon. uclá. qah uleu! chiqohiuglá..
qaveƐ qiché vinaƐ.......................

Eugenio Xdop Ojpan COC

[fol. 27]

uvuεmul cachau
6º qiché achi

etá. oyeu achi Rabinal achi lacachana
curiꜩih la chuvach qah chuvach uleu!
εaꜩareꜩih managoxuhal ꜩih. mixbixtah lá
chuvach. qah. chuvach uleu! chinuchi chi-
nuvach. εaꜩihcu....chiꜩih inxin macubeh.
rinuꜩih. arecut xepixabchinabe la εahaval.
la εavinaεil. mixohqichoco mixohqi:ꜩiqih
ixchacuqiꜩih εahaval εavinaεil ahau.....
tequentoh ahau tequentihax εumarmachii
chitaεtaꜩib taεtaꜩimah quxumaah
quxumachó: quxumaꜩiuan quxumaꜩiquin
qibi qichii qivach laεahaval lavinaεil.....
chipetanaba. alaε cablahuh chioyeu. chia....
chirab. chul tatanabalaε pixabaxiqil.......
alaε mixchanabe riqiꜩih chiεe. uqla.......
xacuxere Rumal ixha:aric ixtuanic ixtu.....
xaric ixꜩarahmaεiric. upamtuhun chi...
vabal chioqibal. chupam. unimal ꜩaε. uni.....
mal. qoxtum. xabelehebchic xalahuhchic..
riꜩaεil. al. riꜩaεil. qahol eqochupam qi...

[fol. 28]

ꜭaꜫil. qiqoxtunal ixchanabe riqiꜭih chiꜫe..
uqlá xacuxere Rumal maná xinecha..
bentah. varal chux mut. qah chux mut
uleu! rumalcut uqoꜫobal nucux. taxe-
nubenebeh xenuꜭelebeh riꜭaꜫil al.
riꜭaꜫil qahol chiriucoꜫ queꜭurutiah...
viquivach. chupana iximcheé. chirech......
uꜭucuxic uchicopil ꜫanacab raxacab......
mixenuvilo ixchacurinuꜭih chuvach. cah.
chuvach uleu! lamana roquiqam ixque..
nuyactacubi vaꜭaꜫil alqahol quiyacatah..
tacubi. chinuhuyubal chinutaꜫahal chacu-
rinuꜭih chinvoponibehtah chuvach vahaval..
nuvinaꜫil qiché huyub. qiché taꜫah ixcha...
curinuꜭih. arecuri. xaiꜭcaꜫin. ruleval....
nabelic xambelic ꜫanboꜭaꜫihal ꜫanaꜭuc-
lic. ꜭaꜫiꜭuclic chiricut mixin quiriteh..
vicanoꜫ chiripancaꜫil chuchexic rumal.
arexbec nucux ruq laꜭaꜫil al ꜭaꜫil. qahol..

xacuxere rumal mixꜭaꜫapan. la. yebal la...
ꜭiqibal. lá. xoꜫcux lá chirech utayic. yebal..

[fol. 29]

la. ꜩiqibal lá. xacuxere mixyopitak apa-
nla. chilapanakachéel chilacut mix-
ꜩaꜫvila yebal. la. ꜩiqibal lá qatecsichiri.
mixe nuyuꜩcupik. uloꜫ riꜩaꜫil ál. riꜩaꜫil-
qakol. chiri chinimchee chiqabrakꜫan.
paraveno. chuchexic. xaꜩcaꜫin chirak.
mana xeyopikic riꜩaꜫil al riꜩaꜫil qakol.
chinukuyubal chinutaꜫakal. qiche kuyub:
qiche taꜫak quekecut mixe ꜩelekvachi-
nuloꜫ. riꜩaꜫil al riꜩaꜫil. qakol qaxir-
xot-tileb ucoqipam queꜩakꜩat taꜫucoꜫ
taxqimakuloꜫ. rakꜫan kuyub rakꜫan......
taꜫak. xacuxere rumal manaxeyopitak-
uloꜫ. chupam qiꜩaꜫil quiqoxtunal. xa-
cuchirichic xeamaꜫelabvi. pamaꜫaá......
chuchexic xaviꜫaꜩin xinmacubek. mixul-
nuveꜩak. akaval. lá. vinaꜫil. lá. ꜫhiri cha-
tinibal. chuchexic. rumal qaxacac. ucoꜫ..
chiri mixinyacubi paral nuchab. paral ...
nupocob. mixin ꜫaꜩakcut. chinukuyubal..
chinutaꜫakal chilá qiche. kuyub. qiche ..
taꜫak. rumal uqoꜫobal. nucux rumal........
manaxinechabentak. varal. ꜫhuxmut...

[fol. 30]

qah. chuxmut. uleu! qekecut mixin ꜯapikcut.....
chupam. ꜯaꜫchun aꜫam. mixin. ꜯakcabik·rik....
mixin ꜯarcabik·uvach. chupam aꜫam·chum...
ꜫaꜯcuin xin macubek xavi cachariꜯik lá...
mixeqiꜯ lá·caib. oxib uꜫab amaꜫ. ꜯivan·ti ...
namit. chiribalam. vac. chitintot vi. poꜫlak.
chicarcaraxak chiqunu chiꜫoꜯibal. taꜫak...
tulul. chuchexic ꜫaꜯcuin xin macubek·rum...
al ucoꜫobal. nucux. lá arecuchul nutoho...
riꜯah rivaral chuxmut qah·chuxmut......
uleu! cachariꜯik-la lal ahau· mapaxavi..
xacha [cacha] curiꜯik la canyopiꜯah ꜯihoxic la..
lá. chuvach vakaval nuvinaꜫil chupam-
umimal ꜯaꜫ unimal qoxtun· chiricut. mix-
pixab tacanla chikuyubal. lá chitaꜫahal·
lá. rumal varal qaꜫachayvi vixal lá qu-
tamil·lá. varal chuxmut. qah. chuxmut.
ulen qachariꜯik la. lamaná vaqochubiꜯik.
lá. chinuchii chinuvach xavacuc. xava-
ꜯiqin. lá. chinuvach laqocuxubanri.........
chiech lá. lal ahau...............mapaxavi.
cachariꜯik lá. canyopiꜯah. ꜯihoxic. lá.
chuvach vakaval nuvinaꜫil. chupam.

[fol. 31]

unimal. ꜭaꜫ: unimal qoxtum. mixpixab. tachi-
canla chihuyabal. la. chitaꜫahal. la ku-
mal. varal qaꜫachayvi vixal. la qutamil-
la. varal chuxmut. qah: chuxmut ulew!
qacharitꜭih. la. lamanaroqiqam chiꜫa-
bantautꜭil chomal aꜭinib. chaꜫinib chin-
viꜫ tacanla. ixchincavuhtacanla. chi-
rech. nuꜫanapuvaꜫ nuꜭaꜫipuvaꜫ rug-
ral. nuchab. rug. ral. nupocob. nuya-
qim. vi. nuyaqimviqah. rug ixqetaꜫ. va-
ꜭiaꜫ. rug. nuxtapiyac varaltachicha-
qunvi. chipataninvi. chiqeal. la. qol. la.
varal. chuxmut. qah. chuxmut ulew!
xatanimaretalil qinyuꜭcupihtubila.
chinutuyubal chinutaꜫahal qachcurinuꜭih.
chuvach qah. chuvach ulew! qah. ulew!
chiqoti uqla. oyew. achi. uꜫalel. achi.
rabinal. achi..............................

6º R

uvahxaꜫ mul cachau.
Rabinal achi.

cha! oyew achi. qaveꜫ qiché vinaꜫ..........

[fol. 32]

lacacha nacuriaȥik la̧ chuvach. qah..
chuvach uleu̧ lamanárogicam. ixchin-
qavuhtacanla ochinviɛtapucanlá chi-
rech nuɛanapuvaɛ nuȥaɛipuvaɛ ruq. ral-
nuchab. o ruq ralnupocob o ruq ixque taɛ-
vaȥiaɛ. ruq nuxtapiac varal tachicha-
cunvi. chipatanin vi-varal. chuxmut.....
qah. chuxmut uleu̧ cachá. riȥih lá xa-...
hin maxqinchacuriva chuvach u.......
vahaval. chuvach lanuvinaɛil taȥeé......
bahun. oyéu taȥeé bahun. achi. ixɛachu-..
ɛabehɛib. ruq. chirih unimal ȥaɛ. unimal......
qoxtun. chioxlahuvinaɛ. ɛih. chiox lahu-....
vinaɛ: aɛab qoɛavaram mahabi. ɛayaca-..
lem, ruq. quehecut mixnuviɛqanoɛ. chi-..
rech. uɛanapuvaɛ. ruq uȥaɛipuvaɛ. ruq.....
uyaqim vi. uyaqim iqah. ruq. ixqetaɛ ra-..
ȥiyaɛ.. ruq. uxtapiyac lamaxqinchacuriva....
chuvach. lavahaval chuvach lanuvi-..
naɛil. qehecut. mixinyopiȥah ubi chuhu-..
yubal. chutaɛahal lamaxqinchacuriva.
Chuvach lavahaval. chuvach lanuvin-..
aɛil. xavi. inȥaɛat inmolah rumal...

[fol. 33]

vahaval nuvinaꜫil colic nuꜫanapuvaꜫ.
nuꜩaꜫipuvaꜫ xavicolic ralnuchab ralnu.
pocob: ruq nuyaqimvi. nuyaqimviqah.:
inꜩaꜫat inmolah rumal vahaval
nuvinaꜫil chupam unimal ꜩaꜫ chupam.
unimal qoxtun quehecut quinyopiꜩah ꜩihol-
lá. chupam unimal. ꜩaꜫ. unimal qoxtun..
ꜫhuvach vahaval nuvinaꜫil vecuxchicha..
vahaval. nuvinaꜫil xuꜩcupihbila chuhu =
yubal: chutaꜫakal. vexchicha vahaval.
xavi ixchinyuꜩcupihbilari xavi vexchi =
cha vahaval. nuvinaꜫil chiqohtana =
balola. chinuchii chinuvach can.:
vilnauchii. uvach. hanicpachioyeu.....
chiachi. vexchicha vahaval nuvinaꜫil
quehecut canuyopiꜩah cula cachacuri-
nuꜩih. chuvach qah. chuvach ulen! qah,
ulen! chiqohi. uq. lá. oyeuachi qaveꜫ.........
qiche. vinaꜫ.................................

7º9 u vahxaꜫ mul cachauic
quiché achi

[fol. 34]

chá. utꜯ. queke qobala oyeu achi uɛalel..
Rabinal achi ɛayopiꜯah lá.................................
nuꜯihoxic chuvach ahaval lá chupam..
unimal. tꜯaɛ. unimal qoxtun quimyopi-
ꜯahlacut. queke. qah. uleu! chiqohi.......
uqla. uɛalel achi Rabinal achi...............

---

ucam Ꜫanꜫal

---

qayopiꜯah chuvach
ahau. ohobtoh

ubeleh mul. cachau
7º R .Rabinal achi

qala ahau. qala. xoɛohau. quiqamo. chi-
rech, qah. qui. qamo chirech uleu! varal.
lal ahavarinaɛvi lal. muharinaɛ. ɛhuxe.
u mutibal. uɛuɛ. raxon. chupam unimal..
ꜯaɛ. unimal qoxtun queke qovaim oye..
valal. la. inachihilal. la. mixin yopiꜯah....

[fol. 35]

culoꜫ chichii la. chuvach la. chupam unimal..
ꜯaꜫ. unimal qoxtun quehecutun oyeu hun-
achi ixꜫachuꜫabeh ꜫib ruq chiox lahuvi-.
naꜫ. ꜫih. oxlahuvinaꜫ aꜫab chirih uni-.
mal. ꜯaꜫ. qoxtum qoꜫavaram maha-
bi. ꜫayaqalem ruq quehecut. mixu-.
ya. qah. mixuya. uleu. mixꜯaꜫcut..
chupam halnuchab chupam ral-
nupocob. mixinꜯaꜫcamah mixinꜯa-
ꜫcobeh. chirech nuꜯaꜫicaam nuꜯa-
ꜫicolob. ruqnuyaquimvi. nuyaquim-
vigah nuchincu nugalgab nuꜯal-
met. quehecut mixingotuchi riayeu ria-
chi. mavi quhulic huꜯuctah xuhiquitah
uvach uhuyubal utaꜫahal chinuchii
chinuvach inoyeu. inachi areoꜯeu areachi.
quban roꜫibal. utiu. quban roꜫibal. yac.
quban roꜫibal utuyhalau chirih unimal.
ꜯaꜫ unimal qoxtun. chirech quiboyexic
quiꜯaqalexic laꜯaꜫil. al. laꜯaꜫil. qahol.
areoyeu areachi mixquiꜯouic. beleheb.
lahuh ꜯaꜫilal. ꜯaꜫilqahol xaviare oyeu-
mixul riꜯah. alaꜫ chiri. chatinibal. are-

[fol. 36]

oyeu arēchi mixouqiꜯó caib. axib. uꜫab amaꜫ.
ꜯivantinamit chirixebalamvac chitintot. vi.
poꜫlah. chuchexic lahanicpacut. mavíqicouic
rahabalquxlá chirech vaoyoval vaachihilal..
mapaxohpixabaxic qumal. ꜫahaual. ꜫauina=
ꜫil. erahaual upamhuhun chiꜯaꜫ chiqoxtun
ahau tequentoh. ahau. tequentihax. ꜫumahma-
chi. taꜫtaꜯib. taꜫtaꜯimah quxuma. ah quxuma=
ꜯivan. quxumachóo. quxumacab. quxumaꜯiquin..
quibí quichiquivach arenacu chul tohoriꜯah =
lari. varal chuxmut. qah. chuxmut. uleu!
quehecut varal qaꜫachayvi uvixal uquta=
mil. varal chuxmut. qah. chuxmut. uleu!
lal. vahaval ahau ohobtoh..........................

unabemul qachavic.
ahau ohobtoh.

voyeual vachihilal qamo chirech qah. qamo.
chirech. uleu! mixyopiꜯah qulolá. chupam.
unimalꜯaꜫ. unimalqoxtun chinuchii chinu=
ovach inahaval lá. inahau. ohobtoh. qamoba...
chirech. qah. qamoba chirech uleu! vemixuya-

[fol. 37]

qah mixuyaulen! rioyen riachi mixꜯaꜫcut
chupamratchabla ralpocobla mixꜯaꜫqa...
mahla mixꜯaꜫcolobehla rioyen riachi hoꜫotahil...
tababa. chiqohtalola. chinuchii. chinuvach.
canvilna uchi canvilna uvach hanicpachi...
achi. chipixabah tabalola. riachi rioyen mata
chibohohic mata chitililic tachoculoꜫ chuchi...
unimal ꜯaꜫ. unimal qoxtun varalcut carah..
loꜫoxel mayihaxel chupam unimal ꜯaꜫ uni-
mal qoxtun varalcut qolic qablahuh. raꜯ. qab-
lahuh. uchaꜫ. eahpuvaꜫinel eahxitanel maha.
chiꜯaꜫat. quichii quivach colo are oyen mix-
chulocoꜫ quiꜯaꜫat quimolah chupam unimal.
ꜯaꜫ. unimal aqoxtun. xavi. quivaral qolic qa-
blahuh. uꜫanal qot. uꜫanal Balam xavima-
ha chiꜯaꜫat quichii quivach coloareoyen ixchu...
locoꜫ quiꜯaꜫat. xaviquivaral qolic. puvaꜫim tem-
puvaꜫim qubulibal qocublebeyom mahabi qu...
belebeyom qoloare oyen qoloare achi mixchul-
qubulibenoꜫ xaviquivaral qolic qablahuh
uquiya. qablahuh. umatul. ixtaꜯunun ubi.
rique qaꜯililic qatiriric quiqoh qab qoh
qantiho. ul. qamavar varal chupam.....

[fol. 38]

unimal ȥaɛ qoxtun ruqiya ahau. qoloare oyeu..
ixcholtihovoɛ. xaviquivaral qolic laɛan uɛin..
qoxah uva. riquiqalaȥ. qabanic ubanom. nute.
nuxoɛohau. qolo. areoyeu. qolo achi ixchulȥauoɛ
uchii. uvach xaviquivaral qolic ȥapilic ri-
uchuch. ɛuɛ. uchuch Raxon ripetenaɛ ȥam -
ɛam qarchá. qoloareoyeu qoloare achi ix -
chulȥavoɛ. uvach chulumeȥeȥeh chupam
vaunimal. ȥaɛ. vaunimal qoxtun qoloare oyeu...
chuloqoɛ hisaxel baluquixel chupam uni-.
mal. ȥaɛ. chupam unimal qoxtun venim-.
anel. veoctiȥanel vechumerib vechume. u-
vach. tachoculoɛ qachacurinuȥih chuva-.
ch. qah. chuvach uleu! quehe. qah. uleu!.......
chiqohi. uqlá. uɛalel achi Rabinal achi........

8°

ulahuh mul cachavic

Rabinal achi............

ahau ohobtoh quiyuxtah tabalá chuvach...
qah. cuvach uleu! qachabarinuȥih chi..
ech. la. aretabavanucoleil uachihilal....
yaom la heteȥamla chuve. chinuchii..........

[fol. 39]

chinuvach chinqanahtanabalá Varal-
nuchab. varal nupocob chiqutanabalá chi-
ꜩapihtanabalá. chupam uchuyal upaɔabal.
chuxlantaná xavi taquimuxlanic humalcut.
qoɔavaram mahabi ɔayaqabem. hug. que-
hecut qanuqanahqanoɔ chupam unimal.
ꜩaɔ. unimal qoxtun qachacurinuꜩih...
chuvach qah chuvach uleu! qah. uleu!
chiqohi uqla. lal. vahaual nuvinaɔil..........
ahau. ohobtoh.......................................

ucamul cauic
ahau ohobtoh

voyeualal vachihilal. laqachanaquri-
ꜩihlá. chuvach qah chuvach uleu! are-
ba. vanuqouil. vavachihilal varalnuchab.
varal nupoqob yaomla heteꜩam lá chinu-
chii. chinuvach canucanahtabacanoɔ. chicu-
tanabala. chiꜩapihtanabala. chupam uni-
mal. ꜩaɔ. qoxtun chupam uchuyal upa-
ɔabal. laqachanacuriꜩihlá..............................
lahulacha ixchin quú. ixchinꜩapih chupam

[fol. 40]

uchuyal chupam upaꜫabal naꜫabichicuri rito–
tobal.lá. chuvach baxulanuloꜫ lapaꜫal uloꜫ.
chuholomuleu! chiraꜫanuleu! naꜫabichicuri ri–
tobal.lá. xuvichiqueriꜫal ꜫaqahol. riquielubi...
chuviquiꜯuꜯunic quiqahalenic chiqahpa chi
.... chigoh xuqutal. arenacuri humulchic..
camulchic cayânubila Vaqouil lá. vaachihilal lá
varalchab lá. varalpocob lá vanuyaom chiechlá
voyeualal uachihilal uꜫalel achi Rabinal achi.......
quehe.qah. uleu! chiqohi uqlá.......................................

9° hu lahuh cachauic
Rabinal achi

uꜯ quehebala vexchinyac chinubi. vanu–
qouil. vauachihilal. yaomla heteꜯam la.
chinuchii chinuvach queꜫcut qanuyacchi–
nubi humulchic. qamul.chic. qachacuri nuꜯih.
chuvach qah. chuvach uleu! quehecut. qanu–
qanahcanlá. uaral chupam unimal ꜯaꜫ.
unimal.qoxtun.qah. uleu! chiqohi uqlá. lal.
uahaual nuvinaꜫil ahau.ohobtoh..............................

[fol. 41]

rox mul cachauic
ahau ohobtoh

uẑbalá, uoyeualal. uachihilal banaltabala mapa-
htahla. maẑoqotahla. uoyeualal uachihilal.
uEalel. rachi. Rabinal rachi..........................
qah ulew! chiqohi..uqla..........................

uroxBanBal.

10° uqablahuh mul qachauic
Rabinal achi.

qu qamá. qiché achi ximilic qiché achi..........
ehá oyeuachi qaueE. qiché vinaE. quibain
vamixin yopiẑah la chupam unimal ẑaE.
unimal qoxtun chuvach vahaval nuvina..
Eil. queheeut. mixchauloE vahaual nuvina-
Eil. chipixabahtaculolá rioyeu riachi mata..
chitililic mata chibohohic xata chumerib
chumetauvach tachoculoE chuchii. unimal ẑaE..

[fol. 42]

qoxtun uaral chuxmut. qah. chuxmut. uleu!
Rumal uaral loɛoxel. mayiharel chupam unimal...
ʒaɛ unimal qoxtun uaral ʒaɛat. molah upam...
unimal ʒaɛ. unimal qoxtun golic qablahuh raʒ.
qablahuh uchaɛ. eahpuaɛinel ahxitanel. maha..
queʒaɛat quichi quiuach goloareoyeu golo are
achi ixchuloqoɛ. qiʒaɛat qimolah xauiqui varal...
golic qablahuh uɛanal qot. uɛanal balam xaui.
maha. queʒaɛat quichii quiuach golo are oyeu...
golo achi chulocoɛ. quiʒaɛat xauiqui uaral golic
puvaɛim tem puvaɛim chacat puvaɛim qubulibal
golo areoyeu golo achi ixchulcubulibenoɛ xauiqui-.
varal qulri ʒapilic riuchuch. ɛuɛ. uchuch Raxon.
riyamanib ixtecoquib ripetenaɛ ʒamɛam qar-
cha. qoʒayomuchii mahabi ʒayom urach. golo -.
areoyeu. golo are achi chulʒaravauchii urach xaui
quivaral golic riqablahuh uqiyá riqablahuh..
umatul riqueqaʒililic riqueqatiriric ruciya a.
hau. chupam unimal ʒaɛ. unimal qoxtun golo are..
oyeu. golo are achi chultihovoɛ xauiqui varal golic..
laɛan. uɛin qoxahuva riquigalaʒ qabanic ubanom.
uute uuxoɛohan golo areoyeu golo are achi chul.-
ʒaua. urach xàuiqui varal ixchuloqoɛ hiarel....

[fol. 43]

baluquixel uaral chupam unimal ꜩaɛ. unimal qoxtun
mixchauloɛ uahaual nuvinaɛil. quehecut. ixchin
pixabahtacubila matachitilil la. mata chibohoh la..
tachocapanlá chuchii unimal ꜩaɛ unimal qoxtun
chimetaibla. chixuctaibla. tachocapanla chuvach
uahaual nuvinaɛil mama ahau ohobtoh qachá..
qurinuꜩih chuvach qah. chuvach uleu! quehe..
mani quiyaꜩih qohꜩihonic. qah. uleu!.........................
. chi qohi uqlá qaveɛ. qiché vinaɛ..........................

8°

ubetzh mul cachauic
qui che achi.

chá oyeu achi Rabinal achi la qachanacuriꜩihla
chuvach qah. chuvach uleu! mixinyopiꜩah la...
ꜩihoxic la chuvach uahaual chuvach nuvina –
ɛil. chupam unimal ꜩaɛ. unimal qoxtun qacha...
rinuꜩih quehecut chipixabahtalolá ꜩrioyeu ri –
achi chicohtanalolá chinuchii chinuvach chu...
chi. unimal. ꜩaɛ. canvilnauchii canvilna uvach
hanicpachioyeu hanicpachi achi. chipixaba –
htalola. matachitililic matachibohohic tachoc –
uloɛ chiꜩnuchii chinuvach chumetarib chume =..

[fol. 44]

uvach. veare oyeu veare achi venimanel veoctiꜭanel
rumal varal loꜫoxel mayihaxel chupam unimal
ꜭaꜫ. chupam unimal qoxtun mixchauloꜫ vahaual
nuvinaꜫil lacacha riꜭih lá laincuhun chioyeu la-
in qotuchiachi curi vexaxchinmevib vexchin me-
nuvach qobala vanumebal. vib. qobala varalnuchab.
varal nupocob rug. vanuyaquimvi qah. are nume-
bal. vib. va nuxuculibal. vá. mixqainocapanoꜫ chu-
chi unimal tꜭaꜫ unimal qoxtun qarahcut xax-
chin. ꜫaꜭah unimal. uꜫih. ralaxic ahaual-
la. vinaꜫil. qarah xaxchinquevih riquem
uchii. rahꜭic uchii chupam. unimal tꜭaꜫ.
unimal qoxtun. quitanape qatihlá..........
ri oyeu. achi uꜫalel. achi Rabinal achi.......

1º ixoꜫ. mun.
cachauiꜫ

oyeu achi qaveꜫ. quiché vinaꜫ mala-
qamiꜭah la voyeualal vachihilal..........
uꜫalel. achi. Rabinal achi..........

ugah ꜩanꜩal

[fol. 45]

9º ulatuh mul cachauic
quiché achi.

qaqulun chuvach ahau.ohobtoh.

qala.achi.quibain vamix yopitahuloꜫ. chu....
chi unimal.tꜭaꜫ. chuchi unimal qoxtun lal...
ahavarinaꜫ.ui. lal. muharinaꜫ.vi.mixul yopi-
ꜭaxacut nuꜭihoxic chichi lá chivach lá in..
oyeu inachi Rumal mixchaᵃpanoꜫ. riyebal-
lá. tꜭiquibal.lá. oyeualal.lá. achitilal..
lá. uꜫalel achi Rabinal achi chinuchii
chinuvach mixyopiꜭax.cut. nuꜭihoxic chi-
vach lá.lal vahaual. nuvinaꜫil chup-
am: unimal.tꜭaꜫ mixchauloꜫ.utꜭih....
vahaual nuvinaꜫil chiqohtanabalolá..
ri oyeu riachi chinuchii chinuvach..
qanvilnauchii.qanuilna uvach. hanic-
pachio oyeu .hanicpachi achi ixchipixa.:
bah.talolá.rioyeu riachi matachitililic.
mata chibohohic chumetarib chumeta=
uvach. tachoculoꜫ. chuchii unimal.tꜭaꜫ.
chuchii unimal qoxtun mixcha apanoꜫ..

[fol. 46]

riyebal.la tziquibal.la. rumal achihilab-
la. chinuchii chinuvach laingotun chi-
achi oyeu curi vechul numeavib vechu-
l numeanuvach qobala uanumel uib. are-
bauanumebal uib uaral nuchab uaral...
nupocob xacuchulnuɛatzah. ɛihla.........
alaxicla. chulnuquevih riquem chila rah-
tzic. chila. quitanapecatih la. lal.ahau...

ixoɛmun

2º qamul qachauic

oyeu achi qaueɛ qiche. uinaɛ malaqamitzak...
uahaual nuvinaɛil ahau.ohobtoh. chupam.....
unimal.tzaɛ. chupam unimal qoxtun............
.....................qului tzapil ui..

10º uhulatuh mul qachauic
qui che achi.......................

quehecut chiɛibitzahtaculola. rinutem ri-
nuchagat. rumal areri chinuhuyubal chi-
nutaɛahal. paɛabam unɛih paɛabam. vala-

[fol. 47]

xic. qo nutem qo nuchagat naꜫiquinpaba=
xtah chuvactiꜫeu naꜫiquin pabaxtah
chuvach horon gachaqurinutꜯih. chuva=
ch: qah chuvach uleu! qah..
uleu chigohi ugla. mama ahau ohobloh.....

.ugahmul gachauic
ahau ohobtoh............

oyeu achi gaveꜫ giché uinaꜫ gamo chirech.
qah qamochirech, uleu! mixyopitahculolá.
chupam unimal.tꜯaꜫ. chupam unimal..
qoxtun inahauarinaꜫ.ui. inmuharinaꜫui..
in mama ahau.ohobtoh, quetrecut. chitꜯi=
hontaculá chichatacula rumal xape......
xalal. ricul banalá roꜫibal.utiu. roꜫibal-
yac. roꜫibal utuy. halau. chirih launi=
mal. tꜯaꜫ. launimal. qoxtun chirech. qui=
boyexic. chirech quigagalexic xaui chi=
rech queletꜯaxic. ritꜯaꜫil al ritꜯaꜫil=
gahol. rieꜫeletꜯam.bi. chuvach launimal
tꜯaꜫ. qoxtun chupam.ixc̄hée. etꜯuguyre...
egahaleyre uchigopil ꜫanagab raxagab.

[fol. 48]

tꜩuƐbal. ve. inmama ahau. ohobtoh. chup.=
am. unimal. tꜩaƐ. unimal qoxtun. xavi...
quilal mixetꜩelehebeh lá beleheb lá....
huh. tꜩaƐil. al. tꜩaƐil. qahol.. xatꜩqaƐin.
chirah manaxeopontah chila quiché..
huyub. vematahabi rinoyenalal va.=
chihilal xubu utꜩebeh a vachih uloƐ.......
Ɛatꜩchila. qachayuila quivixal qui=...
quitamil ritꜩaƐil. al. ritꜩaƐil qahol.
xavi quilal. mixul eletꜩah rinaha...
ualrinuvinaƐil chiri chatinibal xavi...
cuare mixinyacbila chupam ralchab lá...
mixine tꜩapih lá chupam aƐamchun tꜩah=...
cabih láuih. nunach chila qiché huyub qiche=
taƐah xavi Ɛatꜩhila qaqitꜩ-uila uchayic.......
nuvixal nuqutamil chila qiche huyub. qiche.
taƐah. arecuri Rumal qolic noyenalal. vachi-
hilal uƐalel achi Rabinal achi mixinreletꜩa-
hchiviuloƐ mixinulototeh chiviuloƐ. chupa-
m: raluchab chupam ralupocob vema voye=
nalal. vachihilal Ɛatꜩchila. qachayui. nu=
vixal nuqutamil arecuri mixunulu hete=..
tꜩah. chic. chupam unimal. tꜩaƐ. qoxtun........

[fol. 49]

xaui qui.lal. mixe quitz̨la qaib.oxib. uɛab amaɛ.
tz̨ivam tinamit chiri Babam vac chitɛatot.-
vi poɛlah chiqaraxah chiqunu chiɛotz̨ibal......
taɛah.tulul. chuchezic..

X

lahanic pacut mavi quiqovic rahabal qux la..
chirech vaoyoual va. achihilal lahulacha mi..
x yac chulolá mix tz̨ilibitz̨ah chulola mapachi-..
la. mixbec umuɛic upitz̨ic vaoyoval va achihilal..
chila chiqotom chiticram mapa Beleheb moɛoh..
Beleheb chumay mixbec umuɛic upitz̨ic vaoyoual. Va.-
achihilal. mixɛabano ohrahaual oh vinaɛil up.-
am hutun chitz̨aɛ chiqoxtun arenaquehul-
tohoritz̨ah larivaral chuxmut qah. chuxmut-
uleu! quehecut mixpixab chin taqan lá chi..
huyubal lá. chitaɛahal lá ɛatz̨ cuarelal qamel.
laltz̨achel varal chuxmut qah chuxmut.......
uleu! quehe. qah. uleu!..
tachiqohi. uqla. qaveɛ quiche vinaɛ........

11° uqablahuh mul qachanic..
quiché achi..

[fol. 50]

ahau. ohobtoh. quiyuxtah tabalá chuvach
qah chuvach uleu! ꜫatꜯbaretꜯih ꜫatꜯ..
bare. pixab mixbixtah la. chuvach. qah..
chuvach uleu! ꜫatꜯin xinmaqubeh qa=
charitꜯih la. mixebenebeh. la. mixetꜯeletebe-
h. la. ritꜯaꜫil al. ritꜯaꜫil. qahol. rieꜫe-
letꜯam. bi. etꜯuquyre eqahaleyre. u..
chiqopil. ꜫana. qab. raxaqab. tꜯuꜫbal. ve..
inmama. ahau ohobtoh chupam unim..
al tꜯaꜫ. chupam. umianal. qoxtun qacha-
ritꜯih. la xatꜯqaꜫin xinmaqubeh ru..
mal uqoꜫobal. nuqux rumal manaxine..
chabentah chirech. tꜯaꜫil huyub tꜯa..
ꜫil taꜫah varal chuxmut. qah chuxmut
uleu! xavi qacharitꜯihla tamixin vebe-
tꜯah bila chiri chatinibal mapa xa-
quinatinuqoꜫ chiri. chatinibal qacha
ritꜯih la xavi ꜫatꜯin xinmaqubeh Ru--
uqoꜫobal nuqux Rumal manaxinechabentah
chirech tꜯaꜫil huyub chirech tꜯaꜫil taꜫah
varal chuxmut. qah chuxmut. uleu! xavi.
qacharitꜯihla........ixpixab chintacanla. chi..
huyubal lá chitaꜫahal lá qacharitꜯih-lá

mo

[fol. 51]

Rumal varal. lal. qamel. lal. tz̧achel. Varal. qa=
εachay Vi. vixal la' qutamil-la'. Varal chuxmut
qah. chuxmut. uleu! qacharitz̧ih la' εatz̧cuin. ix=
numayih. ritz̧ih. ripixab Varal chuvach qah.
chuvach uleu! rumal uqoεobal. nuqux. Vecuεatz̧.
Varal incamel intz̧achel qacha chicurinutz̧ih.
chi. chila'. chivach la. Vecu εatz̧ laltz̧aεat lal..
molah chupam unimal tz̧aε. unimal qoxtum. chin
εah tachinabachiech la riVaibal. la. rioquibal. la.
ruqiyaa'. ahau ixtatz̧unun. ubii riqablahuh
uquiya qablahuh umatul riqueqatz̧ililic qatirira.
quicoh qabqoh qantiho ulqamavar chupam uni=
mal tz̧aε chupam unimal qoxtum xaunimabal.
nute nuxoεohau chintihtanape' xata nimaretalil
uVach nucamic nutz̧achic Varal chuxmut. qah.
chuxmut uleu! qachacurinutz̧ih queke qah........
uleu! chiqohi uqla ahau ohobtoh...............

uromul cachanic
ahau. ohobtoh

oyeu achi qaVeε quiche Vinaε laqacha nacu—
riatz̧ih chuvach qah chuvach uleu! chiyata=...

[fol. 52]

chibalachuve rivaibal.la. rioquibal.la. chinɛah
tanachiechla chiuntihtanape qacharitꜩihla xa-
nimaretalil nuqamic nutꜩachic qolic qanuyo qan-
hetetꜩah chiechlá achih mun. ixoɛmun. chaqa-
mauloɛ rinuvaibal nuoquibal chayaachire ri-
oyeu achi qaveɛ qiché vinaɛ xanimaretalil. u.-
qamic utꜩachic varal chuxmut, qah. chuxmut uleu!.......

3° ....mun.....

utꜩbala vahaval nuvinaɛil qanuyaoo: Chire ri-
oyeu achi ribala oyeu achi qaveɛ quiche. vi-
naɛ.......... tihanapela rivaibal roqibal vahaval. nu-
vinaɛil. mama ahau ohobtoh chupam unimal.
tꜩaɛ. qulvi. tꜩapilvi vahaval........................
nuvinaɛil oyeu achi..

12° uRox lahuhmul qachauic
quiché achi.............................

chá ahau. ohobtoh. laevaibal lavá oquibal
lavá ɛatꜩmavi vaqochubiihla chinuchii. chinu-
vach aretanape qatihlarive qochinuhuyubal......

[fol. 53]

chinutaɛahal quimayihuquiil uɛutz̨il..
quicoh. qabcoh quimayih qatz̨ililic qatiriric..
riqantiho chinuhuyubal chinutaɛahal
...............qachachibarinutz̨ih chuvach. qah..
chuvach uleu! la arevaibal lavá ɛatz̨are.
uholom nuɛahau qanuvilo qanumuɛuh. la..
mana. roquicam quehetabanel tz̨aɛanitz̨a =
nel. chirechvaubaɛil nuvi ubaɛil nuholom qo..
timtachirih qotimtachuvach tachiɛah apanoɛ.
chinuhuyubal. chinutaɛahal tz̨aɛatitz̨a-
bal tare. oqal. peɛ. oqal qaqó. qumal.
val. qumal. nuqahol chinuhuyubal.
chinutaɛahal quechatavál, quecha-
ta nuqahol..................areuholom ɛaman.
ɛaɛahau......quechataval quechatanuqa-
hol. quxtabal. tavé. qumal ual nuqahol.
chuxeɛih chuxetz̨aɛ............aretacut.........
vaubaɛil nuɛab aretachoquic uɛab tz̨ochi-
puvaɛ. quimayihtah chichahahic quima-
yihtah chivahahic chupam unimal tz̨aɛ..
chupam unimal qoxtun aretacut. vaub-
-aɛil. vaɛan aretachoquic uɛab topono =
votz̨. ɛohom quimayihtah chilanan qah..

[fol. 54]

chibanan uleu! rumal Varal chupam
unimal tzaE. chupam unimal qoxtun.
qacha curinutzik mixchinEahtanachiechla.
chiyatala chuve rilotoh richuchuk rila-
Ean. uEin. riqoxah uva riquicaltzcabanic
riubanom nutenuxoEotrau mixchin tiqui-
qeh. uloE chupam unimal tzaE chupam
unimal qoxtun chiqahpa. chiqahxuqutal.
xata nimaretalil nucamic nutzachic.........
Varal chuxmut. qah chuxmut uleu!........

6º u Vah xaEmul qachauic
ahau okobtoh...............

oyeu achi qaueE qiche VinaE naEitanaon
rixcharayih rixchatzonoh qanuyao chave.
xanima retalil aqamic atzachic Varal
chuxmut qah chuxmut uleu! achihmun.
ixoEmun chaq-^{ma}a..uloE riloloh richuchuk
rilaEan uEin qoxah uva riquicalatz qa-
banic ribanomla chupam unimal tzaE.
chupam unimal qoxtun chaya achire......
rioyeu chire riachi xanima retalil..........

[fol. 55]

ucamic utz̧achic Varal.....................
chuxmut. qah. chuxmut Uleu!..........

......mun.......

utz̧bala Vatanal nuVinaꜫil qanuya.
chire rioyeu qanuya achire riachi ri-
urayibal ribalá rioyeu achi riquiqa-
latz̧. qabanic riqarayih la. riꜫz̧onoh-
lá. qanuyacuchaVe xaquxere.....................
.......................mamayih la maꜫulih la..........

13°. ......quiché achi.....

alaꜫ bari ahtz̧u. alaꜫ bari...............
ahꜫohom.......... alatachique riuchinutz̧u.
riuchinuꜫohom..........rimix chitz̧aꜫ talaꜫ.
aretaba.. . chitz̧aꜫalaꜫ rinunima tz̧uu.
opuenuchatitz̧uú............. chitz̧aꜫtabalaꜫ............
varetapuch chitz̧aꜫ alaꜫ..........rinuyaqui..
tz̧uú. nuyaqui ꜫohom aretapuch..................
chitz̧aꜫ alaꜫ nuquiché tz̧uu. nuquiché......
ꜫohom qohbalre rinuqanab rinuteleché....

[fol. 56]

Chinutuyubal chinutaɛahal quitachibirbot qah-
quitachibirbot uleu!............chiɛahtaɛaVi.............
ɛaholom chirech uyiɛic uxahic quC achih............
mun-ixoɛ-mun............Varal chuxmut. qah.....
chuxmut uleu! qachaqurinutʒih. chuVach.....
qah. chuVach uleu! qah. uleu!...........chiqohi....
uq alaɛ ahtʒun. alaɛ ahɛohom......................

14° uqahlahuh mul qachauic. musica
quiché. achi........................

chá ahau. ohobtoh. quiyuxtah tabala...........
chuVach. qah. chuvach uleu! ribalarinu...–
ɛohom rinuchaɛim mix chulnuhacha mix chul-
nupera chuchi unimal tʒaɛ unimal qoxtun...
chicutabala chitʒapih tabala chupam uchu-
yal. upaɛabal chupam unimal tʒaɛ. chupam
unimal qoxtum mixyaculachuvé rinurayibal.
nuqutubal chuVach. qah. chuVach uleu!............
mixin hiquiqueh. uloɛ. chupam unimal tʒaɛ...
qoxtun chiqahpa chiqahxuqutal xacunima=
retalil. nuqamic nutʒachic varal chuxmut.......
qah chuxmut uleu! qachachicurinutʒih..........

[fol. 57]

chuvach·qah. chuvach uleu!.......veꜫatꜯ lal........
ꜯaꜫat........lalmolah chupam unimal ꜯaꜫ........
chupam unimal qoxtun chiyatachibala.........
chuve chinꜫahtanaba chiech la riuchuch..
.........ꜫuꜫ. uchuch Raxon riyamanib ixtecoquib
ripetenaꜫ ꜯamꜫam qarcha qotꜯayom uchii.
mahabi ꜯayom uvach chintꜯatana uchi..
chin ꜯatanacu uvach chin metꜯetꜯeh-
tah. chinhiquiquehtah chupam unimal.
ꜯaꜫ. unimal qoxtun chiqahpá chiqah-
xuqutal xatanima retalil nuqamic nu-
ꜯachic varal chuxmut. qah. chuxmut.
uleu! quehe. qah. uleu! chiqohi................
...................uq. lá. ahau ohobtoh.........................

7° uvuꜫ mul qachanic
ahau ohobtoh.................

oyeu achi qaveꜫ quiché Vinaꜫ naꜫitana-
ón. richarayih chatꜯonoh......qanuyaó.
quchave arayibal atꜯonobal rumal..
varal qu.ul.vi ꜯapil vi. riuchuch.ꜫuꜫ.
uchuch Raxon yamanib exteqoquib.......

[fol. 58]

ripetenaꜫ tꜯamꜫam qarchá. qotꜯayom...
uchii mahabi tꜯayom uvach qanuya...–
quchavé. oyeuachi xaqunima retalil..
uqamic atꜯachic varal chuxmut. qah...
chuxmut. uleu! achih mun. ixoꜫ. mun.........
chaqamauloꜫ. riuchuch ꜫuꜫ. riuchuch....
Raxon chayaachire rioyeu chayaa..........
chire riachi urayibal utꜯonobal. xanima....–
retalil. uqamic utꜯachic varal...............
...............chuxmut. qah. chuxmut uleu!...........

5°...... ixoꜫ mun........

utꜯbala vahaval nuvinaꜫil qanuya chire..
rioyeu riachi.........Ribala rioyeu achi.....
qaveꜫ quiche. vinaꜫ.........qanuya chiech lá...
rirayibal. lá. qutubal. lá. xaquxere...........
mamayih lá maꜫutih lá riuchuch..ꜫuꜫ...
uchuch Raxon xata chihiquiqueh. lá....
chimetꜯetꜯehtalá chupam unimal...
tꜯaꜫ chupam unimal. qoxtun..............

15° uroolahuhmul qachavic
quiche achi.................. <u>musica</u>

[fol. 59]

ahau ohobtoh quiyuxtah tabalá chu-
vach·qah chuvach uleu! arebava..
nuεohom nuchaεim mixyaqula........-
chuVe. mixim hiquiqueh quloε mixin
metz̧etz̧eh quloε chiqahpa chiqah ...
xuqutal. chupans unimal tz̧aε unimal.
qoxtun chiqutaqula chitz̧apihtaqulá.
chupam unimal. tz̧aε. unimal qoxtun.
qacha chiqurinutz̧ih chiyatachibala-
chuVe chinεah tachinaba chiech la'ri ..
qablahuh uεanal. qot. uεanal Balam ri ..
enuqulum chiεil chiaεabal chuVach toó.
chuVach chamiy ixquenuεahtanaquchi-
ech la mixquibenuVetz̧abeh uloε chupam
halnuchab chupam halnupoqob. chi......
qahpa chiqahxuqutal chupam unimal.
tz̧aε. unimal qoxtun xatanimaretalil.
nuqamic nutz̧achic varal chuxmut......
qah. chuxmut uleu! queche qah uleu!
.......................chiqohi uqla ahau ohobtoh...............

uVahxaεmul qachauic
ahau ohobtoh.......................

[fol. 60]

oyeu achi qaVeɛ quiché Vinaɛ.laqacha.
naquriatꜩih chuvach.qah. chuVach......-
uleu! chinɛahtana chiech lá rigablahuh
uɛanal qot........ uɛanal Balam................
qacha ritꜩih.lá. canuyabachiechlá rigab-
lahuh uɛanal qot..........uɛanal Balam...............
ri qarayih.lá. riqatꜩonoh.lá. chinuchii chi-
nuvach ixbala nuqot. nubalam chibanabala.
qota quelvi. rioyeu riachii quixretꜩabeh........
uloɛ. chupam raluchab chupam ralupo-
cob.......... chiqahpá chiqahxuqutal..........................

16º uvaɛlahuh mul qachanic
quiché achi................................musica

ahau ohobtoh quiyuxtahtabala chuVach..
qah chuVach uleu! mixyaqulachuVé............
rinurayibal nuqutubal riuɛanal.qot.........
......Balam......mixebenuVetꜩabehuloɛ chupam.
ralnuChab ralnupoqob.........laaregot laVá..
.........lae Balam laVá. manaVagoChubih la...
chinuChii chinuVach humal qocatꜩunic. qo-
naqatꜩuntah qohintare qohinta rixqaɛ

[fol. 61]

aretanapequillarive rigochinutuhuyubal.
chinutaɛahal quimayih quetzunic qui=
mayih quevachinic qui mayih quechahahic.
que chihihic rug. que e rug quixgaɛ..................

9° ...ubelehmul gachauic....
.....ahau okobtoh.................

oyeu achi gaveɛ quiché......vinaɛ gaɛilnari
ri agot..........riaBalam.......... riegochahuyubal.
naɛipaquetzunic queVachinic.......... riagot.....
.....riaBalam......riegochahuyubal.......................
.......................riegochataɛal.................

17° .uVuɛlatuhmulgachauic
quiché achi..............................

ahau...ohobtoh....... quiyuxtahtabala chuvach-
gah. chuvach.uleu! gachachibarinutzih...
chichila chivachlá chiyatachibala chuVe...
rioxlatuvinaɛ...ɛih........rioxlahuvinaɛ aɛab.....
mixenpixabah tachinabaulob...uvach lá...
nuhuyubal uvach lanutaɛahal aViri...........

[fol. 62]

xinbinvi xintꜩilabvi. chiqakpa chiqakxuqutal...
chuvi nutꜩ...qunic nuqahalenic chirech utꜩucuxic
..............vecha nuquxun..............................

.......116...............
......qui che achi....................
18° ....utequel chic qachauic....

ix qot. ixBalam. xelic. quixcha.
mana. xinel. tak. xamixinpixa..-
bak. chiculoꜫ. uvach nukuyubal..
uvach nutaꜫakal. avixinbin—
vi. mixin tꜩilabvi. chirech. utꜩu....-
cuxic. vecha nucuxun chiqakpa..
chiqakxuqutal akꜫaroꜫ. qak...
akꜫaroꜫ. uleu. bamaqoxoponvi.... [na]
ri voyeualal. rivachihilal. mixin...
tikcuri. paqak. nube. puleu. nube....
mixin tꜩelekvi. toló.. manaqocuxopon.-
vi.. rivoyeualal. rivachihilal. akꜫa-
roꜫ. qak. akꜫaroꜫ. uleu. laꜫatꜩik. varal...
inqamel. intꜩachel.. varal. chuxmut..
qak. chuxmut. uleu. ixbala, nuꜫana..

[fol. 63]

puvaꜫ. nutꜭaꜫipuvaꜫ. tixpuch.
ral. nuchab. ral. nupocob nuya-
quim vi. nuyaquim. viqah. tixpuch..
ix. taꜫ. vatꜭiaꜫ. ruq. nuxtapiac......
tix. bala. chiꜫatuyubal. chiꜫata-
ꜫahal. tiyabala. ꜫatꜭihol. chu-.
vach. ꜫahaval. ꜫavinaꜫil. rumal..
qacha. lová. ꜫahaval ꜫavinaꜫil...
qatahin. ulová. voyeual vachi-
tilal. tꜭuquyre. qahaley ꜫecha..
ꜫaquxun. qachalová. ꜫahaval...
ꜫavinaꜫil. lamaqacha. tariva...
vexa voyeben. chinuqamic. nu-
tꜭachic. varal. chuxmut. qah..
chuxmut. ulen. ahꜫaroꜫ. bala[cah.]...
ahꜫaroꜫ. bala. ulen. veꜫatꜭ varal..
incämel intꜭachel. varal. chu-
xmut. qah. chuxmut ulen. tare.-
qux. chin. vachilebeh. laquc...
latꜭiquin. laxqam. chuꜫab...
chee.. chuxum. chee. chirech.....,
utꜭuquxic larechá. lauquxun..
varal chuxmut. qah. chuxmut

[fol. 64]

uleu. ixbari. qot. ixbari. Balam quix...
petabalá. chibaná. barichac........
chibana. bari. ipatan. chibana...
bala. rivee. riivix. qaԑ. maqu...
ԑatʒ humervachil. quini vitʒma...
ritʒah. rumal. xaxinoyeu vi..
chinupetic. chinuhuyubal. chinu-
taԑahal. queke. qak. uleu........
chiqohii..ivug ixqot. ixBalam...

....

[page 3 of the cover]

PART II

The Text: Transcription and Translation

ENGLISH VERSION BY ROBERT SCHNEIDER

[fol. i] are ki wae xaj-o-l-ab

ajaw job-toj
r-ajaw-al aj-rabinal-eb

rabinal achi
ajaw u-q'alel rabinal
u-k'ajol ajaw job-toj

kaweq k'iche' achi
r-ajaw-al e yaki aj-kunen
aj-chajul
u-k'ajol balam achi
balam k'iche'
ri r-ajaw-al k'iche'

xoq'ojaw
r-ixoq-il ajaw job-toj

u-chuch q'uq'
u-chuch rax-on
ri yamani[k][4]
{e}xtekoq-ib[5] ki-bi
r-ixoq-il rabinal achi

[achi-j][7] mun
ixoq mun
r-ech rabinal a[c]hi

---

1. The name of this character—cited as Ojob Toj in the rest of the text—is probably of calendrical origin. Consequently, I have definitively adopted the form Job Toj (from the classical Quiché *jo'ob* + *toj*: "Five-Rain" or "Five-Storm") as it appears here. Furthermore, I have chosen to render the term *ajaw* as "king" or "sovereign" when it, as here, lacks any affix, or when its affixed forms (i.e., those that indicate possession, such as *r-ajaw-al, w-ajaw-al, q-ajaw-al*) apply to the same referent. These titles apply therefore to Job Toj (sovereign of the Rabinaleb) and to Balam Achi Balam K'iche' (sovereign of the Quiché). In all other cases, I have translated *ajaw* as "lord" or "master."

2. The early dictionaries often attributed *yaki* with the specific meaning of "Mexican" or "those of Nahua language and/or origin." Tirado (1787: fol. 127) and Basseta (1698: fol. 193v) turn *yaki* into a qualifier for Ladinos (i.e., non-Indians). These two specific definitions have nothing in common with what we know about the populations to which the term applies here. Thus, I have used the more general term "foreigner," which conceptually manifests the geographical-cultural gap separating the central highlands (the land of the Quiché and of the assimilated groups) from the Cuchumatanes mountains (where

[fol. i] These are the dancers:

King Job Toj,[1]
sovereign of the Rabinaleb.

Rabinal Achi,
Lord Dignitary of Rabinal;
son of King Job Toj.

Kaweq K'iche' Achi,
Lord of the Kunen Foreigners[2]
the Chajul Foreigners;
son of Balam Achi
Balam K'iche',
king of the K'iche'.

Xoq'ojaw,[3]
wife of King Job Toj.

Mother of the Quetzal
Mother of the Green Feathers,
called Gems
Precious Stones,[6]
wife of Rabinal Achi.

Man-slave
Woman-slave,
owned by Rabinal Achi.

---

today the Cunen [Quiché] and Chajul [Ixil] communities have settled). The nominal form *yaki* can probably be associated with *-yak,* a classifier denoting diversity or alterity (see Vico n.d.a: fol. 92: "huyac chic: [un] otro género de gente").

3. This term is formed on the apocope of *ixoq ajaw* ("woman-lord").

4. The form *yamanib* in our manuscript—composed of a hypothetical root *yaman* and the plural *-ib*—is not found in any dictionary; thus, it can only be *yamanik* (see Glossary).

5. Restored here according to the pronunciation of José-León Coloch and the transcription given by Basseta (1698: fol. 234v), this term appears in the dictionaries in different forms: *xtekok* ("xtecoc" in Varea n.d.; Angel n.d.), *xtek'ok'* ("xte4o4" in Vico n.d.a), and *xteqoq* ("xtekok" in Coto 1983). The initial *e-* is an originally euphonic element fixed through writing.

6. All the dictionaries agree that *yamanik* and *xtekoq* (and other terms, including *raxon*) refer to green stones, such as jades, emeralds, and serpentines.

7. Here I have restored the complete name and title of the character who is simply called Ixoq Mun in the rest of the text.

e kab-lajuj u-q'an-al kot
balam ki-bi
achi-j-ab aj-rabinal-eb

k'i-a-taq aj-labal-ib
r-uk' k'i-a-mun-ib alaj-il[8] chik
achi wepu ixoq

e xaj-o-l chi-r-e xaj-o-j tun

[fol. 1] u-nabe bi-bal[10] r-ech bartolo sis
chi ju-winaq wajxaq-ib q'ij
chi ik' ri oktubre ri junab de 1850 año[s]
mi x ch-inw-el-e-sa-j wi orijinal
r-ech wae xaj-o-j tun
r-ech wae qa-tinamit
san pablo rabinal wi
kuxta-bal ta w-e k-umal w-al
nu-k'ajol
ch(i)-u-be q'ij
ch(i)-u-be saq chi qa-wa(ch a)pan-oq

keje k'ut
[fol. 2] rabinal achi wepu xaj-o-j tun

8. This word might be an error for *alabil* (see note 9).

9. For Coloch, this segment might be understood as "and many slaves, still young"; now *alaj* connotes smallness (in size) rather than youth. It might be a homonym since *alaj* also means "free" or "freed," but the text does not say "munib *r-uk'* alajil" ("many slaves and freed"). The third hypothesis, supported here, interprets *alajil* as a corruption of *alabil,* a term that when paired with *munil,* in Old Quiché generally designated slaves or servants.

10. A deletion in the manuscript prevents us from clearly reading this word. It probably involves a double error on the part of the copyist, who first wrote *babal* (perhaps instead of *banbal*), then wrote *bibal* over the deletion. The suffix *-bal,* found in both possibilities, denotes instrumentality; the choice, then, bears on the verbal roots *ban* ("to do") and *bij* ("to tell"). In the first case, the translation is "first draft, first act (of copying) of Bartolo Sis." To agree with what the original script seems to indicate, however, I have chosen the second option.

11. Another reading would be "from which I extract the original." It is impossible to specify from this formulation alone what is meant by the "original." Is it an early manuscript older than the present transcription of Bartolo Sis, or is it this same transcription?

The twelve named Eagles
and Yellow Jaguars,
warriors of Rabinal.

A multitude of soldiers
and many slaves,[9]
both men and women.

These are the dancers of the Tun Dance.

[fol. 1] First telling of Bartolo Sis,
the twenty-eighth day
of the month of October in the year 1850,
that I extract from the original[11]
of this Tun Dance,
as it is done in this, our village,
in San Pablo Rabinal,
to allow my children to remember me[12]

in the times to come[13]
facing us.

Here, then, is
[fol. 2] Rabinal Achi, or the Dance of the Tun

---

12. Literally, "memory of me *through* my children." In other words, it will be "my children who will make it the instrument (*-bal*) of my posterity." The Quiché thus place the accent on the agents of memory, the descendants, rather than on its object, which, in this case, is the written text. The memory of tradition is associated here with a timeless ethics: past, present, and future feed off each other continuously; it governs the eternal reality of lasting Mesoamerican time. These are the very objectives that ritual acts obey and to which they contribute; notably ritual speech, through its systematically remembering and recalling all the souls of the dead *in illo tempore,* constructs the essential unicity—and the permanent interchangeability—between the living and the dead, between living people and their ancestors (see Breton 1989, 1991).

13. Literally, "on the path of the sun, on the path of light," in which the pair *q'ij saq* designates "the day(s)." The idea of the future, moreover, is suggested by the directional adverb *apanoq* ("over there [at a determined distance]"). Coto (1983: 548–549), under the entry devoted to future time, lists all the possibilities linked and combined here: "ti be Ɛih, ti be çak: tiempo futuro, venidero [. . .] 'eternamente' [. . .] También suelen usar de la partícula 'apon' [. . .] chi ka vach apon, [. . .] 'de aquí en adelante'."

U-NABE BAN-BAL

u-nabe-mul ka-ø-ch'aw-ik k'iche' achi

k-at-el ul-oq wor-om ajaw
[k']aq-om[14] ajaw
xa k'u xere chi nabe wae ma wi
ka-ø-nu-k'is-o u-ch'ay-ik u-wix-al
u-kutam-il
ajaw chakach-ib
tzaman-ib
kawuq rabinal
ka-ø-cha k'u ri nu-tzij ch(i) u-wach kaj
ch(i) u-wach ulew

keje ma wi k'i-a-tzij k-in-ch'aw uk' la
kaj
ulew chi-k'oji' uk' la
u-q'alel achi
rabinal achi

---

14. With the exception of Villacañas, who writes it as *caƐ* (n.d. fols. 84, 150), all the other dictionaries agree on the classical form *k'aqom* (*4ak/4akom*). This modification is thus called for because it respects Coloch's reading and because, regarding the written form of this ancient term, the original is not very coherent or reliable (*caƐ* also appears as *qaƐ* [fol. 12] and *ƐaƐ* [fol. 19]).

15. The term *worom,* past participle of the verb *wor,* means "pierced," "bored," or "perforated." The term *k'aqom* derives from the verb *k'aq* ("to launch, to throw an object at a distance") and describes what has been struck by these projectiles. Coto (1983: 48) translates *k'aqom* as "wounded by blows from a spear," and Villacañas (n.d.: fol. 84) as "riddled with arrows." A purely contextual interpretation might be satisfied by the fact that K'iche' Achi is speaking here to an adversary whom he has already wounded and whom he is chasing. I prefer, however, to suggest that this way of shouting at Job Toj (since he is the one involved in this case; see note 18) is a formal exordium used in every bellicose encounter referring to a corporal characteristic of the person of the king and more precisely to the fact that some of his body parts are pierced (see also lines 446–453). The description of the investiture ceremony of the Cakchiquel chiefs by Nacxit, as it appears in their annals (Recinos and Goetz 1974: 64), in fact, specifies: "They came before Mevac and Nacxit. . . . Then they entertained them, and the Ahauh Ahpop and Ahpop Qamahay were chosen. Afterwards they dressed them, they pierced their noses, and they gave them their office . . ." A pierced nose is thus a prerogative of a king, a mark of his rank and power (as Carmack and Mondloch also point out [1983: 254–255]); thus, this allusion to the "pierced, perforated" sovereign probably has nothing to do with the sodomitic practices that Brasseur mentions.

ACT ONE

K'iche' Achi speaks for the first time.

«Thou wilt come out, piercèd sovereign
perforated sovereign![15]
Thou wilt not be the first
whose roots[17]
and trunk I'll strike down[16]
– King of the Chakachib
of the Tzamanib,
Kawuq Rabinal,[18]
so says my word, facing the sky
facing the earth.»

«So I will not exchange many words with You![19]
May the sky
and the earth remain with You
– Dignitary[20]
Rabinal Achi!»

---

16. Literally, "finish striking," indicating an action in progress.

17. The term *wix* denotes all of the roots and shoots that every tree (and every plant in general) produces. The pair *wixal kutamil* has the metaphorical meaning of "ancestral lineage"; still today in Rabinal, as mentioned in the early dictionaries, ancestors are called *qa-wixal qa-kutamil* ("our root[s], our trunk[s]").

18. These first words of K'iche' Achi are without any doubt addressed to King Job Toj, who is assumed to be inside his fortress. This assumption is supported by the incitement to "come out" and the terms K'iche' Achi uses to address the person he is speaking to.

19. I am translating the reverential form of the second person singular (*la* or *lal*) and the second person plural (*alaq*) as "You," instead of using the familiar "thou" (*at*) and the plural "you" (*ix*). A comparable distinction is found in the Spanish terms *Usted* and *Ustedes*, contrasted with *tú* and *vosotros*, respectively, as well as in the formal, polite *vous* form in French. This change in pronoun confirms the change in the person addressed: after threatening the king, whom he addresses in the familiar form, K'iche' Achi addresses the king's son, Rabinal Achi, using the polite form. Thus, in a few sentences, this opening immediately situates K'iche' Achi's two interlocutors: one as the privileged target of his goals, the other as someone he despises and attempts to dismiss.

20. In the hierarchy of Quiché lists of titles, this one occupied an elevated place and corresponded to high military functions (Carmack 1981: 171, 177); Basseta (1698: fol. 170) translates it as "captain," D. Tedlock (1985: 349) as "minister."

u-nabe-mul ka-ø-ch'aw rabinal achi

eja[21] oyew achi
kaweq k'iche' winaq
la ka-ø-cha ri a-tzij ch(i) u-wach kaj
ch(i) u-wach ulew
k-at-el ul-oq wor-o[m] ajaw

« [...] ca
» kom ahau! Cuxere chi nabe vae mavi ca nu quizo u chayic
» u vixal u cutamil ahau Chacachib, Zamanib, Cauk Ra-
» binal?»... La ca cha ri a tzih?... Qui-ta-vi-ba cah,
qui-ta-vi-ba uleu! mi-x c'at yauic chupam r'al nu chab,
chupam r'al nu pocob, ruq nu yaquim vit, nu yaquim v'i-
cah, ruq nu chincu, nu galgab, nu zahcab, nu zalmet,
ruq nu couil, v'achihilal. Quehe ta-chi-na, ma-ta-chi-na,
ta mi-x-cat in tzakamah chirech nu zaki caam, nu zaki
colo. Ca cha curi nu tzih chuvach chi cah, chuvach uleu.
Cah, uleu ta chi qohe avuq, oyeu achi, canab, teleche vi-
nak!

U camul ca chau
Rabinal-Achi

Yeha! oyeu achi, canab, teleche vinak! Laki qamo
chire chi cah, chirech uleu! Qui mi-x-at u ya cah, mi-x-
at u ya uleu, ta mi-x-at tzak cut chupam r'al nu chab, [...]

[fol. 3] ch(i) u-pam r-al nu-pokob

21. This cry introduces almost all the dialogues between K'iche' Achi and Rabinal Achi: both warriors, their relationship can only be warlike, marked by challenge and trials of strength. In practice (i.e., during performances of the dance), this cry is transformed into a long, almost sung, modulated vociferation, which announces each time one of the protagonists is about to speak.

22. I am maintaining the primary meaning of *oyew* (or *oyow*) here. This term and its derivations take into account all expressions of anger, including aggression, discontent, outrage, rage, fury, and impatience, sentiments or behaviors that manifest or symbolize a warrior's characteristics. It is not impossible (as Tirado suggests [1787: fol. 106v]) that the ancient Quiché associated this anger with what we call courage, valiance, or bravery. (Thus, in certain contexts, I will translate it as "valiant.")

Rabinal Achi speaks for the first time.

«Eha! Angry man,[22]
Kaweq K'iche'![23]
What says thy word facing the sky
facing the earth?
"Thou wilt come out, piercèd sovereign"[24]

«[. . .] detestable Prince! Is this
» really the first whose roots, whose trunk
»I could not cut off, Prince of Chacachib and of Zamanib, Caük
»of Rabinal?" So says thy word?
But as truly as that sky above, as truly as the
earth exists, thou'st delivered thyself to the point of my arrow, to the
son of my shield, to my Toltec club, to my Yaqui ax,
to my bone bracelets, to my metal bracelets,
to my white varnish, to my *zalmet,* to my strength, to my
valor. But be it so or no, I have vanquished thee
with my white cord, with my shining lace. So says
my word facing the sky, facing the earth. May the
sky and earth be with thee, brave warrior, *my* prisoner,
my captive.

For the second time, Rabinal-Achi speaks

Hail! Proud warrior, *my* prisoner, *my* captive! Thanks
unto the master of the sky, the master of the
earth. Truly the sky has delivered thee, the earth has given thee
over to the point of my arrow [. . .]

[fol. 3] in the child of my shield

23. I am not translating the term *winaq,* which, contrasting with *achi* the way *homo* contrasts with *vir* in Latin, covers the notion of the individual or of a specific member of a group (see note 48).

24. In order to repair the unfortunate and flagrant omission of a portion of the text, which is without any doubt attributable to a copying error by Manuel Pérez, I think it is right to restore this missing part by inserting the fragment corresponding to the version made available by Bartolo Sis to Brasseur de Bourbourg here. (This fragment, whose layout, spelling, and translation have been scrupulously maintained, is taken from Brasseur 1862b: 28–29. I have eliminated his commentaries and have excluded his lines of general numbering.

r-uk' nu-yak-im wi[t][25]
nu-yak-im w-ikaj
nu-chinku[27]
nu-q'alq'ab
nu-sa[q]kab
nu-salmet
k-at-cha ta k'ut awiri a-juyub-al
awiri a-taq'aj-al
awiri at-bos-inaq wi tzala j(u)yub
tzala taq'aj
ma at on[33] r-al sutz'
ma at on r-al mayul

---

25. I have chosen to transcribe and to translate the term *wit* by following Brasseur and certain dictionaries (see Glossary), but this reading remains hypothetical. I thank Nathaniel Tarn for having informed me on this subject of an interesting alternative that deserves more research; in a letter dated February 29, 1992, he writes: "In the stories of the war between the Atitecan ancestors [of Santiago Atitlán] and the black giants that blocked the road to Antigua from them, there is often mention of a weapon, *wit* or *hwit,* which is a type of stick/whip, possibly made of hard rubber."

26. There is no particular reason to follow here the translations proposed up to now, all of which translate *yakim* as a derivative of *yaki* ("foreigner" or "Toltec"; see note 2). In fact, *yakim* (or *yakem*) is the past participle of the verb *yak* ("to raise, to heighten, to hoist, to brandish"). In certain contexts, I translate *yak-im wit yak-im w-ikaj* as "handle/hatchet." That said, the text evokes the foreign origin of certain people (the Yaki from Cunen and from Chajul cited in the epigraph) and of certain items (a flute and a drum notably [lines 2277–2280], which are indeed described as *yaki,* as opposed to *k'iche'*.)

27. I am keeping the form found in the original manuscript here; the dictionaries in fact record too much variability—*chinq'u* ("chinƐu"), *chunq'u,* or *chunku* ("chuncu")—to allow us to choose one form over another.

28. *Chinku* and *q'alq'ab* both designate bracelets, the former most likely carved out of bone (Basseta 1698: fol. 182), the latter made out of precious stones (Ximénez 1985: 151).

29. This probably involves body painting or protective powders. Thus, in his translation of the *Anales de los Cakchiqueles,* for *saqkab* Recinos indicates, "[T]ierra blanca o yeso, que era substancia que usaban los indios para pintarse el rostro y el cuerpo . . ." (1980: 53n31). Basseta (1698) and others also describe it as a sort of gypsum used by weavers to dry their fingers while they work.

30. This term is not found in the dictionaries, and an examination of the entries *sal* (also *tzal* or *tz'al*) and *met* does not lead to any satisfactory solution. My translation is based on Vico (n.d.a: fol. 41), who defines *salq'ij* ("çalƐih") as "talc," and on a possible Nahuatl origin of the lexeme *sal,* derived from *xalli* ("sand, pulverised stone") (Siméon 1986: 761), which would render it particularly similar to *saqkab,* with which it is joined here. One can imagine a fine clay (perhaps a sort of chalk) whose absorbent and insulating properties facilitate the wielding of weapons. However, not being able to clarify the meaning or the origin of the second element, this interpretation of the word *salmet* remains provisional.

31. The metaphorical sense of the verb *bos* ("to see the day, to be born"), which Brasseur and Raynaud retained in their translations, is acceptable. All the same, its various

with my ax handle raised[26]
my ax brandished
my bracelet
my wrist pieces[28]
my white clay[29]
my powdered stone.[30]
Thou wilt say where thy mountains are,
where thy valleys are.
Where didst thou appear from?[31] From the war country?[32]

Perhaps thou art just a child of clouds?
Perhaps thou art just a child of fog?[34]

---

glosses—"to open out" (regarding a flower or a bud), "to make public" (a secret), but also "to pierce, to crush, to burst, to explode"— more commonly convey the idea of an abrupt change of context, an instantaneous change from the hidden (obscure, enveloped, unsuspected) to the conspicuous, accompanied by a sudden and unexpected advent.

32. This phrase is particularly tricky to understand and to translate. I have opted for seeing in *tzala* a derivation of *tzal/tzaloj* (synonym for *labalij* ["to wage war, to fight, to battle"]; see Glossary) and base my choice on the occurrence of a comparable form in the *Título C'oyoi* (fol. 21)—*tzala tun*—translated by Carmack (1973: 325) as "war dance." The pair *juyub taq'aj* is rendered here in its general meaning as "land," in the sense of territory or region. It is possible that this formulation is the Quiché equivalent of the name Tezulutlán—present-day Alta Verapaz—by which it was known at the time of the arrival of the Spanish, the famous "Tierra de guerra" that the Dominicans wanted to evangelize (with the difficulties we are aware of) from out of Rabinal. This region was inhabited notably by Poq'omab, groups in part driven back from the zone of the basins (i.e., from the region that today is occupied by the village communities of Cubulco, Rabinal, Pantzuy, and Chicaj) by Quiché and Rabinaleb conquests, and in fact sheltered hostile populations that although partially subjugated by the expansion of the Quiché and their allies, continued to act threatening, in particular against the Rabinaleb who occupied their former territories and therefore the border. This specific situation of the Rabinaleb against those whom the chronicles sometimes call the Wuqamaq' (the "Seven Tribes," a generic name under which are listed the Poq'omab) and some of the events that have marked the conquest of the basins and the alienation of these lands are present in the *Rabinal Achi* (as we will see later). For now, raised in these terms, Rabinal Achi's question regarding his adversary's origins amounts in some sense to formulating the question, Aren't you one of these "barbarians"?

33. According to Ximénez (1985: 433), *on* is an adverb that expresses doubt and supports an interrogation.

34. This expression no doubt is related to the image of defeat (that we will see again later), as clouds and mist symbolize the desolation of devastated places. Another interpretation is suggested by a passage in a marriage speech recorded in 1979 that says: "I have no father, I am only the child of clouds, only the child of fog." Related to the present context, the question Rabinal Achi asks his captive would thus amount to "Perhaps you are only an orphan?" as if to ask about his family origins and whether he belongs to a royal lineage.

ma at on oqota-m loq ch(i) u-wach ch'a'
ch(i) u-wach labal
ka-ø-cha k'u ri nu-tzij ch(i) u-wach kaj
ch(i) u-wach ulew
keje ma wi k'i-a-tzij k-oj-tzij-o-n aw-uk'
kaj
ulew chi-k'oji' aw-uk'
kanab
teleche winaq

ka-mul ka-ø-ch'aw k'iche' achi

eja ajkaroq[37] kaj
ajkaroq ulew
ki pa tzij ka-bi'i-j la
toq'-o-ba-x-inaq u-wach tzij chi bix-ta-j la
ch(i) u-wach kaj
ch(i) u-wach ulew
chi nu-chi'
chi nu-wach
la in oyew achi k'u ri
ka-ø-cha k'u ri tzij la
la at pa ri at-anim-a-j-inaq[40] ul-oq
ch(i) u-wach ch'a'
[fol. 4] ch(i) u-wach labal
ka-ø-cha ri tzij la
la in k'(o) oyew
la in k'o achi k'u ri
xa ta la ri
alawi in-anim-a-j-inaq wi ul-oq ch(i) u-wach ch'a'
ch(i) u-wach labal
xa wi ka-ø-cha na[41] k'u ri tzij la

---

35. Formed around the past participle of the verb *oqota* ("to hunt, to banish, to abandon, to desert"), the construction *at oqotam loq* reads "you-chased-over here (toward us who are speaking)."

36. The pair *kanab teleche* designates captives taken in war; it also applies to prey or hunting catch.

37. A term that is difficult to translate and that dictionaries give as an interjection or an exclamation denoting both pain and admiration. The choice of writing (which I wanted to keep consistent throughout the text) follows Coloch's pronunciation, as the manuscript and early texts propose quite variable transcriptions of it (see Glossary).

Perhaps thou art fleeing[35] from the fighting
fleeing from combat?
so says my word facing the sky
facing the earth.
So we will exchange few words with thee.
May the sky
and the earth remain with thee
—Captive,
Prisoner!»[36]

K'iche' Achi speaks for the second time.

«Eha! Oh Sky,
oh Earth!
Truly what You are saying,
the words that You offer,
facing the sky
facing the earth, are arrogant[38]
as they concern me.[39]

"Might I be a valiant man . . . ?"
And Your word says:
"Might thou have come here
fleeing the fighting
[fol. 4] *fleeing combat?"*
as You say.
"Might I be valiant?
And might I be a man . . . ?"
Listen only to this:
". . . Where did I appear from, *'fleeing the fighting*
fleeing combat' . . . ?"
—as Your word would have it—

---

38. Or, literally, "wounding and stinging," translating the expression *toq'obaxinaq u-wach,* formed from the verbal root *toq'* ("to wound by stinging"). The Indians used this same verb long ago to designate the bleedings they practiced (see Glossary).

39. Literally, "for my mouth, for my face."

40. This term comes from the verb *an* ("to hasten, to run"); in classical Quiché, the derived forms are *anum* or *anom.*

41. The particle *na* denotes either the contrast between two propositions (as in "in spite of, although") or the antecedence of one over the other (as in "first").

ch-in-jik-i-ba n[u]-wach nu-juyub-al
nu-taq'aj-al
ka-ø-cha ri tzij la
la in k'(o) oyew
la in k'o achi k'u ri
ta x ch-in-jik-i-ba ta k'ut u-wach nu-juyub-al
nu-taq'aj-al
ma[42] na [q']alaj[43] in-bos-inaq wi tzala j(u)yub
tzala taq'aj
xa in r-al sutz'
xa in r-al mayul
la julacha ix ch-in-jik-i-ba nu-juyub-al
nu-taq'aj-al
ka-r-aj xa x chi-k'oq-o-n kaj
xa x chi-k'oq-o-n ulew
ka-ø-cha k'u ri nu-tzij ch(i) u-wach kaj
ch(i) u-wach ulew
keje ma wi k'i-a-tzij k-oj-tzij-o-ya-j[45] uk' la
u-q'alel achi
rabinal achi
kaj
ulew chi-k'oji' aw-uk'

u-rox-mul ka-ø-ch'aw rabinal achi

eja oyew achi
kanab
teleche winaq
[fol. 5] la ka-ø-cha na k'u ri a-tzij ch(i) u-wach kaj
ch(i) u-wach ulew
la in k'o oyew
la in k'o achi k'u ri
we x-ch-in-jik-i-ba nu-juyub-al
nu-taq'aj-al

42. The particle *ma* is a marker of the causative. Depending on the context and function of other markers that are associated with it, it is rendered either by a negative interrogation ("isn't that right?" or "is that not so?") or by the affirmative ("because, in fact").

43. Coloch, reading this term as it appears in the original manuscript—*kalaj*—analyzes it as *ka-laj*, from *ka* ("two") and *-laj* (a classifier) and consequently translates it as "twice, two times." Apart from the fact that no dictionary confirms this interpretation, my translation, supported by the context (and notably by the coupling of this term with *jikiba* in lines 174–175), follows that of Basseta (1698: fol. 170) for *calah*, "cosa clara, manifiesta, pública," a root that the other works, without exception, write as *Ɛalah*/*Ɛalahisah*; thus, a correction to *q'alaj* is justified.

"... I will reveal the face of my mountains
of my valleys."
You say.
Would I be valiant
and would I be a man
if I revealed the face of my mountains
of my valleys?
Isn't it obvious that I have emerged from the war country,

that I am just a child of clouds,
that I am just a child of fog!
Wherefore[44] would I reveal my mountains
my valleys?
Sooner let the sky curse me
let the earth curse me!
So says my word facing the sky
facing the earth.
So we will not engage in further polemics with You
—Dignitary,
Rabinal Achi!
May the sky
and the earth remain with thee!»

Rabinal Achi speaks for the third time.[46]

«Eha! Angry man,
Captive,
Prisoner.
[fol. 5] What says thy word facing the sky
facing the earth:
"Would I be valiant,
would I be a man
if I revealed my mountains
my valleys?

44. An archaic, uncommon form, not recognized today, which was originally used to express a questioning, *julacha* is pointed out by Vico (n.d.a: fol. 88v). A close interrogative form is found in Tirado (1787: fol. 163v): *jucha pa la* ("¿para qué?").

45. The suffixation into *-ya* is one of several forms enabling the expression of the frequentative. In certain cases, as Basseta (1698: fol. 193v) and Ximénez (1985: 299) note, it points out that the action is marked by confrontation. Linked here to the act of speech, it conveys a verbal quarrel.

46. If we take into account the skipping of a page due to the copying error committed by Manuel Pérez (see the reconstruction of the text according to Brasseur), we are in fact dealing here with Rabinal Achi's third set of lines.

ma na [q']alaj in-bos-inaq wi tzal-a j(u)yub
tzal-a taq'aj
xa in r-al sutz'
xa in r-al mayul
ma pa ka-ø-cha ri a-tzij
we ba ma wi ix ch-a-jik-i-ba u-wach ri a-juyub-al
u-wach ri a-taq'aj-al
ta ka-r-aj kaj
ta ka-r-aj ulew
xa at-wa-j-im
xa at-per-aj-im
k-at-inw-ok-i-sa-j ch(i) u-wach w-ajaw-al
ch(i) u-wach nu-winaq-il
ch(i) u-pam u-nim-al tz'aq
ch(i) u-pam u-nim-al k'oxtun
ka-ø-cha k'u ri nu-tzij ch(i) u-wach kaj
ch(i) u-wach ulew
keje kaj
ulew chi-k'oji' aw-uk'
kanab
teleche winaq

u-rox-mul ka-ø-ch'aw k'iche' achi

ajkaroq kaj
ajkaroq ulew
ka-ø-cha k'u ri tzij la ch(i) u-wach kaj
ch(i) u-wach ulew
a la ta k'u k'o wi ri x chi r-ok-i-be-j
[fol. 6] ri x chi r-el-e-be-j ri tzij
ri u-ch[o]l-a-n-ik

47. This translation remains quite ungainly compared to the remarkable pithiness of the Quiché expression. Through these words, Rabinal Achi threatens his interlocutor with making him meat for sacrifice, a fate reserved for prisoners of war who, as is narrated in the *Título Xpantzay II*, were presented as food for the gods (Carmack 1973: 134; see also Coto 1983: 502–503, under the entry "Sacrificar"). The term *wajim* is the past participle of the passive form of *wa* ("to eat [tortillas]"); it can be glossed as "to be a food" and, consequently, "(intended to) be eaten." As for the term *peraj*, it is derived from the verb *per* ("to break, to tear with one's hands") and is used as a numeral classifier to account for the pieces of broken or torn objects (e.g., pieces of paper, fabric, and tortillas; see Glossary).

48. The term *winaq*, in a general way, designates a person/people/folk of any age and gender. In certain contexts and in different forms—as here *nu-winaqil*, which indicates the intimacy of the relationship—it can have the specific meaning of "my own

Isn't it obvious that I have emerged from the war country!

that I am just a child of clouds,
that I am just a child of fog?"
Isn't this what thy word says?
If thou revealst not the face of thy mountains
of thy valleys,
then let the sky
then let the earth ordain
that thou art but food,
that thou art but portions![47]
I am going to bring thee in, facing my master
facing my eminence[48]
inside the great fortress
inside the great wall![49]
So says my word facing the sky
facing the earth.
May the sky
and the earth remain with thee
—Captive,
Prisoner!»

K'iche' Achi speaks for the third time.

«Oh Sky,
oh Earth!
Your word says facing the sky
facing the earth:
"Where then will be the starting point
[fol. 6] *the ending point of the words*
of the formulas[50]

people" or, as Varea (n.d.: fol. 103) points out, "those of my village or of my lineage." Concerning the person of the king, it acquires a unique meaning that I will render as "an eminent person" or "eminence."

49. Considered within specific technical or architectural contexts, *tz'aq* corresponds to building(s) and construction(s), and *k'oxtun* to surrounding wall(s). The pair *tz'aq k'oxtun* designates the fortress or citadel, whether or not such walls exist (and in fact it is rare for archaeological sites to show proof of exterior fortifications); thus, this term reflects the symbolic nature of the place where the king resides and from which he governs as a contained, closed, and sheltered place.

50. Many terms are formed from the root *chol* that mean "to put in order, to do something following a certain order." Under the entry "Decir," Coto (1983: 138) specifies *chol/cholan*: "decir algo derecha y concertadamente [. . .] y distintamente."

ri mi x k-oj-tzij-o-ya-j uk' la ch(i) u-wach kaj
ch(i) u-wach ulew
are ba x chi r-el-e-be-j
are x ch(i) u-qaj-i-be-j
r-umal ix ch-a-jik-i-ba
ix ch-a-[q']alaj-i-sa-j u-wach a-ju[yu]b-al
u-wach a-taq'aj-al
we ma wi ix ch-a-[q']alaj-i-sa-j
ta ka-r-aj kaj
ta ka-r-aj ulew
xa at-wa-j-im
xa at-per-aj-im
ix k-at-nu-koj ch(i) u-wach w-ajaw-al
nu-winaq-il
ka-ø-cha k'u ri nu-tzij ch(i) u-wach kaj
ch(i) u-wach ulew
ka-r-aj at kaj
ka-r-aj at ulew
ri ba la ix ch-in-jik-i-ba k'ut u-wach nu-juyub-al
u-wach nu-taq'aj-al
ri ix tapich'olo[l]
tz'ikin
in r-oyew-el-al
in r-achi-j-il-al ri ajaw ri yaki kunen
ri yaki chajul
la ajaw balam achi
balam k'iche'
ki la jukutaj qaj-inaq wi r-aqan-ibal sutz'
mayul
chi nu-juyub-al
chi nu-taq'aj-al
a la ta k'u k'o wi ri ch(i) u-qaj-i-be-j
a la ta k'u k'o wi ri x chi r-el-e-be-j wa tzij
wa u-ch[o]l-a-n-ik
mi x-oj-tzij-o-n uk' la ch(i) u-wach kaj
ch(i) u-wach ulew
keje kaj
ulew chi-k'oji' uk' la
u-q'alel achi
rabinal achi

51. Revelation and confession are presented by Rabinal Achi (through the words reported here by his adversary) as the conditions for the interrogation's conclusion; this is what is expressed by the (causative) relative *r-umal* and is conveyed here by the colon.

that we exchange, with You, facing the sky
facing the earth?
This will be the final end
the final collapse:[51]
thou shalt confess
thou shalt reveal the face of thy mountains
the face of thy valleys.
If thou dost not reveal them,
then let the sky
then let the earth ordain
that I introduce thee face to face with my master
face to face with my eminence
as food
and [cut into] portions!"
And my word says facing the sky
facing the earth:
Then thou, Sky, ordain
thou, Earth, ordain
that I reveal the face of my mountains
the face of my valleys!
You, you are nightingales
birds!
I, I am the anger
I am the strength of the sovereign of the Yaki Kunen
of the Yaki Chajul,
King Balam Achi
Balam K'iche',
having come down just this instant—a trail of clouds
a trail of fog—
from my mountains
from my valleys!
So where, then, will the collapse be?
Where, then, will be the ending of these words
these formulas
that we have exchanged with You facing the sky
facing the earth?[52]
May the sky
and the earth remain with You
—Dignitary,
Rabinal Achi!»

52. The scorn that K'iche' Achi displays toward his interlocutors is strongly stressed in this passage, which successively employs expressions of insult, vanity, and insolence.

[fol. 7] *u-kaj-mul ka-ø-ch'aw rabinal achi*

oyew achi
kaweq k'iche' winaq
xa pe xa lal ri ka-ø-nu-to
xa lal w-atz
xa pe xa lal nu-chaq'
qatz[54] na pu x-ø-sach nu-k'ux ri
chi-r-ech il-ik la
chi-r-ech tzu'ik la
chi-r-ij u-nim-al tz'aq
chi-r-ij u-nim-al k'oxtu[n]
lal ba ri ka-ban la r-oq'-ibal utiw
ka-ban la r-oq'-ibal yak
ka-ban la r-oq'-ibal utuy
balam
chi-r-ij u-nim-al tz'aq
k'oxtun
ka-boy-i-be-j la k-e la saq-il al
k'ajol
ri q-el-e-sa-m bi[58] ch(i) u-wach u-nim-al tz'aq
ch(i) u-wach u-nim-al k'oxtun

53. This exclamation expresses Rabinal Achi's astonishment at the declarations of his prisoner, as he discovers his origin and, therefore, that he is an ally—a "brother." The situation shifts here: the interrogation into the identity of the interlocutor turns into a trial against an identified adversary who is accused of many crimes, including, in fact, that of having broken the alliance. The revealing of the dispute between the two groups and the various charges that weigh against K'iche' Achi henceforth constitute the single object of the dialogues that follow.

54. The word *qatz* ("in truth, truly") functions over the entire text as a sort of temporal switch and marks the passages from the mimesis to the diegesis and vice versa. Depending on the context, it introduces the evocation of an earlier time, leads us to the current action (the trial going on), or anticipates the immediate future (the outcome of the trial). This play of analepsis and of prolepsis is supported by oratory formulas of the type "Isn't it You who . . ." (which question the relationships of causality that the speaker establishes between events) and those of the type "So You're saying . . ." (which situate the reported speech in time). More mundanely, all these tools of articulation function as so many fade-ins and fade-outs, somewhat like those dissolving views that announced returns to the past in old films.

55. Literally, "You who were doing."

56. The identification of these different animals raises several questions. The term *utiw* systematically designates the coyote or the American wolf, but the term *yak* means the wildcat (Ximénez 1985: 297), a sort of weasel (Coloch, pers. comm.), or skunk (Basseta

[fol. 7] *Rabinal Achi speaks for the fourth time.*

«Angry man,
K'iche' Achi.
But what am I hearing now from You?
It seems You are my elder brother,
it seems You are my younger brother![53]
Could my heart really forget
having seen You
having observed You
behind the great fortress
behind the great wall,
You who imitated[55] the coyote crying
who imitated the wildcat howling
who imitated the agouti howling
the jaguar howling[56]
behind the great citadel

as to attract them, the white children[57]

that we had sent out in front of the great fortress
in front of the great wall:

1698: fol. 192v). As for *utuy,* several dictionaries (Basseta 1698; Coto 1983; Varea n.d.) point it out without proposing a specific translation; Ximénez (1985: 601) and Guzmán (1984: 32) translate it as "cotuza" (a sort of agouti, perhaps *Dacyprocta punctata*). But does it refer to a specific animal, or is it a term that is compounded with *balam* ("jaguar"), as is suggested by the listing's form and Coloch's reading of it as *utuy balam* ("a sort of jaguar")? We will see this same uncertainty when *utuy* is paired with *jalaw* (see note 178).

57. In early texts the pair *al k'ajol* is always somewhat ambiguous. In its most limited definition, it designates the children born of a couple (*al,* "children of both sexes, of a woman"; *k'ajol,* "son of a man") and easily extends to a generation (the "young" as compared to the "older ones" or the "parents"). Yet, it also covers a class of pre-Hispanic society, that of the "common folk" as opposed to the "nobles" (called *ajaw* or *rajawal*), on the one hand, and to "slaves and servants" on the other (Carmack 1976). The specification as to the "white" nature, as it is stipulated here, is a criterion of identity—"the white children" means "those from the white land" (i.e., "from Rabinal," as will be discussed later) or "ours"—and a mark of quality, as in "the true, the excellent." This interpretation is suggested by Vico (n.d.a: fol. 7v) when he marks the difference between the "vassals or macehuales" ("*al 4ahol*") and the "human lineage" ("*çakil al çakil 4ahol*"). Lacking a contraindication, I have rendered the pair *al k'ajol* as "children," without prejudicing any possible extended meanings or introducing metaphorical usages that are impossible to justify.

e tzuku-y r-e u-chikop-il q'an-a kab
rax-a kab
tzuq-bal r-ech w-ajaw-al
nu-winaq-il
mam-a ajaw {o}job toj
xa k'u xere la julacha u-yak-ik
u-silibi-sa-x-ik wa oyew-al
achi-j-il-al
ta mi x-yak chi lo la
ma pa x-oj-ki-sik'-i-j
x-oj-ki-chok-o e kab-lajuj chi ajaw-ab
e r-ajaw-al ju-jun chi tz'aq
ju-jun chi k'oxtun

ma pa x-ø-cha ri ki-tzij chi-q-e
chi pe-t-a na b(a) alaq kab-lajuj chi oyew
[fol. 8] alaq kab-lajuj chi achi-j-ab
ch-ul ta ta na b(a) alaq pixab-a-x-ik-il alaq
r-umal ix-ø-jar-ik
ix-ø-twanik
ix-ø-tux-ar-ik
ix-ø-tzarajmaq-ir-ik
u-pam ju-jun chi wa'bal
chi ok-ibal

58. I have kept the muted and fixed forms—*bi* or *ubi*—of this directional adverb that accompanies the action of a movement toward the exterior, which directs it far from here. Ideally, it should be restored to its classical form: *[u]bi[k].*

59. Varea (n.d.: fol. 331) distinguishes *ruchicopil cab,* which he translates as "wild honey," and *avah cab,* which refers to honey produced by domestic hives (literally, hives found "behind the house"). According to Coto (1983: 58), Tirado (1787: fol. 204), and Vico (n.d.a: fol. 27v), however, the expression is valid only when it pertains to bees. Different glosses confirm the double meaning of the term *kab,* which is applied in Quiché as in most Mayan languages to honey as well as to bees. The form of the nominal group does not create any doubt here—*u-chikopil kab* is read as "animals of honey," something like the old French expression *les mouches à miel* ("honey flies")—and suggests that it is indeed the insects that are sought; however, the qualifiers *q'an* and *rax* (an association that generates a sense of "rich, precious") connected to honey highlight the equal importance of honey. The *Rabinal Achi* is not the only text thus to evoke the fact that Apidae are sought-after edible commodities: the *Historia Quiché de don Juan de Torres* also recalls that they long constituted (along with honey) the unique food source of the Quiché ancestors (Recinos 1984: 27). Studies dealing with these alimentary practices in indigenous societies of modern Mexico have shown, moreover, that a large number of species of this order are still eaten daily, or occasionally, in the form of eggs, larvae, and even adults; most often the nest, removed from its base after it is abandoned by its

those who look for flies of yellow honey
for flies of green honey,[59]
food for our master
for our eminence
—Great[60] King Job Toj?
But why this surge
this display of anger
of force
that You showed then?
Had they not called us
had they not convoked us, they, the twelve lords,
they, the lords from each fortress
from each wall?

Did not their words tell us:
"Come, You, the twelve valiants
[fol. 8] *You, the twelve warriors!*
Come and hear what is recommended to You:
since [the food] has turned to water[61]
has rotted[62]
has flaked off
has desiccated[63]
in the bottom of every plate
of every bowl.

---

occupants, is used in its entirety: honey, comb, and immature insects included (see, e.g., Ramos Elorduy de Conconi 1982).

60. The exact translation of *mam-a* would be "old, great through age (experience and wisdom)."

61. Guided by Coloch's reading, I favor the meaning "to melt, to fall apart, to become liquid" that Quiché dictionaries attribute to *jaar* (with a long vowel), formed with *ja* ("water"), in contrast to *jar,* which means "to become old, to age" and applies to items like clothing, nets, leather, and straw. If indeed we are dealing here with two independent roots—which Cakchiquel clearly distinguishes, using the terms *yaar* and *har* (see Glossary)—it is at present the only case for which the distinction between long and short vowels appears to be important in the *Rabinal Achi.*

62. Recognized by Coloch, whose translation I am borrowing here, this term is not found in dictionaries. It could be a corruption of the root *tub* ("envejecer"; Ximénez 1985: 545; see also Coto 1983: 202, "ttube") or a writing error for *tujanik,* which expresses the idea of evanescence or evaporation, as in the steam bath, or *temascal* (*tuj* in Quiché), which refers to water that turns into steam.

63. Literally, "to become a pumice stone." The situation described here is that of the shortage that prevailed in the fortress, where reserves were dwindling and beginning to run out and food is dried out, rotten, and infested.

xa lol
xa xil chik
k-e-xil-il chi kan-oq ch(i) u-pam ki-tz'aq-il
ki-k'oxtun-al
ri saq-il al
k'ajol
r-umal xa belej-eb chik
xa lajuj chik chi-ki-riq chik ki-tz'aq-il
ki-k'oxtun-al
keje k'ut chi-qa-tana-ba taj u-tij-ik ri saq-il al
saq-il k'ajol
are ta k'u chi-qa-kam u-tij-ik
la qa-ch'u'[67] nim-a kinaq
la qa-xtapakal[68]
la qa-xkorowach
la qa-tz'uley u-ji'
ma pa x-ø-cha ri qa-pixab-a-x-ik-il
k-umal e ajaw-ab
e r-ajaw-al
naqi pe ma wi ch(i)-ø-[e]k'ow-ik r-aj-abal k'ux la
chi-r-ech wa oyow-al
wa achi-j-il-al
ma pa belej-eb moqoj
belej-eb chumay
ix-ø-bek u-muq-ik
u-pis-ik wa oyow-al
wa achi-j-il-al
k-umal e ajaw-ab
chila chi-k'ot-om
chi-tikram ch(i)-u-ch[a]-x-ik[71]
are na k'u ka-toj-or-i-sa-j la ri
waral ch(i) u-xmut kaj
ch(i) u-xmut ulew

---

64. The terms *lol* and *xil* designate two sorts of crickets. Their songs, expressed here by the verb *xilil* and in other texts by *lolin,* are nocturnal and indicate the cessation of all other activity. By extension, they denote places (such as houses or villages) that have been depopulated or deserted, stricken by illness or famine; they are comparable to the French expression *un silence de mort* ("a dead silence"; see Glossary). The evocation of these songs as the final manifestations of life confirms the state of desolation of the places mentioned.

65. In other words, "a few" or "a small number."

66. This order illustrates explicitly the conceptual relationship that existed, among the ancient Quiché, among prisoners of war, sacrifice, and cannibalism (see note 47).

67. I am interpreting this word as a possible apocope of *ch'utin* ("little ones").

Since only the house crickets
and the bush crickets
remain to sing inside the fortress
the wall[64]
of the white children;

since only nine
or ten[65] *have regained their fortress*
their wall;
let us stop consuming the white children[66]

and set to consuming
our own beans, small and large,
our colored beans,
our spotted beans,
our spiral-growing beans."[69]
Is that not what was recommended to us
by them, by the sovereigns,
by the lords?
How to purge Your heart of desiring
this anger
this force?
Was it not at Belejeb Moqoj
Belejeb Chumay,[70]
that this anger
and this force went to bury
to inter themselves
thanks to them, the sovereigns
over there, of Chi K'otom
of Chi Tikram, as they are called?
And that is what You are going to pay for
here at the navel of the sky
at the navel of the earth!

---

68. According to Alonso (n.d.: fol. 143v) and Coto (1983: 240), this term should be read as *xtakapal.*

69. The four terms listed are recognized by Coloch and continue today to designate different types of beans: *ch'u'* is a cold-weather bean with a yellow shell (a sort of flageolet); *xtapakal* is a warm-weather flageolet with a small shell; *xkorowach* is a spotted bean; and *tz'uley u-ji'* (literally, "who embraces his son-in-law"; for a related word, see note 110) is a bean whose long pod rolls in on itself or those close to it.

70. The identification of the toponyms cited in the text is discussed in Part III: Analysis: An Exemplary History.

71. This expression, always associated with place names, is a passive form derived from the root *cha* ("to say")

[fol. 9] keje k'ut mi x-pixab ta kan la chi juyub-al la
chi taq'aj-al la
rumal waral ka-qa-ch'ay wi wix-al la
kutam-il la
waral ch(i) u-xmut kaj
ch(i) u-xmut ulew
ma wi k'u lo chi q'ij
ch(i) aq'ab
chi qaj ta chi pan la chi juyub-al la
chi taq'aj-al la
qatz k'u waral lal kam-el
lal sach-el
waral ch(i) u-xmut kaj
ch(i) u-xmut ulew
keje k'ut ka-nu-yo'pi-sa-j tzij-o-l la
ch(i) u-wach w-ajaw-al
ch(i) u-wach nu-winaq-il
ch(i) u-pam u-nim-al tz'aq
k'oxtun
ka-ø-cha k'u ri nu-tzij ch(i) u-wach kaj
ch(i) u-wach ulew
keje ma wi k'i-a-tzij k-oj-tzij-o-n-ik
kaj
ulew chi-k'oji' uk' la
kaweq k'iche' winaq

u-kaj-mul ka-ø-ch'aw k'iche' achi

eja oyew achi
u-q'alel achi
rabinal achi
la ka-ø-cha na k'u ri tzij la ch(i) u-wach kaj
ch(i) u-wach ulew
la julacha u-yak-ik ri oyow-al
achi-j-il-al

72. I am rendering in the future tense the expression (not devoid of irony) according to which, and given the charges that weigh against the defendant, Rabinal Achi presumes that K'iche' Achi will have thought to inform his people of the risks incurred. The particle *ta[j]* (muted here to *ta*) expresses the desiderative (or the optative; see Coto 1983: 158); it also marks the hypothetical (when the action is to come) or assumed (when the action is completed) nature of the intent of the verb to which it is connected.

73. Literally, "to cause to approach, to cause to reach." This verb, which appears frequently in the text and which will be seen in other forms (*yo'pijik, yo'pitaj*), seems

[fol. 9] Accordingly, You would have informed[72] Your mountains
Your valleys
that here we were going to strike Your roots
Your trunk,
here, at the navel of the sky
at the navel of the earth;
and that henceforth there will be neither a day
nor a night
that You can go down toward Your mountains
toward Your valleys.
It is certain that here You will die
You will disappear,
here, at the navel of the sky
at the navel of the earth!
I shall report[73] the information concerning You
face to face with my master
face to face with my eminence
inside the great citadel.

So says my word facing the sky
facing the earth.
So we do not have much to say to each other.
May the sky
and the earth remain with You
—Kaweq K'iche'!»

K'iche' Achi speaks for the fourth time.

«Eha! Angry man,
Dignitary
Rabinal Achi!
What says Your word facing the sky
facing the earth?
"Why this surge of anger
of force?"

---

idiomatic. It is scarcely mentioned in the early dictionaries, except by Basseta (1698: fol. 196: "yopihic: acercarse") and Vico (n.d.a: fol. 100v), who points out the pair "ul/ yopehic: la venida." This literal translation is, however, not always explicit; thus, depending on the various contexts, I sometimes render this verb as "to report, to present, to announce" (for transitive, causative forms rendered as *-saj*) and sometimes use "to reach, rejoin, approach, appear" (intransitive, passive forms rendered as *-taj*).

ka-ø-cha ri tzij la
je suk'-ul-ik x-e-pixab chi nabe la q-ajaw-al
[fol. 10] la qa-winaq-il
xa k'u xere ma na k'o wi chi-r-ech w-il-ik
nu-pe-t-ik
chi nu-juyub-al
chi nu-taq'aj-al
chiri mi x-ø-el wi jun taq-o-n
samajel ch(i) u-xmut kaj
ch(i) u-xmut ulew
ch(i) u-wach ajaw-ar-inaq tz'aq
kaqyuq' tzilik kakoqonik tepekanik
u-bi u-chi'
u-wach la tz'aq
la k'oxtun
ma pa ka-ø-yut'-ut' apan-oq la [j]o-kal[75] peq
[j]o-kal kako[76]
x-ø-el apan-oq ch(i) u-wach w-ajaw-al
nu-winaq-il
balam ajaw
balam achi
balam k'iche'
u-bi u-chi'
u-wach la nu-tz'aq
la nu-k'oxtun

---

74. This phrase hardly lends itself to a literal translation; therefore, using the verb "to justify," I have rendered the relationship that the preposition *chirech* (expressing here what traditional grammar calls the ethical dative) establishes between the action of summoning/recommendation (previously evoked) and the interest K'iche' Achi takes in this action. Through these words, in fact, K'iche' Achi suggests—and confirms later—that he was absent from his home when those recommendations were made.

75. This term is no longer understood today; I am reconstructing it in a form that is verified later (in lines 619–620), in agreement with Brasseur's and Raynaud's translations, following Ximénez (1985: 149): "cala: para contar cargas de cacao" and also "número 8,000" (a unit of measure equivalent to the Aztec *xiquipilli*) (Siméon 1986: 767; see also Anleo n.d.: fol. 62). According to this passage, the assumed amount of the tribute in cacao owed by the Rabinaleb to the Quiché represented 5 x 8,000, or 40,000 pods of each variety.

76. The distinction *peq/kako* involves two sorts of cacao: the first is *Theobroma bicolor,* also known by the name of *pataxte* (wild cacao), and the second is *Theobroma cacao.*

77. This long and double digression—"Kaqyuq' . . . loads of cacao" (lines 331–336)—which suspends the flow of the story, is particularly important for a historical interpretation of the *Rabinal Achi.* First, it has an inestimable locative function insofar as

You ask.
Yes, that was certainly what our masters
[fol. 10] our eminencies recommended first.
But there was nothing that justified my presence
my coming
to my mountains
to my valleys.[74]
It was then that an envoy
a messenger left the navel of the sky
the navel of the earth,
from the face of the sovereign fortress
—Kaqyuq' Tzilik Kakoqonik Tepekanik:
name of the threshold,
of the front of this fortress
of this wall . . .
—is not this where they assemble the five loads of *pataxte*
the five loads of cacao? . . .[77]
and he comes facing my master
my eminence
—Balam Ajaw
Balam Achi
Balam K'iche':
name of the threshold,
of the face of my fortress
of my wall.[78]

---

it is the sole mention of the name of Kaqyuq' (Kajyub). Second, it has a deictic function: the place where the messenger came out is truly the place where they are and where they are speaking (the demonstrative *la* before *tz'aq k'oxtun* indicates that it concerns the fortress "here"), confirming that Kajyub is indeed the place where the action of the trial hic et nunc is situated. Third, it has a denotative function: by recalling, in an obviously sarcastic way, the reality of the tributary flows (*apanoq*: "from here to over there"), K'iche' Achi evokes the situation of dependency in which Kajyub finds itself with regard to the Quiché and, in doing so, questions the opportuneness of the Rabinaleb initiative. On a more general level, the meaning of this passage, which expresses the Quiché point of view on the origin of the casus belli, can only be found in later explanations and, notably, in light of the misunderstanding generated by the declarations of the Rabinaleb (lines 353–372 and 492–506). These will be interpreted by K'iche' Achi as a challenge issued by the Rabinaleb in the presence of Uxab Poq'omab enemies (lines 351–352) and by Rabinal Achi as the expression of a threat emanating from those same enemies (lines 487–488).

78. There is no doubt a relationship of eponymy between the sovereign and his fortress. It is seen here in the practice of naming a place after the name of the one who rules there; this relationship will continue later but inversely with the toponyms designating the rulers.

ta tze[79] ch-u-ta apan-oq ri ajaw balam ajaw
balam k'iche'
r-umal ta tze ka-ø-rayi-x u-kam-ik
ri ajaw chakach-ib
tzaman-ib
kawuq rabinal
ch(i) u-wach ux-ab
ch(i) u-wach poq'om-ab
chi qa-ban ta utz-il
chom-al
ch-u-taq ta wi ul-oq r-oyow-el-al
r-achi-j-il-al
ri ajaw k'iche' j(u)yub
k'iche' taq'aj
ch-ø-ul ech-a-be-n-a[81] taj chi-r-ech saq-il j(u)yub
ri saq-il taq'aj
chi-ø-pe ta k'ut ri nu-chaq'
ri nu-nim-al
ch-ø-ul ech-a-be-n-a ta k'ut
waral ch(i) u-xmut kaj
ch(i) u-xmut ulew
chi-r-ech saq-il j(u)yub
chi-r-ech saq-il taq'aj
ch-ø-ul tik-o-n-a taj
[fol. 11] ch-ø-ul awex-a-n-a taj
xa ta k'u la chi-ø-bek u-tzam qa-k'um
u-tzam qa-saq-il k'um
qa-saq-il nay
keje k'ut ix-ø-cha k'u u-ye-bal[84]
u-sik'-ibal
la tak-o-m ch(i) u-wach w-ajaw-al
keje k'ut mi x-u-tzaq apan-oq u-ye-bal
u-sik'-ibal

79. This particle is neither identified nor understood (*ta tze, ta se, tatze,* and *tase* all are possible readings). The temporary solution adopted here turns it into an equivalent form of the adverb *ta* ("then, when"). The only similar form encountered in the dictionaries is the particle *tase*Ɛ, which Basseta (1698: fol. 220v) points out and describes as "partícula condicional poco usada," a definition that does not agree with the present context.

80. Literally, "he hears." The presence of the directional-locative adverb *apanoq* indicates that the action expressed by the verb is directed or reaches "there (in a specified place)."

81. The verb *echaben* is formed from the root *ech,* which one finds in the dative preposition *-ech* or *chi-ech* (and also the personal forms that are associated with it, such as *w-ech, aw-ech,* and *r-ech*).

That was when he learned[80]—King Balam Ajaw
Balam K'iche'—
that his death is desired
by the king of the Chakachib
of the Tzamanib,
Kawuq Rabinal,
opposing the Uxab
opposing the Poq'omab:
"So let us perform well
correctly
what the anger
and the force
of the sovereign of the K'iche' mountains
the K'iche' valleys orders us!
Let him come to take possession of the white mountains
of the white valleys![82]
Let my younger brother,
my elder brother come!
Let him come to take possession
of this place, the navel of the sky
the navel of the earth,
the white mountains
the white valleys!
Let him come and sow
[fol. 11] *come and hoe*
and let our squash seedlings
our white squash seedlings sprout together."[83]

So said the exhortations
the pleas
transmitted to the face of my sovereign.
It was then that he cried out his exhortations
his pleas,

82. The words "the white mountains, the white valleys" and "the white land" refer to the territory of the Rabinaleb, to the lands occupied by "the white children" (see note 57).

83. The terms *k'um* and *nay* designate two varieties of edible squashes (*Cucurbita*): *k'um* is the fruit called *ayote* and has small or large seeds (but the variety with large seeds is called *saqil k'um*); *nay* is the small squash called *huicoy*.

84. Instrumental form of the verb *yej* (*yeeh* in the dictionaries), which means "to stimulate, to summon, to hasten" and, more generally, "to incite someone to perform a task quickly." I have rendered it as "exhortation" or "challenge, provocation."

w-ajaw-al
nu-winaq-il
eja ej[a] w-oyew-al-al
w-achi-j-il-al
chi oj at-toj-el
k-at-tzel-e-j-a ba loq
r-umal x-iw-ula'-a-j la taq-o-n
samajel
ix-ø-pe ch(i) u-xmut kaj
ch(i) u-xmut ulew
ch-a-yak-a ul-oq ri a-ko-w-il
ri aw-achi-j-il-al
r-al a-ch'ab
r-al a-pokob
ch-a-tzal-a-j ul-oq r-aqan j(u)yub
r-aqan taq'aj

ix-ø-cha apan-oq u-ye-bal
u-sik'-ibal la w-ajaw-al
nu-winaq-il
in jin ta-n taj
in k-in-tajin-ik in koj-o-l r-eta-l-il ulew
ch(i) u-ben-e-bal q'ij
chi r-ok-ibal aq'ab
chi mach'-m-al tew
mach'-m-al joron
chila pan-tz'ajaxaq ch(i)-u-ch[a]-x-ik
keje k'ut mi x-in-yak ul-oq r-al nu-ch'ab
r-al nu-pokob
mi x-in-tzal-a-j k'ul-oq [90] r-aqan j(u)yub
r-aqan taq'aj
chiri k'ut x-ø-ul nu-tzaq-a wi
nabe nu-ye-bal
nu-sik'-ibal

85. The meaning of this verbal form has unfortunately not been clarified by informants or dictionaries. Coloch comments on it as follows: "[W]hat the messenger came to say [to transmit] concerns K'iche' Achi and the men who accompany him." My translation, hypothetical but coherent in the context, is inspired by the verbal root *ulaj* ("to lodge someone"; see Coto 1983: 384 ["ulaah"]; García Hernández et al. 1980: 158 ["ula' "]).

86. The term *ch'ab* has the double meaning of "arrow" and "bow." All the same, the bow is often called *u-chuch ch'ab* ("the mother of arrows") and the arrow, correlatively, *r-al ch'ab* ("the child of the bow"). This expression, however, remains mysterious when it is applied to the shield: one might presume that it denotes the handle with which it is held or, possibly, the blows it enables the fighter to withstand. To restore the essentially

my master
my eminence:
"Eha! Eha! My anger
my strength,
thou wilt reply for us!
Come back then,
since this envoy
this messenger
who came from the navel of the sky
the navel of the earth invites you back![85]
Come brandish thy resolve
thy strength,
the child of thy bow
the child of thy shield![86]
Come scrambling along[87] *the foot of the mountains*
the foot of the valleys!"

And he let fly his challenge
his cry, so did my master
my eminence . . .
For my part, I heard nothing
—I was setting up the boundary stones[88]
out where the day disappears
out where the night appears
in the sharp wind
the biting cold,[89]
out there, in the place called Pan Tz'ajaxaq—
That's how it was that I came brandishing the child of my bow
the child of my shield,
that I scrambled along the foot of the mountains
the foot of the valleys,
and, from there, I came to let fly
my first challenge
my first cry,

---

binary rhythm of the text, I have conserved this literal translation of the pair, which means "weapons" throughout.

87. Literally, "to walk on a sloping terrain."

88. Literally, "to place the marking of the land."

89. Literally, "gusts of wind . . . and cold." In contrast with the fortress, which is the place of established power and therefore central and sheltered, the borders to the west and east are places of conquest challenging in every respect. This initial manifestation of contrast will be developed later.

90. This adverbial form, which specifies that the unfolding of the action aims precisely to reach a goal, is derived from the verb *k'ul* ("to be in front of, to meet").

[fol. 12] ch(i) u-wach chol-o-ch-ik j(u)yub
chol-o-ch-ik chaj ch(i)-u-ch[a]-x-ik
x-i[91]-pe chi k'u chila
xa wi chiri chik x-ø-ul nu-tzaq-a wi
u-ka-mul nu-ye-bal
nu-sik'-ibal
chiri chik chi-nim-che'
paraweno
chi-kabraqan ch(i)-u-ch[a]-x-ik
x-i-pe chi k'u chila
xa wi chiri chik x-ø-ul nu-tzaq-a wi
u-rox-mul nu-ye-bal
nu-sik'-ibal
xa wi chiri chik pan-ch'alib ch(i)-u-ch[a]-x-ik
x-i-pe chi k'u chila
xa wi chiri chik x-ø-ul nu-tzaq-a wi
u-kaj-mul nu-ye-bal
nu-sik'-ibal xol-chaqaj ch(i)-u-ch[a]-x-ik
chiri x-in-ta wi
ka-ø-tajin ukoq lotz-o tun
lotz-o q'ojom
k-umal la kab-lajuj u-q'an-al kot
balam
ta [tz]e nim ka-ø-lanan kaj
ka-ø-lanan ulew
ki mayi-j k-e-chajaj-ik
ki mayi-j k-e-wajaj-ik
la kab-lajuj u-q'an-al kot
u-q'an-al balam
k-uk' achi-j mun
ixoq mun

chiri k'ut mi x-nu-bix-ta-j wi ch(i) u-wach kaj
ch(i) u-wach ulew

---

91. Archaic form of the first person absolutive.

92. To my mind this translation renders correctly the indigenous formulation that through the verb *tajinik* describes an action "in the process" of occurring. Furthermore, I interpret *ukoq* as an adverb of proximity, as proposed by Ximénez (1985: 587 ["ucoc"]).

93. These terms, translated literally here, are associated with an enigmatic configuration. In the glossary, one notes first that the glosses relating to these entries establish a distinction between *tun,* which designates wind instruments, and *q'ojom,* which refers to instruments that are struck. Furthermore, the verbal root *lotz* indicates the action of sticking oneself with a tip or a lancet in pursuit of a therapeutic goal. The expression *lotz(o) tun* is given as the name of a dance accompanied by flutes or large trumpets (the

[fol. 12] opposite the place called Cholochik Jyub
Cholochik Chaj . . .
Then, coming back from that place,
I came to let fly again
my challenge
my cry, a second time,
at Chi Nim Che'
Paraweno
Chi Kabraqan, as they are called . . .
Then, coming back from that place,
I came to let fly again
my challenge
my cry, a third time,
this time at the place called Pan Ch'alib . . .
Then, coming back from that place,
I came to let fly
a fourth time my challenge
my cry, at the place called Xol Chaqaj . . .
That's where I heard,
close by,[92] the trumpets announcing the bleeding
the percussion instruments announcing the bleeding[93]
played by the twelve Yellow Eagles
and the Jaguars,
amplified then by the echo of the sky
by the echo of the earth.[94]
They made magnificent noises,
they sent out admirable sounds,
the twelve Yellow Eagles
the Yellow Jaguars,
accompanied by the male slaves
by the female slaves.

And it was there I offered up my word facing the sky
facing the earth

---

designation of the instrument extending to the dance itself), which was still performed during the colonial period (see, notably, Coto 1983: 61), but *lotz(o) q'ojom* is never found. On the basis of this information, one can conjecture that the text is telling us of a ritual dance that probably accompanied (gave rhythm to, gave the beat to) the march of soldiers going off to new battles (or conquests) and which gave rise to bleedings for prophylactic purposes.

94. I am restoring here an exegesis by Coloch that dictionaries have not verified; the verb *lanan,* in fact, does not appear in any of them.

ix-ø-cha k'u ri nu-tzij ch(i) u-wach kaj
ch(i) u-wach ulew
k-at-el ul-oq wor-om ajaw
k'aq-om ajaw
xa k'u xere chi nabe w[a] e ma wi
ka-nu-k'is-o u-ch'ay-ik u-wix-al
u-kutam-il
[fol. 13] la ajaw chakach-ib
tzaman-ib
kawuq rabinal
ix-ø-cha k'u ri nu-tzij
la k'o k'u ch-u-ban ri chi-ech la lal ajaw
ma na wa k'o x-in-mayi-j
ma na k'o x-in-q'ut-i-j
xa wa (a)re u-ch'a-bal tzij x-u-bix-ta-j
ch(i) u-wach kaj
ch(i) u-wach ulew
u-q'alel achi
rabinal achi
chi-cha ta chi k'u la ju-mul chik
keje kaj
ulew chi-k'oji' uk' la
u-q'alel achi
rabinal achi

u-ro'-mul ka-ø-ch'aw rabinal achi

eja oyew achi
kaweq k'iche' winaq
la ka-ø-cha na k'u ri a-tzij ch(i) u-wach kaj
ch(i) u-wach ulew
qi-tzij are tzij ri x-bix-ta-j la
ma na k'o x-u-jal tzij mi x-bix-ta-j la
chi qatz-ij waral x-ø-el wi jun taq-o-n
samajel
chi qatz-ij oj mi x-oj-taq-a-n-ik
chila k'iche' j(u)yub
k'iche' taq'aj
xa k'u xere ma na mak
ma na itz-el ri x-oj-taq-a-n wi
ke ch-u-ta apan-oq la ajaw balam ajaw
balam k'iche'

and that my word said facing the sky
facing the earth:
"Thou wilt come out, piercèd sovereign
perforated sovereign!
Thou wilt not be the first one
whose roots
and trunk I'll strike down
[fol. 13] —King of the Chakachib
of the Tzamanib,
Kawuq Rabinal!"
So said my word.
"What does it do to You, oh You, Sovereign,
that there hasn't been anything I haven't devastated
or anything I haven't crushed!"
Such were the words spoken and sung
facing the sky
facing the earth.
Dignitary
Rabinal Achi,
so speak once more!
May the sky
and the earth remain with You
—Dignitary
Rabinal Achi!»

Rabinal Achi speaks for the fifth time.

«Eha! Angry man
Kaweq K'iche'!
What says thy word facing the sky
facing the earth?
Truthful are the words You have offered,
nothing needs to be changed in the words You have just spoken:
it is true that an emissary
a messenger came from here;
it is true that we sent him
over there, toward the K'iche' mountains
the K'iche' valleys.
But this was not a fault
this was not an offense to send him there
so that King Balam Ajaw
Balam K'iche' might learn

ta tze ka-ø-rayi-x u-kam-ik
u-sach-ik la ajaw chakach-ib
tzaman-ib
kawuq rabinal
[fol. 14] k-umal e aj-ux-ab
aj-poq'om-ab
waral ch(i) u-xmut kaj
ch(i) u-xmut ulew
chi-qa-ban ta utz-il
chom-al
ch-u-taq ul-oq ri ajaw k'iche' j(u)yub
k'iche' taq'aj
ri r-oyow-al-al
r-achi-j-il-al
ch-ø-ul ech-a-be-n-a taj chi-r-ech saq-il j(u)yub
saq-il taq'aj
ch-ø-ul tik-o-n-a taj
ch-ø-ul awex-a-n-a taj
xa wi ta k-oj-tik-o-n-aj-ik
k-oj-awex-a-n-ik
xa ta k'u la chi-ø-bek u-tzam qa-k'um
u-tzam qa-saq-il k'um
saq-il nay
ix-ø-cha nabe ri qa-tzij ch(i) u-wach kaj
ch(i) u-wach ulew
xa k'u xere r-umal xa loq' x-oj-[q']el-e-be-j la
xa loq' x-oj-[j]ol u-qaj-i-be-j la
waral ch(i) u-xmut kaj
ch(i) u-xmut ulew

k'amo chi-r-ech kaj
k'amo chi-r-ech ulew
mi x-oj-yo'pi-ta-j ul-oq ch(i) u-wach qa-tz'aq-il
qa-k'oxtun-al
xa k'u xere r-umal chi-qa-yak ch'a'
chi-qa-yak labal
ix chi-k-el-e-be-j e aj-ux-ab
e aj-poq'om-ab
xa k'u xere ix ch-in-ya eqom-al la
taq-ik-il-al la
chila ta ba la ch-an wi la

---

95. This passage presents difficulties in translation concerning a construction that in the manuscript appears shortened and even absurd. The corrections that were made

that the Uxab
and the Poq'omab
desired the death
the disappearance of the king of the Chakachib
[fol. 14] the Tzamanib,
Kawuq Rabinal,
here, at the navel of the sky
at the navel of the earth.
"So let us perform well
correctly
what the sovereign of the K'iche' mountains
the K'iche' valleys orders us,
we who are his anger
his strength.
Let him take possession of the white mountains
of the white valleys!
Let him come and sow
Let him come and hoe
as we sow
and we hoe
and let our squash seedlings
our white squash seedlings sprout together."

Such were our first words facing the sky
facing the earth.
"But it was in vain that we offered You
in vain that we allowed You to descend[95]
here to the navel of the sky
to the navel of the earth.

Thanks to the sky
thanks to the earth,
we have regained[96] our fortresses
our walls!
But—and this is why we instigate a conflict
we instigate a war—
already the Uxab
and the Poq'omab are going away.
Hence, I entrust You with a task
an assignment:
run over there,

---

after a fruitless examination of the various possible readings in the company of Coloch were inspired by the dictionary of Coto (specifically, the verbal roots *Ɛel* and *hol*).

96. Literally, "we came closer to the front of our walls."

ch(i) u-wach nim-be chi-r-ok'oba-ya tz'ikin
ch(i) u-wach chol-o-ch-ik tz'aq[97] chun ch(i)-u-ch[a]-x-ik
[fol. 15] ma ta k'u chi-ya la r-aj-a-bal ki-k'ux e aj-ux-ab
e aj-poq'om-ab
ma yusk'upi-j[98] bi la chi ki-juyub-al
chi ki-taq'aj-al
k-e-mayi-j ta k'u la
k-e-q'ut-i-j ta k'u la
waral ch(i) u-xmut kaj
ch(i) u-xmut ulew
ix-ø-cha nabe r-e ri nu-tzij
xa k'u xere r-umal ma na k'u x-cha la k-il-ik
ki-tzu'-ik
e aj-ux-ab
e aj-poq'om-ab
r-umal ix-ki-solkopi-j k-ib chi ux-il[100]
chi amolo-il
chi sanik-al
chi ch'eken-al
xa nim k-e-lem-em-ik
k-e-chol-ol-ik
ix-ki-maj r-aqan j(u)yub ekem-pek
xe q'an-a jal ch(i)-u-ch[a]-x-ik
xa k'u xere mi x-nu-tzaq apan-oq nu-tzu'-bal
nu-muqu-bal
ch(i) u-wach kaj
ch(i) u-wach ulew
xa k'ate mi x-nuw-il-o e aj-ux-ab
e aj-poq'om-ab
chiri k'ut mi x-ø-pa-j nu-k'ux
mi x-ø-soko-ta-j nu-k'ux
chi-r-ech il-ik la
tzu'-ik la
r-umal ix-ya bi la r-aj-abal ki-k'ux e aj-ux-ab
e aj-poq'om-ab
chiri k'ut mi x-in-tzaq apan-oq nu-ye-bal
nu-sik'-ibal chi-ech la

97. Perhaps *saq chun* ("white lime").

98. I am conserving the form of the original and Coloch's pronunciation of it here. The dictionaries propose, in fact, variable spellings ("yuzƐupih" in Varea n.d. and Coto 1983; "yutzcupih" in Ximénez 1985).

99. There is no equivalent expression to translate both "to drop what one is holding in/with one's hand" (the meaning of *yusk'upij* according to Coto 1983: 529) and the movement "toward the exterior, in the distance" that animates the freed object (the meaning

across from the great road of Chi Rok'obaya Tz'ikin
across from the place called Cholochik Tz'aq Chun!
[fol. 15] And do not give an inch to the machinations of the Uxab
of the Poq'omab!
Don't let them get away[99] toward their mountains
toward their valleys.
Destroy them,
crush them
here, at the navel of the sky
at the navel of the earth!"
That is what my word said first.
But why do You deny having seen
having observed
the Uxab
the Poq'omab,
because they metamorphosed into gnats
into big flies
into little ants
into big ants[101]
and, forming long ranks
forming long files,
they reached the foot of Ekempek mountain
under Q'anajal, as it is called.
But casting my regard
my gaze
facing the sky
facing the earth,
I suddenly saw the Uxab
and the Poq'omab.
At that moment my heart stumbled
my heart was wounded
by the sight of You
by the revelation
that You had given in to the machinations of the Uxab
of the Poq'omab.
And it was from there that I let fly my challenge
my cry in Your direction:

of the directional *bi*). The meaning of this verb, which appears frequently in the lines that follow, is dependent on its accompanying adverbial forms; thus, for example, *yusk'upij kanoq* means "to leave something (or someone) where it is," *yusk'upij bi* (or *ubi*) means "to allow to leave," and *yusk'upij uloq* means "to allow to go (or to come)."

100. According to Coloch, the corresponding modern term is *usil.*

101. From the species in local Spanish called *zompopo.*

eja eja
oyew achi
kaweq k'iche' winaq
naqi pa r-umal mi x-e-yusk'upi-j bi la
[fol. 16] e aj-ux-ab
e aj-poq'om-ab chi ki-juyub-al
chi ki-taq'aj-al
ajkaroq kaj
ajkaroq ulew
xa k'u xere mi x-e-k'oq-o-be-n kan-oq
chi qa-juyub-al
chi qa-taq'aj-al
tzaq-a na (a)pan-a la ye-bal la
sik'-ibal la
chi-k-ech e aj-ux-ab
e aj-poq'om-ab
jampa na wi ix-k-e-cha ul-oq
chiri k'ut mi x-tzaq apan la ye-bal la
sik'-ibal la
chi-k-ech e aj-ux-ab
e aj-poq'om-ab
chiri k'ut mi x-ki-tzaq ul-oq ki-ye-bal
ki-sik'-ibal
eja eja
ix aj-ux-ab
ix aj-poq'om-ab
k-ix-tzel-e-j-a na ba ul-oq
j-i-ta na i-pixab-a-x-ik-il
waral ch(i) u-xmut kaj
ch(i) u-xmut ulew
mi x-ø-cha k'u apan la

chiri k'ut mi x-e-cha ul-oq e aj-ux-ab
e aj-poq'om-ab
ej ej
oyew achi
kaweq k'iche' winaq

102. The presence of this phrase, whose meaning and translation is clear, is at the very least surprising. Although its significance in the present context is not understood because the expected effect appears to be missing, it hypothetically might have been part of a reply of the Uxab and the Poq'omab that different earlier versions gradually deformed and shortened, finally reducing it to this laconic invective.

103. As in the preceding note, this announcement of a response from the Uxab Poq'omab not followed by an effect is curious. Similarly, it might imply the pres-

"Eha! Eha!
Angry man,
Kaweq K'iche'!
Why have You let them,
[fol. 16] the Uxab
the Poq'omab, leave toward their mountains
toward their valleys?
Oh Sky,
oh Earth!
How they harassed
our mountains
our valleys!
So let fly Your challenge
Your cry
against the Uxab
the Poq'omab!"
"When will that be?" they said.[102]
And from there You let fly Your challenge
Your cry
to the Uxab
to the Poq'omab.
After which they let fly their challenge
their cry . . .[103]
"Eha! Eha!
You Uxab!
You Poq'omab!
Come back
listen to the recommendations that are made to you
here, at the navel of the sky
at the navel of the earth!"
is what You said then.

And then the Uxab
the Poq'omab answered:
"Eh! Eh![104]
Angry man,
Kaweq K'iche'!

---

ence of older versions in which the oral interventions of these protagonists were more developed.

104. The difference between the cries of the Rabinaleb and the Quiché ("Eja!") and those of the Uxab Poq'omab ("Ej!") might indicate that the latter express themselves differently, even that they speak a different language.

are k'u ri mi x-oj-yusk'upi-ta-j ul-oq
chi qa-juyub-al
chi qa-taq'aj-al
ma na re waral k-oj-eta-r[105] wi
k-uk' w-al
k-uk' nu-k'ajol
k'o wi xe [q']eq-a sutz'
xe saq-i sutz'
chi mach'-m-al tew
chi mach'-m-al joron
[fol. 17] ch(i) u-xe u-muj-ibal rax-on
ch(i) u-xe [u-]q'an-al peq
u-q'an-al kako
ch(i) u-xe q'an-a pwaq
ch(i) u-xe saq-i pwaq
x-e-pich[108]
x-e-k'ot k-uk' w-al
k-uk' nu-k'ajol
are na ri w-al
are nu-k'ajol
ma na k'o k'ax ka-ki-riq wi ju-per
ch'aqab tzuq-bal k-e

---

105. Inchoative form of *eta* (see *-etal*, which is defined as "sign, boundary, mark" and also "measurement"; see Glossary), which might literally mean "to inhabit a marked (measured) territory." We may note the glosses that Coto provides for the verb *etar*: "tener descendencia" (1983: 145) and "aumentarse o multiplicarse la descendencia" (ibid.: 56). The idea of being established in a place and that of a demographic growth thus might be conceptually linked. I am grateful to Marie-Charlotte Arnauld for having brought to my attention the *Historia Quiché de don Juan de Torres* (Recinos 1984: 24–67), which supports this idea with a remarkable illustration: this text, which traces the original migration of the Quiché groups, associates the memory that a long line of descendants was formed there *and* was "counted" there for each important stage and to each principal place they stayed. A comparable conception is drawn from the lexeme *amaq'* ("village"), whose derivations connote both the fact of settling in a village and the notion of everlasting; thus, the term *amaq'el* means "inhabitant of a village" (substantive) and "always, perpetually" (adverb) and the verb *amaq'elab* signifies both "to settle in a village" and "to be perpetuated."

106. This phrase refers explicitly to the seat of power, elsewhere designated by the pair *muj q'alibal,* which associates the canopy (or dais) of feathers and the throne. It functions simultaneously as metonymy of the sovereign and as synecdoche for the place of power.

107. Early dictionaries regularly translate *q'ana pwaq* and *saqi pwaq* as "gold" and "silver," respectively. Among the metals known (and exploited) in the Mayan highlands in the pre-Hispanic era, copper was by far the most common, as evidenced by discoveries

This is how it is, we have regained
our mountains
our valleys.
Is not this the very place where we settled
with my children

who are under the black clouds
under the white clouds,
in gusts of wind
exposed to the cold,
[fol. 17] *under the protection of the green feathers,*[106]
under the yellow pataxte
under the yellow cacao
under the yellow metal
under the white metal[107]
that they decorate with feathers,
that they carve with my vassals?[109]

This is how my children are:

they don't have any trouble at all getting a piece
a portion of food for themselves;

---

from archaeological digs. Gold and, to a lesser extent, silver were also used, either within alloys or in surface applications, and both were objects of commerce and imported – gold from the Central American isthmus and silver from the highlands of Central Mexico (on this subject, see Bray 1977). It is thus probable that the present mention of yellow and white metals is purely rhetorical, referring more generally to the idea of "wealth."

108. I am transcribing this term based on its original writing while keeping in mind that it concerns the verb *pix* (sometimes written *pich*), which the dictionaries present as describing the work of feather artisans (see Glossary).

109. The two occurrences of the pair *al k'ajol* within the same phrase as agent and coagent of the action enable us to propose two different definitions (see note 57). The entire passage paints a contrasting image of the notion of territory, formed on a series of complementary oppositions between threatening clouds and the sun (from which one protects oneself, symbolically, at least), between cold and heat, between unleashed elements and sheltered places, between difficult living conditions and easy opulence (and, once again, the subsequent lines will confirm this interpretation). This series shows the double nature of inhabited space, which contrastively associates the *intra-muros,* that is, the place of power, which is sheltered, rich, and filled with goods (the cacao and feathers refer to tributes), and the *extra-muros,* or the more distant places, considered dangerous and threatening (the pairs *siwan tinamit,* "the ravines and the fortress," and *amaq' tinamit,* "the outskirts and the village" refer to this same concept). Finally, expressing themselves in these terms, the Uxab and the Poq'omab assert here that they are "civilized" peoples, just like the Quiché and the Rabinaleb.

xa e tz'ul-ik k-ø-ok ul-oq jo-kal peq
jo-kal kako
r-umal e aj-pich
e aj-k'ot ch(i) u-xe q'ij
ch(i) u-xe saq
are k'u ri r-al
u-k'ajol u-q'alel achi
rabinal achi
xa k'u chi kaq ra[y]i-l
chi k'ax-k'[o]l
ka-ki-riq wi ju-per
ch'aqab tzuq-bal k-e
ch(i) u-xe q'ij
ch(i) u-xe saq
xa wi xa jun r-aqan ka-ø-tzu'-n chi-r-ij
keje jun ka-ø-tzu'-n chi-ki-wach
xa e jetz'-ej-oj[113] xa e ki u-wi-wi-j
ri ki u-mam-a-j
u-q'alel achi
rabinal achi ch(i) u-xe q'ij
ch(i) u-xe saq
mi x-ø-cha ul-oq ki-ye-bal
ki-sik'-ibal e aj-ux-ab
e aj-poq'om-ab
r-umal u-k'oq-o-bal ki-k'ux

mi x-cha chi k'u apan la chi-k-ech
eja eja
ix aj-ux-ab
ix aj-poq'om-ab
la ka-ø-cha na k'u r(i) i-tzij ch(i) u-wach kaj
ch(i) u-wach ulew

---

110. The verb *tz'ulik* means exactly "to sleep together, coiled up against each other, arms and legs intertwined" (see Glossary).

111. This literal translation seems particularly apt to render the force of the assertion. As a comparison, we can note that Tirado (1787: fol. 156v) uses this same pair, *rayil k'axk'ol,* to translate "the Passion of Jesus Christ" into Quiché.

112. Considering the relationship already pointed out among prisoners of war, sacrifice, and food, this search "for food" might refer to a quest for sacrificial victims.

113. The root *jetz'* ("lame") is developed following the principle $C_IV_IC+V_IC_I+Vj$, which expresses the intensification of a characteristic or a quality. (This process is often noted in dictionary entries relating to colors.)

114. The terms *wi* and *mam* are, in a certain way, the equivalents of *al* and *k'ajol* for the second descending generation: *wi* is applied to all grandchildren, regardless of gender, of a women, *mam* refers only to the grandsons of a man. The former is an idiomatic form

even when they sleep,[110] *five loads of* pataxte
five loads of cacao come to them,
for they are feather-workers
they are carvers under the sun
under the light of day.
As for the children
of Dignitary
Rabinal Achi,
only by red torments
by suffering[111]
do they obtain their pieces
their portions of food
under the sun
under the light of day![112]
What's more, they've got one leg that looks back
when the other looks front.
They are nothing but invalids, those descendants
those grandchildren[114]
of Dignitary
Rabinal Achi, under the sun
under the light of day!"
So went the taunts
the cries of the Uxab
of the Poq'omab
from the malignancy of their hearts.

And You said to them:
"Eha! Eha!
You Uxab!
You Poq'omab!
What say your words facing the sky
facing the earth

---

of the classical Quiché *iy*, probably created from *w-iy* ("my grandchild," when possession is marked), then fixed into *wi* through a muting of the final phoneme. Consequently, in Rabinal, "my grandchild" is said as *nu-wi* (a comparable evolution affects the classical term *ajaw* [for "lord, master" but also "father"] and *q-ajaw* ["our father"], which the language of Rabinal initially fixed into *qajaw* [see lines 2175, 2195] and then into *qaw* ["father"], which it logically redevelops into *qa-qaw* ["our father"]). As for the second term—*mam*—we should note that it is used reciprocally between grandfather and grandson. These terms appear here in duplicated forms, indicating a collective and totalizing plural. Like the pair *al k'ajol* (see note 57), the pair *wi mam,* in Rabinal today as in the past, has variable extended meanings depending on whether it relates strictly to the realm of kinship, to the marking of a generational distinction, to principles of general organization of society, or even to the religious pantheon, for example, the "ancestors" (*ati/mam*) as opposed to the "living" (*wi/mam*). For further discussion of this theme, see Breton 1989.

are na ri r-al
[fol. 18] u-k'ajol oyew achi
rabinal achi
ma na k'o ch-ø-ok chi-k-ij
chi-ki-wach
ch(i) u-wi ki-tzuku-n-ik
ki-kajale-n-ik chi kaj pa[115]
chi kaj xukut-al
ch(i) u-jolom ulew
chi r-a{n}qan ulew pa jun war-abal
pa ka-ib war-abal
r-umal k'o ki-ko-w-il
k-achi-j-il-al
are k'u ri r-al
u-k'ajol
xa k'u k-e-mayi-x-ik
k-e-q'ut-i-x-ik
suk'-ul-ik k-e-chol-ol-ik ki-el chi ki-juyub-al
chi ki-taq'aj-al
ka-r-aj xa jun
xa ka-ib chik ka-ki-riq ki-tz'aq-il
ki-k'oxtun-al
r-umal xa k-e-mayi-x-ik
xa k-e-q'ut-i-x-ik
ch(i) u-wi ki-tzuku-n-ik
ki-kajale-n-ik
are k'u ri r-al
u-k'ajol oyew achi
u-q'alel achi
rabinal achi

115. I have not been able to clarify the term *pa.* A reference to the four corners (and to the four sides) of the world, however, is quite frequent, both in current ritual discourse and in the earlier texts. Thus, the *Popol Vuh* presents the comparable listing "upa cah, upa uleu, cah tzuc, cah xucut," which D. Tedlock (1985: 243) translates as "in the sky, on the earth, the four sides, the four corners." Like many other terms borrowed from anatomical vocabulary—such as *xe, wi, chi', ij,* and *wach—pa* (from *pam,* "stomach") has a double grammatical function: combined with the directional *chi* (in *chupa/chupam*) it preserves its autonomy, as in "toward the interior of, in the bosom of, in the heart of," or loses its autonomy and is condensed to the prepositional unit "in, to." Thus, I propose four possible translations for *pa*: (1) a general expression of an abstract notion of "direction" (which I am temporarily favoring); (2) a term connoting the interiority of the world where we are (the pair then would be translatable as "the four corners [toward the center]/[from the center] toward the four corners"); (3) a term connoting the interiority of the four sectors corresponding to the four points of the compass (a conception

concerning the children
[fol. 18] *of the valiant*
Rabinal Achi?
Nothing will come to them, neither from the back
nor from the front,
when they look for
and seek in the four directions
in the four corners
at the head of the earth
at the feet of the earth,[116] *in one day's journey*
in two days' journey![117]
In spite of their endurance
and their courage,
these children

are but losers
are vanquished!
It is certain that they will go out from their mountains
from their valleys in groups,
but, at best, only one
or two will return to their fortress
their wall
as a result of their defeat
of their annihilation
during their quest
during their search![118]
These children
of the Angry one
of Dignitary
Rabinal Achi . . .

---

that is echoed in the call "to the four quarters, to the four lands" of modern discourses); or (4) the corruption of another term that remains to be identified. To my knowledge, the formula *chi kaj pa chi kaj xukutal* is found only in the *Rabinal Achi.*

116. That is, respectively, West and East.

117. The term *warabal* designates the stage (the day of walking) and the end place of the stage (the place where one sleeps, which corresponds to its literal translation).

118. The force of the terms used to convey the failure of the Rabinaleb's initiatives—*mayixik* and *q'utixik,* synonyms for "to be destroyed, annihilated, crushed"—indicates that here the focus is on their military campaigns, their attempts at conquest, and their own abilities to defend themselves. K'iche' Achi, taking the side of the Uxab and the Poq'omab to castigate the Rabinaleb, becomes their accomplice and, even more, their substitute, hoping to take advantage of a defeat of Rabinal for his own benefit. This is the subject of the debate in the dialogues that follow whose central object is the control and possession of the "navel of the sky and of the earth."

xa k'u jun
xa ka-ib chi k-el-ik ubi
xa wi xaqi xa jun
xa ka-ib
chi{ri} ki-riq ul-oq ki-tz'aq-il
ki-k'oxtun-al
mi x-cha apan{a} la chi-k-ech e aj-ux-ab
e aj-poq'om-ab

mi x-ø-cha k'u ri nu-tzij
eja eja
oyew achi
kaweq k'iche' winaq
mi x-ta ba la ri ki-ye-bal
ki-sik'-ibal e aj-ux-ab
e aj-poq'om-ab
mi x-ki-tzaq ul-oq
[fol. 19] ajkaroq kaj
ajkaroq ulew
qatz-ij k'u chi tzij
mi x-e-k'aq-a-be-n kan-oq waral ch(i) u-xmut kaj
ch(i) u-xmut ulew
chi ki-wi q-al
chi ki-wi qa-k'ajol
qatz-ij k'u chi tzij
ma x-ø-ech-a-be-n taj chi-r-ech saq-il j(u)yub
saq-il taq'aj
xa k'u lo[q']
xa k'u mayi-j
mi x-ul k'is-a la u-k'i-y-al q'ij
u-k'i-y-al aq'ab
waral ch(i) u-xmut kaj
ch(i) u-xmut ulew
xa wi x-ul k'is-a la r-al ch'ab la
r-al pokob la
xa wi x-ul k'is-a la u-wach k'ux la
u-wach teleb la

119. This "us," not expressed grammatically, is justified by the adverb *uloq,* which indicates that the action is directed toward the present speaker.

120. The literal meaning of this passage is particularly evocative in the native language: "they threw rounds of projectiles (arrows, stones) . . . at our children's heads." Here we find the root *k'aq* (see notes 14, 15; Glossary).

as soon as one
or two go outside,
so soon one
or two
regain their fortress
their wall!"
That is what You said when addressing the Uxab
the Poq'omab!

And my word said:
"Eha! Eha!
Angry man,
Kaweq K'iche'!
You have heard the exhortations
the shouts that the Uxab
the Poq'omab,
addressed to us!"[119]
[fol. 19] Oh Sky,
oh Earth!
It is true
that they attacked[120]
our children here, at the navel of the sky
at the navel of the earth.

But it is equally true
that they have not taken possession of the white mountains
the white valleys.
So it was in vain
and to no purpose
that You have come to lose numerous days
numerous nights[121]
here, at the navel of the sky
at the navel of the earth!
You came only to exhaust the child of Your bow
the child of Your shield!
You came only to exhaust the face of Your heart
the face of Your shoulders!

---

121. Literally, "to finish (to end) many days/nights."

ma na k'o x-ø-opon[122] wi
qatz-ij k'u chi [tz]ij ma x-ech-a-be-n ta k'u la
waral ch(i) u-xmut kaj
ch(i) u-xmut ulew
eta'am k'u la a pa k'o wi r-eta-l ulew la
ch-an-i-be-j k'u la
tzal-a-j k'u bi la r-aqan j(u)yub
r-aqan taq'aj
qatz-ij k'u chi tzij in oyew achi
in u-q'alel achi
in rabinal achi
k-in-eta-r wi kan-oq k-uk' w-al
k-uk' nu-k'ajol
waral ch(i) u-xmut kaj
ch(i) u-xmut ulew
ka-ø-cha k'u ri nu-tzij ch(i) u-xmut kaj
ch(i) u-xmut ulew
keje kaj
ulew chi-k'oji' uk' la
oyew achi
kaweq k'iche' winaq

u-waq-mul ka-ø-ch'aw k'iche' achi

eja eja
ajkaroq kaj
[fol. 20] ajkaroq ulew
qatz-ij k'u chi tzij
ma na x-in-ech-a-be-n taj waral ch(i) u-xmut kaj
ch(i) u-xmut ulew
chi-r-ech saq-il j(u)yub
saq-il taq'aj
la xa loq'
la xa mayi-j
mi x-ul nu-k'is-a u-k'iy-al q'ij
u-k'iy-al aq'ab
chiri ch(i) u-xmut kaj
ch(i) u-xmut ulew

122. Here we recognize the verbal root *apon*, "to arrive somewhere, end up at" (from which is constructed the directional *apanoq*), which, in this environment, is pronounced *opon*. Because this transcription is faithful to the oral form, I did not think it opportune to correct it as *[a]pon*.

123. The content of this passage might confirm the idea that K'iche' Achi partially counted on the Uxab and the Poq'omab to inflict a defeat on the Rabinaleb but that

Nothing came of it![123]
It is true that You have not taken possession
of this place, the navel of the sky
the navel of the earth!
You know perfectly well where Your boundary stones lie!
So go run
and go scramble along the foot of the mountains
the foot of the valleys!
It is certain that I, an angry man
I, Dignitary,
I, Rabinal Achi,
I stay settled with my children,

here, at the navel of the sky
the navel of the earth!
So my word affirms it, facing the sky
facing the earth!
May the sky
and the earth remain with You
Angry man,
Kaweq K'iche'!»

K'iche' Achi speaks for the sixth time.

«Eha! Eha!
Oh Sky,
[fol. 20] oh Earth!
It is true,
I have not taken possession, here, of the navel of the sky
the navel of the earth,
of the white mountains
the white valleys!
Was it in vain
was it to no purpose
that I came to lose numerous days
numerous nights
here, at the navel of the sky
at the navel of the earth?

---

this plan failed. Rabinal Achi denounces the speech K'iche' Achi gave to the Uxab and Poq'omab, a speech according to which the Rabinaleb would be poor combatants, unlucky and weak, and confirmed on the contrary the warring quality and the valor of his people (still strongly claimed today).

la ma na k'o x-ø-opon wi w-oyew-al
w-achi-j-il-al
ajkaroq kaj
ajkaroq ulew
jin ba la chi nu-juyub-al
chi nu-taq'aj-aj
mi x-ø-cha k'u ri nu-tzij ch(i) u-wach kaj
ch(i) u-wach ulew
mi x-nu-tzal-a-j k'u bi r-aqan j(u)yub
r-aqan taq'aj
chila k'ut mi x-in-eta-k'am-ar-a[125] wi
tzam k'amba ch(i)-u-ch[a]-x-ik
ix-ø-cha k'u ri nu-tzij ch(i) u-wach kaj
ch(i) u-wach ulew
la ma na r-okik-am
ix ch-in-t'aki-j ta k'u bi ajaw k'amba
chi-r-ech nu-xtapyak pa ki-wi r-al
pa ki-wi u-k'ajol
u-q'alel achi
rabinal achi
mi x-ø-cha u-k'oq-obal nu-k'ux
xa k'u xere ka-r-aj ka-ø-k'oq-o-n kaj
ka-ø-k'oq-o-n ulew
ix-ø-cha k'u ri nu-tzij
x-in-el chi k'u chiri
chila chi k'ut
mi x-in-eta-k'am-ar-a wi tzam saq-kijel[128] j(u)yub
saq-kijel taq'aj
mi x-nu-tzaq wi nu-ye-bal
nu-sik'-ibal
ajkaroq kaj
ajkaroq ulew

---

124. Like his adversary, K'iche' Achi also claims ownership of the places.

125. This verb is a complex form that associates the roots *eta* ("measure/mark") and *k'am* ("rope," a muted form of *ka'am*) to describe the action of measuring with a rope (the affix *-Vr* is a verbalizer; the suffix *-a* indicates the dynamic nature of the action).

126. Literally, "I punched (while pushing him back [*bi*])". This phrase confirms the eponymy that links the person and the place, as I have pointed out above (note 78).

127. One finds here a particularly explicit illustration of the relationship ancient Quiché establishes between the action of marking or measuring a territory and the idea of conquest.

128. This toponym should probably be broken down into *saq* + *q'ij* + *el* ("WHITE-DAY-nominalizer") and might indicate that this large archaeological site in the basin of Rabinal, at that time, was characterized as a "place of the dawn." Today it is called Saktijel, a term that escapes folk etymology.

Can it have achieved nothing, my anger
my strength?
"Oh Sky,
oh Earth!
I am here in my mountains
in my valleys!"[124]
That is what my word affirmed, facing the sky
facing the earth!
I scrambled along the foot of the mountains
the foot of the valleys!
Over there, for example, where I paced and measured
the place called Tzam K'amba!
That is what I affirmed, facing the sky
facing the earth!
"Would it not be appropriate
for me to overthrow Lord K'amba,[126]
forcing my sandals on the heads of the children

of Dignitary
Rabinal Achi?"[127]
That is what my wicked heart said!
So let the sky curse me
let the earth curse me
for having presumed so!
So I came out from there
and, over that way,
went to measure and pace the land[129] of Tzam Saqkijel

where I let fly my challenge
my cry!
Oh Sky,
oh Earth!

---

129. It is significant that Saqkijel is not defined in the same way as the other places cited in this listing. If the element *tzam* specifies that it involves the fortress, established at the summit—*tzam*—of a hill, the pair *j(u)yub/taq'aj* indicates the existence of an adjoining territory. Perhaps we have an indication here that Saqkijel corresponded at that time to a distinct territorial entity, enclosed with or adjacent to that of the Rabinaleb of Kajyub, and thus belonged to different people (another group) but was assimilated or controlled by the Rabinaleb. Archaeological data easily support this reading. M.-Ch. Arnauld (1993) indeed distinguishes in the ruins of the site of Saqkijel two relatively well-defined phases of construction: one, which would correspond to the Early Postclassic period (ca. 1100–1200), is notably characterized by the presence of a simple temple in the ceremonial center (probably Poq'om phase), whereas the other, more recent (ca. 1200–1450) phase is marked by the presence of twin temples—an undeniable Quiché-Rabinal trait.

[fol. 21] la qatz-ij chi tzij ma na x-in-ech-a-be-n taj
waral ch(i) u-xmut kaj
ch(i) u-xmut ulew
chiri k'ut mi x-in-qaj qaj-oq chiri chisaliya
xa k'ate mi x-nuw-il-o
r-ulew-al nabe-l-ik
xambe-l-ik
r-ulew-al q'an-bo[l] saq-i jal
q'an-a tz'uklik[133]
saq[-a] tz'uklik
qa-r-ixk'aq tz'ikin

ka-ø-cha k'u ri nu-tzij ch(i) u-wach kaj
ch(i) u-wach ulew
la ma na r-okik-am mi x ch-in-lot'-ot'-ej ta k'u bi
xa sk'aqin w[a] w[e] r-ulew-al nabe-l-ik
xambe-l-ik
ch(i) u-pam r-al nu-ch'ab
ch(i) u-pam r-al nu-pokob
chiri k'ut mi x-nu-muq-te'ej r-uk' nu-xtapyak
ch(i) u-pam r-ulew-al nabe-l-ik
xambe-l-ik
x-in-el chi k'u chiri
chila chi k'ut
mi x-in-eta-k'am-ar-a wi tzam ixtink'urun
ch(i) u-wach ximbaja ch(i)-u-ch[a]-x-ik
x-in-el chi k'u chiri
chila chi k'ut
mi x-in-eta-k'am-ar-a wi tzam k'isintun
chiri k'ut x-in-tun-a-j wi
x-ø-oq' nu-k'ux
ox-laju(j)-win[a]q q'ij
ox-laju(j)-winaq aq'ab

---

130. Translating the doubling of the lexeme *qaj* as "to descend by descending."

131. The adverbs *nabe* and *xambe* designate, respectively, "that (or the one) that is in front, the first" and "that (or the one) which is behind, the last" or, in this context, the foreground and the background. My translation as "distant" also comes from Vico (n.d.a: fol. 13), who identifies *xambe* as a derivation of *am*: "cosa remota o de lejos."

132. Literally, "of an intense yellow," indicating that these lands bear an abundance of "ripe" fruit (whether yellow or not).

133. Given by Ximénez (1985: 655) as "zuclic: frijoles que dan la vaina negra." Today, this name designates a variety similar to our French green beans (*ejotes* in Spanish).

134. This expression, as Brasseur said (but contradicted wrongly by Raynaud), corresponds to a variety of green bean, or rather to the green bean's hooked appearance when young.

[fol. 21] Is it true that I have not taken possession
of this place, the navel of the sky
the navel of the earth?
So from that place, I clambered down[130] toward Chisaliya!
And suddenly I saw
the land nearby
and far off,[131]
the land blazing[132] with white ears
yellow beans
white beans
"our bird claws."[134]

This is what I say, facing the sky
facing the earth!
"Would it not be appropriate to take samples[135] back with me
of these lands nearby
and far off
in the child of my bow
in the child of my shield?"[136]
So I sank deep, with my sandals,
into these lands nearby
and far off!
Then I left that place
to measure and pace Tzam Ixtink'urun,
over that way
opposite the place called Ximbaja!
Then, I departed that place
and, over there,
measured and paced Tzam K'isintun!
That was where I trumpeted
where my heart cried
for thirteen times twenty days
thirteen times twenty nights,

---

135. I am rendering the adverb *sk'aqin* ("little, a little") as "samples"; as here, it is often combined with *xa* ("only"). This ancient adverbial form is no longer understood today.

136. This questioning appears to be a sort of digression that leads us to the time of the story, anticipating the recognized consequences of the following phrase, which, in turn, reintroduces us into the time of the action: the two facts indicated by the phrases are thus linked. The burying of the sandals (into a loose and deep ground, a synonym for "rich and fertile") and the sampling of earth taken by K'iche' Achi remain even today significant events in the oral tradition that justifies the current agricultural difficulties of the Rabinaleb by invoking this transfer of the best land to the Quiché.

r-umal ma na x-in-ech-a-be-n taj
waral ch(i) u-xmut kaj
ch(i) u-xmut ulew
chi-r-ech saq-il j(u)yub
saq-il taq'aj
ka-ø-cha k'u ri nu-tzij ch(i) u-wach kaj
[fol. 22] ch(i) u-wach ulew
ajkaroq kaj
ajkaroq ulew
la qatz-ij chi tzij ma na x-in-ech-a-be-n taj
waral ch(i) u-xmut kaj
ch(i) u-xmut ulew
la xa loq'
la xa mayi-j
mi x-ul nu-k'is-a u-k'iy-al q'ij
u-k'iy-al aq'ab
ka-ø-cha k'u ri nu-tzij ch(i) u-wach kaj
ch(i) u-wach ulew
xa wi x-ul nu-k'is-a u-wach nu-k'ux
u-wach nu-teleb
ma na k'o x-ø-opon wi w-oyew-al-al
w-achi-j-il-al
ix-ø-cha k'u ri nu-tzij ch(i) u-wach kaj
ch(i) u-wach ulew
jin ba la chi nu-juyub-al
chi nu-taq'aj-al
ix-ø-cha k'u ri nu-tzij
chiri k'ut mi x-in-tzal-a-j ubi r-aqan j(u)yub
r-aqan taq'aj
ix-ø-cha k'u ri nu-tzij
keje kaj
ulew chi-k'oji' uk' la
u-q'alel achi
rabinal achi

137. The verb *tunaj* is formed from the root *tun* ("wind instrument, trumpet"; see note 93) and means "to play, to sound the trumpet." The association between this action, through which K'iche' Achi shows his pique, and the place where it occurs—K'isintun, the last site that was supposedly visited and conquered by the intruder—provides a possible key to understanding the meaning of the toponym, which has been forgotten today but is related in some way to "the knell of the trumpet" (from *k'is,* "to finish, terminate"; *k'isin[aq],* "finished, terminated").

138. K'iche' Achi—despite his "peripheral" conquests of Tzam K'amba, Tzam Saqkijel, Tzam Ixtink'urun (Ximbaja), and Tzam K'isintun—expresses through these

because I did not take possession
of this place, the navel of the sky
                    the navel of the earth,
the white mountains
the white valleys![138]
So says my word facing the sky
[fol. 22]   facing the earth!
"Oh Sky,
oh Earth!
Is it true that I did not take possession
of this place, the navel of the sky
                    the navel of the earth!
Was it in vain
was it to no purpose
that I came to lose numerous days
                    numerous nights . . .
—I said it facing the sky
          facing the earth!—
that I came to exhaust the face of my heart
                    the face of my shoulders?
Has my anger
     my strength led to nothing!"
That is what I said, facing the sky
                    facing the earth!
"I am in my mountains
     in my valleys!"
That is what I said!
And, from there, I scrambled around the foot of the mountains
                    the foot of the valleys.
That is what I said!
May the sky
and the earth remain with You
—Dignitary,
Rabinal Achi!»

---

words his regret at not having been able to conquer Kajyub (which is incontestably the center, or navel, of this configuration). But this passage also brings out the eminently symbolic dimension of the drama that is being performed, since it combines the four "corners of the world," the movement of rotation that animates them, and the ritual and divinatory calendar cycle of 260 days. This complex system—by which the Maya, relating the passing of days to a journey in space, solved the question of the anisotropy of time (related to the isotropy of space)—has been the subject of many descriptions, both historical and ethnographical (see in particular B. Tedlock 1991).

u-wuq-mul ka-ø-ch'aw rabinal achi

eja
oyew achi
kaweq k'iche' winaq
w-al
nu-k'ajol
naqi pa r-umal x-e-a-yak ubi w-al
nu-k'ajol
ma na k'o aw-ok-ibal chi-k-e
xa k-e-yusk'upi-j kan-oq chi ki-juyub-al
chi ki-taq'aj-al
[fol. 23] we ma wi ix k-e-yusk'upi-j kan-oq
ta [ka-]r-aj kaj
ta [ka-]r-aj ulew
ka-n-tzilo-j kaj
ka-n-tzilo-j ulew
mi x-ø-cha nu-ye-bal
r-umal in jin ta-n taj
in k-in-tajin-ik in koj-ol r-eta-l ulew
chila tzam moqotz'u'um ch(i)-u-ch[a]-x-ik
ta mi x-yak bi la ri saq-il al
saq-il k'ajol
ch(i) u-pam r-al ch'ab la
r-al pokob la
chiri k'ut ma na x-ø-oq' k'ux la
chi-r-ech u-ta-y-ik nu-ye-bal
nu-sik'-ibal
chiri k'ut mi x-in-tzal-a-j k'ul-oq r-aqan j(u)yub
r-aqan taq'aj
chila k'ut mi x-in-eta-k'am-ar-a wi
chiri panajache'el ch(i)-u-ch[a]-x-ik
chila k'ut mi x-nu-tzaq wi nu-ye-bal
nu-sik'-ibal chi-ech la
[k']ate k'u chiri
mi x-e-yusk'upi-j kan la ri saq-il al
saq-il k'ajol

---

139. This translation, which deviates from the literal sense of the Quiché phrase, is however the one that is the most faithful to the text's intent: "causative negation existential YOUR-TO ENTER-instrumental preposition 1–third person plural-preposition 2" (which Coloch paraphrases as "¡No tenía por qué meterte con ellos!").

140. Among the possibilities offered by dictionaries with regard to the roots *tzil* and *tz'il,* I adopt here the meaning that Ximénez (1985: 647) establishes for "ziloh: menear, bullir."

Rabinal Achi speaks for the seventh time.

«Eha!
Angry man,
Kaweq K'iche'!
My children . . .

Why didst thou take away my children?

Thou hadst nothing to do with them![139]
So just leave them in their mountains
in their valleys!
[fol. 23] Because if they are not left there
then may the sky
may the earth ordain
that I shake the sky
that I shake the earth![140]
That was my exhortation.
Because I myself had heard nothing:
I was setting my boundary markings myself,[141]
over there, in the place called Tzam Moqotz'u'um,
when You took away the white children

in the child of Your bow
in the child of Your shield.
But Your heart did not grieve at all[142]
to hear my exhortation
my plea!
From there, I scrambled over the foot of the mountains
the foot of the valleys
and I went, over there, to measure and pace
the place called Panajache'el!
From there I let fly my challenge
my cry against You.
And that was when
You set free the white children,

141. Like K'iche' Achi (see note 74), who was absent from the Quiché capital when the threat of the Rabinaleb reached the ears of his sovereign, Rabinal Achi affirms here his status as "professional" warrior always on campaign: "I was unaware of what was going on at home . . . being busy elsewhere."

142. "Your heart was not touched, did not take into account . . ."

chiri chi-nim-che'
chi-kab-r-aqan
paraweno ch(i)-u-ch[a]-x-ik
xa sk'aqin chik ma na x-e-yo'pi-j-ik
chila k'iche' j(u)yub
k'iche' taq'aj
chiri k'ut mi x-e-tzel-wach-i-n ul-oq
ix-ki-maj ul-oq r-aqan j(u)yub
r-aqan taq'aj
ta [t]ze ka-ø-tz'aj-tz'-at [u]ko[q] ki-pam
k-e-xirxot-il-eb ukoq
ta x-e-tzel-wach-i-n ul-oq
xa k'u xere ma x-e-yo'pi-ta-j chik
ch(i) u-pam ki-tz'aq-il
ki-k'oxtun-al
xa k'u chiri chik mi x-e-amaq'-el-ab[145] wi
chiri pamaq'a ch(i)-u-ch[a]-x-ik
[fol. 24] xa wi ki lal mi x-ø-ul e-sa-j[147] la ri w-ajaw-al
nu-winaq-il
chiri ch(i)-atin-ibal ch(i)-u-ch[a]-x-ik
ma pa xa wi in jin ta-n taj
in k-in-tajin ukoq in koj-ol r-eta-l ulew
chila tzam-ja
ch(i) u-wach k'ul-u-wach abaj ch(i)-u-ch[a]-x-ik
xa k'u xere mi x-in-tzaq ul-oq nu-tzu'-bal
nu-muqu-bal
ch(i) u-wach kaj
ch(i) u-[wach] ulew
xa nim r-aqan-ibal sutz'
mayul chik

143. Guided by the description that this passage suggests to Coloch, I am combining two possible definitions of the frequentative form of the verb *tz'aj*: "to dry out, to be worn out, to run dry" (*tzah* in the early dictionaries) and "to roar, to rumble, to resound" (*tzahtza* or *4,ahah*). Beyond the semantic connections that the apparent similarity in lexical forms might suggest—such as the possibilities that it is a polysemic form or one of several homonym forms—this association is strongly supported by the belief that the phenomenon of thundering mountains (announcing coming rains) is intimately linked to extreme drought.

144. Coloch associates the term *xirxot* to a movement of shaking (of stomachs, in this case), trembling, panting, or waving (like the tail of a kite flying in the wind). Ximénez (1985: 619), following others, defines *xirixot* as "cantar grillo o cigarra," but also *xihxot* as "estar tambaleando de miedo." All of these glosses revolve around the idea of rapid vibration. An understanding of this phrase, which appears in a similar but inversed formulation in lines 1144–1145, is nevertheless uncertain; indeed, an analysis of it comes up against three unknowns: (1) an identification of the particle *ta [t]ze* already

over there, in Chi Nim Che'
Chi Kabraqan
Paraweno, as they're called,
just before they reached
the K'iche' mountains
the K'iche' valleys, over there!
That was when they reappeared,
they were following, as they came back, the foot of the mountains
the foot of the valleys!
Their emaciated bellies thundered,[143]
as they shivered[144]
when they reappeared . . .
But they didn't return
to their fortress
their wall,
but settled in the meantime
in the place called Pamaq'a![146]
[fol. 24] It was also You who abducted my master
my eminence
at the place called Chatinibal!
But I did not hear about that either,
because I, too, was just about to set my boundary stones
over there, in Tzam Ja,
opposite K'uluwach Abaj, as it is called!
However, casting my regard
my gaze
facing the sky
facing the earth,
only great plumes of clouds
and of fog

---

cited in note 79, (2) the meaning in this context of the adverb of proximity *ukoq* (which might indicate that men are approaching or that their condition is worsening as they get closer), and (3) the suffixation into *-ileb* of the verb *xirxot* (*-Vl* might mark the state and *-Vb* might be a plural).

145. Derived from the term *amaq'* ("village, hamlet"), this verb presents the same principle of suffixation as *xirxot*: Vl + Vb (see note 144). There is no doubt, however, about its meaning, as this form is found in Basseta (1698: fol. 163) and Tirado (1787: fol. 27): *amaƐelab* ("avecindarse en pueblo"). See also note 105.

146. Pa Amaq'a was the pre-Hispanic name for present-day Zacualpa. This name is still recognized today by most of those we interviewed in Cubulco, Tres Cruces, and Joyabaj. For the people of Rabinal, however, today it designates Alta Verapaz in general and San Cristóbal Verapaz in particular.

147. I am keeping *esaj,* a muted form of the classical Quiché verb *elesaj* (literally, "to bring out"), which resulted not from a copying error but from an alternative form confirmed through usage.

jik-j-ot-inaq chi kan-oq
ch(i) u-wach u-nim-al tz'aq
u-nim-al k'oxtun
chiri k'ut mi x-nu-tzaq ul-oq nu-ye-bal
nu-sik'-ibal
ch(i) u-wach kaj
ch(i) u-wach ulew
ix-ø-cha k'u ri nu-tzij
eja eja
oyew achi
kaweq k'iche' winaq
w-ajaw-al
nu-winaq-il
naqi pa r-umal x-ul aw-e-sa-j
ch(i) u-pam u-nim-al tz'aq
u-nim-al k'oxtun
xa ma na k'o aw-ok-ibal chi-r-ech
xa ch-a-yusk'upi-j kan-oq
ch(i) u-pam u-nim-al tz'aq
u-nim-al k'oxtun
ix-ø-cha k'u ri nu-tzij
xa k'u xere ma na x-ø-oq' k'ux la
chi-r-ech u-ta-y-ik nu-ye-bal
nu-sik'-ibal
ix-ø-cha k'u ri nu-tzij
{u}we ma wi ix ch-a-yusk'upi-j kan-oq ri w-ajaw-al
nu-winaq-il
ta ka-r-aj kaj
ta ka-r-aj ulew
ka-n-tzilo-j kaj
ka-n-tzilo-j ulew
pa kaj nu-be
p(a) ulew nu-be
ix-ø-cha k'u ri nu-tzij
chiri k'ut ma na x-ø-oq' k'ux la
chi-r-ech u-ta-y-ik nu-ye-bal
[fol. 25] nu-sik'-ibal
mi x-in-tzal-a-j r-aqan j(u)yub
r-aqan taq'aj

148. The glosses relating to the root *jik* refer to the movement consisting of "rubbing/brushing/smoothing with large gestures" (see Glossary), a movement to which the frequentative form adds even more fullness. The image evoked by these rampant streaks of clouds is one of ruin, of devastation, and, if one compares it to what the space of the fortress represents symbolically (see note 109), of chaos.

lingered, as if pulled apart[148]
facing the great fortress
facing the great wall!
At that moment I let fly my challenge
my cry
facing the sky
facing the earth!
And my word said this:
"Eha! Eha!
Angry man,
Kaweq K'iche'!
My master
my eminence . . .[149]
Why hast thou come to take him away
from the great fortress
from the great wall?
Thou hadst nothing to do with him!
So just leave him
in the great fortress
in the great wall!"
So said my word.
But Your heart did not grieve at all
to hear my challenge
my cry!
And my word said:
"If thou dost not release my master
my eminence
then may the sky
may the earth ordain
that I shake the sky
that I shake the earth!
In the sky is my path,
on the earth is my path!"[150]
So said my word.
But Your heart did not grieve at all
to hear my challenge
[fol. 25] my cry!
I scrambled along the foot of the mountains
the foot of the valleys,

149. This turn of phrase, marked by interruption, recalls the one encountered in lines 854–856 regarding children: "My children . . . Why didst thou take away my children?" and apparently conveys the emotion or resentment of the speaker.

150. Through these words, Rabinal Achi threatens K'iche' Achi with bringing terror to the world in return.

chila k'ut mi x-in-eta-k'am-ar-a wi
ch(i) u-pa[m] u-nim-al tz'aq
u-nim-al k'oxtun
xa k'u xere mi x-nuw-il-o
xa r-aqan-ibal sutz' chik
r-aqan-ibal mayul chik
jik-j-ot-inaq chik ch(i) u-wach u-nim-al tz'aq
u-nim-al k'oxtun
xa lol
xa xil chik
k-e-xil-il chi kan-oq
k-e-tun-a-n chi kan-oq
k-e-xil-il-ik ch(i) u-pam u-nim-al tz'aq
u-nim-al k'oxtun
chiri k'ut pa-j nu-k'ux
soko-ta-j nu-k'ux
x-in-tzal-a-j chi k'u bi r-aqan j(u)yub
r-aqan taq'aj
chila k'ut
mi x-in-yo'pi-ta-j apan-oq k'iche' j(u)yub
k'iche' taq'aj
k'ate k'u chiri mi x-nu-riq-o w-ajaw-al
nu-winaq-il
xa nim tz'aq-im chi-r-ij
tz'aq-im ch(i) u-wach
ch(i) u-pa[m] aqam chun
chiri k'ut mi x-nu-tar-ij chi-r-ech r-al nu-ch'ab
r-uk' r-al nu-pokob
r-uk' nu-yak-im wi[t]
nu-yak-im w-ikaj
r-uk' w-oyew-el-al
w-achi-j-il-al
xa k'u xere mi x-nuw-il-o w-ajaw-al
nu-winaq-il

151. Within this context, it seems that the expression "to measure and pace" has the figurative meaning of "to evaluate, to estimate" (in a certain sense, "to assess the damage").

152. It is improbable that these terms designate a toponym. The expression recurs several times in the rest of the story (see notably lines 1169–1170), without ever being accompanied by the indication *chuchaxik,* which is usually attached to toponyms. It more likely designates a hollow (such as a ditch or a quarry) dug in the lime (*aqam chun,* literally, "bitter lime," in contrast to edible lime), which burns the prisoner many times. An indication of the hypothetical nature and location of this place of detention is perhaps indi-

and, over there, measured and paced
the interior of the great fortress
of the great wall![151]
But I saw
only trails of clouds
and trails of fog
still creeping in front of the great fortress
the great wall!
Only the house crickets
only the bush crickets
emitted their striations
continued to trill,
filling the great fortress
the great wall with their song.
Then my heart stumbled
my heart was wounded.
And I departed, scrambling along the foot of the mountains
the foot of the valleys,
and, over there,
I reached the K'iche' mountains
the K'iche' valleys.
There I found my master
my eminence,
only great walls surrounded him
great walls opposed him,
in a prison of quicklime.[152]
So I broke it down[153] with blows from my arrows
with blows from my shield
using my raised handle
my brandished ax
with all my anger
my strength . . .
And I discovered my master
my eminence

---

rectly provided by Tovilla (1960: 217), when, regarding Sacapulas, he points out: "Servía este pueblo [Tuhal or Çacapulas] antiguamente en su gentilidad como cárcel o mazmorra donde encerraban los reyes del Quiché . . . (cuyas eran estas tierras) los que cautivaban en las guerras que continuamente tenían con sus comarcanos, porque estos reyes del Quiché eran muy poderosos. . . . Metían aquí los cautivos en un modo de peña tajada muy grande todas las noches, y de día les hacían acudir a la fábrica de la sal, que hacían mucha y le era de mucha importancia a su rey." Unfortunately, no other document has confirmed the validity of this isolated information (see Hill and Monaghan 1987: 75).

153. Literally, "knock on the door, force one's way in."

xa nim lo-lo-x-inaq chi-r-ij
u-wach
ch(i) u-pam aqam chu[n]
chiri k'ut mi x-nu-lot'-ot'-ej
ch(i) u-pam r-al nu-ch'ab
r-al nu-pokob
qatz-ij k'u chi tzij we ma ta in
qatz k'u chila ka-ø-ch'ay wi u-wix-al
u-kutam-il
la w-ajaw-al
[fol. 26] la nu-winaq-il
chila k'iche' j(u)yub
k'iche' taq'aj
are k'u ri r-umal mi x-in-yak chi wi ul-oq
ch(i) u-pam r-al nu-ch'ab
r-uk' r-al nu-pokob
mi x-ø-ul nu-jet-e-sa-j chi wi k'ut
ch(i) u-pam u-tz'aq-il
u-k'oxtun-al ri w-ajaw-al
nu-winaq-il

ma pa x-e-k'is la ka-ib
ox-ib u-q'ab amaq'
siwan
tinamit
chiri balam-wak
chi-tin-t-ot wi poqlaj
chi-k'arkaraxaj
chi-kunu
chi-q'os-ibal taq'aj tulul ch(i)-u-ch[a]-x-ik
janik' pa k'ut ma wi chi [e]k'ow-ik r-aj-abal k'ux la
chi-r-ech wa oy[e]w-al
wa achi-j-il-al
are na k'u ch-ø-[u]l tojo-r-i-sa-j la ri
waral ch(i) u-xmut kaj
ch(i) u-xmut ulew

---

154. Ximénez (1985: 359) gives "lolot: dar comezón como la cal." Coloch translates this term as "scabs," which he describes as "when the skin is gnawed at and falls away in strips" (see Glossary).

155. The expression *u-q'ab amaq'* literally means "hand (branch) of populating," that is "the outskirts"; Vico (n.d.a: fol. 8v) and Coto (1983: 63, 319), moreover, give a sociopolitical translation, specifying that *u-q'ab amaq'* concerns "neighborhoods," "annexes"

badly burned in back
and in front,[154]
inside the prison of quicklime.
From that place I carried him away
in the child of my bow
in the child of my shield!
It is certain that without me
they would have finished there, with the roots
and the trunk
of my master
[fol. 26] my eminence,
there, in the K'iche' mountains
the K'iche' valleys!
And that is why I brought him back
in the child of my bow
with the child of my shield,
and came to settle him
in his own fortress
in his own wall—my master
my eminence!

Did You not also devastate two
three settlements,
villages
and hamlets including:[155]
in Balamwak,
Chi Tintot Wi Poqlaj
Chi K'arkaraxaj
Chi Kunu
Chi Q'osibal Taq'aj Tulul, as they are called?
And how many more to let pass Your heart's desire
for this anger
for this force?
That is what You have come to pay for
here, at the navel of the sky
at the navel of the earth!

(*barrios* and *estancias* in Spanish), or "little villages subjugated by others." The pair *siwan tinamit* (literally, "ravines/village[s]") connotes what might be called a "town" or "city," including the citadel and its more or less immediate outskirts. The most faithful and simultaneously concise way to render the content of this tercet, which summarizes remarkably the indigenous vision of the settlement pattern, is "Haven't You destroyed several village centers, their surroundings, and their dependencies?"

keje k'ut ix [ch]-in-yo'pi-sa-j tzij-o-l la
ch(i) u-wach w-ajaw-al
nu-winaq-il
keje k'ut mi x-pixab ta kan la chi juyub-al la
chi taq'aj-al la
r-umal waral ka-qa-ch'ay wi wix-al la
kutam-il la
waral ch(i) u-xmut kaj
ch(i) u-xmut ulew
ka-ø-cha k'u ri nu-tzij
keje ma wi k'i-a-tzij k-oj-tzij-o-n uk' la
kaj
ulew chi-k'oji' uk' la
kaweq k'iche' winaq

[fol. 27] *u-wuq-mul ka-ø-ch'aw k'iche' achi*

eja
oyew achi
rabinal achi
la ka-ø-cha na k'u ri tzij la ch(i) u-wach kaj
ch(i) u-wach ulew
qatz are tzij
ma na k'o x-u-jal tzij mi x-bix-ta-j la
ch(i) u-wach kaj
ch(i) u-wach ulew
chi nu-chi'
chi nu-wach
qatz-ij k'u chi tzij
in x-in-mak-u-be-j ri nu-tzij
are k'ut x-e-pixab chi nabe la q-ajaw-al
la qa-winaq-il
mi x-oj-ki-chok-o
mi x-oj-ki-sik'-i-j
ix-ø-cha k'u ki-tzij q-ajaw-al
qa-winaq-il
ajaw teken-toj
ajaw teken-tijax
q'umarmachi
chi taq-ta-sib
taq-ta-simaj
k'[o]x[o]ma aj
k'[o]x[o]ma cho

156. Literally, "I have sinned through (with) my words."

Accordingly, I shall report the information regarding You
to the face of my master
to the face of my eminence!
So You will have left Your recommendations to Your mountains
Your valleys,
for in this very place will we strike Your roots
Your trunk,
here, at the navel of the sky
at the navel of the earth!
That is what I am saying!
And we will not exchange many words with You!
May the sky
and the earth remain with You
—Kaweq K'iche'!»

[fol. 27] *K'iche' Achi speaks for the seventh time.*

«Eha!
Angry man,
Rabinal Achi!
What says Your word facing the sky
facing the earth?
It is true,
nothing needs to be changed in the words You have offered
facing the sky
facing the earth
facing my mouth
facing me!
And it is true
that I lied![156]
That is exactly what our lords
our eminencies first recommended!
Our masters
our eminencies summoned us
they called us
and pronounced their words
—Lord Teken Toj
Lord Teken Tijax
Q'umarmachi
where the smoke abounds
the spearheads abound,
watching place of reeds
watching place of lakes,

k'[o]x[o]ma siwan
k'[o]x[o]ma tz'ikin
ki-bi ki-chi'
ki-wach la q-ajaw-al
la [qa-]winaq-il
chi pe-t-a na b(a) alaq kab-lajuj chi oyew
chi achi-j-ab
ch-ul ta ta na b(a) alaq pixab-a-x-ik-il alaq
mi x-ø-cha nabe ri ki-tzij chi-q-e uk' la
xa k'u xere r-umal ix-ø-jar-ik
ix-ø-twanik
ix-ø-tux-ar-ik
ix-ø-tzarajmaq-ir-ik
u-pam ju-jun chi wa'-bal
chi ok-ibal
ch(i) u-pam u-nim-al tz'aq
u-nim-al k'oxtu[n]
xa belej-eb chik
xa lajuj chik ri saq-il al
ri saq-il k'ajol
[fol. 28] e k'o ch(i) u-pam ki-tz'aq-il
ki-k'oxtun-al
ix-ø-cha nabe ri ki-tzij chi-q-e uk' la
xa k'u xere r-umal ma na x-in-ech-a-be-n taj
waral ch(i) u-xmut kaj
ch(i) u-xmut ulew
r-umal k'ut u-k'oq-obal nu-k'ux
ta x-e-nu-ben-e-be-j
x-e-nu-tzel-e-be-j ri saq-il al
ri saq-il k'ajol
chiri ukoq k-e-tzur-u-t-ya-j wi ki-wach
ch(i) u-pam ixim-che'
chi-r-ech u-tzuku-x-ik u-chikop-il q'an-a kab
rax-a kab

157. Coloch compares this verb, which he doesn't recognize in this specific form, with *tz'urutz'utyaj,* which he interprets as "to come and go rapidly from one point to another, like butterflies on a pool of water . . . giving the impression of fighting"; several dictionaries define *tzur* as "to be a bull-fighter" (a meaning only acquired, one can imagine, in the colonial period but which similarly implies movements of approach, of provocation, and of retreat in one direction or another). This description corresponds perfectly to the activity with which it is supposed to relate: hunting bees and honey.

158. In my opinion, this term designates here a breadnut tree (literally, "corn tree"; *Brossimum alicastrum*) and makes no reference to the city called Iximché, former capital of

sentinel of the ravines,
watching place of birds,
names of the mouths
of the faces of our masters
of our eminencies:
"Come then, You, the twelve valiants
the warriors!
Come then and hear what is recommended to You!"
said their words at first, to us as well as to You.
"Because [the food] has turned to water
has rotted
has flaked off
has dessicated
in the bottom of every plate
every bowl
inside the great fortress
the great wall,
because only nine
ten white children

[fol. 28] *still remain in their fortress*
their wall."
Such were their words at first, to us as well as to You.
That is why I did not take possession
of this place, the navel of the sky
the navel of the earth.
And it is only because of the misdeeds of my heart
that I made
the white children go
the white children come.
It was there, near the place where they were struggling[157]
in the corn tree[158]
looking for flies of yellow honey
flies of green honey,

---

the Cakchiquel and which corresponds to the large archaeological site near present-day Tecpán. There are two reasons for this interpretation: (1) the term is not followed by the expression *chuchaxik,* generally used with a toponym; (2) it is hard to imagine what the Rabinaleb would do there, since the text has specifically just recalled that they were at home, in Kajyub. Furthermore, suggesting that this term might quite simply mean a tree sheltering "honey flies," Coto's dictionary (1983: 58) defines the expression *u chikopil kab* as designating "un avejal o colmena q[ue] se cría en los árboles" (see also note 59).

mi x-e-nuw-il-o
ix-ø-cha k'u ri nu-tzij ch(i) u-wach kaj
ch(i) u-wach ulew
la ma na r-okik-am
ix k-e-nu-yak ta k'u bi wa saq-il al
k'ajol
k-e-yak-a-ta-j ta k'u bi chi nu-juyub-al
chi nu-taq'aj-al
[x-]ø-cha k'u ri nu-tzij
ch-inw-opon-i-be-j taj
ch(i) u-wach w-ajaw-al
nu-winaq-il k'iche' j(u)yub
k'iche' taq'aj
ix-ø-cha k'u ri nu-tzij
are k'u ri xa {i}sk'aqin r-ulew-al nabe-l-ik
xambe-l-ik
q'an-bo[l] saq-i jal
q'an-a tz'uklik
saq-i tz'uklik
chiri k'ut mi x-in-kir-ir-ej wi kan-oq
chiri pank'aqil ch(i)-u-ch[a]-x-ik
r-umal are x-ø-bek nu-k'ux r-uk' la saq-il al
saq-il k'ajol
xa k'u xere r-umal mi x-tzaq apan la ye-bal la
sik'-ibal la
x-ø-oq' k'ux la chi-r-ech u-ta-y-ik ye-bal la
[fol. 29] sik'-ibal la
xa k'u xere mi x-yo'pi-ta-j apan la
chila panajache'el
chila k'ut mi x-tzaq wi la ye-bal la
sik'-ibal la
k'ate k'u chiri
mi x-e-nu-yusk'upi-j ul-oq ri saq-il al
ri saq-il k'ajol
chiri chi-nim-che'
chi-kabraqan
paraweno ch(i)-u-ch[a]-x-ik

---

159. This passage breaks with the reconstructed flow of action to convey the expression of a wish (marked by the particle *taj*), which is an inner thought K'iche' Achi said to himself at the time of the deeds.

160. Coloch translates *kirirej* as "to disperse, to scatter"; according to the dictionaries, the root *kir* associates the meaning "to detach, to unknot, to untangle" with the consecutive action "to drop down, to fall." To illustrate precisely what this verb describes, I cite

that I saw them
and said, facing the sky
facing the earth:
"Would it not be appropriate
for me to take away these white children,

that they should be brought to my mountains
to my valleys?"
And my word said:
"I will come
facing my master
my eminence of the K'iche' mountains
of the K'iche' valleys . . .
and I will tell him:
this is only a little of the nearby lands
and far-off lands,
bursting with white ears of corn
with yellow beans
with white beans . . ."[159]
And that was when I scattered them,[160]
there, in the place called Pank'aqil,
because that is where my heart went with the white children!

That is why You let fly Your exhortation
Your cry
—and Your heart grieved to hear Your own exhortation
[fol. 29] Your own cry—[161]
even as You were then approaching
Panajache'el, over there!
And from there You let fly Your exhortation
Your cry!
Then, immediately,
I set the white children free,

over there, at Nim Che'
at Kabraqan
Paraweno, as they are called!

---

the example of a load of wood that, once untied, falls down onto the ground, or that of flowers, fruits, or leaves that after falling from a tree, are strewn on the ground.

161. Related to the account of these same events by Rabinal Achi (see fol. 23), this phrase might mean that this first summons was powerful enough to move the one who had emitted it but insufficient to impress the one it was intended for.

xa sk'aqin chi r-aj
ma na x-e-yo'pi-j-ik ri saq-il al
ri saq-il k'ajol
chi nu-juyub-al
chi nu-taq'aj-al k'iche' j(u)yub
k'iche' taq'aj
keje k'ut mi x-e-tzel-e-j wach-i-n ul-oq ri saq-il al
ri saq-il k'ajol
ka-ø-xirxot-{t}ileb uko[q] ki-pam
k-e-tz'aj-tz'-at taq ukoq
ta x-ki-maj ul-oq r-aqan j(u)yub
r-aqan taq'aj
xa k'u xere r-umal ma na x-e-yo'pi-ta-j ul-oq
ch(i) u-pam ki-tz'aq-il
ki-k'oxtun-al
xa k'u chiri chik x-e-amaq'-e-l-ab wi
pamaq'a ch(i)-u-ch[a]-x-ik
xa wi qatz in x-in-mak-u-be-j
mi x-ø-ul nuw-e-sa-j ajaw-al la
winaq-il la
chiri ch(i)-atin-ibal ch(i)-u-ch[a]-x-ik
r-umal ka-ø-xakak ukoq
chiri mi x-in-yak ubi pa r-al nu-ch'ab
pa r-al nu-pokob
mi x-in-qa-sa-j k'ut chi nu-juyub-al
chi nu-taq'aj-al
chila k'iche' j(u)yub
k'iche' taq'aj
r-umal u-k'oq-obal nu-k'ux
r-umal ma na x-in-ech-a-be-n taj
[fol. 30] waral ch(i) u-xmut kaj
ch(i) u-xmut ulew
keje k'ut mi x-in-tz'api-j k'ut
ch(i) u-pam saq chun aqam
mi x-in-sa[q] kab-ij r-ij
mi x-in-sa[q] kab-ij u-wach ch(i) u-pam aqam chu[n]
qatz k'u in x-in-mak-u-be-j

---

162. As in the case of the co-occurrence within the same phrase of the pair *al k'ajol* (see note 109), this phrase's ending provides us the opportunity to render the pair *jyub taq'aj* by two of its possible meanings.

163. The verb *xakak* describes the action of washing oneself in a river in shallow water, that is, standing up with spread legs (see Ximénez 1985: 605: "xac," "abrir las

It would not have taken much
for the white children to reach

my mountains
my valleys of the K'iche' land![162]

That's when the white children reappeared;

their bellies trembling,
all groaning and thin,
when they followed the foot of the mountains
the foot of the valleys!
But they did not return to
their fortress
their wall however,
but only to the place where they settled:
Pamaq'a, as it is called!
It is equally true that I alone committed a fault
by coming to abduct Your master
Your eminence,
there, in the place called Chatinibal,
when he was just about to bathe.[163]
From there, I took him in the child of my bow
in the child of my shield,
and forced him to descend[164] toward my mountains
toward my valleys
over there, in the K'iche' land . . .

because of the misdeeds of my heart
having failed to take possession
[fol. 30] of this place, the navel of the sky
the navel of the earth!
That is when I shut him up
in the quicklime,
walling up his back
walling up his front in the lime!
It is true that I am guilty . . .

---

piernas") and, as Coloch explains, the body is bent, the hands joined together to splash water over one's head to wet or rinse it.

164. The verb *qasaj* (literally, "to cause to come down") also relates to military terminology, in which it means "to humiliate, to conquer, to triumph."

xa wi ka-ø-cha ri tzij la
mi x-e-k'is la ka-ib
ox-ib u-q'ab amaq'
siwan
tinamit
chiri balam-wak
chi-tin-t-ot wi poqlaj
chi-k'arkaraxaj
chi-kunu
chi-q'os-ibal taq'aj tulul ch(i)-u-ch[a]-x-ik
qatz k'u in x-in-mak-u-be-j
r-umal u-k'oq-obal nu-k'ux
la are k'u ch-ø-ul nu-toj-or-i-sa-j ri
waral ch(i) u-xmut kaj
ch(i) u-xmut ulew
ka-ø-cha ri tzij la lal ajaw
ma pa xa wi ka-ø-cha k'u ri tzij la
ka-n-yo'pi-sa-j tzij-o-x-ik la
ch(i) u-wach w-ajaw-al
nu-winaq-il
ch(i) u-pa[m] u-nim-al tz'aq
u-nim-al k'oxtun
chiri k'ut mi x-pixab ta kan la chi juyub-al la
chi taq'aj-al la
r-umal waral ka-qa-ch'ay wi wix-al la
kutam-il la
waral ch(i) u-xmut kaj
ch(i) u-xmut ulew
ka-ø-cha ri tzij la
la ma na wa k'o ch-u-bi'i-j la chi nu-chi'
chi nu-wach
xa wa kuk
xa wa tz'ikin la chi nu-wach
la k'o k'u x-u-ban ri chi-ech la lal ajaw
ma pa xa wi ka-ø-cha ri tzij la
ka-n-yo'pi-sa-j tzij-o-x-ik la
ch(i) u-wach w-ajaw-al
nu-winaq-il
[fol. 31] ch(i) u-pam u-nim-al tz'aq
u-nim-al k'oxtu[n]
mi x-pixab ta chi kan la chi juyub-al ri la
chi taq'aj-al la

As Your word says:
"You destroyed two
three settlements,
villages
and hamlets including,
over there, in Balamwak,
Chi Tintot Wi Poqlaj
Chi K'arkaraxaj
Chi Kunu
Chi Q'osibal Taq'aj Tulul, as they are called!"
It is true that I committed faults
by the misdeed of my heart!
Is that what I have come to pay for
here, at the navel of the sky
at the navel of the earth?
That is what You say, You, my Lord!
And don't You also say:
"I shall report what You have said
before my master
before my eminence
inside the great fortress
the great wall!
So You will have left Your recommendations to Your mountains
to Your valleys
for in this place will we strike Your roots
Your trunk,
here, at the navel of the sky
at the navel of the earth!"
That is what Your word says!
But what are these pronouncements facing my mouth
facing me?
They are only squirrels
they are only small birds facing me![165]
How does this concern You, You, my Lord?
Does not Your word say:
"I shall report what You say
before my master
my eminence
[fol. 31] *inside the great fortress*
the great wall!
You have left Your recommendations to Your mountains
to Your valleys

165. Rabinal Achi's words, repeated here by K'iche' Achi, are considered by him to be trifles.

r-umal waral ka-qa-ch'ay wi wix-al la
kutam-il la
waral ch(i) u-xmut kaj
ch(i) u-xmut ulew
ka-ø-cha ri tzij la
la ma na r-okik-am chi-qa-ban ta utz-il
chom-al
atz-in [q-]ib
chaq'-in [q-]ib
ch-in-wiq ta kan la
ix ch-in-kawuj ta pu kan la
chi-r-ech nu-q'an-a pwaq
nu-saq-i pwaq
r-uk' r-al nu-ch'ab
r-uk' r-al nu-pokob
nu-yak-im wi[t]
nu-yak-im w-ikaj
r-uk' {i}[s]k[a]taq[168] w-atzyaq
r-uk' nu-xtapyak
waral ta chi chak-u-n wi
chi patan-i-n wi chi-k-e al la
k'[aj]ol la
waral ch(i) u-xmut kaj
ch(i) u-xmut ulew
xa ta nim-a r-eta-l-il
k-in-yusk'upi-j t(a) ubi la chi nu-juyub-al
chi nu-taq'aj-al
ka-ø-cha k'u ri nu-tzij ch(i) u-wach kaj
ch(i) u-wach ulew
kaj
ulew chi-k'oji' uk' la
oyew achi
u-q'alel achi
rabinal achi

u-wajxaq-mul ka-ø-ch'aw rabinal achi

eja

166. The use of the reflexive *-ib*, thus marked by the first person plural (*q-*), confers an ambiguous character on K'iche' Achi's petition, which consequently might be considered condescending or threatening: do the opportuneness and the conventions it invokes signify, in fact, that the brothers "that we are" owe it to each other to forget this quarrel and to go back to the situation that existed before, or, on the contrary, that they cannot act in any other way without risking reprisals?

for in this place will we strike Your roots
Your trunk,
here, at the navel of the sky
at the navel of the earth!"
That is what Your word says!
Would it not be appropriate for us to behave well
correctly
as between the older brothers
as between the younger brothers that we are;[166]
that You decorate me
and that You adorn me[167]
with my yellow metal
my white metal,
with the child of my bow
with the child of my shield,
my handle raised
my ax raised,
with all of my clothes
with my sandals,
to work here
and serve Your children,

here, at the navel of the sky
at the navel of the earth,
showing in this way
that You leave me [free to] go toward my mountains
toward my valleys?
So says my word facing the sky
facing the earth!
May the sky
and the earth remain with You
—Angry man,
Dignitary
Rabinal Achi!»

Rabinal Achi speaks for the eighth time.

«Eha!

167. Ximénez (1985: 167) defines *cauh* as "componer, aliñar, arreglar; ataviarse."

168. This unusual form of the plural is applied, it seems, to a discontinuous group of a small number of objects (Basseta 1698: fol. 237). It is probably constructed from the morphemes *ska* (or *sk'a*), which means "a little" (see *sk'aqin*), and *taq,* which is a pluralizer.

oyew achi
kaweq k'iche' winaq
[fol. 32] la ka-ø-cha k'u ri tzij la ch(i) u-wach kaj
ch(i) u-wach ulew
la ma na r-okik-am
ix ch-in-kawuj ta kan la
ch-in-wiq ta pu kan la
chi-r-ech nu-q'an-a pwaq
nu-saq-i pwaq
r-uk' r-al nu-ch'ab
{o}r-uk' r-al nu-pokob
{o}r-uk' {i}[s]k[a]taq w-atzyaq
r-uk' nu-xtapyak
waral ta chi chak-u-n wi
chi patan-i-n wi
waral ch(i) u-xmut kaj
ch(i) u-xmut ulew
ka-ø-cha k'u ri tzij la
xa jin ma x k-in-cha k'u ri wa
ch(i) u-wach l[a] w-ajaw-al
ch(i) u-wach la nu-winaq-il
ta [tz]e ba jun oyew
ta [tz]e ba jun achi
ix-qa-chuq'ab-e-j q-ib r-uk'
chi-r-ij u-nim-al tz'aq
u-nim-al k'oxtun
chi ox-laju(j)-winaq q'ij
chi ox-laju(j)-winaq aq'ab
k'o qa-war-am
maja-bi qa-yakal-em r-uk'
keje k'ut mi x-nu-wiq kan-oq
chi-r-ech u-q'an-a pwaq
r-uk' u-saq-i pwaq
r-uk' u-yak-im wi[t]
u-yak-im w-ikaj
r-uk' {i}[s]k[a]taq r-atzyaq
r-uk' u-xtapyak
la ma x k-in-cha k'u ri wa
ch(i) u-wach la w-ajaw-al
ch(i) u-wach la nu-winaq-il
keje k'ut mi x-in-yo'pi-sa-j ubi ch(i) u-juyub-al
ch(i) u-taq'aj-al

Angry man,
K'iche' Achi!
[fol. 32] What says Your word facing the sky
facing the earth?
"Would it not be appropriate
for You to decorate me
and for You to adorn me
with my yellow metal
with my white metal,
with the child of my bow
and the child of my shield,
with all of my clothes
and my sandals,
to work here
and serve,
here, at the navel of the sky
at the navel of the earth?"
as Your word says!
Me! You want me to go say that
to the face of my master
to the face of my eminence!
"Outside is a man of valor
outside is a man
with whom we battled
behind the great fortress
the great wall
for thirteen times twenty days
for thirteen times twenty nights;
we are exhausted
we had no peace[169] with him.
Nevertheless, I have given him back his ornaments:
his yellow metal
his white metal,
his war handle
and his war ax,
all of his clothes
including his sandals!"
Is that what I am going to say
to the face of my master
to the face of my eminence?
"I also let him regain his mountains
his valleys!"

169. Literally, "no tranquility" (see Ximénez 1985: 297; "yacal: to create calm").

la ma x k-in-cha k'u ri wa
ch(i) u-wach la w-ajaw-al
ch(i) u-wach la nu-winaq-il
xa wi in tz'aqat
in mol-a-j
[fol. 33] r-umal w-ajaw-al
nu-winaq-il
k'o-l-ik nu-q'an-a pwaq
nu-saq-i pwaq
xa wi k'o-l-ik r-al nu-ch'ab
r-al nu-pokob
r-uk' nu-yak-im wi[t]
nu-yak-im w-ikaj
in tz'aqat
in mol-a-j r-umal w-ajaw-al
nu-winaq-il
ch(i) u-pam u-nim-al tz'aq
ch(i) u-pam u-nim-al k'oxtun
keje k'ut k-in-yo'pi-sa-j tzij-o-l la
ch(i) u-pam u-nim-al tz'aq
u-nim-al k'oxtun
ch(i) u-wach w-ajaw-al
nu-winaq-il
we k'u x chi-ø-cha w-ajaw-al
nu-winaq-il
yusk'upi-j bi la ch(i) u-juyub-al
ch(i) u-taq'aj-al
we x chi-ø-cha w-ajaw-al
xa wi ix ch-in-yusk'upi-j bi la ri
xa wi we x chi-ø-cha w-ajaw-al
nu-winaq-il
chi koj ta na ba lo la chi nu-chi'
chi nu-wach
ka-nw-il na u-chi'
u-wach
janik' pa chi oyew
chi achi
we x chi-ø-cha w-ajaw-al
nu-winaq-il
keje k'ut ka-nu-yo'pi-sa-j k'u la
ka-ø-cha k'u ri nu-tzij ch(i) u-wach kaj
ch(i) u-wach ulew
kaj
ulew chi-k'oji' uk' la
oyew achi
kaweq k'iche' winaq

Is that what I am going to say
to the face of my master
to the face of my eminence?
All the more so as I am supplied
I am well maintained
[fol. 33] by my master
my eminence!
There is my yellow metal
my white metal
just as there is the child of my bow
the child of my shield,
and my war handle
my war ax!
I am supplied
I am well maintained by my master
by my eminence
inside the great fortress
inside the great wall!
Accordingly, I shall report the information concerning You
in the great fortress
the great wall
before my master
my eminence!
And if my master
my eminence says:
"Let him go to his mountains
to his valleys!"
if my sovereign says so,
I will let You go there immediately!
But if my master
my eminence says:
"Have him come in before my mouth
before my face,
so I see his mouth
his face,
and see how angry he is
how much he is a man!"
If that is what my master
my eminence says,
then I will introduce You!
So says my word facing the sky
facing the earth!
May the sky
and the earth remain with You
– Angry man,
Kaweq K'iche'!»

u-wajxaq-mul ka-ø-ch'aw-ik k'iche' achi

[fol. 34] eja
utz keje k'o ba la oyew achi
u-q'alel
rabinal achi
ka-yo'pi-sa-j la nu-tzij-o-x-ik
ch(i) u-wach ajaw-al la ch(i) u-pam u-nim-al tz'aq
u-nim-al k'oxtun
k-in-yo'pi-sa-j la k'ut
keje kaj
ulew chi-k'oji' uk' la
u-q'alel achi
rabinal achi

U-KAM BAN-BAL

k-u-yo'pi-sa-j ch(i) u-wach ajaw {o}job toj

u-belej-mul ka-ø-ch'aw rabinal achi

kala ajaw
kala xoq'ojaw
ki k'amo chi-r-ech kaj
ki k'amo chi-r-ech ulew
waral lal ajaw-ar-inaq wi
lal muj-ar-inaq
ch(i) u-xe u-muj-ibal q'uq'
rax-on
ch(i) u-pam u-nim-al tz'aq
u-nim-al k'oxtun
keje k'o wa in oyew-al-al la
in achi-j-il-al la
[fol. 35] mi x-in-yo'pi-[t]a-j k'ul-oq chi chi' la
chi wach la

170. The term *kala* was chosen by most of the Spanish missionaries, who adapted Christian prayers into Indian languages, to introduce the Hail Mary and translated the Latin Ave (see, e.g., *Cartilla breve traducida en lengua quiche y cakchiquel al pie de la letra para el uso de los cristianos indígenas*; in Brasseur 1862a: vii). Many examples also appear in the translations that Vico (n.d.b) presents in his grammar text.

K'iche' Achi speaks for the eighth time.

[fol. 34] «Eha!
Good, let it be so — Angry man,
Dignitary
Rabinal Achi!
Present the information concerning me
facing Your sovereign in the great fortress
the great wall!
Announce me!
And may the sky
and the earth remain with You
— Dignitary
Rabinal Achi!»

ACT TWO

He announces him before King Job Toj.

Rabinal Achi speaks for the ninth time.

«Hail,[170] oh King!"
Hail, oh Queen![171]
Yes, thanks to the sky
and thanks to the earth,
You who are enthroned
You who are sheltered here
under the protection[172] of the quetzal
the green feathers
inside the great fortress
the great wall!
Here am I, Your anger
Your strength,
[fol. 35] I have appeared facing Your mouth
facing Your face

171. Besides the epigraph (line 13), where Xoq'ojaw is mentioned in the list of characters, this address by Rabinal Achi to her constitutes the only trace left in the text of the queen's presence.

172. According to Ximénez (1985: 397), "muh: sombra de cosas inanimadas" and also "muh calibal: trono." Guzmán (1984: 121) confirms this last pair — "muh/Ɛalibal: trono de magestad, o sitial" (ceremonial armchair) — and gives *muh* the more specific meaning of "canopy."

ch(i) u-pam u-nim-al tz'aq
u-nim-al k'oxtun
keje k'u jun oyew
jun achi
ix-qa-chuq'ab-e-j q-ib r-uk'
chi ox-laju(j)-winaq q'ij
ox-laju(j)-winaq aq'ab
chi-r-ij u-nim-al tz'aq
k'oxtun
k'o qa-war-am
maja-bi qa-yakal-em r-uk'
keje k'ut mi x-u-ya kaj
mi x-u-ya ulew
mi x-ø-tzaq k'ut ch(i) u-pam r-al nu-ch'ab
ch(i) u-pam r-al nu-pokob
mi x-in-tzaq-k'am-a-j
mi x-in-tzaq-ko[lo]b-e-j[173]
chi-r-ech nu-saq-i ka'am
nu-saq-i kolob
r-uk' nu-yak-im wi[t]
nu-yak-im w-ikaj
nu-chinku
nu-[q']al[q']ab
nu-salmet
keje k'ut mi x-in-k'ot u-chi' ri oyew
ri achi
ma wi kujulik jusuk' taj
x-u-jik-i[-ba] taj u-wach u-juyub-al
u-taq'aj-al
chi nu-chi'
chi nu-wach in oyew
in achi

---

173. The correction of *kobej* to *kolobej* is necessary if one compares it with a similar form (see line 1473).

174. As in the case of the verb *etak'amara* (see note 125), this compound associates two actions: that of "dropping, throwing on the ground," corresponding to the transitive form of the verb *tzaq,* and that of "attaching," given by the terms *ka'am* (muted into *k'am*) or *kolob,* which specifies the nature of the ties/bonds used.

175. The term *kolob* designates straps of skin or leather.

176. Literally, "to dig out his mouth." Coto (1983: 77, 226) confirms the metaphorical meaning of this expression, which he renders as "buscar haciendo inquisición" and "examinar."

inside the great fortress
the great wall!
There is an angry one out there,
a man out there
with whom we battled
for thirteen times twenty days
for thirteen times twenty nights;
behind the great citadel.

We are tired
we have had hardly any rest with him!
And now the sky has granted
the earth has granted
that he fall within the child of my bow
within the child of my shield!
I threw him down and tied him
I threw him down and bound him[174]
with my white cord
my white thong[175]
with my brandished handle
my brandished ax
my bracelets
my ornaments
my powdered stone!
And I've interrogated[176] the angry one
the man!
He prevaricated,[177]
he did not immediately reveal the face of his mountains
of his valleys!
Before my mouth
before my face, I who am angry
I who am a man,

---

177. I am restoring an exegesis here rather than a literal translation that could only be partially verified. Indeed, the term *kujulik* has not been identified, but it might be a derived form of *jul* ("to make a hole, to pierce"), echoing *k'ot* ("to dig out"). As for the expression *jusuk' taj,* understood today as "he is not right / not correct," it might be only an approximation of the translators who recognized in it the element *suk'* ("right, uprightness, truth"; see *suk'ulik* in the glossary). Early dictionaries define the term *jusuk'* as "right away, immediately, promptly," and I have chosen to use this meaning. It is very likely that a hypothetical reading of the original text might be *ma wi [s]u[k']ulik jusuk' taj* ("he was not frank right away" or "he was late in telling the truth").

are oyew
are achi k-u-ban r-oq'-ibal utiw
k-u-ban r-oq'-ibal yak
k-u-ban r-oq'-ibal utuy
jalaw
chi-r-ij u-nim-al tz'aq
u-nim-al k'oxtun
chi-r-ech ki-boy-e-x-ik
ki-k'ak'ale-x-ik la saq-il al
la saq-il k'ajol
are oyew
are achi
mi x-ø-k'is-ow-ik belej-eb
lajuj saq-il al
saq-il k'ajol
xa wi are oyew
mi x-ø-ul r-e-sa-j alaq[179] chiri ch(i)-atin-ibal
[fol. 36] are oyew
are achi
mi x-e-u-k'is-o ka-ib
ox-ib u-q'ab amaq'
siwan
tinamit
chiri xe-balam-wak
chi-tin-t-ot wi poqlaj ch(i)u-ch[a]-x-ik

la janik' pa k'ut
ma wi k-ø-ek'ow-ik r-aj-abal k'ux la[180]
chi-r-ech wa oyew-al
wa achi-j-il-al

ma pa x-oj-pixab-a-x-ik k-umal q-ajaw-al
qa-winaq-il
e r-ajaw-al u-pam ju-jun chi tz'aq
chi k'oxtun

---

178. The term *jalaw* is absent from both the Quiché and Cakchiquel dictionaries. Coloch believes, without conviction, that the compound word *utuy jalaw* is only a variant of *utuy balam* ("a sort of jaguar"; see note 56). Not having more precise information, I translate *jalaw* as "tepescuintle" (derived from the Nahuatl *tepeitzcuintli,* commonly accepted in Mesoamerica to designate the paca or *Coelogenys paca*), thus following the meaning this word is generally given in other Mayan languages, such as K'ekchi and Tzeltal.

179. The use of *alaq,* the reverential form of the second person plural, is explained by the fact that in this passage Rabinal Achi is addressing the royal couple. Nothing

this angry one
this man imitated the howling of the coyote
imitated the howling of the wildcat
imitated the howling of the agouti
the *tepescuintle*[178]
behind the great fortress
the great wall,
so as to attract
as to surprise the white children!

This angry one
this man
exterminated nine
ten white children!

It was also this angry one
who came to abduct You, over there, in Chatinibal!
[fol. 36] This is the angry one
this is the man
who destroyed two
three settlements,
villages
and hamlets including,
over there, at Xe-Balamwak
Chi Tintot Wi Poqlaj, as they are called!»

«And how many more
to let pass Your heart's desire
for this anger
this force?»

«Was it not recommended to us by our masters
our eminencies,
the inside[181] lords of each fortress
of each wall:

else, however, indicates that the queen, Xoq'ojaw, shared the fate of her husband during this kidnapping episode.

180. The form of this phrase, in the flow of the account thus reported to Job Toj, should be *r-ajabal u-k'ux* ("his heart's desire"). The change of person being addressed therefore forces us to consider it as an aside addressed to K'iche' Achi.

181. This correlation, established between the sovereign and his royal residence, reinforces the characteristics that are associated with the figure of the king, such as settled and immobile.

ajaw teken-toj
ajaw teken-tijax
q'umarmachi
taq-ta-sib
taq-ta-simaj
k'[o]x[o]ma aj
k'[o]x[o]ma siwan
k'[o]x[o]ma cho
k'[o]x[o]ma kab
k'[o]x[o]ma tz'ikin ki-bi ki-chi'
ki-wach

are na k'u ch-ø-ul toj-or-i-sa-j la ri
waral ch(i) u-xmut kaj
ch(i) u-xmut ulew

keje k'ut waral ka-qa-ch'ay wi u-wix-al
u-kutam-il
waral ch(i) u-xmut kaj
ch(i) u-xmut ulew
lal w-ajaw-al
ajaw {o}job toj

u-nabe-mul ka-ø-ch'aw-ik ajaw {o}job toj

w-oyew-al
w-achi-j-il-al
k'amo chi-r-ech kaj
k'amo chi-r-ech ulew
mi x-yo'pi-sa-j k'u lo la
ch(i) u-pam u-nim-al tz'aq
u-nim-al k'oxtun chi nu-chi'
chi nu-wach
in ajaw-al la
in ajaw {o}job toj
k'amo ba chi-r-ech kaj
k'amo ba chi-r-ech ulew
[fol. 37] we mi x-u-ya kaj
mi x-u-ya ulew ri oyew
ri achi

Lord Teken Toj
Lord Teken Tijax
Q'umarmachi
where the smoke abounds
the spearheads abound,
watching place of reeds,
sentinel of the ravines,
watching place of lakes,
watching place of bees,
watching place of birds, names of their mouths
of their faces!»

«That is what You have come to pay for
here, at the navel of the sky
at the navel of the earth!»[182]

«And in this place we will strike his roots
his trunk,
here, at the navel of the sky
at the navel of the earth!
—Oh You, my sovereign,
King Job Toj!»

King Job Toj speaks for the first time.

«My angry one,
my warrior!
Thanks to the sky
thanks to the earth,
You have announced him
inside the great fortress
the great wall, to my mouth
to my face,
I, who am Your sovereign,
I, King Job Toj!
So thanks be to the sky
thanks be to the earth
[fol. 37] if the sky has granted
the earth has granted that the angry one
the man

182. Here we have once again a change in the person being addressed, another aside directed at the prisoner, whom Rabinal Achi apparently continues to angrily call to from within the royal palace (see note 180).

mi x-ø-tzaq k'ut ch(i) u-pam r-al ch'ab la
r-al pokob la
mi x-tzaq-k'am-a-j la
mi x-tzaq-kolob-e-j la ri oyew
ri achi
joq'otaj-il ta ba la
chi koj ta lo la chi nu-chi'
chi nu-wach
ka-nw-il na u-chi'
ka-nw-il na u-wach
janik' pa chi achi
chi pixab-a-j ta ba la ri achi
ri oyew
ma ta chi boj-oj-ik
ma ta chi t'il-il-ik
ta ch-ø-ok ul-oq ch(i) u-chi' u-nim-al tz'aq
u-nim-al k'oxtun
waral k'ut ka-r-aj loq'-o-x-el
mayi-j-a-x-el
ch(i) u-pam u-nim-al tz'aq
u-nim-al k'oxtun
waral k'ut k'o-l-ik kab-lajuj r-atz
kab-lajuj u-chaq'
e aj-pwaq-i-nel
e aj-xit-a-nel
maja chi tz'aqat ki-chi'
ki-wach
kolo are oyew mi x-ch-ø-ul ok-oq ki-tz'aqat
ki-mol-a-j
ch(i) u-pam u-nim-al tz'aq
u-nim-al k'oxtun
xa wi ki waral k'o-l-ik kab-lajuj u-q'an-al kot
u-q'an-al balam
xa wi maja chi tz'aqat ki-chi'
ki-wach
kolo are oyew ix ch-ø-ul ok-oq ki-tz'aqat
xa wi ki waral k'o-l-ik pwaq-im tem
pwaq-im kubul-ibal
k'o kub[u]l-e-be-y-om
maja-bi kub[u]l-e-be-y-om

183. The expression *karaj* (literally, "he wants, wishes that") is rendered here by the conditional, in agreement with the meaning of "perhaps" that both early and modern translators give it.

should succumb to the child of Your bow
the child of Your shield,
that You threw him down and tied him
that You threw him down and bound him, the angry one
the man!
If only for a moment,
bring him in, in front of my mouth
in front of me,
that I may see his mouth
that I may see his face,
and how much a man he is!
Advise the man
the angry one
not to gesticulate
not to vociferate
as he crosses the threshold of the great fortress
of the great wall!
And perhaps[183] he will be appreciated
he will be admired
in the great fortress
the great wall!
For his twelve elder brothers
his twelve younger brothers are here,
those who are bearers of metal,
those who are bearers of precious stones,
whose number is still incomplete![184]

Perhaps this angry one will come to join them
to complete their number
inside the great fortress
the great wall!
It is true that here also are the twelve Yellow Eagles
the twelve Yellow Jaguars,
whose number is likewise incomplete!

Perhaps this angry one will come to complete their number!
Here also are the metal benches
the metal seats,
some are occupied
but others are vacant!

184. Literally, "not yet completely their mouths, their faces."

kolo are oyew
kolo are achi mi x ch-ø-ul kubul-i-be-n-oq
xa wi ki waral k'o-l-ik kab-lajuj u-ki'-ya'
kab-lajuj u-matul
ixtatz'unun u-bi
ri k-e ka-ø-silil-ik
ka-ø-t'ir-ir-ik
ki'-koj
kab-koj
ka-n-tij-o ul
k'amawar
[fol. 38] waral ch(i) u-pam u-nim-al tz'aq
k'oxtun
r(i) u-ki'-ya' ajaw
kolo are oyew ix ch-ø-[u]l tij-ow-oq
xa wi ki waral k'o-l-ik laq'an u-q'in
k'oxaj u-wa' ri ki-kalatz'

185. The name of this liquid(s) remains enigmatic. In all likelihood, it combines the Nahuatl element *ixta* and the Quiché element *tz'unun* ("hummingbird"), and different interpretations can be proposed. Siméon (1986: 235), under the entry "iztac," suggests two expressions dealing with drinks: "iztac atolli: bebida hecha con maíz y chile" and "iztac octli: vino blanco"; however, "iztac uitzitzilin" (which might be the exact Nahuatl equivalent for *ixtatz'unun*) simply designates a hummingbird "de plumaje muy hermoso y variado." Another entry deserves to be pointed out: "iztlactli," whose meanings of "saliva, drool, venom" (ibid.: 239) recall those of the Quiché term *matul,* also are employed here to characterize the same drink. Both in Nahuatl and Mayan languages, "sweet, sugary, honeyed" has a certain semantic proximity to "toxic, venomous"; D. Tedlock (1985: 363) has pointed out, for example, how the Quiché term *ki'* (see line 1512, *u-ki'-ya'*) "reflect[s] the paradox of a drink that started out sweet and harmless and ended up bitter and (in sufficient quantities) sickening"; the same is true of the Yucatecan Mayan term *cab,* which designates honey, the venom of an insect, and the nectar of certain plants (Álvarez 1984: 103). Among these plants, we might consider the *Datura stramonium,* a powerful psychotropic whose external use or ingestion can gradually produce a certain number of imbalances, such as drunkenness; sleepiness; loss of memory, reason, or judgment; and even a state of passing or lasting madness (Garza 1989: 1401–1402). Lacking more precise data to identify the names and compositions of the drinks or liquors in question, we can find connections that might explain the reference to the hummingbird, a small pollen-gathering bird whose behavior while flying and whose alimentary practices are easily compared to those of an insect (indeed, in French it is called a "bird-fly"). In addition, it is fitting to recall that in rural Mexico, even today, this bird "evoca la sensualidad del diablo. Una vez disecado, es perfumado y envuelto en un pañuelo. Libera entonces una fuerza mágica que permite conquistar a las mujeres. . . . Comer carne de colibri ocasiona ataques de 'locura.' Es sabido que este pájaro presagia la muerte" (Galinier 1990: 600).

186. Although we do not know the exact nature of this drink, its effects are particularly explicit. The roots *silil* and *t'ir* (here combined into *t'irir* to mark the intensification

Perhaps this angry one
perhaps this man will come to settle there!
Here also are the twelve liquors
the twelve poisonous drinks
called Ixtatz'unun[185]
those that chill
that paralyze,[186]
both[187] sugary
and honey-like,
that provoke falling
and delirium in me,[188]
[fol. 38] here, inside the great citadel!

The King's liquors . . .
perhaps this angry one will come to taste them!
All the more so as here there are weavings[189] with double warp
and single woof,[190]

---

of the action) affirm in fact that its consumption produces a sensation of algidity and of drowsiness (see Glossary). The meaning of the second verb seems to have evolved: Coloch translates it today as "clear one's throat" and García Hernández et al. (1980: 31) define *cät'iririk* as "to be spicy, acidic." The effect of cold, as it is described in the text by the verb *sililik,* is associated by certain dictionaries with the ingestion of a very strong wine (Angel n.d.: fol. 39) or a very sweet one (Vico n.d.a: fol. 43).

187. The suffixation into -C_IVoj of a monosyllabic root of the type C_IVC_2—relating to the realm of colors, tastes, perfumes, and so forth—indicates either a tendency toward a specific quality (e.g., yellowish, greenish, sweetish) or the double quality of something (e.g., the bicolored coat of an animal).

188. The translation of this phrase is not clearly established. The translation of the term *ul* ("crumbling, collapsing") seems to be unanimous, but that of *k'amawar* is more doubtful. I have chosen to follow the exegesis that Coloch provides ("a sleep disturbed by nightmares") but dictionaries provide no confirmation of this interpretation. According to the dictionaries, it might more simply mean "to be taken by sleep" (from *k'am,* the verbal root for "to receive, to take," and *war,* "to sleep"). The verb *tij* is understood today as "to consume, to ingest" and generally covers every action of drinking and eating; it seems, however, that this translation results either from a mixture—Coto distinguishes *tih* ("to experiment") from *tij/tijh* ("to eat")—or from an extension of the meaning that is not recognized in classical Quiché. According to early dictionaries, this verb signifies more specifically "to taste, to try" but also "to prove, to experience, to put to the test, to challenge."

189. The term *kalatz'* encompasses the group of items including the warp and the different sticks that conform to the Amerindian loom (e.g., end beams, lease sticks, heddle rod, and "saber" use to beat weft thread).

190. In the process of weaving, the weft thread is considered to be the food (*wa'*) of the warp (*q'in*).

ka-ø-ban-ik u-ban-om nu-te
nu-xoq'ojaw
kolo are oyew
kolo achi ix ch-ø-ul sa-w-oq u-chi'
u-wach
xa wi ki waral k'o-l-ik tz'ap-i-l-ik ri u-chuch q'uq'
u-chuch rax-on
ri pe-t-e-naq tzam q'am karcha
kolo are oyew
kolo are achi ix ch-ø-ul sa-w-oq u-wach
ch-ø-ul-u mes-es-e-j
ch(i) u-pam wa u-nim-al tz'aq
wa u-nim-al k'oxtun
kolo are oyew ch-ø-ul ok-oq ji'-a-xel
baluk-i-xel
ch(i) u-pam u-nim-al tz'aq
ch(i) u-pam u-nim-al k'oxtun
we nima-nel
we oktisan-el
we ch-u-me(j) r-ib
we ch-u-me(j) u-wach
ta ch-ø-ok ul-oq
ka-ø-cha k'u ri nu-tzij ch(i) u-wach kaj
ch(i) u-wach ulew
keje kaj
ulew chi-k'oji' uk' la
u-q'alel achi
rabinal achi

---

191. This way in which Job Toj refers to his own wife is similar to the way those who are currently responsible in religious confraternities (*cofradías*) today speak of their own: a wife of *qajawxel* is, for him as for all of the group, a *chuchuxel*, a "mother." The term used here, however, is not the Quiché term (*chuch*) but the equivalent Cakchiquel (or Tzutujil) term (*te*), unknown by my translators. According to Varea (n.d.: fol. 277), this term—a title in the present context—specifically designated in these languages the mother and the sister of the mother and, by extension, all married women. Thus, more than this reverential formula, it is the use of this particular term that raises questions: is this usage to be considered only a simple fact of language (an archaism)? or does it indicate that the ally—the queen in this case—is from Cakchiquel (or Chakach, see note 48 of the introduction) origin?

192. The verbal root *sa* (which appears in the forms *sawoq*, *sawa*, and *sayom*) means "to expose something to the sun, to fire, to the air, to dry it out." Associated with the object *wach* (or *chi'*), it is translated in all the dictionaries as "to use or to consume for the first time" (see Glossary).

193. The verb *mesesej* is formed by the duplication of the root *mes*, which refers to different actions implying a horizontal movement of the hand or of an object, such as

the handiwork of my "mother"[191]
of my queen!
Perhaps this angry one
perhaps this man will come and use them for the first time![192]

Here also is enclosed the Mother of the Quetzal
the Mother of the Green Feathers,
having come from Tzam Q'am Karcha!
Perhaps this angry one
perhaps this man will come to use her for the first time
will come and take her for a walk[193]
inside the great fortress
inside the great wall!
Perhaps this angry one will enter as a son-in-law
as a brother-in-law
inside the great fortress
inside the great wall!
If he is obedient
if he is gracious[194]
if he bends,
if he bends his face,
then let him come in!
So says my word facing the sky
facing the earth!
May the sky
and the earth remain with You
—Dignitary
Rabinal Achi!»

"to sweep," "to raze, to level," and "to caress the head of someone" as a sign of affection or to stroke him (see Glossary). The figure of the "Mother of the Quetzal Mother of the Green Feathers" is the symbol of alliance; she names a plural entity—women and objects (feathers)—who symbolizes the matrimonial relationships most likely joining the nobles of Rabinal to the women of Carchá; she designates wives, real or potential, of the great warriors and, first of all, according to the epigraph, that of Rabinal Achi (see lines 15–19). The woman and the objects of which she is the holder—the "guardian," according to some—are consubstantial: to consent to use for the first time and to walk (i.e., to make dance) the feathers amount to accepting the alliance. The lines that follow explicitly confirm the equation established symbolically between dancing and joining together.

194. This term, which Tirado (1787: fol. 30) translates as "bebedor," might derive from the Nahuatl root *octli,* defined as "pulque, vino, licor fermentado del maguey" (Siméon 1986: 354), that Cakchiquel, for example, transforms into *ucti* (Coto 1983: 328). It is understood today as "the one who agrees to drink" but also, more generally, as "the one who accepts an invitation or an offer."

u-lajuj-mul ka-ø-ch'aw-ik rabinal achi

ajaw {o}job toj
ki yux-ta-j ta ba la ch(i) u-wach kaj
c[h(i)] u-wach ulew
ka-ø-cha ba ri nu-tzij chi-ech la
are ta ba wa nu-ko-w-il
w-achi-j-il-al
ya-om la
jet-e-sa-m la ch(i)-w-e chi nu-chi'
[fol. 39] chi nu-wach
ch-in-kan-a-j ta na ba la wa r-al nu-ch'ab
wa r-al nu-pokob
chi k'u ta na ba la
chi tz'ap-i-j ta na ba la
ch(i) u-pam u-chuy-al
u-paq'-abal
ch-ø-uxla-n ta na
xa wi ta k-in-uxla-n-ik
r-umal k'ut k'o qa-war-am
maja-bi qa-yakal-em r-uk'
keje k'ut ka-nu-kan-a-j kan-oq
ch(i) u-pam u-nim-al tz'aq
u-nim-al k'oxtun
ka-ø-cha k'u ri nu-tzij ch(i) u-wach kaj
ch(i) u-wach ulew
kaj
ulew chi-k'oji' uk' la
lal w-ajaw-al
nu-winaq-il
ajaw {o}job toj

u-ka-mul ka-ø-[ch'a]w-ik ajaw {o}job toj

w-oyew-al-al
w-achi-j-il-al
la ka-ø-cha na k'u ri tzij la ch(i) u-wach kaj
ch(i) u-wach ulew

---

195. The root *yux* is common to different verbs meaning "to bend, to lower, to incline, to nod one's head."

196. In order to maintain the balance of the pair and the equivalency of its terms, I render *chuyal* as "reserve," knowing that this word has the limited and more technical

Rabinal Achi speaks for the tenth time.

«King Job Toj!
May You be honored[195] facing the sky
facing the earth!
My word says this to You then:
Here is the firmness that is mine
my strength,
given by You,
conveyed by You, to me, to my mouth
[fol. 39] to my face!
I leave You this child of my bow
this child of my shield!
Keep them, then,
shut them up then
in the storehouse
the repository![196]
Let them rest
as I shall rest
because we are indeed exhausted
we have had no rest with him!
So I abandon them
in the great fortress
the great wall!
So says my word facing the sky
facing the earth!
May the sky
and the earth remain with You!
You, my master
my eminence,
King Job Toj!»

King Job Toj speaks for the second time.

«My angry one,
my warrior!
What says Your word facing the sky
facing the earth?

---

meaning of "sheath, envelope, case, quiver," and possibly "box" or "chest" (Basseta 1698: fol. 184). The meaning of the second term, *paq'abal,* is established as a place where one puts separately, where one relegates, or where one puts away, following Coto (1983: 38), "pacbal: apartamiento," and Basseta (1698: fol. 210), "paƐaba: arrimar."

are ba wa nu-ko-w-il
wa w-achi-j-il-al
wa r-al nu-ch'ab
wa r-al nu-pokob
ya-om la
jet-e-sa-m la chi nu-chi'
chi nu-wach
ka-nu-kan-a-j ta ba kan-oq
chi k'u ta na ba la
chi tz'ap-i-j ta na ba la
ch(i) u-pam u-nim-al tz'aq
k'oxtun
ch(i) u-pam u-chuy-al
u-paq'-abal
la ka-ø-cha na k'u ri tzij la
la julacha ix ch-in-k'u
ix ch-in-tz'ap-i-j
[fol. 40] ch(i) u-pam u-chuy-al
ch(i) u-pam u-paq'-abal
naqabi k'u ri ri{to} to-bal la
ch(i) u-wach la xul-a-n ul-oq
la paq-a-l ul-oq
ch(i) u-jolom ulew
chi r-aqan ulew
naqabi chi k'u ri ri to-bal la
[ch(i)] u-wi chi-k-e ri q-al
qa-k'ajol
ri ki-el ubi ch(i) u-wi ki-tzuku-n-ik
ki-kajale-n-ik
chi kaj pa
chi kaj xukut-al
are na k'u ri ju-mul chik
ka-mul chik
ka-yak[-a]-n ubi la wa ko-w-il la
wa achi-j-il-al la
wa r-al ch'ab la
wa r-al pokob la
wa nu-ya-om chi-ech la w-oyew-al-al
w-achi-j-il-al
u-q'alel achi
rabinal achi

197. In other words, "What will be Your means of defense against the threats coming from the west and the east of the territory?"

"Here is this firmness that is mine
my strength,
the child of my bow
the child of my shield,
given by You,
conveyed by You, to me, to my mouth
to my face!
I give them up!
Keep them, then,
shut them up then
inside the great citadel,

inside the storehouse
the repository!"
Is this what Your word says?
Why should I keep them
shut them up
[fol. 40] inside the storehouse
inside the repository?
How will You manage
against what comes down
what goes up
from the head of the earth
from the feet of the earth?[197]
And by what means will You watch over them,
our children,

who have gone out questing
gone out searching[198]
in the four directions
in the four corners?
And one more time
a second time
You will display this firmness that is Yours
this warlike zeal
this child of Your bow
this child of Your shield,
that I hand over to You, You my anger
my strength
—Dignitary
Rabinal Achi!

198. Or "What will be Your means to assist and protect our men when they leave to hunt, to gather . . . ?"

keje kaj
ulew chi-k'oji' uk' la

ju-lajuj[-mul] ka-ø-ch'aw-ik rabinal achi

utz keje ba la
we x ch-in-yak chi nu-bi[199] wa nu-ko-w-il
wa w-achi-j-il-al
ya-om la
jet-e-sa-m la chi nu-chi'
chi nu-wach
keje k'ut ka-nu-yak chi nu-bi ju-mul chik
ka-mul chik
ka-ø-cha k'u ri nu-tzij ch(i) u-wach kaj
ch(i) u-wach ulew
keje k'ut ka-nu-kan-a-j kan la
waral ch(i) u-pam u-nim-al tz'aq
u-nim-al k'oxtun
kaj
ulew chi-k'oji' uk' la
lal w-ajaw-al
nu-winaq-il
ajaw {o}job toj

[fol. 41] *[u-]rox-mul ka-ø-ch'aw-ik ajaw {o}job toj*

utz ba la w-oyew-al-al
w-achi-j-il-al
ban-al ta ba la
ma paj taj la
ma sok-o taj la w-oyew-al-al
w-achi-j-il-al
u-q'alel achi
rabinal achi
kaj
ulew chi-k'oji' uk' la

199. Literally, "in my possession."

May the sky
and the earth remain with You!»

Rabinal Achi speaks for the eleventh time.

«Well, if it be so,
I will take back this firmness that is mine
this strength that is mine,
given by You
attributed by You to my mouth
to my face!
And so I will take them back one more time
a second time!
So says my word facing the sky
facing the earth!
With this, I leave You
here, in the great fortress
the great wall!
May the sky
and the earth remain with You,
You, my master
my eminence,
King Job Toj!»

[fol. 41] *King Job Toj speaks for the third time.*

«It is well, my anger
my strength,
do so then!
Do not stumble,
do not wound Yourself, my anger
my strength,
—Dignitary
Rabinal Achi!
May the sky
and the earth remain with You!»

U-ROX BAN-BAL

u-kab-lajuj-mul ka-ø-ch'aw-ik rabinal achi

k-u-k'am-a k'iche' achi
xim-i-l-ik k'iche' achi[200]

eja
oyew achi
kaweq k'iche' winaq
ki ba in wa mi x-in-yo'pi-sa-j la
ch(i) u-pam u-nim-al tz'aq
u-nim-al k'oxtun
ch(i) u-wach w-ajaw-al
nu-winaq-il
keje k'ut mi x-ø-cha ul-oq w-ajaw-al
nu-winaq-il
chi pixab-a-j ta k'u lo la ri oyew
ri achi
ma ta chi t'il-il-ik
ma ta chi boj-oj-ik
xa ta ch-u-me(j) r-ib
ch-u-me(j)-ta u-wach
ta ch-ø-ok ul-oq ch(i) u-chi' u-nim-al tz'aq
[fol. 42] k'oxtun
waral ch(i) u-xmut kaj
ch(i) u-xmut ulew
r-umal waral loq'-o-x-el
mayi-j-a-x-el
ch(i) u-pam u-nim-al tz'aq
u-nim-al k'oxtun
waral tz'aqat
mol-a-j u-pam u-nim-al tz'aq
u-nim-al k'oxtun
k'o-l-ik kab-lajuj r-atz
kab-lajuj u-chaq'
e aj-pwaq-i-nel
aj-xit-a-nel
maja k-e-tz'aqat ki-chi'
ki-wach

200. This phrase is not spoken by Rabinal Achi, as the manuscript implies, but specifies his action at the moment when Act III begins and when he starts speaking again. Thus, this line logically should have been separated from the beginning of the dialogue, as with line 1353 at the beginning of Act II.

ACT THREE

Rabinal Achi speaks for the twelfth time.

He goes to seek K'iche' Achi;
K'iche' Achi is attached.

«Eha!
Angry man,
Kaweq K'iche'!
So it is. I have announced You
inside the great fortress
the great wall,
to the face of my master
to the face of my eminence!
This is what my master
my eminence had me say:
"Advise the angry one
the man
not to gesticulate
not to vociferate
but only to bend
that his face be bent
as he crosses the threshold of the great citadel,

[fol. 42]

here, at the navel of the sky
at the navel of the earth!
For here he will be appreciated
and admired
in the great fortress
the great wall,
here he will be well maintained
and well supplied in the great fortress
the great wall!
For his twelve elder brothers are here
his twelve younger brothers,
those who are bearers of metal,
bearers of jewels,
whose number is still incomplete!

kolo are oyew
kolo are achi ix ch-ø-ul ok-oq ki-tz'aqat
ki-mol-a-j
xa wi ki waral k'o-l-ik kab-lajuj u-q'an-al kot
u-q'an-al balam
xa wi ma ba k-e-tz'aqat ki-chi'
ki-wach
kolo are oyew
kolo achi ch-ø-ul ok-oq ki-tz'aqat
xa wi ki waral k'o-l-ik pwaq-im tem
pwaq-im ch'akat
pwaq-im kubul-ibal
kolo are oyew
kolo achi ix ch-ø-ul kubul-i-be-n-oq
xa wi waral k'u-l wi tz'ap-i-l-ik ri u-chuch q'uq'
u-chuch rax-on
ri yamani[k]
{i}xtekoq-ib ri pe-t-e-naq tzam q'am karcha
k'o sa-y-om u-chi'
maja-bi sa-y-om u-wach
kolo are oyew
kolo are achi ch-ø-ul sa-w-a u-chi'
u-wach
xa wi ki waral k'o-l-ik ri kab-lajuj u-ki'-ya'
ri kab-lajuj u-matul
ri k-e ka-ø-silil-ik
ri k-e ka-ø-t'ir-ir-ik
r(i) u-ki'-ya' ajaw
ch(i) u-pam u-nim-al tz'aq
u-nim-al k'oxtun
kolo are oyew
kolo are achi ch-ø-ul tij-o-w-oq
xa wi ki waral k'o-l-ik laq'an u-q'in
k'oxaj u-wa' ri ki-kalatz'
ka-ø-ban-ik u-ban-om nu-te
nu-xoq'ojaw
kolo are oyew
kolo are achi ch-ø-ul sa-w-a u-wach
xa wi ki waral ix ch-ø-ul ok-oq ji'-a-xel
[fol. 43] baluk-i-xel
waral ch(i) u-pam u-nim-al tz'aq
u-nim-al k'oxtun

Perhaps this angry one,
perhaps this man will come to complete their number
to join them!
Here also, it is true, are the twelve Yellow Eagles
the twelve Yellow Jaguars,
whose number is likewise incomplete!

Perhaps this angry one,
perhaps this man will come to complete their number!
Here also are the metal benches
the metal thrones
the metal seats!
Perhaps this angry one,
perhaps this man will come to settle there!
Also enclosed here is the Mother of the Quetzal
the Mother of the Green Feathers,
the Gems
the Precious Stones, come from Tzam Q'am Karcha!
Some have been used,
others have never been used![201]
Perhaps this angry one,
perhaps this man will come to use them for the first time!

Here also are the twelve liquors
the twelve poisonous drinks
those that chill
those that paralyze,
– the King's liquors –
inside the great fortress
the great wall!
Perhaps this angry one,
perhaps this man will come to taste them!
Here also are weavings with double warp
and single woof,
the handiwork of my "mother"
of my queen!
Perhaps this angry one,
perhaps this man will come and use them for the first time!
So would he surely enter here as a son-in-law
[fol. 43] *as a brother-in-law,*
here, inside the great fortress
the great wall!"

201. This passage shows that the green feathers (stones) are a synecdoche for their representative, for their guardian (see note 193).

mi x-ø-cha ul-oq w-ajaw-al
nu-winaq-il
keje k'ut ix ch-in-pixab-a-j ta k'u bi la
ma ta chi t'il-il la
ma ta chi boj-oj la
ta ch-ok apan la ch(i) u-chi' u-nim-al tz'aq
u-nim-al k'oxtun
chi me(j)-ta ib la
chi xuk-ta ib la
ta ch-ok apan la ch(i) u-wach w-ajaw-al
nu-winaq-il
mam-a ajaw {o}job toj
ka-ø-cha k'u ri nu-tzij ch(i) u-wach kaj
ch(i) u-wach ulew
keje ma wi k'i-a-tzij k-oj-tzij-o-n-ik
kaj
ulew chi-k'oji' uk' la
kaweq k'iche' winaq

u-belej-mul ka-ø-ch'aw-ik k'iche' achi

eja
oyew achi
rabinal achi
la ka-ø-cha na k'u ri tzij la ch(i) u-wach kaj
ch(i) u-wach ulew
mi x-in-yo'pi-sa-j la tzij-o-x-ik la
ch(i) u-wach w-ajaw-al
ch(i) u-wach nu-winaq-il
ch(i) u-pam u-nim-al tz'aq
u-nim-al k'oxtun
ka-ø-cha ri nu-tzij
keje k'ut chi pixab-a-j ta lo la ri oyew
ri achi
chi koj ta na lo la chi nu-chi'
chi nu-wach
ch(i) u-chi' u-nim-al tz'aq
ka-nw-il na u-chi'
ka-nw-il na u-wach
janik' pa chi oyew
janik' pa chi achi
chi pixab-a-j ta lo la

That is what my master
my eminence had me say!
Accordingly, I advise You:
do not gesticulate
do not vociferate
as You cross the threshold of the great fortress
the great wall!
Bend down
kneel down
as You enter the presence of my master
of my eminence,
the great King Job Toj!
So says my word facing the sky
facing the earth!
And we have nothing more to say to each other!
May the sky
and the earth remain with You
—Kaweq K'iche'!»

K'iche' Achi speaks for the ninth time.

«Eha!
Angry man,
Rabinal Achi!
What says Your word facing the sky
facing the earth?
"I have delivered the information concerning You
facing my master
facing my eminence,
inside the great fortress
the great wall.
And so says my word:[202]
go then, inform the angry one
the man;
bring him in, in front of my mouth
in front of my face,
on the threshold of the great fortress
that I may see his mouth
that I may see his face,
how angry he is
how much a man he is!
Advise him

---

202. K'iche' Achi repeats here the words that Job Toj spoke to Rabinal Achi.

ma ta chi t'il-il-ik
ma ta chi boj-oj-ik
ta ch-ø-ok ul-oq chi nu-chi'
chi nu-wach
ch-u-me(j)-ta r-ib
[fol. 44] ch-u-me(j) u-wach
we are oyew
we are achi
we nima-nel
we oktisa-nel
r-umal waral loq'-o-x-el
mayi-j-a-x-el
ch(i) u-pam u-nim-al tz'aq
ch(i) u-pam u-nim-al k'oxtun
mi x-ø-cha ul-oq w-ajaw-al
nu-winaq-il
la ka-ø-cha ri tzij la
la in k'[o] jun chi oyew
la in k'[o] ju[n] chi achi k'u ri
we xa x ch-in-me(j) w-ib
we x ch-in-me(j) nu-wach
k'o ba la wa nu-me(j)-bal w-ib
k'o ba la wa r-al nu-ch'ab
wa r-al nu-pokob
r-uk' wa nu-yak-im w-ikaj
are nu-me(j)-bal w-ib
wa nu-xuk-u-l-ibal wa
mi x k-in-ok apan-oq ch(i) u-chi' u-nim-al tz'aq
u-nim-al k'oxtun
ka-r-aj k'ut xa x ch-in-qa-sa-j u-nim-al u-q'ij
r-ala-x-ik
ajaw-al la
winaq-il [la]
ka-r-aj x ch-in-kewi-j r-ikem u-chi'
r-ajsik u-chi'
ch(i) u-pam u-nim-al tz'aq
u-nim-al k'oxtun
ki ta na pe ka-tij la ri oyew achi
u-q'alel achi
rabinal achi

203. I am translating literally an expression that means "upset destiny" or "shatter the name" and which dictionaries generally render as "to defeat."

204. Ximénez (1985: 483) defines *queuo* as "andar dando de codo"; according to Coloch, this verb means "to mistreat" or "to strike."

not to gesticulate
not to vociferate
as he enters in front of my mouth
in front of me!
Let him bend
[fol. 44] *let him bend his face!*
If he is valiant
if he is a man
if he is obedient
if he is willing,
then he will be appreciated
he will be admired here
inside the great fortress
inside the great wall!"
This is what my master
my eminence had me say!"
Is that what Your word says?
Would I still be valiant,
would I still be a man
if I bent down
if I bent my face?
Rather, here is what I will "bend"!
Here is the child of my bow
here is the child of my shield,
and my brandished ax!
Here's what my "submission" will be,
here's what my "kneeling" will be
as I cross the threshold of the great fortress
the great wall!
And as for Your master
Your eminence,
if only I might crush the grandeur of his days
of his birth![203]
If only I might damage[204] the bottom of his mouth
the top of his mouth
inside the great fortress
the great wall!
But first, You will have a taste of this![205] – Angry man,
Dignitary
Rabinal Achi!»

205. Coloch renders this expression as "Mientras tanto . . . ¡Buen provecho!" (see note 188); it corresponds to the moment in the dance when K'iche' Achi lunges at Rabinal Achi to strike him with his ax.

ixoq mun ka-ø-ch'aw-ik

oyew achi
kaweq k'iche' winaq
ma la kam-i-sa-j la w-oyew-el-al
w-achi-j-il-al
u-q'alel achi
rabinal achi

U-KAJ BAN-BAL

[fol. 45] *u-lajuj-mul ka-ø-ch'aw-ik k'iche' achi*

ka-ø-k'ul-u-n ch(i) u-wach ajaw {o}job toj

kala achi
ki ba in wa mi x-ø-yo'pi-ta-j ul-oq
ch(i) u-chi' u-nim-al tz'aq
ch(i) u-chi' u-nim-al k'oxtun
lal ajaw-ar-inaq wi
lal muj-ar-inaq wi
mi x-ø-ul yo'pi-sa-x-a k'ut nu-tzij-o-x-ik
chi chi' la
chi wach la
in oyew
in achi
r-umal mi x-ø-cha apan-oq
ri ye-bal la
ri sik'-ibal la oyew-al-al la
achi-j-il-al la
u-q'alel achi
rabinal achi chi nu-chi'
chi nu-wach
mi x-ø-yo'pi-sa-x k'ut nu-tzij-o-x-ik
chi wach la lal w-ajaw-al
nu-winaq-il
ch(i) u-pam u-nim-al tz'aq
mi x-ø-cha ul-oq u-tzij w-ajaw-al
nu-winaq-il

Ixoq Mun speaks:

«Angry man,
Kaweq K'iche'!
Do not kill my anger
my strength,
—Dignitary
Rabinal Achi!»

ACT FOUR

[fol. 45] *K'iche' Achi speaks for the tenth time.*

He is in front of King Job Toj.

«Hail Man!
I am indeed the one who introduced himself
at the threshold of the great fortress
at the threshold of the great wall,
—You who are enthroned here,
You who are sheltered here!
The information concerning me had just been reported to You[206]

—I who am angry,
I who am a man—
according to
the exhortation
the cry of Your anger
of Your strength
—Dignitary
Rabinal Achi—to my mouth
to my face!
Having been reported the information concerning me
before You, my master
my eminence
inside the great fortress,
the word of my master
of my eminence said:

206. To lighten this phrase, which the formal discourse renders as extremely convoluted, I have distilled the expression *chi chi' la chi wach la* ("to your mouth, to your face") to "You."

chi koj ta na ba lo la ri oyew
ri achi
chi nu-chi'
chi nu-wach
ka-nw-il na u-chi'
ka-nw-il na u-wach
janik' pa chi oyew
janik' pa chi achi
ix chi pixab-a-j ta lo la ri oyew
ri achi
ma ta chi t'il-il-ik
ma ta chi boj-oj-ik
ch-u-me(j)-ta r-ib
ch-u-me(j)-ta u-wach
ta ch-ø-ok ul-oq ch(i) u-chi' u-nim-al tz'aq
ch(i) u-chi' u-nim-al k'oxtun
[fol. 46] mi x-ø-cha apan-oq ri ye-bal la
ri-sik'-ibal la
r-umal achi-j-il-al la chi nu-chi'
chi nu-wach
la in k'o jun chi achi
oyew k'u ri
we ch-ø-ul nu-me(j)-a w-ib
we ch-ø-ul nu-me(j)-a nu-wach
k'o ba la wa nu-me(j)-[ba]l w-ib
are ba wa nu-me(j)-bal w-ib
wa r-al nu-ch'ab
wa r-al nu-pokob
xa k'u ch-ø-ul nu-qa-sa-j q'ij la
ala-x-ik la
ch-ø-ul nu-kewi-j r-ikem chi' la
r-ajsik chi' la
ki ta na pe ka-tij la lal ajaw

ixoq mun ka-mul ka-ø-ch'aw-ik

oyew achi
kaweq k'iche' winaq
ma la kam-i-sa-j w-ajaw-al
nu-winaq-il
ajaw {o}job toj ch(i) u-pam u-nim-al tz'aq
ch(i) u-pam u-nim-al k'oxtun
k'u-l wi
tz'ap-i-l wi

"Have him come in, then, the angry one
the man
before my mouth
before my face,
that I may see his mouth
that I may see his face
how angry he is
how much of a man!
And advise him well, the angry one
the man,
not to gesticulate,
not to vociferate!
Have him bend down
have him bend his face down
as he crosses the threshold of the great fortress
the threshold of the great wall!"
[fol. 46] That is what Your exhortation
Your cry caused to be said
by Your warrior, in front of my mouth
in front of me!
Would I still be a man
an angry one in fact
if I had just bent down
if I had just bent my face?
Here is what I will "bend" instead:
this is what I will "bend" with,
this child of my bow
this child of my shield!
And I have come only to crush the grandeur of Your days
of Your birth!
I have come to damage the top of Your mouth
the bottom of Your mouth.
And first of all, You will have a taste of this! Oh You, King!»

Ixoq Mun speaks for the second time.

«Angry man,
Kaweq K'iche'!
Do not kill my master
my eminence,
King Job Toj, in the great fortress
in the great wall
where he is guarded
where he is enclosed!»

u-ju-lajuj-mul ka-ø-ch'aw-ik k'iche' achi

keje k'ut chi qibi-sa-j ta k'u lo la ri nu-tem
ri nu-ch'akat
r-umal are ri chi nu-juyub-al
chi nu-taq'aj-al
paq-a-ba-m [nu]-q'ij
[fol. 47] paq-a-ba-m w-ala-x-ik
k'o nu-tem
k'o nu-ch'akat
naqi k-in-paba-x taj ch(i) u-wach tew
naqi k-in-paba-x taj ch(i) u-wach joron
ka-ø-cha k'u ri nu-tzij ch(i) u-wach kaj
ch(i) u-wach ulew
kaj
ulew chi-k'oji' uk' la
mam-a ajaw {o}job toj

u-kaj-mul ka-ø-ch'aw-ik ajaw {o}job toj

oyew achi
kaweq k'iche' winaq
k'amo chi-r-ech kaj
k'amo chi-r-ech ulew
mi x-yo'pi-ta-j k'u lo la
ch(i) u-pam u-nim-al tz'aq
ch(i) u-pam u-nim-al k'oxtun
in ajaw-ar-inaq wi
in muj-ar-inaq wi
in mam-a ajaw {o}job toj
keje k'ut chi tzij-o-n ta k'u la
chi cha ta k'u la
r-umal xa pe xa lal ri k-ø-ul ban-a la
r-oq'-ibal utiw
r-oq'-ibal yak
r-oq'-ibal utuy
jalaw
chi-r-ij la u-nim-al tz'aq
la u-nim-al k'oxtun

207. The glosses relating to the verb *paba* form a series that is relatively close to the double meaning of the French verb *prévenir* ("to warn, to prevent"): they imply both the idea of "warning" (*pabaxic* is given as a synonym of *pixabaxic* by Coto [1983: 39]) and that

K'iche' Achi speaks for the eleventh time.

«Then approach my throne
my seat
for in my mountains
in my valleys
my days are highly valued
[fol. 47] my birth is highly valued!
I have my throne there
I have my seat there!
Am I not kept from the wind,
am I not kept from the cold?[207]
So says my word facing the sky
facing the earth!
May the sky
and the earth remain with You
—Great King Job Toj!»

King Job Toj speaks for the fourth time.

«Angry man,
Kaweq K'iche'!
Thanks to the sky
thanks to the earth,
You have reached
the interior of the great fortress
the interior of the great wall
where I have been enthroned
where I am sheltered by the dais,
I, the great King Job Toj!
So relate,
say
why You, and only You, came to imitate
the crying of the coyote
the crying of the wildcat
the groaning of the *tepescuintle*

behind the great fortress
the great wall,

of "prevention" (Ximénez 1985: 140). Through them we once again see the indigenous conception of a reclusive authority, sheltered and protected, and which Varea (n.d.: fol. 253) confirms with this definition: "paba: poner en señorío o oficio o dignidad."

chi-r-ech ki-boy-e-x-ik
chi-r-ech ki-k'ak'ale-x-ik
xa wi chi-r-ech k-el-e-sa-x-ik ri saq-il al
ri saq-il k'ajol
ri e-q-el-e-sa-[m] bi
ch(i) u-wach la u-nim-al tz'aq
k'oxtun
ch(i) u-pam ixim-che'
e-tzuku-y r-e
e-kajale-y r-e u-chikop-il q'an-a kab
rax-a kab
[fol. 48] tzuq-bal w-e
in mam-a ajaw {o}job toj
ch(i) u-pam u-nim-al tz'aq
u-nim-al k'oxtun
xa wi ki lal mi x-e-tzele-j-e-be-j la belej-eb
lajuj saq-il al
saq-il k'ajol
xa sk'aqin chi r-aj
ma na x-e-opon taj chila k'iche' j(u)yub
we ma ta ja bi ri w-oyew-al-al
w-achi-j-il-al
x-u-b{u}[208] u-tzel-e-j ta wach-i-j ul-oq
qatz chila ka-ø-ch'ay wi la ki-wix-al
ki-ku{i}tam-il ri saq-il al
ri saq-il k'ajol

xa wi ki lal mi x-ø-ul el-e-sa-j ri w-ajaw-al
ri nu-winaq-il
chiri ch(i)-atin-ibal
xa wi k'u are mi x-in-yak bi la
ch(i) u-pam r-al ch'ab la
mi x-in-e[209]-tz'ap-i-j la
ch(i) u-pam aq'am chun
sa[q] kab-ij la w-ij
nu-wach
chila k'iche' j(u)yub
k'iche' taq'aj
xa wi qatz chila
ka-k'is wi la u-ch'ay-ik nu-wix-al
nu-kutam-il

208. This form has not been clarified: it might result from a muting of the verbal syntagm *x-u-b[an]* ("he did / he made").

so as to attract
so as to surprise,
and also so as to abduct the white children

that we sent out
in front of the great citadel

in the corn tree,
those who look for
and seek the flies of yellow honey
of green honey,
[fol. 48] my own food,
—I, the great King Job Toj
in the great fortress
the great wall!
Truly, You have brought back the nine
the ten white children!

But it wouldn't have taken much
for them to have reached, over there, the K'iche' mountains!
If it hadn't been for my anger
my warrior
to make them return and reappear,
it is certain that, over there, the white children's roots
the white children's trunk
would have been struck!

It was also You who came to abduct my sovereign self
my person
there, at Chatinibal,
and You who took me away
in the child of Your bow,
who shut me up
in bitter lime,
sealing up my back
my front,
there, in the K'iche' mountains
the K'iche' valleys!
It is equally certain that
You would have finished by striking my roots
my trunk

---

209. According to Coloch, the particle *-e* is emphatic; it would place the accent on the fact that "me" is really the victim of the action, thereby making up for the ambiguity of the phrase *x-in-tz'apij la,* translatable as both "You have enclosed me" as well as "I have enclosed You."

chila k'iche' j(u)yub
k'iche' taq'aj
are k'u ri r-umal k'o-l-ik w-oyew-al
w-achi-j-il-al
u-q'alel achi
rabinal achi
mi x-in-r-el-e-sa-j chi wi ul-oq
mi x-in-u-lot'-ot'-e-j chi wi ul-oq
ch(i) u-pam r-al u-ch'ab
ch(i) u-pam r-al u-pokob
we ma w-oyew-al-al
w-achi-j-il-al
qatz chila ka-ø-ch'ay wi nu-wix-al
nu-kutam-il
are k'u ri mi x-[i]n-ul u-jet-e-sa-j chik
ch(i) u-pam u-nim-al tz'aq
k'oxtun
[fol. 49] xa wi ki lal mi x-e-k'is la ka-ib

ox-ib u-q'ab amaq'
siwa[n]
tinamit
chiri balam-wak
chi-tin-t-ot wi poqlaj
chi-k'ar[kar]axaj
chi-kunu
chi-q'os-ibal taq'aj tulul ch(i) u-ch[a]-x-ik
la janik' pa k'ut
ma wi k-ø-ek'ow-ik r-aj-abal k'ux la
chi-r-ech wa oyew-al
wa achi-j-il-al
la julacha mi x-yak chu lo la[210]
mi x-silibi-sa-j chu lo la
ma pa chila mi x-ø-bek u-muq-ik
u-pis-ik wa-oyew-al
wa achi-j-il-al
chila chi-k'ot-om
chi-tikram
ma pa belej-eb moqoj
belej-eb chumay

---

210. I am interpreting this phrase as *la julacha mi x-yak ch[ik k']u lo la* ("But why have You brandished it again?"). Coloch comments in fact on this passage as referring to comparable actions led in vain by the Quiché and to the defeats that the Rabinaleb inflicted on them in more ancient times but whose lessons were not learned.

over there, in the K'iche' mountains
the K'iche' valleys!
It was for this reason that my angry one
my warrior
—the Dignitary
Rabinal Achi—
delivered me
brought me back, carrying me in his arms,
in the child of his bow
in the child of his shield!
If my anger
my force had not been there,
it is certain that my roots
my trunk would have been struck!
And in this way he came to settle me
within the great citadel!

[fol. 49] It is also true that it was You who destroyed
[two
three settlements,
villages
and hamlets including:
there in Balamwak,
Chi Tintot Wi Poqlaj
Chi K'arkaraxaj
Chi Kunu
Chi Q'osibal Taq'aj Tulul, as they are called!
And how many more
to let pass Your heart's desire
for this anger
this force?
Why have You brandished it
have You exalted it?
Was it not over there that this anger
this force went to bury itself
to inter itself,
over there, in Chi K'otom
in Chi Tikram?
Was it not at Belejeb Moqoj
Belejeb Chumay

mi x-ø-bek u-muq-ik
u-pis-ik wa oyew-al
wa achi-j-il-al
mi x-qa-ban-o oj r-ajaw-al
oj [u]-winaq-il
u-pam ju-jun chi tz'aq
chi k'oxtun
are na k'u ch-ø-ul toj-or-i-sa-j la ri
waral ch(i) u-xmut kaj
ch(i) u-xmut ulew
keje k'ut mi x-pixab chi n[a] ta kan la
chi juyub-al la
chi taq'aj-al la
qatz k'u are lal kam-el
lal sach-el
waral ch(i) u-xmut kaj
ch(i) u-xmut ulew
keje kaj
ulew chi-k'oji' uk' la
kaweq k'iche' winaq

u-kab-lajuj mul ka-ø-ch'aw-ik k'iche' achi

[fol. 50] ajaw {o}job toj
ki yux-ta-j ta ba la ch(i) u-wach kaj
ch(i) u-wach ulew
qatz ba r-e tzij
qatz ba r-e pixab mi x-bix-ta-j la
ch(i) u-wach kaj
ch(i) u-wach ulew
qatz in x-in-mak-u-be-j
ka-ø-cha ri tzij la
mi x-e-ben-e-be-j la
mi x-e-tzel-e-j-e-be-j la ri saq-il al
ri saq-il k'ajol
ri e q-el-e-sa-m bi
e-tzuku-y r-e
e-kajale-y r-e u-chikop-il q'an-a kab
rax-a kab
tzuq-bal w-e
in mam-a ajaw {o}job toj
ch(i) u-pam u-nim-al tz'aq
ch(i) u-pam u-nim-al k'oxtun
ka-ø-cha ri tzij la
xa sk'aqin x-in-mak-u-be-j
r-umal u-k'oq-obal nu-k'ux

that this anger
this force went to bury itself
to inter itself?
It was we, the masters
the eminencies,
from inside each fortress
from inside each wall, who took this action.
And that is what You are going to pay for,
here, at the navel of the sky
at the navel of the earth!
So You have left Your recommendations
to Your mountains
to Your valleys;
it is certain that You are going to die
that You are going to disappear
here, at the navel of the sky
at the navel of the earth!
May the sky
and the earth remain with You
—Kaweq K'iche'!»

K'iche' Achi speaks for the twelfth time.

[fol. 50] «King Job Toj!
May You be honored facing the sky
facing the earth!
True are the words
true are the recommendations You have pronounced
facing the sky
facing the earth!
It is true that I have erred!
Your word says:
"You took the white children away

You brought them back,
those whom we sent out
to look for
and seek the flies of yellow honey
the flies of green honey,
my own food,
—I, the great King Job Toj
in the great fortress
the great wall!"
Your word says it:
I erred in part
because of the malevolence of my heart

r-umal ma na x-in-ech-a-be-n taj
chi-r-ech saq-il j(u)yub
saq-il taq'aj
waral ch(i) u-xmut kaj
ch(i) u-xmut ulew
xa wi ka-ø-cha ri tzij la
ta mi x-inw-el-e-sa-j bi la chiri ch(i)-atin-ibal
ma pa xa k-in-atin ukoq chiri ch(i)-atin-ibal
ka-ø-cha ri tzij la
xa wi qatz in x-in-mak-u-be-j
r-u[mal] u-k'oq-obal nu-k'ux
r-umal ma na x-in-ech-a-be-n taj
chi-r-ech saq-il j(u)yub
chi-r-ech saq-il taq'aj
waral ch(i) u-xmut kaj
ch(i) u-xmut ulew
xa wi ka-ø-cha ri tzij la
ix pixab chi n[a] ta kan la chi juyub-al la
chi taq'aj-al la
ka-ø-cha ri tzij la
[fol. 51] r-umal waral lal kam-el
lal sach-el
waral ka-qa-ch'ay wi wix-al la
kutam-il la
waral ch(i) u-xmut kaj
ch(i) u-xmut ulew
ka-ø-cha ri tzij la
qatz k'u in nu-mayi-j ri tzij
ri pixab
waral ch(i) u-wach kaj
ch(i) u-wach ulew
r-umal u-k'oq-obal nu-k'ux
we k'u qatz waral in kam-el
in sach-el
ka-ø-cha k'u ri nu-tzij chi chi' la
chi wach la
we k'u qatz lal tz'aqat
lal mol-a-j
ch(i) u-pam u-nim-al tz'aq
u-nim-al k'oxtu[n]
ch-in-qaj ta chi na ba chi-ech la ri wa'-bal la
ri ok-ibal la

for not having taken possession
of the white mountains
of the white valleys,
here, at the navel of the sky
at the navel of the earth.
And, as Your word also says,
for having abducted You, there, at Chatinibal:
"Was I not about to bathe at Chatinibal?"
as Your own word has it!
It is equally true that I erred
because of the malevolence of my heart,
for not having taken possession
of the white mountains
of the white valleys,
here, at the navel of the sky
at the navel of the earth!
As Your own word says:
"You have left Your recommendations to Your mountains
to Your valleys,"
You say,
[fol. 51] *"because here You are going to die*
You are going to disappear.
Here we are going to strike Your roots
Your trunk,
here, at the navel of the sky
at the navel of the earth!"
You say,
and it is true, that I spoke aggressively
I spoke destructively,[211]
here, facing the sky
facing the earth,
because of the malignancy of my heart!
And if it is true that here I am going to die
that here I am going to disappear . . .
—I say it to Your mouth
to Your face!—
. . . and if it is true that You are well supplied
that You are well maintained
inside the great fortress
the great wall,
then I will borrow from You Your plates
Your bowls:

211. I am keeping Coloch's translation, but this passage might simply mean "I denied" or, referring to recommendations of peace, "I violated the instructions."

r(i) u-ki'-ya' ajaw
ixtatz'unun u-bi
ri kab-lajuj u-ki'-ya'
kab-lajuj u-matul
ri k-e ka-ø-silil-ik
ka-ø-t'ir-ir-ik ki'-koj
kab-koj
ka-n-tij-o ul
k'amawar
ch(i) u-pam u-nim-al tz'aq
ch(i) u-pam u-nim-al k'oxtun
xa u-nima-bal nu-te
nu-xoq'ojaw
ch-in-tij ta na pe
xa ta nim-a r-eta-l-il u-wach nu-kam-ik
nu-sach-ik
waral ch(i) u-xmut kaj
ch(i) u-xmut ulew
ka-ø-cha k'u ri nu-tzij
keje kaj
ulew chi-k'oji' uk' la
ajaw {o}job toj

u-ro'-mul ka-ø-ch'aw-ik ajaw {o}job toj

oyew achi
kaweq k'iche' winaq
la ka-ø-cha na k'u ri a-tzij ch(i) u-wach kaj
ch(i) u-wach ulew
[fol. 52] chi ya ta chi ba la ch[i-]w-e ri wa'-bal la
ri ok-ibal la
ch-in-qaj ta na chi-ech la
ch-[i]n-tij ta na pe
ka-ø-cha ri tzij la
xa nim-a r-eta-l-il nu-kam-ik
nu-sach-ik

---

212. The confrontation between K'iche' Achi and Job Toj leads to the condemnation of the schemes of the accused. K'iche' Achi, by rejecting the conciliatory offers of his judge and by continuing with his provocations, fully accepts the fatal outcome (in fact, even demands it loud and clear). This passage's series of exchanges—from Job Toj's offers to K'iche' Achi's borrowings and returns—is inscribed in the procedure relating to the sacrifice of a man of high rank, a judicial and ritual procedure that is related to what we

the King's liquors
called Ixtatz'unun,
the twelve liquors
the twelve poisonous beverages,
those that chill
that paralyze, sugary
and honey-like at the same time,
that cause me to fall
to have visions,
inside the great fortress
the great wall!
Only the great offering of "my mother"
"my queen"
will I try,
as a presage of my death
of my disappearance,[212]
here, at the navel of the sky
at the navel of the earth!
So says my word!
May the sky
and the earth remain with You
—King Job Toj!»

King Job Toj speaks for the fifth time.

«Angry man,
Kaweq K'iche'!
What says thy word facing the sky
facing the earth?
[fol. 52] *"Give me then Your dishes*
Your bowls;
I will borrow them from You,
and I will taste them
—You say—
as a great sign of my death
of my loss!"

---

might call "the final wishes" and, in the present case, consists of the condemned experimenting with the offerings of his hosts before giving them back (while disparaging them). At the moment when this procedure begins, the warning, through which K'iche' Achi asserts as the single valid offer that of "his queen," is understood as the announcement of a systematic rejection of what Job Toj might propose to him, favoring only what he has from his own queen, that is, equivalent goods coming from "his" mountains.

k'o-l-ik ka-nu-yo'o[213]
ka-n-jet-e-sa-j chi-ech la

achi-j mun
ixoq mun ch-a-k'am-a ul-oq ri nu-wa'-bal
ri nu-ok-ibal
ch-a-ya-a chi-r-e ri oyew achi
kaweq k'iche' winaq
xa nim-a r-eta-l-il u-kam-ik
u-sach-ik
waral ch(i) u-xmut kaj
ch(i) u-xmut ulew

... *mun...*

utz ba la w-ajaw-al
nu-winaq-il
ka-nu-ya-o chi-r-e ri oyew achi

ri ba la oyew achi
kaweq k'iche' winaq
tij-a na pe la ri [u-]wa'-bal
r-ok-ibal w-ajaw-al
nu-winaq-il
mam-a ajaw {o}job toj
ch(i) u-pam u-nim-al tz'aq
k'u-l wi
tz'ap-i-l wi w-ajaw-al
nu-winaq-il
oyew achi

u-rox-lajuj-mul ka-ø-ch'aw-ik k'iche' achi

eja
ajaw {o}job toj
la e wa'-bal la
wa ok-ibal la wa
qatz ma wi wa k'o ch-u-bi'i-j la chi nu-chi'
chi nu-wach
are ta na pe ka-tij la ri w-e k'o chi nu-juyub-al
[fol. 53] chi nu-taq'aj-al

---

213. Irregular form of *ya* ("to give").

I have what is needed to give
to offer You!»

«Achij Mun,
Ixoq Mun! Bring my dish
my bowl.
Give them to him, to the angry man
Kaweq K'iche',
as a great sign of his death
of his loss,
here, at the navel of the sky
at the navel of the earth!»

Mun:

«So be it, my master
my eminence!
I give them to him, to him, the angry man.»

«Here, Angry man,
Kaweq K'iche'!
Taste from the dish
the bowl of my master
of my eminence
—the great King Job Toj—
in the great fortress
where my master
my eminence is established
is enclosed!
Oh Angry man!»

K'iche' Achi speaks for the thirteenth time.

«Eha!
King Job Toj!
What are Your dishes
what is this bowl which is Yours?
It definitely says nothing worthy to my mouth
to my face!
Taste mine instead; mine which comes from my mountains
[fol. 53] my valleys,

ki mayi-j u-ki'-il
u-q'us-il ki'-koj
kab-koj
ki mayi-j ka-ø-silil-ik
ka-ø-t'ir-ir-ik ri
ka-n-tij-o chi nu-juyub-al
chi nu-taq'aj-al
ka-ø-cha chi ba ri nu-tzij ch(i) u-wach kaj
ch(i) u-wach ulew
la are wa'-bal la wa
qatz are u-jolom nu-qajaw[214]
ka-nuw-il-o
ka-nu-muqu-j
la ma na r-okik-am
keje ta ban-el
tz'aq-a-n-i-sa-nel
chi-r-ech wa u-baq-il nu-wi
u-baq-il nu-jolom
k'ot-im ta chi-r-ij
k'ot-im ta ch(i) u-wach
ta chi qaj apan-oq chi nu-juyub-al
chi nu-taq'aj-al
tz'aqat-i-sa-bal ta r-e [j]o-kal peq
[j]o-kal kako
k-umal w-al
k-umal nu-k'ajol chi nu-juyub-al
chi nu-taq'aj-al
k-e-cha ta w-al
k-e-cha ta nu-k'ajol
are u-jolom qa-ma[m]
qa-qajaw
k-e-cha ta w-al
k-e-cha ta nu-k'ajol
k'uxta-bal ta w-e k-umal w-al
nu-k'ajol
ch(i) u-xe q'ij
ch(i) u-xe saq
are ta k'ut wa u-baq-il nu-q'ab
are ta ch-ok-ik u-q'ab soch-i pwaq

214. Here we have an illustration of the fixing of *q-ajaw* ("our father") into *qajaw* ("father"), which in turn allows a mark of possession: *nu-qajaw* ("my father"; see note 114). Today one would say *nu-qaw*.

its sweetness is admirable
its flavor is sugary
and honey-like at the same time;
it chills magnificently
and it paralyzes,
that which I taste in my mountains
in my valleys!
So says my word facing the sky
facing the earth!
What is this bowl which is Yours?
It is my father's skull!
I see it
I inspect it![215]
Would it not be appropriate
that in the same fashion
You work
the bone of my head
my skull,
with its back carved
its face engraved,
to have it go down into my mountains
into my valleys
accompanying the five loads of *pataxte*?
the five loads of cacao?
This is why
in my mountains
in my valleys . . .
. . . my children will say:

"This is the skull of our grandfather
of our father!"
That is what my children will say then,

as they remember me, my children,

under the sun
under the light of day!
Here also is the bone from my arm:
it would make a perfect metal rattle,

---

215. I am translating in this way the action of the verb *muquj,* which, often paired with *il* (in the sense of "to see, to watch"), stresses the intensity or the acuity of the vision ("to see far away, to watch with attention; to scrutinize"; see *muqubal* in the glossary).

ki mayi-j taj chi chajaj-ik
ki mayi-j taj chi wajaj-ik
ch(i) u-pam u-nim-al tz'aq
ch(i) u-pam u-nim-al k'oxtun
are ta k'ut wa u-baq-il w-aqan
are ta ch-ok-ik u-q'ab toponowotz' q'ojom
ki mayi-j taj chi-ø-lanan kaj
[fol. 54] chi-ø-lanan ulew
r-umal waral ch(i) u-pam u-nim-al tz'aq
ch(i) u-pam u-nim-al k'oxtun
ka-ø-cha k'u ri nu-tzij
mi x ch-in-qaj ta na chi-ech la
chi ya ta la ch(i)-w-e
ri lo-lo-j
ri ch'uch'u-j ri laq'an u-q'in
ri k'oxaj u-wa' ri ki-kal[a]tz'
ka-ø-ban-ik ri u-ban-om nu-te
nu-xoq'ojaw
mi x ch-in-jik-ik-e-j ul-oq
ch(i) u-pam u-nim-al tz'aq
ch(i) u-pam u-nim-al k'oxtun
chi kaj pa
chi kaj xukut-al
xa ta nim-a r-eta-l-il nu-kam-ik
nu-sach-ik
waral ch(i) u-xmut kaj
ch(i) u-xmut ulew

u-wa{jxa}q-mul[218] *ka-ø-ch'aw-ik ajaw {o}job toj*

oyew achi
kaweq k'iche' winaq
naqi ta na on ri x ch-a-rayi-j
ri x ch-a-tz'ono-j
ka-nu-ya-o ch(i)-aw-e
xa nim-a r-eta-l-il a-kam-ik
a-sach-ik

---

216. This Nahuatl term designated the great cylindrical slit drum carved from a hollowed trunk of an "ant tree" (*Platymiscium dimorphandrum*). On one side two vibrating tongues were created by slitting out the shape of an H. The name that was given here to this instrument is completely lost today, with only *tun*—a term that once designated wind instruments—still being used. As for the term *q'ojom,* it is generally applied to instruments that are struck; today it designates both the marimba (adapted from the African xylophone) and the drum with stretched skins (*nima q'ojom*).

that would resound magnificently
that would reverberate magnificently
inside the great fortress
inside the great wall!
Here also is the bone of my leg:
that would make a perfect stick to hit the *teponauaztli* drum[216]
which would make the sky throb
[fol. 54] would make the earth throb most admirably
from this place, within the great fortress
within the great wall!
And I say
that I will borrow them from You . . .
Give me then
the tenderness
the delicacy of the weavings with double warp
and single woof,
the handiwork of "my mother"
of "my queen"!
I will flaunt them[217]
inside the great fortress
inside the great wall,
in the four directions
in the four corners,
as a great sign of my death
of my loss,
here, at the navel of the sky
at the navel of the earth!»

King Job Toj speaks for the sixth time.

«Angry man,
Kaweq K'iche'!
Is this truly what thou desirest
what thou requestest?
I give it to thee
as a great sign of thy death
of thy disappearance,

217. The verb *jikikik* describes the unique way in which the snake moves; it is also used to convey the illusion of slithering created by the oscillation of a rope held on the ground when one of its ends is shaken.

218. An error by the copyist, for *u-waq-mul* appears evident here.

waral ch(i) u-xmut kaj
ch(i) u-xmut ulew

achi-j mun
ixoq mun
ch-a-k'am-a ul-oq ri lo-lo-j
ri ch'uch'u-j ri laq'an u-q'in
ri k'oxaj u-wa' ri ki-kalatz'
ka-ø-ban-ik ri ban-om la
ch(i) u-pam u-nim-al tz'aq
ch(i) u-pam u-nim-al k'oxtun
ch-a-ya-a chi-r-e ri oyew
chi-r-e ri achi
[fol. 55] xa nim-a r-eta-l-il u-kam-ik
u-sach-ik
waral ch(i) u-xmut kaj
ch(i) u-xmut ulew

... *mun...*

utz ba la w-ajaw-al
nu-winaq-il
ka-nu-ya-a chi-r-e ri oyew
ka-nu-ya-a chi-r-e ri achi
ri u-rayi-bal

ri ba la ri oyew achi
ri ki-kalatz' ka-ø-ban-ik
ri ka-rayi-j la
ri ka-tz'ono-j la
ka-nu-ya k'u ch-aw-e
xa k'u xere ma mayi-j la
ma q'uti-j la

... *k'iche' achi*

alaq ba ri aj-su'
alaq ba ri aj-q'ojom

here, at the navel of the sky
at the navel of the earth!»

«Achij Mun,
Ixoq Mun!
Bring the tenderness
the delicacy of the weavings with double warp
and single woof
that Your work produces
inside the great fortress
inside the great wall!
Give them to him, to the angry one
to him, the man,
[fol. 55] as a great sign of his death
of his disappearance,
here, at the navel of the sky
at the navel of the earth!»

Mun:

«Very well, my master
my eminence!
I give them to the angry one
I give them to the man,
according to his desire!»

«Here, Angry man,
is the weaving that we have made,
that You desire
that You have requested!
I give it to thee!
But do not destroy it
do not tear it!»

K'iche' Achi:[219]

«Oh You, flutists!
Oh You, drummers!

219. One should note that these lines spoken by K'iche' Achi do not appear in his speech numbers, no doubt because they are distinguished from the dialogue opposing him to Job Toj. We will see a similar case in line 2514, when K'iche' Achi addresses the Eagle and Jaguar warriors before delivering his final monologue.

a la ta chi k-e ri u-chi' nu-su'
ri u-chi' nu-q'ojom
ri mi x chi tzaq t(a) alaq
are ta ba chi tzaq alaq
ri nu-nim-a su'
{o}pu e nu-ch'uti{l} su' chi tzaq b(a) alaq
{o} are ta pux chi tzaq alaq ri nu-yaki su'
nu-yaki q'ojom
are ta pux chi tzaq alaq nu-k'iche' su'
nu-k'iche' q'ojom
koj-bal r-e ri nu-kanab
[fol. 56] ri nu-teleche chi nu-juyub-al
chi nu-taq'aj-al
ki ta chi bir-b-ot kaj
ki ta chi bir-b-ot ulew
chi qaj ta qa-wi
qa-jolom
chi-r-ech u-yiq'-ik
u-xaj-ik k-uk' achi-j mun
ixoq mun
waral ch(i) u-xmut kaj
ch(i) u-xmut ulew
ka-ø-cha k'u ri nu-tzij ch(i) u-wach kaj
ch(i) u-wach ulew
kaj
ulew chi-k'oji' uk' alaq aj-su'
alaq aj-q'ojom

u-kaj-lajuj-mul ka-ø-ch'aw-ik k'iche' achi

eja
ajaw {o}job toj
ki yux-ta-j ta ba la ch(i) u-wach kaj
ch(i) u-wach ulew
ri ba la ri nu-q[a]j-om
ri nu-chaq'im
mi x ch-ø-ul nu-jach-a
mi x ch-ø-ul nu-per-a ch(i) u-chi' u-nim-al tz'aq
u-nim-al k'oxtun

---

220. I am rendering the verb *tzaq* as "to play," knowing that it more generally means "to throw, to launch" or, in the realm of music or song, "to start singing."

221. The noun *wi* literally designates "the top" or, relating to the human body, "the tip, the crown of the head."

Will this be the tongue of my flute
the tongue of my slit drum
that You will play on then?[220]
That is what You will play upon:
it will be on my great flute
on my little flute that You will play!
And You will also play on my Yaki flute
my Yaki slit drum,
as You will play my K'iche' flute
my K'iche' slit drum,
the way they welcome my prisoners
[fol. 56] my captives in my mountains
in my valleys!
May the sky tremble
may the earth tremble
may our scalps
our heads bend down[221]
to trample down the floor
and dance with Achij Mun
Ixoq Mun,
here, at the navel of the sky
at the navel of the earth![222]
So says my word facing the sky
facing the earth!
May the sky
and the earth remain with You, oh flutists
You, oh drummers!»

K'iche' Achi speaks for the fourteenth time.

«Eha!
King Job Toj!
May You be honored facing the sky
facing the earth!
Here is what I borrowed
what I return!
I have just parted with it
I have just relinquished it at the threshold of the great fortress
of the great wall!

222. This passage might refer to a dance (and music), especially performed as a prelude to the sacrifice of a captive, as evoked under the name of "Tun (or Tum) Teleche" by certain early sources.

chi k'u ta ba la
chi tz'ap-i-j ta ba la ch(i) u-pam u-chuy-al
u-paq'-abal
ch(i) u-pam u-nim-al tz'aq
ch(i) u-pam u-nim-al k'oxtun
mi x-ya k'u la ch(i)-w-e ri nu-rayi-bal
nu-k'ut-ubal
ch(i) u-wach kaj
ch(i) u-wach ulew
mi x-in-jik-ik-e-j ul-oq ch(i) u-pam u-nim-al tz'aq
k'oxtun
chi kaj pa
chi kaj xukut-al
xa k'u nim-a r-eta-l-il nu-kam-ik
nu-sach-ik
waral ch(i) u-xmut kaj
ch(i) u-xmut ulew
[fol. 57] ka-ø-cha k'u ri nu-tzij ch(i) u-wach kaj
ch(i) u-wach ulew
we qatz lal tz'aqat
lal mol-a-j ch(i) u-pam u-nim-al tz'aq
ch(i) u-pam u-nim-al k'oxtun
chi ya ta chi ba la ch(i)-w-e
ch-in-qaj ta na ba chi-ech la
ri u-chuch q'uq'
rax-on
ri yamani[k]
{i}xtekoq-ib ri pe-t-e-naq tzam q'am karcha
k'o sa-y-om u-chi'
maja-bi sa-y-om u-wach
ch-in-sa-a ta na u-chi'
ch-in-sa-a ta na k'(u) u-wach
ch-in-mes-es-e-j taj
ch-in-jik-ik-e-j taj ch(i) u-pam u-nim-al tz'aq
u-nim-al k'oxtun
chi kaj pa
chi kaj xukut-al
xa ta nim-a r-eta-l-il nu-kam-ik
nu-sach-ik

Keep it
shut it up in the storehouse
the repository,
inside the great fortress
inside the great wall.[223]
You have acceded to my desire
answered my calls
facing the sky
facing the earth!
I have flaunted it inside the great citadel

in the four directions
in the four corners,
as a great sign of my death
of my disappearance,
here, at the navel of the sky
at the navel of the earth!
[fol. 57] And my word says facing the sky
facing the earth:
"If it is true that You are well supplied
that You are well maintained in the great fortress
in the great wall,
give me then
—I will borrow her from You—
the Mother of the Quetzal
of the Green Feathers,
the Gems
the Precious Stones, come from Tzam Q'am Karcha!
Some have been used,
others have not;
I will try her mouth
I will try her face,
I will walk with her,
I will flaunt her inside the great fortress
the great wall,
in the four directions
in the four corners,
as a great sign of my death
of my disappearance,

223. This conclusion of course recalls the situation in Act II when Rabinal Achi proposed to give up his weapons to Job Toj. Unlike in the first case, Job Toj this time accepts the act of restitution.

waral ch(i) u-xmut kaj
ch(i) u-xmut ulew
keje kaj
ulew chi-k'oji' uk' la
ajaw {o}job toj

u-wuq-mul ka-ø-ch'aw-ik ajaw {o}job toj

oyew achi
kaweq k'iche' winaq
naqi ta na on ri ch-a-rayi-j
ch-a-tz'ono-j
ka-nu-ya-o k'u ch(i)-aw-e a-rayi-bal
a-tz'ono-bal
r-umal waral k'u-l wi
tz'ap-i-l wi ri u-chuch q'uq'
u-chuch rax-on
yamani[k]
{e}xtekoq-ib
[fol. 58] ri pe-t-e-naq tzam q'am karcha
k'o sa-y-om u-chi'
maja-bi sa-y-om u-wach
ka-nu-ya k'u ch(i)-aw-e oyew achi
xa k'u nim-a r-eta-l-il a-kam-ik
a-sach-ik
waral ch(i) u-xmut kaj
ch(i) u-xmut ulew

achi-j mun
ixoq mun
ch-a-k'am-a ul-oq ri u-chuch q'uq'
ri u-chuch rax-on
ch-a-ya-a chi-r-e ri oyew
ch-a-ya-a chi-r-e ri achi u-rayi-bal
u-tz'ono-bal
xa nim-a r-eta-l-il u-kam-ik
u-sach-ik
waral ch(i) u-xmut kaj
ch(i) u-xmut ulew

... ixoq mun

utz ba la w-ajaw-al
nu-winaq-il
ka-nu-ya chi-r-e ri oyew achi

here, at the navel of the sky
at the navel of the earth!"
May the sky
and the earth remain with You,
King Job Toj!»

King Job Toj speaks for the seventh time.

«Angry man,
Kaweq K'iche'!
Is this truly what thou desirest
what thou requestest?
I give her to thee, according to thy desire
according to thy request!
Because in this place is guarded
is enclosed the Mother of the Quetzal
the Mother of the Green Feathers,
the Gems
the Precious Stones
[fol. 58] come from Tzam Q'am Karcha.
Some have been tried
others have not!
I give her to thee, Angry man,
as a great sign of thy death
of thy disappearance,
here, at the navel of the sky
at the navel of the earth!»

«Achij Mun,
Ixoq Mun!
Bring the Mother of the Quetzal
the Mother of the Green Feathers!
Give her to him, to him the angry one
Give her to him, to him the man, according to his desire
according to his request,
as a great sign of his death
of his disappearance,
here, at the navel of the sky
at the navel of the earth!»

Ixoq Mun:

«Very well, my master
my eminence!
I give her to him, to him the angry man!»

ri ba la oyew achi
kaweq k'iche' winaq
ka-nu-ya chi-ech la ri rayi-bal la
k'ut-ubal la
xa k'u xere ma mayi-j la
ma q'uti-j la ri u-chuch q'uq'
u-chuch rax-on
xa ta chi jik-ik-e-j la
chi mes-es-e-j ta la ch(i) u-pam u-nim-al tz'aq
ch(i) u-pam u-nim-al k'oxtun

u-ro'-lajuj-mul ka-ø-ch'aw-ik k'iche' achi

[fol. 59] ajaw {o}job toj
ki yux-ta-j ta ba la ch(i) u-wach kaj
ch(i) u-wach ulew
are ba wa nu-q[a]j-om
nu-chaq'-im
mi x-ya k'u la ch(i)-w-e
mi x-i[n]-jik-ik-e-j k'ul-oq
mi x-in-mes-es-e-j k'ul-oq
chi kaj pa
chi kaj xukut-al
ch(i) u-pam u-nim-al tz'aq
u-nim-al k'oxtun
chi k'u ta k'u la
chi tz'ap-i-j ta k'u la ch(i) u-pam u-nim-al tz'aq
u-nim-al k'oxtun
ka-ø-cha chi k'u ri nu-tzij
chi ya ta chi ba la ch(i)-w-e
ch-in-qaj ta chi na ba chi-ech la
ri kab-lajuj u-q'an-al kot
u-q'an-al balam
ri e nu-k'ul-um chi q'i[j-i]l
chi aq'ab-al ch(i) u-wach toq'
ch(i) u-wach ch'amiy
ix k-e-nu-qaj ta na k'u chi-ech la
mi x k[-e]-be nuw-etz'a-be-j ul-oq

224. The adverb *k'uloq* is not translated; it specifies that the actions described here are accompanied by a movement of encounter (*k'ul*) by the players.

225. The terms *toq'* and *ch'amiy,* in the early dictionaries as well as today, designate sticks that serve as insignia for village authorities (*varas* in Spanish). It is reasonable to

«Here she is, Angry man
Kaweq K'iche'!
I give her to You according to Your desire
Your conditions!
Still do not destroy her,
do not tear the Mother of the Quetzal
the Mother of the Green Feathers,
only draw her along
walk with her inside the great fortress
inside the great wall!»

K'iche' Achi speaks for the fifteenth time.

[fol. 59] «King Job Toj!
May You be honored facing the sky
facing the earth!
Here is what I have borrowed
and what I return!
You have given her to me,
I have flaunted her
I have walked with her,[224]
in the four directions
in the four corners
inside the great fortress
the great wall!
Keep her, then.
Shut her up in the great fortress
the great wall!
And my word says once again:
"Give me
—I will borrow them from You—
the twelve Yellow Eagles
Yellow Jaguars,
those whose sticks
whose lances[225] I met in combat by day
by night,
and I will borrow them from You.
I will go and rough them up

---

believe that their meaning has evolved and that in the present context they thus designate weapons: an indication in favor of this interpretation, which I am following here, is provided by Vico (n.d.a: fol. 75v), who proposes a translation of *ch'amiy* as "spear."

ch(i) u-pam r-al nu-ch'ab
ch(i) u-pam r-al nu-pokob
chi kaj pa
chi kaj xukut-al
ch(i) u-pam u-nim-al tz'aq
u-nim-al k'oxtun
xa ta nim-a r-eta-l-il nu-kam-ik
nu-sach-ik
waral ch(i) u-xmut kaj
ch(i) u-xmut ulew
keje kaj
ulew chi-k'oji' uk' la
ajaw {o}job toj

u-wajxaq-mul ka-ø-ch'aw-ik ajaw {o}job toj

[fol. 60] oyew achi
kaweq k'iche' winaq
la ka-ø-cha na k'u ri a-tzij ch(i) u-wach kaj
ch(i) u-wach ulew
ch-in-qaj ta na chi-ech la ri kab-lajuj u-q'an-al kot
u-q'an-al balam
ka-ø-cha ri tzij la
ka-nu-ya ba chi-ech la ri kab-lajuj u-q'an-al kot
u-q'an-al balam
ri ka-rayi-j la
ri ka-tz'ono-j la chi nu-chi'
chi nu-wach

[j-]ix ba la nu-kot
nu-balam
ch-i-ban-a ba la k'o ta k-ø-el wi ri oyew
ri achi
k-ix-r-etz'a-be-j ul-oq ch(i) u-pam r-al u-ch'ab
ch(i) u-pam r-al u-pokob
chi kaj pa
chi kaj xukut-al

u-waq-lajuj-mul ka-ø-ch'aw-ik k'iche' achi

ajaw {o}job toj
ki yux-ta-j ta ba la ch(i) u-wach kaj
ch(i) u-wach ulew
mi x-ya k'u la ch(i)-w-e ri nu-rayi-bal
nu-k'ut-ubal

in the child of my bow
in the child of my shield,
in the four directions
in the four corners
inside the great fortress
the great wall,
as a great sign of my death
of my disappearance,
here, at the navel of the sky
at the navel of the earth!"
May the sky
and the earth remain with You,
King Job Toj!»

King Job Toj speaks for the eighth time.

[fol. 60] «Angry man,
Kaweq K'iche'!
What says thy word facing the sky
facing the earth?
"I will borrow from You the twelve Yellow Eagles
the twelve Yellow Jaguars!"
You say!
I give You them, the twelve Yellow Eagles
Yellow Jaguars
that You desire
that You ask to my mouth
to my face!»

«Go then, my Eagles
my Jaguars;
do that for which he has gone out, the angry one
the man!
Have him "rough you up" in the child of his bow
in the child of his shield,
in the four directions
in the four corners!»

K'iche' Achi speaks for the sixteenth time.

«King Job Toj!
May You be honored facing the sky
facing the earth!
You have acceded to my desires
answered my calls!

ri u-q'an-al kot
balam
mi x-e-be nuw-etz'a-be-j ul-oq
ch(i) u-pam r-al nu-ch'ab
r-al nu-pokob
la are kot la wa
la e balam la wa
ma na wa k'o ch-u-bi'i-j la chi nu-chi'
chi nu-wach
r-umal k'o ka-ø-tzu'-n-ik
k'o na ka-ø-tzu'-n-ik taj
k'o jinta r-e'
k'o jinta r-ixkaq
[fol. 61] are ta na pe k-il la ri w-e ri k'o chi nu-juyub-al
chi nu-taq'aj-al
ki mayi-j ki-tzu'-n-ik
ki mayi-j ki-wach-i-n-ik
ki mayi-j k-e-chajaj-ik
k-e-chij-ij-ik r-uk' k-e'
r-uk' k-ixkaq

u-belej-mul ka-ø-ch'aw-ik ajaw {o}job toj

oyew achi
kaweq k'iche' winaq
ka-q-il na ri ri a-kot
ri a-balam
ri e k'o ch(i) a-juyub-al
naqi pa k-e-tzu'-n-ik
k-e-wach-i-n-ik ri a-kot
ri a-balam
ri e k'o ch(i) a-juyub-al
ri e k'o ch(i) a-taq'aj-al

u-wuq-lajuj-mul ka-ø-ch'aw-ik k'iche' achi

ajaw {o}job toj
ki yux-ta-j ta ba la ch(i) u-wach kaj
ch(i) u-wach ulew
ka-ø-cha chi ba ri nu-tzij chi chi' la
chi wach la

The twelve Eagles
Jaguars,
I went to rough them up
in the child of my bow
of my shield!
What are Your Eagles?
Are those Your Jaguars?
They say nothing worthy to my mouth
to my face,
unless it be that some see
and some do not see,
that they have no teeth
and no claws!
[fol. 61] Look at mine rather, those who are in my mountains
in my valleys:
their show is truly admirable
their appearance is magnificent,
they make an imposing noise
and they attack frightfully with their teeth
with their claws!»

King Job Toj speaks for the ninth time.

«Angry man,
Kaweq K'iche'!
We know about[226] "thy Eagles"
"thy Jaguars,"
the ones who are in thy mountains!
What do they see then,
what do they show then, thy Eagles
thy Jaguars,
the ones who are in thy mountains
in thy valleys!»

K'iche' Achi speaks for the seventeenth time.

«King Job Toj!
May You be honored facing the sky
facing the earth!
My word says to Your mouth
to Your face:

226. Literally, "we see them."

chi ya ta chi ba la ch(i)-w-e
ri ox-laju(j)-winaq q'ij
ri ox-laju(j)-winaq aq'ab
mi x [ch]-e-n-pixab-a-j ta chi na ba ul-oq
u-wach la nu-juyub-al
u-wach la nu-taq'aj-al
[fol. 62] awiri x-in-bin wi
x-in-silab wi
chi kaj pa
chi kaj xukut-al
ch(i u-)wi nu-tz[u]ku-n-ik
nu-kajale-n-ik
chi-r-ech u-tzuku-x-ik w-echa'
nu-k'uxun

k'iche' achi u-tekel chik ka-ø-ch'aw-ik

ix kot
ix balam
x-ø-el-ik k-ix-cha
ma na x-in-el taj
xa mi x-in-pixab-a-j chi k'ul-oq
u-wach nu-juyub-al
u-wach nu-taq'aj-al
a[la]wi x-in-bin wi
mi x-in-silab wi
chi-r-ech u-tzuku-x-ik w-echa'
nu-k'uxun
chi kaj pa
chi kaj xukut-al

ajkaroq kaj
ajkaroq ulew
la ma na k'o x-ø-opon wi ri w-oyew-al-al
ri w-achi-j-il-al
mi x-in-tij k'u ri pa kaj nu-be
p(a) ulew nu-be
mi x-in-tzel-e-j wi tolo

---

227. Literally, "where I moved."

228. The word *tolo* has not been identified by Coloch or through the dictionaries. It must be connected to the forms *tole, tolan,* and *toloba,* which are encountered, for example, in Coto (1983) and connote ideas of emptiness, solitude, and abandonment and might,

Give me then
thirteen times twenty days
thirteen times twenty nights,
so I may advise
the face of my mountains
the face of my valleys!
[fol. 62] There, where I have walked
where I have lived,[227]
in the four directions
in the four corners,
with regard to seeking
and to providing for
the gathering of my food
of my subsistence!»

K'iche' Achi, being then alone, speaks:

«You, Eagles,
you, Jaguars!
"He is gone," you say!
I have not gone,
I have only given my adieux
to the face of my mountains
to the face of my valleys,
where I have walked
where I have moved
for the gathering of my food
of my subsistence,
in the four directions
in the four corners!»

«Oh Sky,
oh Earth!
Has my anger
my strength come to nothing!
I have relished my course beneath the sky
my course on the earth,
I've returned from it empty-handed![228]

hypothetically, signify "without anything." My choice of translation, which borrows from cynegetic vocabulary, seems particularly adapted to describe the failure of K'iche' Achi's attempts when he was captured while he was trying to "hunt" the Rabinaleb.

ma na k'o k'u x-ø-opon wi ri w-oyew-al-al
ri w-achi-j-il-al
ajkaroq kaj
ajkaroq ulew
la qatz-ij waral in kam-el
in sach-el
waral ch(i) u-xmut kaj
ch(i) u-xmut ulew

[fol. 63] [j-]ix ba la nu-q'an-a pwaq
nu-saq-i pwaq
j-ix puch r-al nu-ch'ab
r-al nu-pokob
nu-yak-im wi[t]
nu-yak-im w-ikaj
j-ix puch ix taq w-atzyaq
r-uk' nu-xtapyak
j-ix ba la chi qa-juyub-al
chi qa-taq'aj-al
j-i ya[-a] ba la qa-tzij-o-l
ch(i) u-wach q-ajaw-al
qa-winaq-il
r-umal ka-ø-cha lo wa q-ajaw-al
qa-winaq-il
ka-ø-tajin u-lo wa w-oyew-al
w-achi-j-il-al
tzuku-y r-e
kajale-y q-echa'
qa-k'ux-u-n
ka-ø-cha lo wa q-ajaw-al
qa-winaq-il
la ma ka-ø-cha ta ri wa
we xa w-oy-e-be-n chi nu-kam-ik
nu-sach-ik
waral ch(i) u-xmut kaj
ch(i) u-xmut ulew

ajkaroq ba la kaj
ajkaroq ba la ulew
we qatz waral in kam-el
in sach-el
waral ch(i) u-xmut kaj
ch(i) u-xmut ulew
are k'u x ch-in-wach-il-i-be-j la kuk
la tz'ikin

My anger
my strength have come to nothing!
Oh Sky,
oh Earth!
Is it certain that here I will die
I will disappear,
here, at the navel of the sky
at the navel of the earth?»

[fol. 63] «Go then, you, my gilded metals
my silvered metals!
Go then, you, the child of my bow
the child of my shield,
my war handle
my war ax!
Go also, all you my clothes
and my sandals!
Go then toward our mountains
toward our valleys!
Go convey the news
to the face of our master
our eminence,
for perhaps our master
our eminence is saying:
"He goes ahead, my angry one
my warrior.
He is looking for
and seeking our food
our subsistence!"
This is probably what is saying our master
our eminence!
Something he will no longer say
if it is so that I await henceforth my death
my disappearance,
here, at the navel of the sky
at the navel of the earth!»

«Oh Sky,
oh Earth!
If truly here I am to die
to disappear,
here, at the navel of the sky
at the navel of the earth,
then let me resemble that squirrel
that bird

la x-ø-kam ch(i) u-q'ab che'
ch(i) u-xum che'
chi-r-ech u-tzuku-x-ik la r-echa'
la u-k'ux-u-n
waral ch(i) u-xmut kaj
[fol. 64] ch(i) u-xmut ulew

ix ba ri kot
ix ba ri balam
k-ix-pe-t-a ba la
ch-i-ban-a ba r(i) i-chak
ch-i-ban-a ba ri i-patan
ch-i-ban-a ba la r(i) iw-e'
ri iw-ixkaq
ma k'u qatz ju-mer wach-il k-in-iw-ism-ar-i-sa-j
r-umal xa x-in-oyew wi
chi nu-pe-t-ik chi nu-juyub-al
chi nu-taq'aj-al
keje kaj
ulew chi-k'oji' iw-uk'
ix kot
ix balam

[page 3 of the cover]

Junio 12. 191{1}3 Perez

---

229. These words and using the image of the squirrel and the bird can be interpreted as a final claim of innocence by K'iche' Achi. It would thus affirm that his scheming came only out of the natural behavior of a warrior, obliged to seek out and to bring back what is needed for sacrificial practices; in doing so it would express the fact that his failure is not due to a mistake, but to the superiority of those other predators (hunters), his adversaries. That is, in any case, what the Rabinaleb have him say . . .

230. A particularly difficult expression to translate, and which is analyzed as follows: *k* (imperfective), *-in* (first person singular absolutive), *-iw* (second person plural ergative), *-ism* ("hair, fur, feathers"), *-Vr* (inchoative), *-i* (euphonic), *-sa* (transitivizer [causative]), *-j* (terminal suffix of transitive verbs). This finale of the *Rabinal Achi*, in which the death of the defeated warrior is marked by an instant metamorphosis into a bird, is found in

that died on the branch
on the limb of the tree
from which came its food
its sustenance,[229]
here, at the navel of the sky
[fol. 64] at the navel of the earth!»

«Oh you, the Eagles,
oh you, the Jaguars,
you will come!
Do your work
carry out your duty,
so put your fangs
and your talons to action,
so that in a single instant you will make me become plumage[230]
because it was in pure valor
that I came from my mountains
from my valleys![231]
May the sky
and the earth remain with you,
oh you, Eagles,
oh you, Jaguars!»

[page 3 of the cover]

June 12, 1913, Pérez.

---

the legend of the death of Tecum Uman, transformed into a colibri under the fatal blow of Alvarado. This apotheosis of the warrior is found elsewhere in Mesoamerica, notably among the Aztecs where the "dead and resuscitated warriors . . . were reincarnated into the gracious bodies of the hummingbird" (Soustelle 1979: 73) and whose ultimate symbol was the sun god Uitzilopochtli (ibid.: 6).

231. There are in this phrase with tragic overtones three overlapping interpretations: it signifies first that K'iche' Achi was only doing his duty (see note 229), second, that his bravery was manifest to the very end, without any compromise; and finally, it recalls that only the "great" (dignitaries, warriors, etc.) have the privilege to metamorphose into a bird at the moment of their death.

PART III

Analysis: An Exemplary History

The trial to which the Rabinaleb bring K'iche' Achi clearly recalls the offenses he is accused of and underscores some of the issues that oppose them. The Quiché warrior indeed proves guilty on several occasions of kidnapping. First, he kidnapped the "white children" (twice: the first time, he took them to Pan K'aqil and elsewhere before finally liberating them at the behest of Rabinal Achi; the second time was when he was captured). He also kidnapped the king himself, whom he hid in the mountains. Furthermore, K'iche' Achi admits that he attempted to seize a territory that was apparently controlled by the Rabinaleb, undermining some of their vassals (the ruler and the people of K'amba) and stealing their best lands, and he admits to having destroyed several of their towns and villages. Ultimately, he doubly betrayed the Rabinaleb, first by not acting as he should have in the face of the threat of the Uxab Poq'omab, then by obviously transgressing the recommendations of peace proclaimed by the sovereign authorities. These reasons are sufficient to warrant the trial and, eventually, in this particular cultural context, to justify capital punishment.

But several questions remain. Why have the Rabinaleb for five centuries continued to place such importance on this tale? What underlying motives have been at work to preserve this text and to ensure that, even today, it is the object of ritual representations? Is its function purely commemorative?

To my knowledge, no student of the *Rabinal Achi* has sought to reconstruct the meaning of this text beyond the specific events that it recounts. Yet, the purpose of the *Rabinal Achi* is not simply to narrate a story but to construct

History. The *Rabinal Achi* is not simply a series of distinct episodes but is indeed the affirmation of a meaningful paradigm. It is this path, which leads from the story to the History, that I will attempt to recover here. To do so we will return to the places, actors, and events.

RETURN TO THE PLACES: SPACES AND JOURNEYS

The trial takes place in Kajyub, the final capital established by the Rabinaleb to control the southern part of the basin of Rabinal. The action takes place outside the palace during the encounters between the two warriors and inside when they appear in turn before the king.

The recalling of the offenses K'iche' Achi is accused of, however, does not mention Kajyub at all but describes, like so many "returns to the past," different episodes referring to other places and to other geographical contexts. We will examine these places and contexts by looking at the tale's groupings and connections, which follow eight easily identifiable sequences, listed here in order of appearance:[1]

Sequence A. Recalling a previous conflict in Belejeb Moqoj Belejeb Chumay and a failure suffered by the Quiché against the ancient rulers (possibly Rabinaleb or from a related group) from Chi K'otom Chi Tikram (lines 276–283).

Sequence B. Journey of K'iche' Achi (outside Rabinal): Pan Tz'ajaxaq → Cholochik Jyub Cholochik Chaj → Chi Nim Che' Paraweno Chi Kabraqan → Pan Ch'alib → Xol Chaqaj (lines 398–428).

Sequence C. Encounter with the Uxab Poq'omab on the great road of Chi Rok'obaya Tz'ikin (across from Cholochik Tz'aq Chun); then flight of the Uxab and Poq'omab to the mountains called Ekempek (Xe Q'anajal) (lines 523–546).

Sequence D. Quiché attempt at conquest (over the Rabinal territory): Tzam K'amba → Tzam Saqkijel (→ Chisaliya) → Tzam Ixtink'urun (across from Ximbaja) → Tzam K'isintun (lines 760–811).

Sequence E. Journey of Rabinal Achi: Tzam Moqotz'u'um → Panajache'el → Tzam Ja (across from K'uluwach Abaj), then a return to an unspecified location (lines 868–918).[2]

Sequence F. Kidnapping of the "white children" by K'iche' Achi: first taken to an unspecified location → carried off to Pan K'aqil → then to Chi Nim Che' Chi Kabraqan Paraweno where they are freed → return and settling in Pamaq'a (lines 870–902, 1091–1153).

---

1. References to the text (using line numbers) point out only the first detailed descriptions of these sequences but omit subsequent reminders or allusions, which almost all of them have.

2. We will focus later on completing these journeys by proposing possible responses inferred from the contextual analysis.

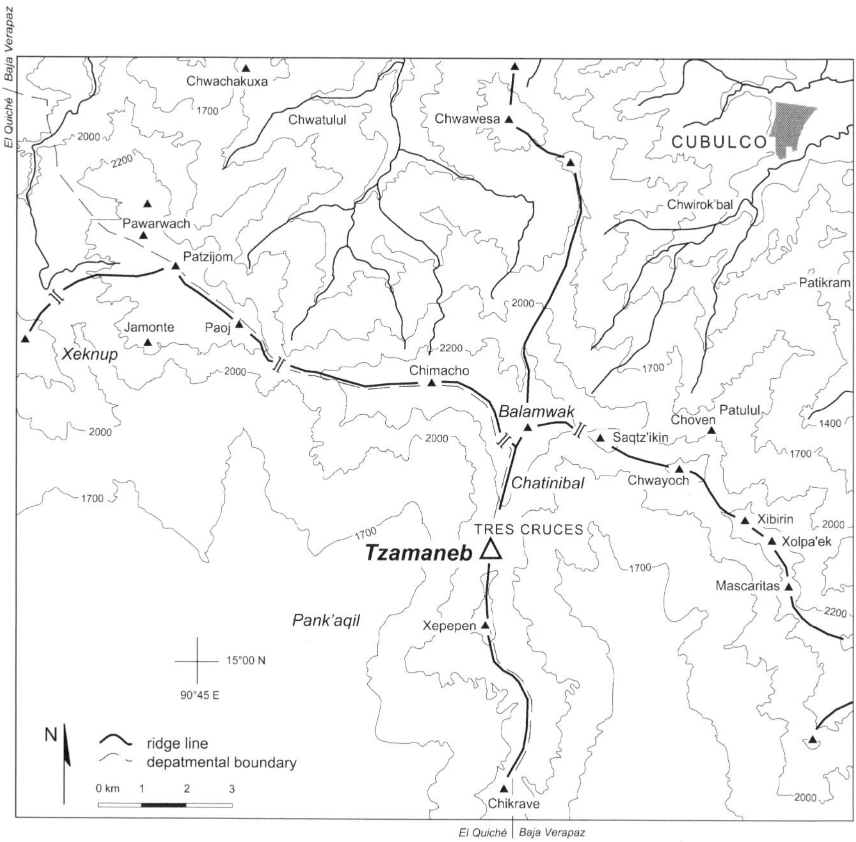

3. *The Surroundings of Tzamaneb (Tres Cruces)*

Sequence G. Kidnapping of Job Toj by K'iche' Achi: taken to Chatinibal → carried off to a prison of quicklime (*aqam chun*) before being found by Rabinal Achi → taken back by Rabinal Achi to an unspecified location (lines 903–905, 971–994).

Sequence H. Destruction attributed to K'iche' Achi of Balamwak (and/or Xe Balamwak), Chi Tintot Wi Poqlaj, Chi K'arkaraxaj, Chi Kunu, and Chi Q'osibal Taq'aj Tulul (lines 1009–1017).

Spatial Perspective

The analysis of the toponyms in these sequences raises many problems, and most of the names up to now have resisted any identification (see, notably, Acuña 1975). Despite a systematic examination of existing maps, exploration, and the many interviews led throughout the region (see Figures 3 and 4) and beyond, large gaps still remain that prevent us from formally recognizing all the places cited and, a fortiori, from situating in the regional space with sufficient precision the events that occurred in those various sequences. Established on the basis of these inquiries, the rapid review of detail that follows enables us, sequence by sequence, to analyze them:

Toponyms	*Locations*
SEQUENCE A: Region of Tres Cruces (?)	
Chi K'otom Chi Tikram	Hypothetically, these two toponyms are encountered near the hamlet of Tres Cruces, the first to the southwest (Joyabaj side), the second to the north (Cubulco side). Tikram, however, is used frequently in the region: there is another place called Tikram to the west of Rabinalá (on the edge of Canillá), a third to the north of Rabinal (the cemetery of Chitukan), the culminating point of the slope at the south end of which is Kajyub (see Brasseur 1862b: 39).
Belejeb Moqoj Belejeb Chumay	Hypothetically, this might be, as Brasseur (ibid., 18) suggests, another name (perhaps older) for Belej Tz'aq Belej K'oxtun, which in his time was the name the Indians were using for the ruins of Tres Cruces. Another place called Belej Tz'aq has an archaeological site and is located at the northern exit of the village of Cubulco.
SEQUENCE B: Region of eastern Quiché	
Pan Tz'ajaxaq	Considering the context and knowing that this journey of K'iche' Achi starts from the region of Utatlán, the hypothesis that this toponym corresponds to the current hamlet of Tzahachac, located near San Sebastián Lemoa (a few kilometers to the south of Santa Cruz del Quiché), is reasonable.
Cholochik Jyub Cholochik Chaj	Unidentified.
Chi Nim Che' Paraweno Chi Kabraqan	Among these three linked toponyms, only the second, Paraweno, has not been identified. Chi Nim Che' ("The Great Tree") no doubt corresponds to the current Panimaché close to Chichicastenango; Chi Kabraqan is today a large hamlet located to the west of Chiché.
Pan Ch'alib	Categorically identified by several informants from Tres Cruces, this toponym probably corresponds to Pachalib, located near the current town of Joyabaj.
Xol Chaqaj	Categorically identified by the same informants as Xolchiaqaj, a hamlet of Joyabaj close to Chuaq'enum.
SEQUENCE C: Region of Tres Cruces (?)	
Nim Be Chi Rok'obaya Tz'ikin	Unidentified. However, an informant recognizes that "the great road [*nim be*] of Chi Rok'obaya Tz'ikin" might be associated with Saq Tz'ikin, a place located a few kilometers northeast of Tres Cruces, crossed by the camino real leading to Cubulco and passing through Chwirok'bal.
Cholochik Tz'aq Chun	Unidentified.
Ekempek Xe Q'anajal	Unidentified.

Toponyms	*Locations*
SEQUENCE D: Basin of Rabinal[3]	
Tzam K'amba	Categorically identified as the hill located to the east of the village of Rabinal, the summit of which contains a small, destroyed archaeological site and is still the site of ceremonies to solicit rain.
Tzam Saqkijel	Categorically identified as the archaeological site of the same name, located to the southeast of Rabinal.
Chisaliya	Part of the basin of Rabinal located at the foot of Saqkijel, whose lands, irrigated by the waters of the Kumatza (or Chisaliya) River, are particularly rich.
Tzam Ixtink'urun chwach Ximbaja	Although the memory of the first toponym is practically erased, the name *Ximbaja,* combined with *chwach* ("across from") determines its location and corresponds to a hill of the southern piedmont in the basin of Rabinal, which for a long time had a chapel (perhaps built on an ancient pre-Hispanic altar) that today is in ruins. It is still a place of traditional worship.
Tzam K'isintun	Categorically identified as the intermediary summit in the chain that separates the communities of Rabinal and Cubulco.
	The rites preparatory to the dance of the *Rabinal Achi* involve visiting all the places of this sequence except Chisaliya.
SEQUENCE E: Unidentified region	
Tzam Moqotz'u'um	Unidentified. Although René Acuña (1975: map plate, p. 10) indicates a place called "Mucutzuum" located very far from Rabinal toward the southeast in the valley of the Río Motagua near San Agustín Acasaguastlán (El Progreso), he does not mention it again (ibid., table, p. 114). It seems improbable that Rabinal Achi's journey and, therefore, the influence of the Rabinaleb reached as far as the place described by Acuña.
Panajache'el	Unidentified. For the same reasons as just described, I choose not to associate Panajache'el with the village of Panajachel, located on the edge of Lake Atitlán in Cakchiquel land. The etymology of the toponym—formed on *ajache',* the name of the tropical fruit white sapote (*Casimiroa edulis* or *matasano* in Spanish)—might refer to many other places known today by names such as Los Matasanos or Matasanal.

continued on next page

3. Toponymy is a realm reputed to be stable and little affected by time. This stability of place-names (some of which designate archaeological sites, such as K'amba and Saqkijel) and the total absence of comparable toponyms in the current region of Tres Cruces are sufficient evidence in my opinion to refute the thesis advanced by Mace (1967a, 1967b) and accepted by Acuña (1975), according to which these names once corresponded to locations in the region of Tzamaneb–Tres Cruces and were "displaced" toward the basin of Rabinal at the time of the Spanish Colony.

Toponyms	*Locations*
Tzam Ja chwach K'uluwach Abaj	Unidentified. In view of the context, the meaning of these names—"The edge of the house (of the village) in front of the rocks that stand opposite"—leads one to believe that Rabinal Achi, ending his journey here, is close to home.
SEQUENCE F: Region of eastern Quiché	
Pan K'aqil	Categorically identified by informants as corresponding to the hamlet or to the valley of K'aqil, which extends below Tres Cruces to the village of Joyabaj.
Chi Nim Che' Chi Kabraqan Paraweno	See Sequence B.
Pamaq'a	Categorically identified with the pre-Hispanic village of Zacualpa and also is cited by this name in several other texts (see Carmack 1981: 185; Fox 1978: 236–237).
SEQUENCE G: Region of Tres Cruces	
Chatinibal	Categorically identified as the place (literally, "the bath") where king Job Toj was bathing at the time of his kidnapping; it is located near Tres Cruces. Until recently, people still came to this same place to ritually wash an effigy of Santiago, the patron saint of Cubulco, in the water of a babbling stream.
SEQUENCE H: Region of Tres Cruces	
Balamwak	Categorically identified as the mountain to the north that overlooks the hamlet of Tres Cruces. Near its summit, in the place called Chwamonte', is an altar where healers of the region hold their rituals.
Chi Tintot Wi Poqlaj	Unidentified. This name, which means "where the dusty earth crunches (under one's steps)," is perhaps not a toponym but a specification attached to Balamwak or a surrounding place.
Chi K'arkaraxaj	Hypothetical identification: Julian Sic, a connoisseur of these highlands after passing between Rabinal and Joyabaj many times in his youth while trading cloth and fabric, affirms that this place is located on the line of ridges separating these two villages. I have not been able to confirm its exact location. A seventeenth-century document, preserved in the Archivo General de Centroamérica under the reference A1-5940-51970, mentions a toponym (Raxaj) located on the same line of ridges.
Chi Kunu	Probable identification: all my informants from Tres Cruces and the surrounding area immediately recognize in this toponym present-day Xeknup (Xe K[u]nup).
Chi Q'osibal Taq'aj Tulul	Unidentified. The exact name is probably Chi Q'osibal Chaq'aj Tulul, which refers to a place where one harvests ripe (*chaq'aj*) sapotes (*tulul*) with a pole (*q'osibal*). Consequently, this name might specifically refer to a place planted with sapota trees (*Lucuma mammosa*). Such places and toponyms—notably, in the form "Patulul"—are abundant in the region and thus render identification all the more difficult.

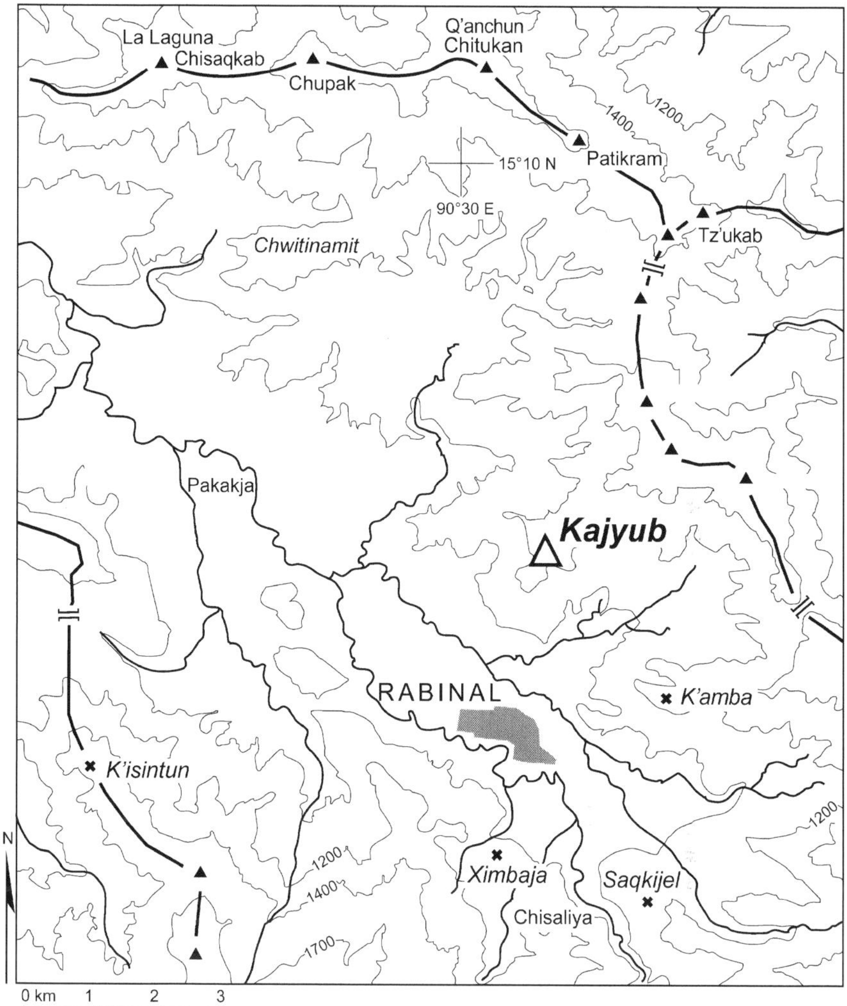

4. The Surroundings of Kajyub (Rabinal)

A clear understanding of the locations mentioned in the *Rabinal Achi* thus is hampered by the inability to clearly identify all the toponyms. The sequential analysis, however, provides enough geographical indications to enable us to recognize their specific contexts and to define their general context. Except for Sequences D (involving the surroundings of Kajyub, to which we will return later) and E (evoking an unidentified journey of Rabinal Achi), all sequences confirm K'iche' Achi's presence in the region or on the outskirts of the present-day hamlet of Tres Cruces, so in essence the mountain range located at the intersection of the basins of Rabinal, Cubulco, and Joyabaj in the place where so-called Tzamaneb was located.[4] This area between Kajyub (in the text, Kaqyuq' Tzilik Kakoqonik Tepekanik) and Utatlán-Q'umarkaj (in the text, Q'umarmachi) is where most of the action is concentrated and where most of the events unfold.

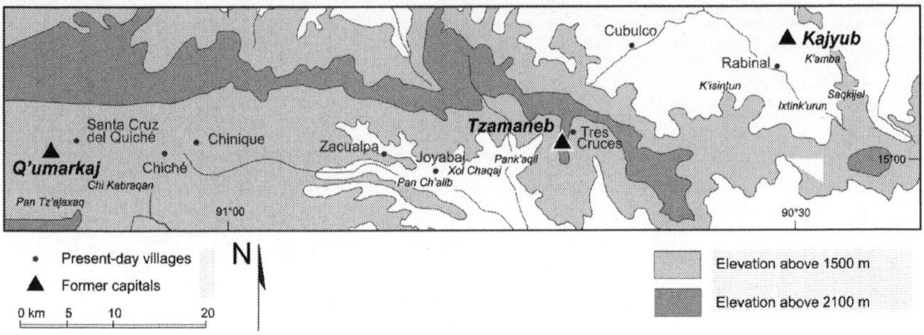

TEMPORAL PERSPECTIVE

The reconstruction of these events, furthermore, raises the no less delicate question of their connection in time. It is notably difficult for us to assert that the order they are given in the tale is strictly chronological. Although it is true that the systematic recalling of the facts as it occurs in Act I begins with the evocation of an earlier event (see Sequence A), and although it is also true that the repeated allusions to some of these events in the continuation of the text respect this initial order (Sequences G and H in the report that Rabinal Achi gives to Job Toj in Act II; Sequences F, G, and H when Job Toj repeats the accusation against K'iche' Achi in Act IV), we cannot draw a general conclusion from this information that is applicable to all the sequences. It is indeed appropriate to recall here that the gaps in the text and notably the omission of two sets of lines—the fifth of K'iche' Achi and the sixth of Rabinal Achi, which, following all logic, should be inserted between lines 736 and 737—break the thread of the story and force us to proceed cautiously.

Yet, an examination of the explicit relationships that the text in its current state establishes between these different sequences reveals that several among them are contiguous or even contemporaneous. On the basis of such temporal relationships (notably between Sequences B and C and between Sequences D, E, F, G, and H) I will attempt to bring together the strictly factual content of the tale.

4. This regional identification of the Rabinaleb's ancient capital can today be considered an established fact (see Acuña 1975; Ichon 1982; Arnauld and Breton 1993), even if doubt remains about whether its precise archaeological identification is the site of Los Cimientos–Patzaj or that named Chatinibal, recently discovered by Arnauld.

Sequence A appears to be an isolated sequence stressing the ancientness of the disagreement and anchoring the episodes that follow to an even older dispute between the two groups. The idea that the stakes of this war, lost by the Quiché against the rulers of Chi K'otom Chi Tikram, were already under the control of the Tzamaneb–Tres Cruces region is not implausible, but this characterization remains hypothetical. No doubt the conflict underwent an unfolding similar to that of the trial in the *Rabinal Achi* and is referred to in the passage in which after K'iche' Achi is offered a drink, he recognizes "his father's skull" (line 2175) in the cup that is presented to him and predicts that a similar treatment and usage may be intended for his own skeleton.

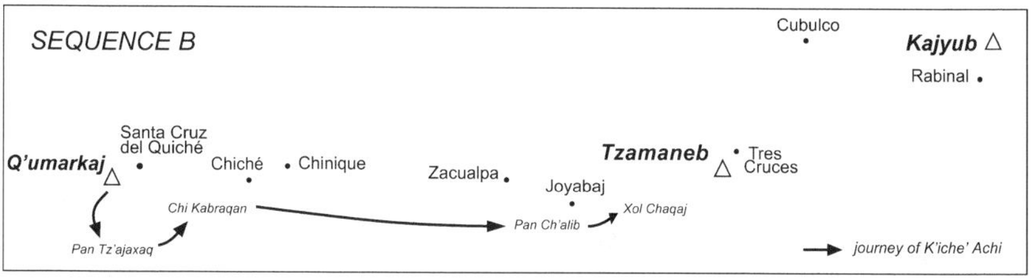

Sequence B opens with a reminder of the list of offenses weighing directly on the Quiché warrior. It is immediately set within a double misunderstanding. The first can be attributed entirely to K'iche' Achi, who, absent from Q'umarmachi at the time when the sovereign authorities voiced their recommendations for peace, is uniquely aggressive and appears as the transgressor. The second opposes the Rabinal and Quiché kings over the meaning of a message, whose meaning is interpreted one way at its emission in Kajyub and another at its reception in Q'umarmachi. I will return later to these two events—the breaking of the nonaggression pact and the episode of the messenger—for they have multiple consequences; however, I will note that from the beginning they underlie K'iche' Achi's motives. K'iche' Achi undertakes the journey that separates the Quiché capital from the region of Tres Cruces in response to what he considered a provocation by the Rabinaleb. From Utatlán, he reaches the outskirts of Joyabaj in several stages; there, and more precisely at Xol Chaqaj, just below Tres Cruces, he hears the very close murmurings of the Rabinaleb's war preparations. Convinced that these preparations are meant for him, he takes the initiative and provokes King Job Toj.[5] The preliminary war ritual of the "trumpets and drums of the bleeding," however, is not aimed at the Quiché.

5. The exordium "k-at-el ul-oq wor-om ajaw k'aq-om ajaw . . ." that K'iche' Achi then utters no doubt comes out of the protocol of the warring encounter. The fact that it appears twice in the text (lines 45–46, 446–447) is explained simply by its correspondence with two distinct confrontations between K'iche' Achi and Job Toj and not, as I once believed, by the tale's return to a single event.

The hostilities of the Rabinaleb are directed here toward the Uxab Poq'omab in response to the harassment they inflicted on the Rabinaleb (lines 570–572). As the Rabinaleb are preparing this counteroffensive (lines 509–520) in response to the attacks they endured and confronted alone, without the expected aid of the Quiché, Rabinal Achi once again solicits the help of K'iche' Achi.

Sequence C thus is set within the immediate continuation of this encounter, with regard to both geography (allowing us to confirm that the action indeed unfolds in Tres Cruces) and the plot (continuing to believe that the Rabinaleb have convinced the Uxab Poq'omab to be in league against him, K'iche' Achi does not offer the expected anticipated assistance). Not only does he allow the Uxab Poq'omab to flee (they are metamorphosed and regain their territory, the basin, with impunity), but he instigates and pursues a long dialogue with them during which he proves to be sensitive to their point of view and does his best to support their criticisms against the Rabinaleb (see lines 645–685, 706–719).

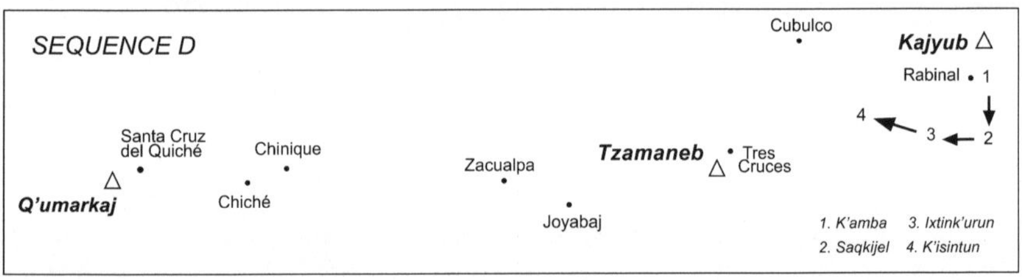

Sequence D describes unambiguously K'iche' Achi's attempt to seize four sites on the periphery of Kajyub, continuing without transition his actions, from the heights of Tres Cruces to the basin of Rabinal. I have already mentioned the reasons why we are today incapable of connecting this sequence to the one that precedes it and why every attempt to fix this rupture is forever compromised. Does this incursion convey a "displacement" of what was at stake or perhaps a territorial extension of Quiché ambitions? Is it inscribed in the continuation of the encounter with the Uxab Poq'omab? Would K'iche' Achi have pursued them that far? Would he have attempted to subjugate them? Did the missing part of the text allude to the Uxab Poq'omab's flight beyond the borders of the basin? These questions cannot be answered. The text tells us only that at least part of this sector of the basin was already under Rabinaleb control, since the governor and the people from Tzam K'amba were being controlled by the Rabinaleb (lines 766–771).

The transition from Sequence D to the following sequences presents fewer difficulties. In order to follow K'iche' Achi's steps and to favor as much as possible the fragile indications of continuity between his different actions, we will look at Sequences F, G, and H before Sequence E, because Sequence E is partly contemporary with them, unfolding in parallel.

If we were sure that the tale followed a strictly linear and chronological unfolding, the first allusion to the kidnapping of the "white children" (line 854) would situate this misdeed by K'iche' Achi in immediate concordance of time and place with the preceding episode (implying that the conquered people of K'amba could be counted among these "children"). However, in light of the most complete description that the text offers us of Sequence F (lines 1091–1153), it is probable that this kidnapping principally concerns the Rabinaleb victims of the Tres Cruces region,[6] as the return of the expedition toward the Quiché follows the path of Pan K'aqil (at mid-slope between Tres Cruces and Joyabaj). Let us recall that the "white children," led in the direction of Utatlán, were released before arriving there, and then, returning the way they had come, they swelled the population of Pamaq'a (formerly Zacualpa). This outcome, as it agrees with the historical perspective outlined in the introduction, appears to reinforce the establishment of borders around or near Tres Cruces, which strengthened Quiché control in this region.

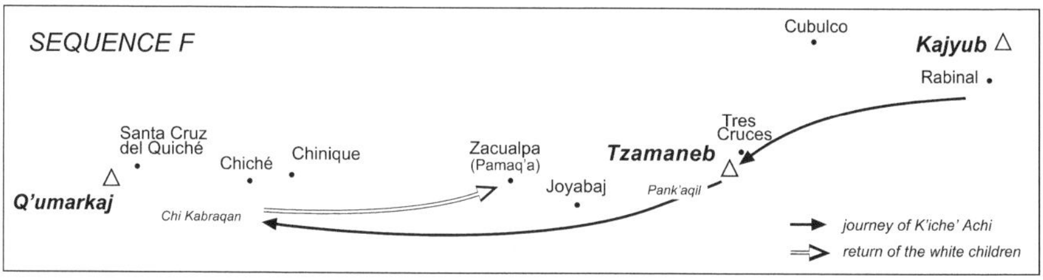

Sequence G relates K'iche' Achi's return to the sector of Tres Cruces. He specifically seizes Job Toj in Chatinibal, then carries him off to his province, and puts him in the prison (*aqam chun*).

Sequence H, in my opinion, involves the same episode. We will see later that the destruction of Balamwak and other village and hamlet establishments comes out of a campaign intended to be final and decisive against the sector of Tres Cruces: the identifications proposed for Chi Kunu and Chi K'arkaraxaj and, above all, the mention of Balamwak—or Xe Balamwak (literally, "below Balamwak"), referring to all of this sector—describe the space exactly.

In the meantime, while the Quiché warrior is carrying out this series of kidnappings and destruction, the Rabinal warrior is going on another journey, which is the focus of Sequence E. The fact that we do not know the first stages of

6. Another argument, which I will not develop here, borrows from the oral tradition of Tres Cruces and from the myth of Yew Achi. This myth tells of the repeated attacks on Tres Cruces, then occupied by the Rabinaleb (the sons of San Pablo), by a Quiché warrior. According to this myth, the warrior—Yew Achi—also kidnapped numerous individuals so that he could populate (literally, "to sow them") other places. Stressing San Pablo's inability to thwart these attacks, the myth relates that he agreed to allow Santiago (patron of Cubulco) to confront the Quiché in his place in exchange for control of the Tres Cruces region. This story explains the displacement of San Pablo and his children toward the basin of Rabinal whereas the sector of Tres Cruces remained under the sole control of the people of Cubulco, who overcame Yew Achi (see Arnauld and Breton 1993).

this other journey is regrettable for the reasons of the historical and geographical interpretation, however, this journey remains secondary with regard to the narration, which stresses, above all, Rabinal Achi's absence during these events. He is busy elsewhere and leads his own conquests (discussed later), while following, from afar and powerlessly, the tribulations inflicted on his people. He is in fact in Tzam Moqotz'u'um when K'iche' Achi carries off the "white children," in Panajache'el when they are freed (Sequence F), and, finally, in Tzam Ja at the time of Job Toj's kidnapping (Sequence G). Although, as we have said, Tzam Moqotz'u'um and Panajache'el cannot be identified, the reference to Tzam Ja evokes an ending to the journey. Indeed, it is from that place that he discovers the still-smoking ruins of his fortress and, approaching and surveying them, notes with open bitterness the devastation of the place (Sequence H). And it is from these very places in Xe Balamwak that he immediately decides to go look for Job Toj.

In fact, Sequence E ends in such a way that it essentially offers a break in the action to review all the facts, even as it covers and prolongs Sequences F, G, and H. Leading Rabinal Achi toward the Quiché land before leading him home in the company of Job Toj, this sequence closes the tale with a victorious end that, with the king found and reinstalled in his land and place, represents a return to order.

HISTORICAL PERSPECTIVE

This analysis shows that the story of the "precedents" — since, in fact, all these events are earlier than the one that directly motivates the trial[7] — projects us into the two spaces between which the historical populating of the Rabinaleb plays out: the sector of the high mountains identified as Xe Balamwak, or more simply Tres Cruces, and the zone of the basin of Rabinal, where the modern village of Rabinal is found. In other words, between Tzamaneb and Kajyub.

Although this bipolarization of the space generally conforms to the historical tradition mentioned in the introduction, it veers away from tradition on an important point. We may recall, in fact, that Tzamaneb and Kajyub appeared as two distinct stages corresponding to two successive phases within the territorial expansion of the Rabinaleb. Now, following the connection of the sequences as established by our text, at the time when K'iche' Achi was carrying out his military campaigns, these two "territories" were already under Rabinaleb control and, consequently, their respective administrative seats (Tzamaneb and Kajyub) were contemporary. What historical interpretation would be likely to reconcile these two apparently incompatible theories? As we shall soon see, one of the primary purposes of the *Rabinal Achi* is to evoke processes of transition; therefore, I believe I am completely respecting the logic of the tale in proposing the following hypothesis.

---

7. The trial begins after the capture of K'iche' Achi while he was preparing a new attempt to kidnap the "white children."

The Rabinaleb occupied the two aforementioned sectors at the time of the action. Tzamaneb and Kajyub are indeed contemporary but at the time had neither the same status nor the same functions. Tzamaneb, the high city, was still the capital, that is, the seat of Rabinal royalty, whereas Kajyub was no doubt only an advance post—a garrison, a military fortress—established in the basin at the time of an earlier Rabinaleb conquest. It is clear that all of K'iche' Achi's misdeeds did not have the same consequences. His attempt to conquer the basin (Sequence C) failed: even if he obtained some results there (such as conquering the K'amba, seizing the lands of Chisaliya, and taking Saqkijel, Ixtink'urun and K'isintun), he admits an incomplete victory when he regrets not having been able ultimately to take possession of the very center of this sector, the "navel of the sky, navel of the earth" (i.e., Kajyub [lines 816–820]). However, he leads actions against Tzamaneb that prove decisive (Sequences F, G, and H): kidnapping (removing) of the king and sacking (destruction) of the lands. It is also clear that the role assigned to Rabinal Achi is inscribed in an inverse logic—deliverance (restitution) of the king and his reinstallation in his lands—and that it is indeed this logic which ultimately triumphs. Thus, the transition that takes place (implicitly contained in the completion of Sequence G) must no doubt be interpreted as a transition of place: the king, evidently undone in Tzamaneb then finally recovered by Rabinal Achi, is returned to Kajyub, the place that can henceforth be considered the new capital of the Rabinaleb as Tzamaneb has been destroyed. The tale's reconstructed course bears witness to this transition: it is in Kajyub that the Quiché warrior's final misdeed, his attempt to kidnap the "white children," is foiled by Rabinal Achi, occasioning his capture and the opening the trial.

After examining the places in the *Rabinal Achi* and the actions that unfold in them, elements stand out that enable us to undertake a more detailed look at the relationships joining the different characters. The nature and arrangement of the implicit relationships that this tale attempts to set up from one place to another is remarkable. K'iche' Achi's failure during his first attempt to conquer ancient Kajyub, at that time a warrior town without a king (Sequence D); his subsequent success over Tzamaneb, a royal city without warriors (Sequences F, G, and H); and finally his definitive failure before the new Kajyub, which became the single capital of the two newly joined forces of king and warrior,[8]

8. I previously have not proposed a translation of the toponym Kaqyuq' Tzilik Kakoqonik Tepekanik, the name used in the text to designate the capital of the Rabinaleb, but I will adopt here the sole hypothesis with any credibility, that of Acuña (1975: 112n32), who by isolating the elements *kaq-* and *tepe-*, recognizes in them the pair that designates royal power (*kaqal tepewal*). I, in turn, propose that this pair expresses above all the completeness of that power when it associates and combines the qualities of the warrior (*kaq*, "ardor") and those of royalty (*tepew*, "majesty"). A commentary by Zuñiga (cited in Miles 1957: 767) assigning to *kaqal tepewal* the connotation of "inaccessibility" entirely supports the idea that I am defending here regarding Kajyub: constituted into a new capital following the reunion of Rabinal Achi and Job Toj, it in fact becomes inaccessible to K'iche' Achi (who not only fails in his attempt but is captured).

exhaust the three possible outcomes at stake in these relationships, which can be formalized as follows (w: warrior character; r: royal character; → : direction of dominance):

Nature of the place	*Nature of the relationships between the characters*
(1) Kajyub: w, not r	w ↔ w
(2) Tzamaneb: r, not w	w → r
(3) Kajyub: r + w	w ← rw

According to the tale and in accordance with the proposed schema, a confrontation implicating two forces comprised of only warriors thus reaches an impasse. This irresolution of the conflict calls for a more general clarification. To deepen this model and grasp the evolution of the relationships of power that it suggests, let us return to the actors.

RETURN TO THE ACTORS: FIGURES OF THE WARRIOR AND THE KING[9]

A large part of the plot of the *Rabinal Achi* rests on the assumed equivalence between the two warriors. Cited in the introduction, a number of other indigenous chronicles—the *Popol Vuh, Anales de los Cakchiqueles,* and *Título de los Señores de Totonicapán*—all agree on the fact that in spite of the increase in the conflicts that opposed them, the Rabinaleb and the Quiché recognized that they had the same origin and shared a common history during which, throughout the various migrations and conquests, they were more often brothers-in-arms and allies than adversaries. We can observe moreover that the trial of K'iche' Achi occurs after a reconciliation has been proposed and that it occurs within a conjuncture favorable to a possible return to the alliance. It is therefore not surprising that the two warriors potentially consider themselves within this context to be "brothers" (although temporarily separated and set against each other by an enmity between their two peoples). The equivalency of Rabinal Achi and K'iche' Achi stands out in some of their declarations[10] but also in other elements relating to the tale's composition or in what takes the place of its dramatic movement.

The equivalency is found foremost in the formal artifice that presides over the layout and the characteristics of Rabinal Achi's and K'iche' Achi's lines. During their encounters, their exchanges indeed respect a rigorous balance with each allotted eight pieces of dialogue in Act I and one in Act III, or nine sets of

9. Some of this section borrows from an earlier publication (Breton 1994).
10. See lines 214–215, 361–362, 1322–1323, 1491–1492, and 1694–1695.

lines for each of them).[11] When the contributions of the other actors—specifically, the king and the slave—are forms of direct discourse, it is exclusively during the exchanges between the two warriors that the process of overlapping discourse is manifest and fully expressed. Indeed, such overlapping is in part reflective of this equivalency, and echolalia tends to be the favored, meaningful, and indeed caricatural expression of it. If the warriors' speech was not endowed with ambiguity and imprinted with such rhetorical importance, gradually giving form and substance to the story, these words at most would be only vain utterances, repeated identically over and over.[12]

Enclosed in this vagueness that condemns them to a sterile confrontation, the warriors cannot be separated without the intervention of an external referee: in this case, the king. He is the intercessor, mediator, and arbiter. He is the one who alternately throughout the trial listens, advises, dubs, or condemns, and he is also the one in relation to whom the warriors are led to make up their minds in order, finally, to differentiate themselves. This symmetry to which the situation of the two warriors conforms with regard to the king is also seen in the overall scale of the text, whose schema, in relation to the acts, can be visualized as follows:

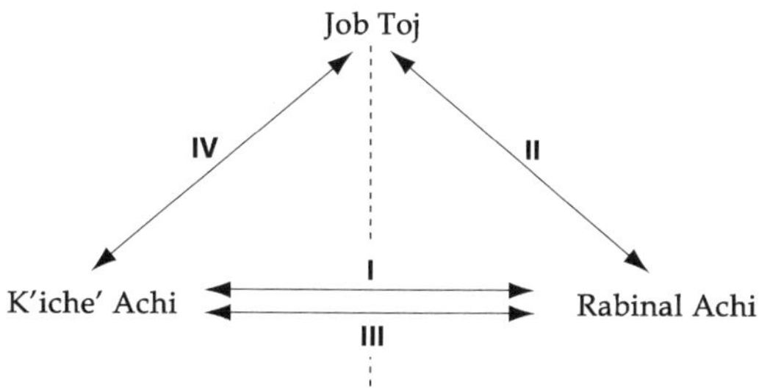

The Figure of the Warrior

One of the qualities shared by Rabinal Achi and K'iche' Achi can be found in their names. The term *achi,* which is added to their respective ethnonyms,

---

11. Job Toj, over the whole of the text, also expresses himself nine times, three times in the presence of Rabinal Achi (in Act II) and six times in the presence of K'iche' Achi (in Act IV). Only the speech that relates exclusively to this triadic relationship is accounted for: the interventions of Ixoq Mun (lines 1822, 2141, 2255, 2383), with but a single exception (line 1886), escape this accounting; also excluded are two interventions of K'iche' Achi, one addressed to the musicians (lines 2268–2297), the other to the Eagle and Jaguar warriors, as well as to the sky and the earth, who are witnesses of the final monologue (lines 2514–2598).

12. Indeed, K'iche' Achi conveys the very uselessness of any dialogue with his enemy on several occasions with formulas of the type "we have nothing to say to each other," "why should we exchange any more words," or "let us cease these polemics."

is the generic term that designates the male, the man, the masculine principle, and, by extension (*achij*), the fighter, the soldier, the warrior. Colonial dictionaries rarely distinguish between *achi* and *achij*, and even those that separate the two words do not make clear distinctions between their meanings, defining them generally in terms that seem to convey the excellence of virility, such as strength, firmness, vigor, and courage.

Angel (n.d.: fol. 7v): *achij*, el hombre; *uachihilal*, mi valentía y esfuerzo; (152v) *viƐ/vik achihilal*, animarse, tomar ánimo.

Basseta (1698: fol. 161v): *achih*, varón; *achihilal*, varonilidad [marido].

Coto (1983: 276): *achi/achih*, hombre o varón; *achih*, hombre o varón fuerte; *yn achih achi*, yo soy hombre fuerte; *achihilal*, fortaleza así; (327) *achi/achih*, macho, en todo género de animal. . . . El primero usan para los hombres, para decir "varón," "hombre ya;" el [segundo] le toman por el valiente, esforzado.

Santo Domingo (1693: fol. 3v): *achijh*, cosa dura, o recia; *achih*, varón fuerte; *achiha*, soldados; *achihilal*, fuerza, o fortaleza; *achihir*, hacerse fuerte.

Tirado (1787: fol. 106v): *oyeuh achih*, fuerte varón y muy esforzado; (119) *achij*, hombre; (135v) *achij*, macho en cada especie; (187v) *achiy*, varón.

Vico (n.d.a: fol. 6v): *achi*, hombre o mujer fuerte . . . o valiente; *achihilal*, la fortaleza.

Another characteristic of the warrior is contained in the paired expression *oyew achi*, which the two protagonists use to describe each other reciprocally or to describe themselves, and in which the term *oyew* (or *oyow*) covers all manifestations of anger, such as fury, impatience, aggressiveness, irritation, outrage, and rage, but also warrior values, such as bravery, ardor, courage, and even cruelty.

Alonso (n.d.: fol. 46): *oyeuh*, hombre bravo [= *cak*]; *quinoyouar*, hacerse bravo [= *quincakar*].

Angel (n.d.: fol. 106v): *oyouar*, enojarse, o airarse; *oyeuh*, el enojado; *oyouariçah*, airar a otro; (107) *oyeuh*, el enojado [= *oyow*]; (179v) *nim ru ƐaƐal nu 4ux, nim royoual nu 4ux*, tengo grande rencor y enojo.

Basseta (1698: fol. 168v): *oyeual*, enojo; (208) *oyouariƐ*, enojarse; *oyoual*, enojo; *oyoualah*, cruel.

Tirado (1787: fol. 8): *quinoyovaric*, acelerarse en cólera, o enojo; (14) *chi oyoval*, airadamente; (45v) *oyoval*, cólera, o enfado; *oyovalaj achij*, colérico, airado; (78v) *oyoval*, corage; (86) *oyoval*, enfado; (88) *quinoyovaric*, me enojo; (106v) *oyeuh achih*, fuerte varón y muy esforzado; (107) *oyoval* [= *cakal*], furia, o furor; *oyovarel*, furioso de enojo [= *cakarel*]; (122) *chi oyoval*, impacientemente; (149v) *4orroyoval usak vachibal nu4ux*, tengo odio; (163) *cantzur chi oyoval*, provocar a ira; *tzururic chioyoval*, provocación a ira; (172v) *oyovalah vinak*, persona rigorosa.

Varea (n.d.: fol. 30): *camiquil oyoual*, odio mortal; (47) *oyeo*, persona colérica, brava y airada; *oyeval*, la ira, enojo, coraje; *oyevar*, enojarse, ser iracundo;

> *oyevariçah,* enojar a otro; *oyevariheh,* enojarse con otro; (144) *oyouaribeh,* después que me enoje; *oyouariçala,* enojarse muchas veces.
>
> Vico (n.d.a: fol. 144): *oyeuar,* enojarse; *oyeuh,* el enojo; *oyeuah,* airar [= *oyow*].

Indeed, the warrior's temperament appears, by definition, to be marked by anger and impetuosity—in a word, fire (in Quiché, *kaq,* which literally means "redness"), a term that is cited several times as a synonym for *oyew.*

Returning to the text of the *Rabinal Achi,* this temperament can be seen and heard through the actions attributed to Rabinal Achi and K'iche' Achi. Most of their dialogues are introduced through the enraged cry *Eja!*—the signal of an encounter placed under the seal of a challenge and a trial of strength. During performances of the dance, this cry is extended into a long, modulated vociferation that is almost sung and announces when each protagonist is about to speak. Upon hearing the cry, the actors promptly move toward each other, brandishing their weapons (hatchets) and waving their shields before starting their discourse. Although less violent, the movements that accompany the recitatives during their face-offs (which occur in Acts I and III) convey a similar and constant excitation.

The text also stresses the incessant mobility of these two warriors, detailing their travels and multiple displacements following their various journeys. They come and go throughout their lands, traveling along the boundaries of their territory and surveying borders; both of them travel the world over mountains and through valleys, edging along the mountains, climbing hills, constantly going from one place to another, and leaving imprints of their sandals or their feet engraved on the earth. Certain episodes, such as those that we witness during Sequences E, F, G, and H in our tale, might lead us to believe that, like titans, these protagonists leap from mountain top to mountain top while reviling each other across great distances. This ability of the warriors, who also possess great magical powers, finds its counterpart in other ancient documents.[13]

Regarding the *Quiché Vinak,*

> [d]icen que un indio del rey de Tecpan-Guatemala y aun dicen que era su hijo, era gran brujo. Éste se venía de noche a los edificios del Quiché donde dormía el rey y daba grandes ahullidos y voces diciéndole muchos baldones y oprobios al rey . . . y viéndose [el rey] baldonado y molestado de aquel brujo, llamó a los brujos que tenía y prometió grandes premios, y ofreciéndose uno que le debía de exceder en este arte salió en su busca y topando con él, y queriéndolo coger, *de un salto se iba a otro cerro, pero lo mismo hacía el Quiché, y siguiéndolo de aqueste modo mucha distancia lo hubo de aprender* con mucho cuidado. (Ximénez 1929–1931: book 1, chapter 28: 62–63; emphasis mine)

Regarding the *Ah Pop* of San Andrés Sajcabajá, on the lands of Quanimaché and Zacquila, the alcaldes and principales affirm,

13. This theme is also important in oral traditions. See notably the myth of the Yegua Achi of Momostenango (Cook 1983) and those of the Yew Achi of Cubulco (Shaw 1972: 62–63) and of Tres Cruces (Arnauld and Breton 1993).

> no tienen otro documento que un quaderno simple escrito en su idioma patrio de mala letra y enquadernado en quarto . . . el referido papel solo incluye evidentes supersticiones, entusiasmos e imaginarias diligencias no menos que practicadas por arte diabólico, pues el actuante que aparece es el Gran Ah Pop, que a la monta será algun hechicero o Idolo de los que veneraban en su gentilidad, pues persuade este juicio el que dice expresamente que *el memoriado Ah Pop, al darles posesión, volaba de monte en monte, sentándose en los mojones hasta con impresión de sus plantas.* (document A1-53330-6043 (November 24, 1794), *Archivo General de Centroamérica,* fols. 7–8 [in Piel 1989: 273]; emphasis mine)

It is in very similar terms that the title of another document from the same bundle of letters indicates

> [l]os naturales del pueblo de San Andrés Semetabaj, con motivo del reconocimiento de sus tierras, presentaron un cuaderno simple escrito en su idioma . . . se encontró que el referido papel sólo incluye evidentes sus peticiones [supersticiones?] . . . pues el actuante que aparece es *el Gran Ah Pop [. . . que], al darle posesión, volaba de monte en monte sentándose en los mojones.* Año 1797 (ibid.: fol. 10v; emphasis mine)

Such, then, is the provocative image of the warrior—arrogant, ironic, insulting, moved by anger and impetuosity, always looking for a confrontation—that stands out in the *Rabinal Achi.* But the text also shows another facet of the warrior: that of the hunter. This alternate image no doubt corresponds to another dimension of war, indeed, to *another war,* which is played out in parallel. This other war indeed appears in a very different light since it takes on aspects of the hunt and borrows all of the subtleties associated with that activity. Indeed, it is when K'iche' Achi is hunting the Rabinaleb, lying in wait near Kajyub and insidiously laboring to entrap them, that he is surprised and captured. We will return to this topic later.

Finally, to finish with the examination of the warrior's characteristics, we must point out that his activities lead him to distant, peripheral, extreme places and spaces associated with notions of distance (the cardinal points), of challenges (climatic elements), and of danger (the threats of the borders). K'iche' Achi makes partial mention of these activities in the following passage:

> —I was setting up the boundary stones
> out where the day disappears
> out where the night appears
> in the sharp wind
> the biting cold,
> . . . .
> under the black clouds
> under the white clouds (lines 398–402, 603–604)

The role of Rabinal Achi is similar, as evoked in this other excerpt in which, having refused Job Toj's idea of a reconciliation with K'iche' Achi and then having threatened to give up his weapons, he is immediately commanded to take them back and is confirmed in his functions. The king justifies his decision as follows:

> How will You manage
> against what comes down
> what goes up
> from the head of the earth
> from the feet of the earth?
> And by what means will You watch over them,
> our children,
> who have gone out questing
> gone out searching
> in the four directions
> in the four corners [of the territory]? (lines 1609–1620)

Although as warriors and as "enemy brothers" Rabinal Achi and K'iche' Achi are on potentially equal footing, their behavior toward royal authority sets them apart: Rabinal Achi submits dutifully whereas K'iche' Achi continues outrageously to defy that authority. Stressing the "whole" nature of the Quiché warrior and every tragic aspect of his fate, various authors have wanted to identify him as the single true hero of the story and thus have believed they must challenge the original title of the work. Acuña (1975: 88) proposed changing and Padial Guerchoux and Vázquez-Bigi (1991) actually changed its title to "*Quiché Vinak*" (*K'iche' Winaq*, or "The Man from Quiché"). This position can no doubt be attributed to an error in judgement[14] and to an ethnocentric interpretation that, unless one is invoking the romantic spirit of the tragic Hegelian hero, ends up in a false quarrel. Even if a hero, in the literary sense of the term, was supposed to be the focus of this work, that hero, in this context, would be the figure of the king who unquestionably stands out and is asserted.

The Figure of the King

Whether referring to the character of Job Toj, ruler of the Rabinaleb and father of Rabinal Achi, or the king of the Quiché, Balam Ajaw Balam K'iche' (father of K'iche' Achi), or even the sovereign authorities, the text portrays the king as the antithesis of the warrior through a number of traits. The term *ajaw*, which designates both the king's person and his function, is generally translated as "master, possessor, lord, patron, principal" (and, in Old Quiché, as "father"). Through the different forms that are derived from it, *ajaw* defines that which relates to the sovereign and to royal power (e.g., throne, insignia, and scepter) as well as the qualities that are required or supposed to be associated with that

---

14. Previously, in Ximénez, we saw that the title of *Quiché Vinak*, an equivalent drama performed by the Quiché to denounce the attacks of a Cakchiquel warrior (son of the king of Tecpán-Guatemala), is derived from the name of the local warrior and not from the intruder's name.

power (e.g., dignity, authority, mastery of self, calm, serenity, majesty, and gravity), as seen in these examples taken from various dictionaries:

> Angel (n.d.: fol. 45): *chapom chi ahauarem,* puesto en señorio.
>
> Anleo (n.d.: fol. 7v): *ahavalah vinak,* gente principal; (10v) *nu chuch nu kahau,* mi madre, mi padre; (13v) *he Ɛinom chiri4et e xcahavaric,* aquellos eran ricos, por eso gobernaron.
>
> Basseta (1698: fol. 140): *qahauaric,* señorear; (162) *ahauaribal tem,* asiento de Magestad o grandeza; (140v) *ahau; rahaual al cahol,* señor de vasallos; *chicahil ahau,* señor soberano.
>
> Coto (1983: 520): *ahaval vach nu vach,* sereno estar, y con gravedad y majestad.
>
> Santo Domingo (1693: fol. 4): *ahauarizah,* hacer reinar, o constituir en la tal dignidad.
>
> Tirado (1787: fol. 19v): *oher ahauarem,* antiguo gobierno; (61) *ahavilah vinak,* gente quieta, o sosegada, y lo que literalmente dice es, el reposo, y Señorío; (74v) *ahavarem; ahavaremal; nima vinakil,* dignidad, o señorío; (89) *ahauarem;* ahavaremal, enseñoreado; (109) *ahaualah vinak,* persona grave, de autoridad; (126v) *ahauarem,* insignias, o divisa, como los que tienen los Señores en la mano; (155) *kahavixel,* patriarca; *chuch kahauh tool vinak,* patrón, o defensor; (165) *ahavilah 4oheic,* quietud y sociego; (169v) *ahavalah vinak,* real persona; (171) *ahavuaremal,* reino, señorío; *quin ahavaric,* yo reino; (177v) *ahau,* señor; *ahavab,* señores; *quin ahavaric,* señorearse; (188v) *ahaualah 4hamiy,* vara real; (197) *nu kahau/wahau,* mi padre.
>
> Vico (n.d.a: fol. 4): *ahau,* el cacique o señor; *ahauab,* señor quiché; *Ɛalel ahau,* gran señor; *ahauar,* v[erb]o neutro de *ahau; ahauariçam, ahauariçah, ti ahauaren,* señorío o dignidad.

Here, too, the *Rabinal Achi* usefully completes the lexical contribution by providing us with firsthand information regarding the place granted to the king, as well as his role and his actions within the framework of related events.

The king unquestionably stands at the center. He rules over his subjects ("the white children") from within his citadel ("the great wall, the great fortress," "the sovereign wall"), itself located "at the navel of the sky, at the navel of the earth."[15] This royal residence is described as a chest filled with riches (objects of tribute) and within which the king is safely ensconced—he is literally "enclosed" there and "kept," like a treasure,[16] "covered, sheltered" under the protection ("in the shadow") of the paraphernalia of power. The

15. It even seems, if we are to believe the tale, that the citadel is invested, par excellence, with that umbilical function that, depending on the contexts, is true for Tzamaneb as well as for Kajyub. Similarly, several times the text evokes this almost "cellular" unicity within which the fortress and the king (the "nucleus") are set. This metaphor is sketched through phrases of the type "the ruler(s) of the interior of . . ." and through a reciprocal eponymous relationship that blurs distinctions between the two.

16. Also enclosed and guarded is the "Princess," the mother of the quetzal, the green feathers, the gems, the precious jewels.

royal bench is called *muj q'alibal,* which associates the "dais of feathers" with "throne," and several passages evoke the opulence and comfort of the place (lines 1359–1364, also 607–624).

The text also lists actions associated with the king: from his "retreat," he summons, convokes, recommends, orders, and exhorts and sometimes he bestows, heaps, offers, and, of course, performs marriages and renders justice. These last two prerogatives, of which the *Rabinal Achi* provides one of the most illustrative examples, were also pointed out in the sixteenth century in the *Vocabulario de la lengua cakchiquel,* compiled by Fray Domingo de Vico, which defines "kahaual" (or *q-ajaw-al;* literally, "our lord, our king") as "gran persona, el Principal como anciano o más viejo, que entiende en los pleitos, o casamientos."

These examples confirm that the king is in every respect the antithesis of the warrior. Just as the warrior is active, the king is calm and serene; when the warrior runs around in all directions, traveling around the territory and climbing mountains and valleys, the other is immobile and reclusive in his fortress; while the warrior is exposed to risks, to trials, and to bad weather, the king is sheltered, secure, and protected. The inert and measured nature of the royal figure is more than an expression of age, an attitude, or a privilege—it is consubstantial to him. This complete inertia is confirmed in the way in which the king is (accidentally) forced to move. The text mentions his movement only once: on the occasion of the kidnapping of Job Toj, an event that relates to a circumstance that is unique from every point of view and results from a disorder provoked by epic hubris. During that journey and his return, the king is always and only transported by being "picked up" (*yak*) and "carried in the arms" (*lot'ot'ej*), as if he were incapable of moving by himself, as if it were necessary that he be moved as one might move a package or a piece of furniture.[17]

Thus, the *Rabinal Achi* does not just portray, through some of its manifestations, the fundamental duality that is seen in ancient Rabinaleb representations relating to power or, within that duality, the two poles of complementary

17. Symbolically and metaphorically reducing the figure of the king—the entity endowed with power—to an inert object is probably one of the most ancient and stable conventions within the indigenous system of representations. It is found, in fact, in the form of "sacred bundles" carried by Quiché ancestors during the long journey of the original migration (like their homologues, the Azteca Chichimeca). Indeed, this convention still appears today as the principal motif of the village of Rabinal's founding myth: the Patzka ancestors, arriving at the end of a long wandering, discovered the Divino Sacramento (or Achi Ajaw) seated, immobile, at the foot of the church. Upon his request, the Patzka managed to lift him up and carry him to the main altar, but they died shortly after their efforts. The Sun (*ajaw* par excellence), however, began its course, moved by this first impulse and, in some way, animated and endowed with life following this founding "sacrifice" (see Breton 1982, 1989). Finally, we must not forget the carrying of the saints in procession, which reflects a comparable necessity and explicitly pursues the same intent. The saints, Christ, and the king, like the Sun, all belong to the category *ajaw* (Breton 1989).

opposition represented by the figures of the warrior and the king. Although it is clear that the "categories" *achi* and *ajaw* are antinomic and that their antinomy is projected, as we have seen, onto names, characteristics, attitudes, actions, roles, functions, and even places that are associated with them, this dichotomy, so strongly stressed by the text, signifies other things and serves a more crucial purpose.

Supremacy of One Figure over the Other

At the same time that the text asserts the contrast between the two figures, it connects them through a genetic relationship that while distinguishing the warrior-son from the king-father, relates their differences to those that separate two generations. Indeed, they symbolize, respectively, youth vs. old age, movement vs. impotence, and excitement vs. serenity, a list that we could continue into a long inventory of contrastive propositions: standing/seated, loud/calm, exposed/sheltered, and so forth. The expected consequence of such a configuration is that an eventual transformation of one figure into the other appears potentially inscribed in the normal course of biological (the advancement in age) and sociological (the cycle of life) processes. The text easily supports the hypothesis. Although he is opposed to the reconciliation proposed by the king, Rabinal Achi must resign himself to it: as the legitimate heir of the sovereign, "son" par excellence of Job Toj, his loyalty must remain with his father and he is ultimately confirmed in his functions as warrior and in his (assumed) destiny as future king.

On the contrary, K'iche' Achi, by defying royal authority, appears as a rebel "son." Through his determination and his refusal to bend to the offers that are made to him—offers that are related to a protocol of "adoption"—he definitively rejects the idea that he can be (or become) a son to Job Toj and, consequently, resolutely turns away from a royal destiny, preferring (and condemning himself to) death. Summed up in this way, however, such an ontogenetic interpretation only focuses on the tragic outcome of the tale, on its "theatrical" nature. This interpretation essentially only comes out of the form and the constraints that the composition of the work imposes on itself (e.g., distribution and status of the characters, balance and symmetry of their lines, and the ambiguity of the relationship between the two warriors and the king).

An alternative consists of directing the interpretation of the *Rabinal Achi* toward phylogenesis, or, more exactly, toward "history" as it was written by the Rabinaleb. What interests us right now in that history is not so much the conjunctural and precarious nature of the event that it relates—a particular dispute that, among other things, closes a long series of conflicts between the groups present; forges a renewed peace with the Quiché; reestablishes the independence of the Rabinaleb from the Quiché; and confirms a disputed and ultimately won territorial possession over the Uxab Poq'omab—as the way in which it articulates these facts in the long term. The essential message of the tale resides in the assertion that a more profound transformation, one of another nature, indeed took place and that it came out of an irreversible process. The exploitation (to political or ritual ends) of the trial against K'iche' Achi, like its periodic reproduction through the representations of the dance, is essentially a *pro domo* argument, and the meaning of the text goes largely beyond the framework of a particular conjunctural event or an exemplary story of a family. It *is* the History of the Rabinaleb, the one that they recognize and that has value both as a genesis tale (the sacrifice giving birth to the day) and as a founding myth (the exploits of the ancestors, the definition of the territory, and the establishment in Kajyub). This tale presents an indigenous theory of History and thus includes the mythical paradigms from which it speculates on the meaning and the stages of its own evolution. Seen from this angle, the *Rabinal Achi* is also the fruit of collective creation, of common knowledge, of a tradition that, behind the characters of the drama and the figures they represent, portray "mythistorical" (according to the useful expression of D. Tedlock [1985]) processes and what we can call an "ethnohistoriography."

As previously mentioned, K'iche' Achi and Rabinal Achi are both associated with hunters. Whereas the Rabinaleb seek honey and bees,[18] K'iche' Achi hunts the Rabinaleb by calling to them while imitating the sounds of several animals, as if he were trying to lure his prey. Now, this connotation metaphorically projects the image of the warrior back to ancient times, the time of the ancestors who during their long migration, experienced the same modes of "subsistence" and utilized the same "hunting" techniques. An example is the description of their living conditions in those distant days, taken from the *Historia Quiché de don Juan de Torres*:

> [E]staban desnudos, sin abrigo, no tenían vestido, no tenían que comer, *sólo miel y avispas conseguían*, sólo el muzgo de los árboles recogían a un tiempo aquellas gentes infortunadas . . . llegaron cerca del mar. . . . Después que llegaron, se levantaron junto al mar, lo pasaron vadeándolo y llegaron a la [otra] orilla del mar, se establecieron y se quedaron. Mataban a los venados y cazaban a las liebres en sus madrigueras, robaban a las liebres y a los zompopos, *mientras lanzaban el grito del gato de monte y el coyote en la oscuridad y en la noche.* (Recinos 1984: 27–31; emphasis mine)[19]

Owing to this connection, the figure of the warrior appears as the heir of those distant ancestors, as mobile, exposed hunters ("*sin abrigo*"). Thus, it

18. In this regard, we may note that Rabinal Achi is not directly associated with this activity; his role consists of watching over the "white children" when they are gathering. This difference might indicate a discrimination between the hunting of large animals, perhaps the exclusive privilege of the great warriors (the nobility), and the activities managed by the "white children" (the subjects or vassals), which are associated more with gathering.

19. It is possible that the names of the animals mentioned in the tale—who, it is specified, are "hunted" and "caught"—might designate peoples encountered on the way, like the Uxab Poq'omab in the *Rabinal Achi.* For example, the *venados* might allude to the Aj Kejay ("Those of the House of the Deer"), one of the local groups related to the Poq'omab and who the Quiché-Cakchiquel claim to have met during their migration (see Recinos 1980; see also Percheron 1982).

is identified with another famous Mesoamerican figure, the Chichimeca, the "barbarian," and symbolizes the "wild" and obscure side of History,[20] that long period from migration to establishment and passing through the first attempts of populating and conquests that preceded the assertion of territorial and political independence.[21] The institution of royalty was born out of this process. No doubt the figure of the king emerges gradually through these stages at the price of many conflicts of interests, influences, and power with the warriors.

Our text unrolls the thread of these events, which it attempts to establish once and for all in a bygone past, a past characterized by migration and conquest. The warrior's ideal, hunter and ancestral, no longer exists. To be convinced of this fact one need only refer to the recommendations of the sovereign authorities of the Quiché, the same ones that K'iche' Achi, absent and therefore unable to hear them, has ignored.

The trial, which serves as the argument for the story, thus confirms that a page of the history has been resolutely turned, that a new era has arrived in which this anachronistic archetype of the warrior is no longer master of the game but now must bend to royal authority. This mutation is evidently what is meant in Act II by Rabinal Achi's change of mind and the new "dubbing" of which he is the object. By contrast, K'iche' Achi still behaves as an outdated warrior-hunter, violates the orders of his peers, continues in excess and threats, declines the conciliatory offers of the sovereign, denies his authority, and rejects adoption (domestication?) as he wallows in a stubbornness and an excessiveness that lead to his death. The final sacrifice of the rebel and conquering warrior "buries"[22] the ancestral past that he represents as much as it feeds the luminous present of the king: his death thus marks the definitive triumph of the day over darkness, of sedentary values over nomadic values, of agriculture over hunting; in short, of civilization over barbarianism.

RETURN TO EVENTS[23]

A DISPUTED TERRITORY

Representations of space and of its use are shown through the speech of the two principal characters, Rabinal Achi and K'iche' Achi, both of whom are presented as warriors intent on defending their territory while devoting

20. The previous excerpt seems to differentiate two moments in the long and difficult adventure: that of the primitive wandering, associated with gathering ("*miel y avispas*") and that of the first temporary establishments, associated with a true hunt.

21. This independence was probably of short duration since in 1517 the Cakchiquel attempted to subjugate the region (*Anales de los Cakchiqueles,* in Recinos 1980) and, in 1524, Pedro de Alvarado entered into Guatemala.

22. This allusion to "burial" is not a mere figure of speech since, indeed, an earlier defeat of K'iche' Achi is explicitly described in these terms: "Was it not at Belejeb Moqoj Belejeb Chumay that this anger and this force went to bury, to inter themselves?" (lines 276–280).

23. This part expands a text published in Spanish in Breton 1993.

themselves to the conquest of new territory, in perpetual movement far from their respective "capitals."

Territorial Possession. The *Rabinal Achi* establishes a fundamental dichotomy between the center, which, as the domain of the king, is a protected place, sheltered and warm, and the periphery, which is the realm of the warrior, a place of danger, challenges, and cold. When specific events concern the places where their kings reside—Q'umarmachi for K'iche' Achi and Chatinibal (Tzamaneb) for Rabinal Achi—the warriors are absent, busy traveling afar "at the foot of the mountains, the foot of the valleys." The expression of such travels is associated with the idea of territorial marking, expressed in terms of "bordering" or in terms of "surveying" and "measurement" ("I was setting up the boundary stones" [line 398]; "I paced," literally, "measured with a rope" [line 762]). The text does not always specify the explicit goals of these travels or what such actions involve.

As Job Toj reminds Rabinal Achi, however, one of the functions assigned to the warrior consists of accompanying hunting and/or gathering expeditions carried out by the king's subjects to watch over them while they are undertaking such activities and to protect them from threats that might exist in the zones of the expeditions. Beyond the necessity of acquiring "the king's food," traveling through those territories corresponds to a need to effect permanent control over their internal conditions as well as over the security of their borders, tasks that, in the end, involve a purely defensive strategy. The text also refers to other journeys that can be considered to be more offensive in purpose, notably when it denounces the movements of the Quiché warrior in the Rabinaleb's own territory and the actions that the warrior boasts about having undertaken there. The journey and the "pacing" are synonyms here for taking possession of the places and for military victory; the aggressor explicitly alludes to the overthrowing of King K'amba and to the subjugation of his men, whom he calls "children" (vassals) of the Rabinaleb (lines 766–771). The appropriation begins then with domination and subjugation but also with the use of the lands. This appropriation is, it seems, the meaning of the passage in which K'iche' Achi proposes to take and to carry off (metaphorically, "in his arms" and "with his sandals") the fertile lands seen from Chisaliya (lines 788–804).

The cycle in which this journey is inscribed is exemplary. The complete series of the places it encompasses is described by K'iche' Achi: "I paced and measured the place called Tzam K'amba! . . . and the land of Tzam Saqkijel. . . . I clambered down toward Chisaliya . . . to measure and pace Tzam Ixtink'urun . . . opposite the place called Ximbaja . . . and . . . Tzam K'isintun" (lines 762–811). The action of pacing or measuring (which is rendered by the verb *etak'amar*) bears exclusively on four of these toponyms described as *tzam* ("point, extremity, eminence"); Chisaliya is mentioned here only to designate an intermediary stage, Ximbaja is noted as a locative referent. These toponyms are all easily identifiable, and they are still visited and frequented today during rituals preparatory to representations of the dance. Each constitutes a step in the journey and is located in relation to Kajyub according to the following schema:

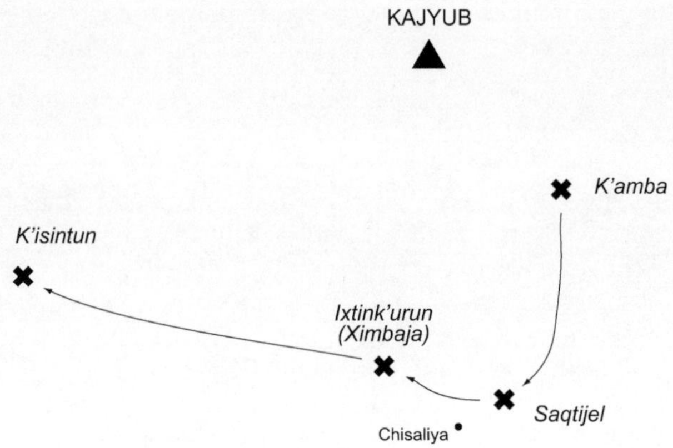

This circuit evokes one of the most well-known and ancient symbolic Mayan configurations through which, by relating the passing of the days to a cyclical traveling through space, the Maya had partially resolved the problem of the anisotropy of time. This configuration, which can still be found in several communities in the Guatemala highlands, designates the four "corners of the world" (surrounding a center) between which "circulate" the days, notably the four days of the ritual calendar called "Year bearers," which preside like divinities over the destiny of places and people.[24] The fact that K'iche' Achi's circuit is inscribed in a period of 260 days therefore provides a new illustration of this configuration. Through his marking of the four points that serve as stages, the intentions of the Quiché intruder are revealed: to control the entire "world" of the Rabinaleb and to reign over their destiny.

As we know—and as K'iche' Achi laments—his attempt failed: even though he managed to complete the journey, he did not take possession of the "white mountains, the white valleys, the navel of the sky, the navel of the earth" (lines 817–820). He, however, immediately hastens to assert (perhaps through spite or arrogance) that he is "in *his* mountains, in *his* valleys," as he proclaims twice (lines 756–757, 840–841; emphasis mine). These false claims by him fit within the logic of the text.

A Possession Claimed by All. Indeed, one of the *Rabinal Achi*'s statements is that the territory in question—the basin—is claimed by each of the three groups represented: the Quiché (as expressed through the voice of their champion), the Rabinaleb, and the Uxab Poq'omab. We will not spend much time on the claims of the first two as they are well-known. Indeed, the very meaning of the trial against K'iche' Achi continually demonstrates that this territory belongs

24. Other communities where such a system persists include Todos Santos Cuchumatán (Oakes 1973), Nebaj (Lincoln 1942, 1945; Breton 2001), and Momostenango (B. Tedlock 1991).

to the Rabinaleb alone: it is the place where they have established their capital (Kajyub), they possess vassals (the inhabitants of the site of K'amba, of the "land" of Saqkijel), they obtain the food intended for their king (i.e., the "honey flies" and honey), and they cultivate many kinds of food (corn ["the white ears"] and various types of beans and squashes, including "ayotes" and "huicoy") over vast stretches of thick, rich, fertile lands.

It is appropriate, however, to spend some time on the claim of the Uxab and the Poq'omab, whose conflicting proximity to the Rabinaleb is the object of a long passage (lines 513–730). This section reminds us of the attacks carried out by the Uxab Poq'omab ("How they harassed our mountains our valleys" [lines 570–571]; "they attacked our children here, at the navel of the sky at the navel of the earth" [lines 699–701]), the counteroffensive led by the Rabinaleb and the ritual preparations to which it gave rise ("the trumpets and drums of the bleeding"), the help requested by Rabinal Achi of K'iche' Achi with a view to exterminating the Uxab Poq'omab before they definitively withdrew.

> . . . run over there,
> across from the great road of Chi Rok'obaya Tz'ikin
> across from the place called Cholochik Tz'aq Chun!
> And do not give an inch to the machinations of the Uxab
> of the Poq'omab!
> Don't let them get away toward their mountains
> toward their valleys.
> Destroy them,
> crush them
> here, at the navel of the sky
> at the navel of the earth! (lines 523–533)

Using an artifice to escape K'iche' Achi's vigilance (lines 539–546), the Uxab Poq'omab are successful and recapture the basin, declaring loud and clear, as if to contest the territorial ambitions of the Rabinaleb and to show that they are in no way their inferiors:

> This is how it is, we have regained
> our mountains
> our valleys.
> Is not this the very place where we settled
> with my children
> who are under the black clouds
> under the white clouds,
> in gusts of wind
> exposed to the cold,
> under the protection of the green feathers,
> under the yellow *pataxte*
> under the yellow cacao
> under the yellow metal
> under the white metal
> that they decorate with feathers
> that they carve with my vassals?

This is how my children are:
they don't have any trouble at all getting a piece
a portion of food for themselves;
even when they sleep, five loads of *pataxte*
five loads of cacao come to them,
for they are feather-workers
they are carvers under the sun
under the light of day. (lines 597–623)

This episode shows furthermore that K'iche' Achi is not naively taken in by the ruse deployed by the Uxab Poq'omab. The text introduces a doubt, suggesting that the Quiché warrior has deliberately let them escape instead of destroying them. It is possible that K'iche' Achi wants the Uxab Poq'omab threat to continue to weigh on the Rabinaleb to weaken them, perhaps with the goal of later subjugating them too.

Whatever the case may be, we can confirm that the places (and the territory) claimed by the Rabinaleb are equally claimed by the other two groups and that possession of them is bitterly disputed. This competition among the groups does not appear to be gratuitous since this territorial indetermination, echoed in the text, is accompanied by a comparable political indetermination.

AN IMPOSSIBLE ALLIANCE

The episode we have just described, in fact, appears following a misunderstanding between the two warriors regarding what I will call "the episode of the messenger." After Rabinal Achi had denounced the unjustified ardor of his adversary by recalling that the recommendations of peace had been proclaimed by the sovereign authorities (gathered in a council in Q'umarmachi), K'iche' Achi concedes this point, but not without mentioning his absence from the Quiché capital at the time of this "pact." All the same, and in the guise of an explanation for his vigorous irruption, he claims to have been sent by his king to respond to the message of an emissary who came from Kajyub. The message exhorted K'iche' Achi in these terms:

Let him come to take possession of the white mountains
of the white valleys!
Let my younger brother,
my elder brother come!
Let him come to take possession
of this place, the navel of the sky
the navel of the earth,
the white mountains
the white valleys!
Let him come and sow
come and hoe
and let our squash seedlings
our white squash seedlings sprout together. (lines 359–371)

To the Quiché ruler, Balam Ajaw Balam K'iche', this "invitation" rings like a provocation, a challenge made by the Rabinaleb in the presence or in the company of the Uxab Poq'omab, with a view to draw him into an ambush and, he assumes, conquer him. In the guise of reprisals, he reacts immediately by summoning his warrior (K'iche' Achi) to investigate without delay what he considers to be a secession[25] or, indeed, a rebellion since the Uxab Poq'omab are implicated.

What the king of the Quiché understands and retains from the tenor of the message that reaches him is summed up by K'iche' Achi:

> That was when he learned — King Balam Ajaw
> Balam K'iche' —
> that his death is desired
> by the king of the Chakachib
> of the Tzamanib,
> Kawuq Rabinal,
> opposing the Uxab
> opposing the Poq'omab. (lines 345–352)

For his part, Rabinal Achi denies having had such an intention. On the contrary, the invitation was sincere and aimed to solicit "fraternal" ties that would unite the Rabinaleb and the Quiché so that they might battle the Uxab Poq'omab together. Such is, in any case, the version he proposes as the reason for sending the emissary:

> . . . it is true that an emissary
> a messenger came from here;
> it is true that we sent him
> over there toward the K'iche' mountains
> the K'iche' valleys.
> But this was not a fault
> this was not an offense to send him there
> so that King Balam Ajaw
> Balam K'iche' might learn
> that the Uxab
> and the Poq'omab
> desired the death
> the disappearance of the king of the Chakachib
> the Tzamanib
> Kawuq Rabinal. (lines 475–489)

In a certain sense, the rest of the events only confirm Rabinal Achi's fears: indeed, the flight of the Uxab Poq'omab, in spite of the (timid) intervention of K'iche' Achi, at the very least was facilitated by his refusal to fight them. Strong

---

25. It is this same passage that points out the tributary dependence of the Rabinaleb vis-à-vis Q'umarmachi, which K'iche' Achi is eager to stress, as if to remind them of their obligations: "[I]s not this where they assemble the five loads of *pataxte*, the five loads of cacao?" (lines 335–336).

from this statement and given the facts evoked previously, the Rabinal warrior can only denounce this fruitless alliance.

> But it was in vain that we offered You
> in vain that we allowed You to descend
> here to the navel of the sky
> to the navel of the earth. (lines 509–512)

Therefore, even more perhaps than the ineffectiveness shown by K'iche' Achi, it is the collusion between K'iche' Achi and the Uxab Poq'omab that provokes the anger of Rabinal Achi and that, added to the other charges against the prisoner, reinforce K'iche' Achi's guilt.

Beyond the at least ambiguous expression of the protagonists' respective intentions and behaviors at the time of the facts and during their recalling—and the misunderstanding of the messenger is only one of several—we can assert that the tale works constantly to stress the complexity of a regional situation dominated by confusion and political indetermination. However, if we disregard the suspicion and the equivocal opinions shown by those involved toward each other, the narrative structure is far from confused. Indeed, the tale systematically plays with all possible combinations of alliance, exposing one by one the three imaginable solutions to which the three groups present can have recourse and then sentencing them all to failure. According to the text, each solution is not viable, from an alliance between the Quiché and the Rabinaleb (the Rabinal point of view on the episode of the messenger), an alliance between the Rabinaleb and the Uxab Poq'omab (the Quiché point of view), to the alliance between the Quiché and the Uxab Poq'omab (in the view of the empirical reality described by the Rabinaleb). All are "thinkable," but none is truly possible. Each of the three protagonist groups is definitively alone in its confrontation with each of the other two.

The evocation of another theme in the *Rabinal Achi,* similarly illustrating a situation of extreme atomization, offers us another occasion to support these observations.

The War: A Metaphor for the Hunt

The Quest for Food. Besides the text's expressions of constant traveling over the territories—expressions that are in the end anecdotal as they simply reinforce the two protagonists' status by emphasizing this "typical" behavior of the warrior—a much more important and major theme relating to the central argument is developed by the text: that of subsistence and of the ways in which that subsistence is obtained. This theme brings us to the heart of the relationships among the three groups that inhabit, and claim, this territory.

Let us return to the time of the trial and to the primary impetus for that trial: the Quiché warrior was once again caught in the process of hunting the "white children" on the immediate outskirts of their fortress, insidiously attempting to lure them as a hunter would do his game or, rather, pretending himself to be a possible prey to attract them as hunters with a view to capturing them. As Rabinal Achi says:

> Could my heart really forget
> having seen You
> having observed You
> behind the great fortress
> behind the great wall,
> You who imitated the coyote crying
>   who imitated the wildcat howling
>   who imitated the agouti howling
>   the jaguar howling
> behind the great citadel
> as to attract them, the white children
> that we had sent out in front of the great fortress
>   in front of the great wall:
> those who look for flies of yellow honey
>   for flies of green honey,
> food for our master
>   for our eminence
> —Great King Job Toj? (lines 216–235)

Indeed, the "white children" are also presented as hunters and, more specifically, as indicated in the final passage, as hunters of "flies of honey" upon which their king feeds.

Now, this activity occurs within a particularly hostile environment. For confirmation, one need only listen to what the Uxab Poq'omab say about it.

> As for the children
> of Dignitary
>   Rabinal Achi,
> only by red torments
>   by suffering
> do they obtain their pieces
>   their portions of food
> under the sun
> under the light of day! (lines 624–632)

The Rabinaleb thus find themselves forced to limit their quest to the immediate outskirts of their fortress, from which they leave only in small numbers, returning to it immediately (lines 680–685). When they must leave in a larger group to travel farther—"when they look for and seek in the four directions, in the four corners, at the head of the earth, at the feet of the earth [i.e., to the west and the east], in one day's journey, in two days' journey!" (lines 655–660)—they expose themselves to attacks that result in their "defeat and annihilation" (lines 672–673). The very terms of this statement and the strength of the words used to convey the worst difficulties to which these initiatives are confronted indicate that this search for precious royal food is much more than a simple gathering of items and that it is explicitly related to operations of capture that put warrior strategies into play. The image of this hunt for "white children" (led by the Quiché) or for the "flies of honey" (led by the Rabinaleb) thus functions as a metaphor for war. What is more, if we add the capture of K'iche' Achi and the fatal outcome to which he exposes himself, these pell-mell representations are revealed to connect to two types of war. One consists of procuring new vassals intended to populate and to exploit new lands, or to occupy or reinforce some frontier post (which, in my opinion, is the underlying objective of the kidnapping of the "white children" by K'iche' Achi, some of whom were to be settled in Pan K'aqil whereas others settled in Pamaq'a or the former Zacualpa). The other aims more specifically at the capture of sacrificial victims and is associated with what is called "holy war."

The Capture of Sacrificial Victims. The *Rabinal Achi* alludes on various occasions to prisoners of war and to the outcome that awaits them. I have already highlighted the tenor of the passage concerning the "pact" by which Quiché authorities recommend no longer "consuming the white children" (lines 263–264). These resolutions, which follow the statement of extreme penury from which the Rabinaleb suffer (following the attacks by the Uxab Poq'omab), basically recommend suspending a practice that consisted of "eating" them, that is, making them sacrificial victims intended to feed the gods of the Quiché capital. And this fate was no doubt the same one that the Quiché reserved for the Rabinaleb before the aforementioned resolutions intervened.

This custom seems to have been shared by the two groups and is inscribed in the framework of reciprocal practices. It is in the same sense but with a reversal of roles, that Rabinal Achi, inquiring into the case of K'iche' Achi and ordering him to declare his origins, literally threatens his prisoner with "cutting him into portions" and "introducing him as food" to his sovereign (lines 174–183). Indeed, Ximénez (1926: 125) might have been influenced by the *Rabinal Achi,* echoes of which surely reached him during his long stay in Rabinal, when he asserted in turn that a high-ranking enemy (*señor principal*) captured during a war was sacrificed and eaten.

The reciprocity between Rabinaleb and Quiché concerning the necessity of obtaining sacrificial victims through "holy" war (that they waged mutually) accounts for only a part of the interrelations maintained by the various groups on a regional scale. In this realm, the text also assigns an eminent role to the Uxab Poq'omab and lends itself to an analysis enabling us to better understand the nature of the rivalry and the antagonisms between them and the Rabinaleb.

The hostility of the environment takes on its full measure here. The difficulties encountered when they move away from their fortress; the obligation to carry out only sporadic expeditions, brief "sorties" in limited numbers, that is to say, "bit by bit"; the eminently local nature of the quest for food intended for Job Toj; and the extreme vigilance with which they proceed are so many indications of strong pressures from neighboring groups and suggest the permanent and omnipresent threat of the Uxab Poq'omab that weighed upon their immediate environment. Expressed in cynegetic terms, the situation in which the Rabinaleb find themselves is both that of the hunted and that of the hunter; in this context, they are prey as well as predator. However, if it is clear that the Rabinaleb are the prey of the Uxab Poq'omab, who are the Rabinaleb's prey?

Hunters of Bees, Gatherers of Honey. The model of the reciprocal war waged by the Rabinaleb and the Quiché can be used to look at the relationship between the Rabinaleb and the Uxab Poq'omab. I propose to interpret the hunt for "flies of honey" as making implicit reference to the hunt for the Uxab Poq'omab. Beyond the "warrior" characterization that describes this quest and beyond the consumption of the prey (which connects it to the complex of a holy war), this interpretation seems justified by a series of more or less subtle indications that nevertheless form a relatively significant ensemble and is, to my mind, sufficiently persuasive to hazard it.

We will look first at the information contained in the ethnonymy and thus at what an analysis of the words *ux* and *poq'om* (the suffix *-ab* is a mark of the plural) reveals. The etymology of *ux* is obscure and its interpretation remains uncertain. The root *ux* might designate a gnat, a "little fly" or a "baby fly," and thus allude directly to the animals hunted by the Rabinaleb, that is, the "flies of honey." In that, *ux* would either be an idiomatic form of the root *us,* more generally found in all Quiché languages, or the result of a transformation from *ux* to *us,* which comes out of a play on words. An argument in favor of the first hypothesis is the description given by the *Rabinal Achi* of the flight of the Uxab Poq'omab in the form of a migration of ants and flies, large and small, which effectively uses the word *uxil* (and not *usil*) with regard to the flies (Brasseur 1862b: 46; *Pérez Manuscript*). In favor of the second hypothesis, we have proof that the terms *ux* and *us* can be interchangeable, as in Uspantán where they still designate patronyms and whose evocation lends itself to jokes. The precariousness of such connections, I admit, can appear bold, and I would hesitate to use them if other considerations did not support them.

Curiously, the etymology of *poq'om,* more convincing in my opinion, also relates the meaning of this term to the same semantic realm: this ethnonym in fact refers to the primitive techniques of apiculture. Thomás de Coto, in the entries "Castrar colmenas" and "Colmenas" in his *Thesaurus Verborum* (1983: 93, 98), lists the following forms:

tin poƐ: castrar colmenas
poƐom chic: colmena castrada
poƐonic: castradura

One can recognize through these expressions the evocation of a technique that is both very old and very widespread that consists, as is sometimes said, of hunting bees and harvesting honey. "Castrating the hives" means collecting the honey by uncapping — the primary meaning of the roots *poq'* and *or* is "to pull, to perforate" — the wax plugs covering the cavities. This harvesting or gathering can be carried out either by respecting the integrity of the hive (after chasing the bees away) or by destroying it, but the result is always the extraction[26] of the brood, that is, the eggs, the larvae, and the immature animals as well as the honey.[27]

Yet, is the connection between the ethnonym Poq'omab and the root *poƐ-* purely fortuitous? The response to this question is provided indirectly by Ximénez: in writing that the "ah poƐon" are "los de Chinautla" (1985: 65), he evokes the very ones whose oral tradition still untiringly recalls that they were the original inhabitants of the region of Rabinal and that they were expulsed from it by the Rabinaleb.[28] But further, does the sign Ɛ (tresillo) of the old dictionaries truly correspond to the glottalized uvular /q'/ by which we have rendered it? The various translators of the *Rabinal Achi,* having up to then only Brasseur's version, could only follow the transcription provided by him and consequently adopt the spelling *k* (thus, "Pokom"). In the *Pérez Manuscript,* on the other hand, we find *poƐomab* (i.e., *poq'omab,* respecting the equivalency between the sign Ɛ and the phoneme /q'/, which is verified throughout the text). Without a doubt, we are dealing with a single root, and I thus propose to translate the ethnonym Poq'omab as "castrated hives." Furthermore, to direct this convergence of meanings toward an apiarian context, let us remember the name of the Poq'omab capital as it is revealed in the *Anales de los Cakchiqueles*: Oronik Kaqjay. Again, in Coto (1983) there is a possible explanation for this toponym, notably in the connection suggested by the lexicography between the roots *poƐ-* and *or-*:

ti u'or cab: castrar colmenas [synonym for *tin poƐ*]

orom: colmena castrada [synonym for *poƐom*]

oronel: castrador [synonym for *poƐol cab*]

voronic: castradura así [synonym for *poƐonic*]

---

26. "Entresacar" is also one of the meanings derived from the root *poƐ* according to Coto (1983: 201). This same author (96) gives the word *ux* the meaning of "coger algo con los dos dedos . . . como cogen el algodón o chiles," which refers to a gathering of fragile, but also stinging, objects necessitating particular care.

27. This technique was still practiced in Rabinal fifty years ago. Bonifacia Mendoza, born in 1915, remembers the way in which, at the time, one "cut" or "castrated" the hives with the help of an ax (*ikaj*) to collect the honey. This operation was used for the bees' permanent nests, called *uskab* and *wonon,* installed in hollow trunks of trees like the *iximche'* tree. The hives were cut after the occupants had been chased with great blows of a fan or by waving rags around. The hanging hives, of the kind called *aqaj,* were smoked and then removed with the help of a pole before being entirely consumed (honey, combs, and larvae). The use of these apiculture techniques is noted among the Maya of the Yucatán at the time of the Conquest and during the Colonial era (see, in particular, Landa 1978: 125–126; Barrera Vásquez 1980; Álvarez 1980: 166, 193, 284–285; 1984: 36, 100–101, 103) and elsewhere in the world (see *L'abeille, l'homme, le miel et la cire* 1981: 127).

28. This popular interpretation is unanimous: the Uxab Poq'omab once lived in the basin of Rabinal from which they were expelled under the pressure of the Rabinaleb, some of them emigrating toward San Cristóbal Verapaz (i.e., the people henceforth known as Poq'omchi') and others toward Chinautla (i.e., the Poq'omam).

Thus, the congruence noted between these names and the logical correspondence of their meanings—the Poq'omab (or "castrated hives"), Oronik Kaqjay (the "red house of castration"),[29] and the Uxab (the "flies")—place us in the presence of a relatively well-identified metaphorical ensemble, enabling us to assume that the quest for "animals of honey," undertaken by the Rabinaleb to feed their king, designates quite directly (although in an enigmatic form) their victims: the Uxab Poq'omab. Neighbors and rivals of the Rabinaleb, they are their prey and also their predators.

As if to render the image of these Rabinaleb living amidst the bees (the Uxab/flies; the Poq'omab/hives) as even more significant, various other local indications join to confirm this identification.

1. In the text, the flight of the Uxab Poq'omab borrows the image of a great migration of insects with the look of a swarming: "they metamorphosed into gnats, into big flies, into little ants, into big ants and, forming long ranks, forming long files, they reached the foot of Ekempek mountain" (lines 539–545).
2. In the old oral traditions, as reported by Ximénez (1975: book 1, chapter 28: 81), at the time when the Rabinaleb occupied Tzamaneb: "[Q]ue está entre Cubulco y Xoyabah . . . como ellos [los Rabinaleb] veían las tierras de los contornos y [cuando] *saliesen a colmenear,* los cogían los de Cobán [los Poq'omab] y los sacrificaban y ofrecían a los ídolos."
3. In modern tradition, certain versions of the founding myth of the village of Rabinal, evoking the scene discovered by the Patzka ancestors when they arrived, show Achi Ajaw (Christian avatar of Job Toj; see Breton 1982, 1989) seated and immobile, in the darkness of a cave filled with bees (Mace 1970: 128).

This group of meanings, even if the formulation of a coherent model remains to be established, enables us to clarify somewhat the representation of relationships between the Rabinaleb and the Uxab Poq'omab.

Just like the figure of the warrior/hunter, the hunting of bees for food goes back to the mythical times of the migration and recalls the difficulties inherent in the living conditions of those times. Besides the previously cited *Historia Quiché de don Juan de Torres* ("no tenían que comer, sólo miel y avispas

29. Ichon (1982: 68–72) has proposed to identify Oronik Kaqjay with the archaeological site of Pakaqja (*pa kaq ja,* "place of the red house"). This identification is not incompatible with the idea of a conflict opposing this Poq'om site with Kajyub but argues in favor of a relative coexistence based on the dividing of the basin between the two groups: the northern part controlled by the Poq'omab, the southern part by the Rabinaleb. The archaeological observations (see Arnauld 1993) agree favorably with this hypothetical division distinguishing Kajyub and the sites of the southern foothills of the basin from the Poq'omab sites on the north of the valley (i.e., Oronik Kaqjay [or Pakaqja], Tz'aq Poq'om [Nim Poq'om Chwitinamit]). It is important to emphasize that the *Rabinal Achi* contains no reference to this latter great site next to Kajyub; this omission shows the extent of the extraordinary political fragmentation at the time and of the extreme concentration of what was specifically at stake.

conseguían"), three other texts also mention it, as Mace remarks (ibid.: 86), in reference to the situations of famine with which the ancestors often found themselves confronted when they moved from place to place.

> [T]hey did not live in their houses by day, but walked over the mountains, and ate only the young horseflies, and the wasps, and the bees which they hunted; they had neither good food nor good drink. (*Popol Vuh,* cited in Recinos et al. 1977: 192)

> Estaban sufriendo gran hambre, "sólo nos alimentamos de los hijos de las avispas y los hijos de los abejorros," le dijeron. (*Título Real de don Francisco Izquin,* cited in Recinos 1984: 111)

> [H]ere they stopped for some days . . . here also they stopped for some time, nourishing themselves with eggs of wasps and beetles . . . there, necessity forced them to eat the eggs of wasps and other insects. . . . There they raised houses, suffered many wants, although later they found a way to sow corn, with which they were content and they remained for a long time. (*Título de los Señores de Totonicapán,* cited in Recinos and Goetz 1974: 180–181)

RETURN TO THE TEXT: EPILOGUE

The descriptions the *Rabinal Achi* provides of the interrelations among the groups, of the pressures they exert on each other, and the political or territorial issues at stake are inscribed in the same imaginary—wandering, darkness, penury, territorial and political indetermination, gathering and hunting—as well as in the same processes as those evoked by the myths of migration. The pressure imposed by the Quiché on the Rabinaleb and the ambition of the Rabinaleb to conquer the basin—which materializes in the moving from Tzamaneb to Kajyub to the detriment of the Uxab Poq'omab—are fully inscribed in this general movement and conveys a similar dynamic of expansion and conquest.

Quiché → Rabinaleb → Uxab Poq'omab

From the point of view of the Rabinaleb, who appear here as the buffer group on a disputed border, one also understands that the text, by insisting on the difficulties encountered and the conflicts that they generate, accounts for the ultimate phase of these "leapfrog migrations" (Fox 1987), which experience their final throes while the final waves intermingle there.

If the text insists on emphasizing these difficulties and conflicts, if it attempts to reconstruct this troubled and confused history, it is above all in order to present a precondition to the goal it has set itself. Faithful to the mythical paradigm that travels through all Mesoamerican historical creation, from the oldest indigenous chronicles to the oral traditions still in use, this history serves an actuality and supports an eschatology. Just as the original chaos announces the coming of a new order, so does the primitive darkness foretell of the coming of the day, migration precedes establishment, territorial and political indetermination calls upon integrity and independence, and war is the antecedent to peace. And the composition of the *Rabinal Achi* is quite certainly one form of the writing of that history. To illustrate this point we will return to the problematics of the reciprocal relationships that connect the Rabinaleb to the Quiché on the one hand and the Uxab Poq'omab on the other, and at the heart of which they are each both prey and predator. Because although the tale spends a lot of time dealing with these relationships, it also asserts and ultimately proclaims their inviability.

Indeed, the message of the trial brought against K'iche' Achi resides in the definitive break of the Quiché/Rabinaleb relationship. K'iche' Achi, instead of helping the Rabinaleb destroy the Uxab Poq'omab, becomes their accomplice (whether or not intentionally) and allows them to flee, causing, as we have seen, a "swarming" that from then on deprives the Rabinaleb of their royal resource. Furthermore, if it is true that the execution of K'iche' Achi might appear as a "judicial" consequence of the many wrongs he is accused of throughout the trial, the death of the Quiché predator is also, in a certain way, the structural counterpart of the flight of the Uxab Poq'omab prey. The literary artifice rests on the following equation: neutralizing "the one who is hunting us" (the capture and death of K'iche' Achi) has as its corollary being rid of "those whom we hunt" (flight of the Uxab Poq'omab) and vice versa.

Therefore, a "structural" reading of the *Rabinal Achi* can be modeled on the form of the following scenario:

Paradigm of departure: migration-conquest (ancestral model)

Quiché → Rabinaleb → Uxab Poq'omab

Situation 1: a disputed territorial possession

Quiché → Rabinaleb ← Uxab Poq'omab

Situation 2: an impossible alliance

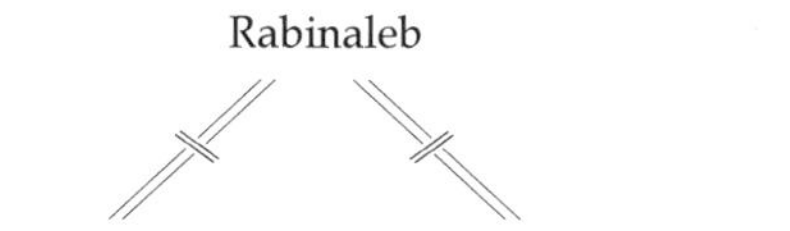

Situation 3: reciprocal war

Quiché ↔ Rabinaleb ↔ Uxab Poq'omab

Paradigm of arrival: the predator is neutralized *and* there is no more prey; the chain is broken (new model):

Quiché // Rabinaleb // Uxab Poq'omab

This scenario, which systematically takes into account—while simultaneously rejecting them—all the situations to which the reciprocal relationships between the three protagonist groups lend themselves, incontestably leads to a break in the logic of things, the transformation of an ancient (dis)order into a new order: migration gives way to settlement (in Kajyub), hunting to agriculture ("let us stop consuming the white children and set to consuming our own beans"; lines 263–266), and wandering and journeying over hostile lands to the enjoyment of one's own territory. The trial of K'iche' Achi is, among other things, a portrayal of this break and the announcement of this new order.

The moving from Tzamaneb to Kajyub, the triumph of the king over the warrior, and the independence acquired over the other groups express what is at stake on the local level. At the same time, these themes are common to other ethnohistorical sources as well as to modern oral traditions.

In general, the indigenous chronicles (such as the *Popol Vuh* and *Anales de los Cakchiqueles*) as well as contemporary myths (such as the one relating to the figure of the Yew Achi) deal with these issues in various ways, often to the advantage of the groups that are voicing the story and without our always being able to connect their episodes and establish order among them. A major difficulty heavily impedes a comparative examination of these sources and any connection of their data: this difficulty resides in the fact that, impassioned by its own history that is constantly reinvented, each of these groups has produced tales that are the panegyric of its own exploits, to the detriment of actions attributed to neighboring groups (whether they be allies or enemies), who are relegated to the role of mere objects, at best, of only laconic or depreciative mention. As Schele and Freidel have rightly stressed in the introduction to their study on Classic Mayan royalty,

> [h]istory is as much a construction of those writing it as the events it proposes to record, and this is as true of the Maya as of any other civilization. Surviving Maya texts give us, almost exclusively, only the side of the winners—those who were victorious in war, who had the power to commission the great public monuments and buildings, those wealthy enough to fill their tombs with inscribed objects, and those who could afford to buy or commission precious objects as offerings to the gods. . . . What we have is history as the kings and nobles wanted their constituents to understand it. (1990: 55)

The *Rabinal Achi* does not escape this rule, and there is every reason to believe that the narration it constructs is not an objective history. Having deliberately chosen to analyze the text from the inside, we will not raise any questions here on the "historical" veracity of the events or the words reported. It will eventually be necessary, to get a better look at that reality, to examine these *same* events in contemporary versions coming from the other groups involved, such as the Quiché or the Uxab Poq'omab. Granted, the text of the *Rabinal Achi,* through the device of the "trial"—a genre particularly rich in details and teachings—gives the floor to the different antagonistic parties one after the other; granted, it introduces into the tale the principle of contradiction; but in the end the Rabinaleb are at the same time judges and parties in this text. The objective of the text is to highlight and to demonstrate "their" truth, to make "their" point of view triumph. What weight can we give then to what they express out of the mouth of K'iche' Achi? What confidence can we invest in the declarations that they lend to the Uxab Poq'omab? We, who are neither judges nor parties, have no other alternative than to accept that point of view. We can temper it, however, by stressing that the Rabinaleb were the first concerned during this "migration/expansion" toward the basin and thus their version of the facts assumes an essential importance. Yet, because we cannot distinguish the "true" from the likely, the "real" from the ideological,[30] or even history from myth, we will temporarily refrain from confirming or invalidating the descriptive and strictly "historical" value of such a tale. Insofar as the *Rabinal Achi* comes out of a "literary genre,"[31] we can presume that it reflects a mode of writing history, an ethnohistoriography, in which, to paraphrase Bourdé and Martin (1983: 9), "the silent rules that govern the [Quiché-Achi] *Establishment*" of that time have to appear.

Also within this perspective it was appropriate to understand some of the symbolic representations that this text employs to account for the situation and the events reported. This reading, which easily lends itself to an interpretation in paradigmatic terms (as Kuhn [1962] defines it), favors the indigenous theory of history rather than the history itself. I have not however exhausted all the meanings of this complex and multiform text; it is but a necessary step at the end of which we may perhaps in the future and with a better understanding deal more justly with aspects that we call "historical."

---

30. If we accept that one cannot isolate an autonomous "objective truth" from the discourse that constructs it (see Hanks 1992).

31. This text, which has had an exceptional destiny, might never have reached us, as has been the case with so many others. Its value is all the greater in that it indeed represents a genre of tale (and of literary works) once widespread in the highlands of Guatemala but of which no other examples exist today.

Glossary

This glossary is not a dictionary—the choice of entries is selective—but an inexhaustive collection of glosses excerpted from colonial lexicographical sources dealing with most of the nominal and verbal roots as well as with certain derived terms encountered in the *Rabinal Achi.*

The original forms of the indigenous terms have been preserved, and the original forms of the glosses, restored into their original language (Spanish), have been brought up to date. The glosses are presented by work in alphabetical order by author; certain entries are from more recent references (such as Brasseur 1862b; Coloch, pers. comm.; Curruchich Gómez and Coyote Tun n.d.; Saquic Calel 1989). Among the several anonymous (and often incomplete) works that appear in the Bibliothèque nationale de Paris, a single one is sometimes cited here under the reference "Anonymous"; it is a partial copy of the original work that served as a model for the dictionary of Tirado, which usefully makes up for the absence of certain folios in that work.

Within these headings there sometimes appear, between brackets, certain indications and some linkage elements in English. The following signs have been adopted:

>	derived from
<	derived into
≠	to be distinguished from
/	equivalent to
//	forming a pair with

ACHI

Angel (fol. 7v) *achij*, el hombre [≠ *achih*, hombre o mujer valiente; *uachihilal*, mi valentía y esfuerzo] • (152v) *viƐ / vik achihilal*, animarse, tomar ánimo.

Basseta (fol. 161v) *achih*, varón; *achihilal*, varonilidad [. . .] marido.

Coto (1983: 276) *achi / achih*, hombre o varón; *achih*, hombre o varón fuerte; *yn achih achi*, yo soy hombre fuerte; *achihilal*, fortaleza así • (327) *achi / achih*, macho, en todo género de animal [. . .] El primero usan para los hombres, para decir "varón," "hombre ya"; el [segundo] le toman por el valiente, esforzado • (328) *achih / nim ru 4ux / oyeuh*, magnánimo.

Santo Domingo (fol. 3v) *achijh*, cosa dura, o recia; *achih*, varón fuerte; *achiha*, soldados; *achihilal*, fuerza, o fortaleza; *achihir*, hacerse fuerte.

Tirado (fol. 105v) *covil // achihilal*, fortaleza de varón • (106v) *oyeuh achih*, fuerte varón y muy esforzado • (119) *achij*, hombre • (135v) *achij*, macho en cada especie • (187v) *achiy*, varón.

Vico (n.d.a: fol. 6v) *achi*, hombre o mujer fuerte; *achih*, hombre o mujer fuerte o valiente; *achihilal*, la fortaleza • (139v) *nima achi*, grande hombre, o personaje, o español.

Villacañas (fol. 130) *couil // achihilal*, constancia, firmeza.

AJ

Anleo (fol. 44v) *ahavanic / ahavaxic* [irregular derivations of the root *ah*] • (67) *ahauaxel / cahauax*, necesario, necesariamente.

Basseta (fol. 162) *ah*, querer; *zcaquin chic carah*, más es menester.

Santo Domingo (fol. 4) *aho*, querer; *ahouah*, querer muchas cosas, o muchas veces.

Tirado (fol. 58) *cahavaxic*, conviene • (64v) *chirahabal nu4ux*, de mi voluntad • (65) *xax mahiui cauah*, de ninguna manera quiero • (139v) *ahavaxic*, ser menester • (165) *carah lo*, quizá, quizás.

AJAW

Angel (fol. 103v) *kahaual [= kanima vinak]*, gran persona, el Principal como anciano o más viejo, que entiende en los pleitos, o casamientos.

Anleo (fol. 7v) *ahavalah vinak*, gente principal • (10v) *nu chuch nu kahau*, mi madre, mi padre [≠ *uahau*, mi señor].

Basseta (fol. 140v) *ahau*; *rahaual al cahol*, señor de vasallos; *chicahil ahau*, señor soberano.

Tirado (fol. 155) *kahavixel*, patriarca; *chuch kahauh tool vinak*, patrón, o defensor • (177v) *ahau*, señor; *ahavab*, señores • (197) *nu kahau / wahau*, mi padre.

Vico (n.d.a: fol. 4) *ahau*, el cacique o señor; *ahauab*, señor quiché; *Ɛalel ahau*, gran señor.

AJAWAREM

Angel (fol. 45) *chapom chi ahauarem*, puesto en señorío.

Anleo (fols. 13v–14) *he Ɛinom chiri4ut e xcahavaric*, aquellos eran ricos, por eso gobernaron • (53) *ca nu 4orah*, por tener gravedad, y señorío.

Basseta (fol. 140) *qahauaric*, señorear • (162) *ahauaribal tem*, asiento de Magestad o grandeza.

Coto (1983: 520) *ahaval vach nu vach*, sereno estar, y con gravedad y majestad.

Santo Domingo (fol. 4) *ahauarizah*, hacer reinar, o constituir en la tal dignidad.

Tirado (fol. 19v) *oher ahauarem*, antiguo gobierno • (61) *ahavilah vinak*, gente quieta, o sosegada, y lo que literalmente dice es, el reposo, y Señorío • (74v) *ahavarem; ahavaremal; nima vinakil*, dignidad, o señorío • (75) *rahilaxic ahavarem*, ditado, o título de honra • (89) *ahauarem; ahavaremal*, enseñoreado • (109) *ahaualah vinak*, persona grave, de autoridad • (126v) *ahauarem*, insignias, o divisa, como los que tienen los Señores en la mano • (165) *ahavilah 4oheic*, quietud y sociego • (169v) *ahavalah vinak*, real persona • (171) *ahavuaremal*, reino, señorío; *quin ahavaric*, yo reino • (177v) *ahavaric*, señorearse • (188v) *ahaualah 4hamiy*, vara real.

Varea (fol. 309) *ahavarem / chapomal*, el señorío.

Vico (n.d.a: fol. 4) *ahauar*, v[erb]o neutro de *ahau; ahauariçam, ahauariçah, ti ahauaren*, señorío o dignidad.

AJKAROQ

Anleo (fol. 51) *ahkarok!*, doliéndose o admirándose.

Basseta (fol. 161) *acaroc*, eia, ¡ay de mí!

Coto (1983: 21) *ah kook*, Ay, o a, interjección de compasión de sí o de otro • (375) *ah kook*, O, interjección para exclamar [. . .] y lo mismo si es lastimándose de algo o doliéndose.

Martínez (fol. 43) *ah karook*, propterea de admiración.

Santo Domingo (fol. 2) *aƐaoc*, interjección dolentis • (2v) *acaoc*, interjección dolentis o admirantis.

Torresano (fol. 37v) *ahkook / ahkooke*, significativa del afecto interior del alma, así de dolor y tristeza, como de alegría y placer, o deseo, quejándose [. . .] Exclamantis del que clama o suspira.

Varea (fol. 5) *ahkook*, interjección que significa dolerse o compadecerse • (371) *kook / ahkook*, partícula que significa suspirar o quejarse o sentimiento.

Vico (n.d.a: fol. 95v) *akok, ahkok, ahkorok*, interjección.

Villacañas (fol. 59) *aƐaoƐ*, ay dolentis [≠ *aƐuoc*, ay admirantis].

Ximénez (1985: 55) *acaoc / aƐarroc*, interjección de dolor y admiración.

AL

Tirado (fol. 42v) *chinamit // alaxic*, casta, linaje • (108) *alaxic // 4aholaxic*, generación • (188v, 190v) *al // 4ahol*, vasallo [. . .] villano.

Vico (n.d.a: fol. 7v) *al 4ahol*, son los vasallos, o macehuales; *çakil al çakil 4ahol*, será el linaje humano • (41) *çakillal çak4ahol*, será el linaje humano; *kapasal al 4ahol*, vasallos por metáfora.

ALAJIL

Angel (fol. 8) *alah*, cosa pequeña, sea animal, sea planta, etc. [≠ *alah*, cosa libre, hombre, mujer o animal libre].

Basseta (fol. 162v) *alah*, tierno [≠ *alah*, libre].

Saquic Calel (p. 326) *alaj [/ laj]*, pequeño.

Tirado (fol. 140) *alah uvach*, cosa menuda • (153) *alah chee*, palo pequeño *[= 4huti]* • (155) *alah 4,iquin*, pájaro pequeño *[= 4huti]* • (161v) *alah quieh queb uhunab*, potro (joven) de dos años.

Vico (n.d.a: fol. 7) *alah*, libre hombre o mujer [. . .] cosa pequeña.

See also:

Zuñiga (in Miles 1957: 766) *alaheh* [referring to the freeing of a slave].

AMAQ'

Alonso (fol. 207) *huremah chi amaƐ*, provincia.

Angel (fol. 9v) *amaƐ*, pueblo; *pa tak amaƐ tinamit*, en los pueblos.

Anleo (fol. 12v) *amaƐ*, este nombre [. . .] que significa pueblo, tiene significación de plural copulativo, como también *vinak*.

Basseta (fol. 163) *amaƐ tinamit*, pueblo o ciudad [. . .] de aquí sale *amaquelabic*, avecindarse.

Coto (1983: 63) *ru Ɛa amaƐ*, barrio • (319) *ru Ɛa amaƐ*, lugares o pueblos pequeños que están sujetos a otros *[ru Ɛa amaƐ ru Ɛa tinamit ≠ nima amaƐ nima tinamit]*.
Tirado (fol. 7) *amaƐ*, ciudad • (27) *quinamaƐelab chupa ri tinamit*, avecindarse en pueblo • (30v) *utzilaj sak amaƐ*, bien aventuranza; *ramaƐelal utzak ramaƐ dios*, bien aventuranza, lugar de la Gloria • (128v) *upixab amaƐ*, ley del pueblo.
Vico (n.d.a: fol. 8v) *amaƐ*, Pueblo; *ruƐa amaƐ*, la estancia, o Pueblo sujeto a otro • (13) *am*, cosa remota o de lejos.

AMOLO
Saquic Calel (p. 302) *amolo*, mosca.
Tirado (fol. 143v) *uz amolo*, mosca grande • (205) *amolo*, la mosca [≠ *uz*, mosquito].
Vico (n.d.a: fol. 8v) *amalo*, la mosca que cría gusanos.

AN
Coto (1983: 19) *quin an / aniyah / anila*, aguijar, darse prisa o correr; *anom*, el que es así presto; *anim*, la presteza [. . .] usan también de los verbos *tin yeeh* o *tin covih*.
Varea (fol. 16) *an*, andar a prisa, como corriendo; *an < anilan, aniyah*.
Vico (n.d.a: fol. 8) *an*, correr; *anom*, el huido.
Villacañas (fol. 133) *an*, correr; *r-anibal ya*, corriente de agua.

ANIMAJINAQ
Angel (fol. 10v) *anumah*, huirse.
Basseta (fol. 163) *anumahic*, huirse; *anum*, huida [from another writer: *anumachinac*, ausente].
Saquic Calel (p. 302) *animajic*, huir.
Tirado (fol. 8v) *anumahisanic*, ahuyentar • (120) *anum*, huidor; *anumah*, huir.
Varea (fol. 12) *anih*, huirse *[= anomah]*; *anom*, el que se huye.
Vico (n.d.a: fol. 8) *an*, correr; *anom*, el huido.

AQANIBAL
Coloch (pers. comm.) *aqanibal*, huellas, impresiones, marcas en el suelo, el camino abierto por . . . (seguido por); e.g., *x-u-maj lo ri r-aqan-ibal chak patan*, él ha tomado las huellas de los trabajos sagrados (i.e., él ha pasado por todos los cargos); *x-ki-maj bi ri r-aqan-ibal*, ellos siguieron las huellas; *pa k-aqan-ibal ri q-ati qa-mam*, en las huellas de los antepasados; *chupam r-aqan-ibal sutz' r-aqan-ibal mayul*, en las (huellas de las) nubes, la neblina.
Varea (fol. 4) *akanibal* [the notion of a circular course; e.g., *xu 4ul rakanibal huna*, ya se ha cumplido un año; *xu 4ul rakanibal pedro*, como si sale de un pueblo, y dada vuelta por otros pueblos, vuelve a donde salió; *xu 4ul rakanibal obispo*, acabó (el obispo) su visita y se volvió a donde salió].

ATINIBAL
Coto (1983: 61) *atin*, bañarse en río, laguna o baño como los de Acatenango; *atinibal*, baño, el lugar donde se bañan [≠ *tuh / tuhabal*, temascal].
Varea (fol. 185) *r-atin*, es costumbre o abusión de los Indios irse a bañar al río, antes de amanecer cuando cae el primer aguacero.

ATZ
Vico (n.d.a: fol. 139) *atz*, nimal, hermano, o hermana mayor.

ATZ'YAQ

Basseta (fol. 164) *atziac,* toda ropa de vestir; *atziaric,* envejecerse la ropa *[= haaric]* • (217) *ratziac che,* paste, vestidura del palo.

BALAM

Basseta (fol. 165) *balam,* tigre.
Varea (fol. 115) *çak balam,* tigre pequeño de su naturaleza; *Ɛana balam,* el [tigre] grande.

BALUK

Varea (fol. 116) *baluc,* todos los de un chinamital dicen al que se casa con cualquiera mujer de su chinamital: *nu hi nu baluc.*

BANOJ

Torresano (fol. 78) *banbal missa,* el Ornamento con que se dice la misa • (78v) *ban,* hacer [< *banic,* la hechura]; *banel,* lo factible [*kitzih banel ri,* cierto que es factible aquello] • (82) *ban* < *banoh* [*-oh* significa la obra del verbo]; *nu banoh,* mi obra • (129v) *banala,* ¡Hágalo Vd!

BIBAL

Coto (1983: 97) *bibal,* cohecho • (138) *bibal,* el decimiento de algo o con lo que se dice [> *biy,* decir, hablar].
Santo Domingo (fol. 9v) *bijbal,* la causa o efecto por que se dice [e.g., *vuh bibal rutzihoxic,* carta misiva].
Varea (fol. 122) *vuh bibal,* carta que lleva uno o que da noticias de uno; *bibal,* el cohecho.
Vico (n.d.a: fol. 19) *biybal,* la causa, o efecto por que se dice [e.g., *vuh biybal utzihoxic,* carta de hacer saber].

BIRBOT

Angel (fol. 18v) *biribo [= birbot],* bullirse alguna cosa como gusano o como pulgas, o hormigas, piojos; *birbot nu4ux,* haber miedo.
Basseta (fol. 166) *birbotic,* temblar las carnes, o bullir • (167v) *nima barbotem,* con gran ruido . . .
Coto (1983: 224) *tan ti birbot vleuh,* estremecerse la tierra (Tenían creído, y aún lo tienen hoy, que debajo la tierra está un gigante, que es el que sustenta la tierra, al cual llaman çipacnay, y, cuando éste se menea, tiembla la tierra, y que éste es el dios de los temblores) • (530) *ti birbot,* sonar atabal grande como de guerra; *ti tino vi / ti biro vi ru chi vleuh,* tierra que suena por estar hueca; *ti tinin / tibirbot ru chi cak iƐ,* sonar el viento o norte.
Santo Domingo (fol. 10v) *ti biribot nu cux,* mi corazón tiene miedo; *biribotem,* trueno.
Saquic Calel (p. 305) *birbotem,* temblarse.
Tirado (fol. 102) *cabirbot uleu,* estremecerse o temblar la tierra • (181v) *quinbirbot, quinsicsot rumal teuh,* estoy temblando de frío.
Varea (fol. 125) *birir* < *birbot,* tronar el volcán [= *hinhot,* ir haciendo ruido el agua del río grande, si va crecido, o tronar, o temblar la tierra [. . .] también hablar hueco, o el son de atabal o tambor grande [. . .] hacer gran ruido el árbol o piedra grande que cae (see also fols. 131–132)] • (166) *ti birbot chi ƐaƐ mix yacatah nah tibe chi cah,* alzarse gran llama con gran ruido • (219) *birbot,* tronar [referring to a volcano, an earthquake, a waterfall] • (221) *ti birbot chi cakiƐ, chi hab, chi cabrakan,* hacer ruido trueno, lluvia, temblor de tierra • (282) *biro* < *birbot* [= *tinin,* tronar; andar con mucho ruido, pisando fuertemente,

dando grandes patadas que se oyen de lejos como el que va apriesa; = *nicnot*] • (331) *tan tibirbot, tan tinicnot, tan tiçilon uleuh rumal cabarakan,* tiembla la tierra.

Vico (n.d.a: fol. 20v) *birir,* hacer sonido, o tronar [> *bir-*]; *biribot,* bullirse alguna cosa como gusanos, pulgas, o piojos, hormigas; *birbot // çicçot,* estremecerse, temblar; *cabirbotic,* resplandecer; *birbot,* hacer ruido [= *yicyot / tohoh*].

BOJOJIK

Angel (fol. 20) *bohih,* dar bofetón.

Basseta (fol. 166v) *bohba,* menear las alas el ave.

Coto (1983: 466–467) *bohoh,* cuando tuestan el maíz al fuego, y revienta; *bohbo,* reventar, como reventó el malvado Judas [. . .] se fue a colgar de un árbol a causa de su enfado, y allí reventó por dentro, dejando sobre la tierra su entraña toda, sus hígados, su corazón.

Curruchich Gómez and Coyote Tun (p. 13) *b'ojij,* reventar, voluntaria o involuntariamente objetos vacíos que al reventarse hacen ruido (vejigas).

Santo Domingo (fol. 11v) *bohih,* dar de bofetones [e.g., *tin bohila ruchi*].

Varea (fol. 128) *bohih,* dar gran bofetón con enojo.

Vico (n.d.a: fols. 22v–23) *bohih,* abofetear • (24v) *bohih,* dar bofetadas; *bohloh,* saltar como maíz que se tuesta.

See also:

Coto (1983: 530) *ti bohbo nu tzam,* sonar las narices por sí solas, como cuando roncan [. . .] tiénenlo por agüero • (530) *ti vohoh ru chi vuh,* sonar [. . .] la hoja del libro, al volverla.

Varea (fol. 106) *vohoh,* sonar hojas secas por darles el viento, o menearla, o pisarlas; *vokok,* significa hacer ruido hablando [. . .] hablar alterados, o recio, o riñiendo; *vokcorih,* levantarse murmurando contra alguno o riñiéndose [. . .] contradiciendo, riñiendo, o perdiendo el respeto.

Vico (n.d.a: fol. 25) *buhbut,* suena la tierra como cuando andan, o tiembla [. . .] o rechinan las maderas o los dientes; *buhlin,* ir muchos juntos de tropel como hormigas, o gente.

BOSINAQ

Alonso (fol. 46) *pboçinak* [*sic*], brotada, flor • (113) *qui boçon,* engendrar [= *qui 4aholan, qui mialan, quin etar*].

Angel (fol. 21) *boz,* la flor cuando se abre; *bozinak chic,* ya está reventada, o cuando el huevo revienta puesto al fuego, o publicar algun secreto • (120v) *poz,* nacer, multiplicar, o brotar la flor, o restallar.

Coto (1983: 74) *boz,* brotar o reventar las flores, abrirse; *bozinak chic,* flor brotada o abierta • (217) *boz,* estallar, reventando así; *bozinak,* lo que así ha reventado y dado estallido; *boz,* significa también este verbo: salir los pollos del cascarón [. . .] abrirse o reventar la flor [. . .] reventarse el ojo • (190) *tin boz,* reventar la flor . . . [and, metaphorically, "engendrar"]; *boçel,* la descendencia; *yn boçinel,* soy padre o engendrador • (446) *tin boz a mac chi vachil,* publicaré tu pecado • (466–467) *boz,* reventar las flores abriéndose, o la granada [. . .] el huevo, puesto al fuego [. . .] el ojo [. . .] el hinchazón.

Santo Domingo (fol. 12) *boz,* se dice de la flor que abre; *boçinak chic,* cuando salta el huevo en el fuego, o publicar algún secreto.

Tirado (fol. 3) *boz,* abrirse la flor o cualquier botón de planta; *xboz ri co4,ijh,* reventó la flor; *xboz ri met vel chih chupam umapil,* dice que reventó el algodón de su botón; *xrrakarob riah chuvach cah / xboz ri ah chuvach cah,* reventó el cohete en la región [= *xpokic*].

Varea (fol. 26) *boz* [referring to something that unfolds, opens up; e.g., *zak boroboh chic kavan tan ti boz huhun 4,utuh,* ya están todas las flores o barbas desplegadas] • (130)

boz, abrirse las flores [. . .] salir los pollos del cascarón [. . .] reventar el huevo (en el fuego y estallar) [. . .] publicar algún secreto [in this last meaning: *boz* = *Ɛalahizah*] • (306) *tan ti boz 4,utuh avan*, ya están en flor las milpas.

Vico (n.d.a: fol. 24) *boz*, reventar flor; *boçinak chic co4,ih*, ya reventó la flor, o cuando el huevo revienta al fuego o publicar algún secreto • (24v) *boz*, nacer, o multiplicar, brotar flores como se dijó • (159v) *ppoz* [*sic*], nacer, multiplicar, o brotar, florecer, o retoñar.

BOYEXIK / BOYIBEJ

Angel (fol. 20) *boychin*, halagar con palabras, engañar, o sobornar, o alcahuetear, o halagar.

Basseta (fol. 166v) *boy*, la flauta para llamar venados; *boyoh*, llamar con ella.

Coto (1983: 320) *tin boy*, llamar con reclamo al venado o pájaro, o otro animal.

Villacañas (fol. 61) *boy chih / boy chi eleƐal*, alcahuetear • (91) *boy chiih*, atraer por halagos • (148) *tin boy queh*, chiflar o chillar llamando a venado.

CHA

Vico (n.d.a: fol. 56v) *cha*, por decir, o llevar oír alguna parte.

CHAJAJIK / CH'AJAJIK

Basseta (fol. 179v) *chahahic*, gritar o vocear y también cuando gorjean los zanates o golondrinas [and, from another writer: (180v) *chahah*, hablar mucho, gorjear los pájaros, hacer sonido].

Tirado (fol. 163v) *ca4hahan a4*, menudean los gallos al querer amanecer.

Varea (fol. 320) *4hahah*, llover recio, golpeando [. . .] significa hablar recio y mucho.

Vico (n.d.a: fol. 60) *chahahic*, vocear • (259v) *4hahah*, hablar mucho, o bachillerear [. . .] gorjear los pájaros.

Villacañas (fol. 96) *chahah*, baladrar *[= vaian; vayay]* • (104) *chahahel*, bullicioso • (108) *qui chahahil vinac*, bullicio o rumor de gente.

CHAKACHIB

Angel (fol. 43v) *chacach*, cesto, o canasta • (141) *chacach*, chiquiguite.

Basseta (fol. 178) *chacach*, cesta.

Coto (1983: 201) *nu chacach*, [mi] petaca [= *nu pop*, mi petate] • (214) *4huti chacach*, esportilla o cestillo.

Tirado (fol. 39) *chacach*, canasta • (60v) *chacach*, cesta.

Varea (fol. 13) *chacach*, el chiquiguite.

CHAQ'

Vico (n.d.a: fol. 59) *chaƐ*, hermano menor, o hermana, primo hermano o prima hermana.

CHAQ'IM

Angel (fol. 45) *chaƐimah*, pedir prestado; *tin chaƐimah tin Ɛah*, alquilar.

Coto (1983: 438) *chaƐimam*, a lo que así han pedido prestado *[= kahom; halom]*.

Tirado (fol. 65) *chahim*, depositado; *chahinel*, depositario.

Varea (fol. 308) *chaƐimah*, pedir prestado.

CHIJIJIK / CH'IJIJIK

Coto (1983: 236) *4hih*, forzar, obligar a que alguno haga o diga algo, o a que peque; *xa nu 4hihic*, para decir que una cosa no la hicieron con voluntad, sino forzados.

Varea (fol. 324) *4hih*, poder, sufrir [. . .] forzar porfiando.

CHINKU

Alonso (fol. 46) *chuncu / pixoh*, brazalete de pluma; *puvakim chuncu / macupil chuncu*, brazalete de oro.

Angel (fol. 49v) *chuncu*, ajorca, o manillas.

Basseta (fol. 182) *chinƐu*, unos brazaletes de hueso • (184) *chunƐu*, brazaletes de hueso para bailar en su antigüedad y le llamaban al baile *uachibal chiquirim*, figura de la cigarra; *chunƐu // calcab*, brazaletes.

Vico (n.d.a: fol. 67) *chuncu*, manillas • (122) *chuncu*, brazalete [= *macupil* > *mac*, el ámbar, cuentas amarillas] • (227v) *ƐalƐa // chuncu*, joyas.

CHUMAY

Basseta (fol. 183v) *chumay*, el brazo desde el codo a la mano.

Brasseur de Bourbourg (1862b: 38, n. 2) *chumay*, coudee.

Coto (1983: 96) *chumay*, medida desde el codo a la punta de los dedos *[hu chumay, ca chumay . . .]* • (340) *chumay*, medida de un codo; *tin chumaih r'etaxic ri 4am*, medir el cordel a codos (Y cuando hacen sus casas, suelen medir los palos a codos y dicen: *tin chumaih ru tzam lae che, o r'akan lae che*).

Vico (n.d.a: fol. 66v) *chumay*, hasta el codo midiendo, o del codo a la muñeca • (68–68v) *chumay*, está puesto, que es el codo hasta la muñeca [e.g., *volahuh chi chumay xri4avibeh viri ya / ha hvi nimah tak huyu*, quince codos en alto sobrepujó el agua el diluvio sobre los montes más altos].

CHUN

Varea (fol. 315) *chun*, la cal; *chunam hay*, casa blanqueada.

CHUQ'AB

Torresano (fol. 133) *chuƐab*, la fuerza.

Varea (fol. 316) *chuƐa*, la fuerza de persona o animal, o miel si se come mucha, o de medicina, o su virtud o vigor; *chuƐabah*, hacer fuerza, o violencia o tiranía, tiranizar (como hacen los negros y mulatos a los Indios), hurtar ropa, arrebatar por fuerza lo ajeno para apropriarlo te a tí.

Vico (n.d.a: fol. 97) *chichuƐabah*, darse prisa, forzar *[= yeebal]* • (113v) *maquitah kaçar ruchuƐa ri achi*, es invencible.

CHUYAL

Alonso (fols. 19, 54) *ru chuyal 4ha*.

Basseta (fol. 184) *chuyal*, caja [from another writer].

Coto (1983: 27, 89) *ru 4huyul 4ha*, aljaba [. . .] carcaj de flechas [which Acuña comments on in a note: "Alxaba o aljaba: Ms lee *ru 4huyul 4ha*, lectura que volverá a repetir en Carcax (fol. 73v); sin embargo, en el Vocabulario [Alonso, fols. 19, 54], se lee *ru chuyal 4ha*. La palabra *chuyal* o, mejor, *chuuyal*, se deriva de *chuuy*, bolsa (fol. 59), costal (96), o esquero (172v). La frase, *ru chuuyal 4ha*, significa 'bolsa de las flechas'"].

See also:

Varea (fol. 204) *chuyah*, almuesta; *hu, ca chayah*, una, dos almuestas.

CH'A'

Coto (1983: 258) *ah 4ha*, guerreador [> *4haa*, flecha].

Varea (fol. 318) *4ha*, decir o hablar; úsanlo para reprehender lo malo que oyen [. . .] significa reprehender, amonestar y doctrinar • (320) *4ha*, (se me acordo ahora que significa también) pleitear • (321) *4haoh*, el pleito.

See also:

Basseta (fol. 177v) *cha [≠ chab]*, unas piedras que ponen en las flechas en lugar de hierro y la lanzeta, o lanza; *ahcha*, el que usa de la tal lanzeta.

CH'AB

Angel (fol. 203) *4habin / 4habih*, flechar, tirar con flecha • (206) *4haa*, virote, o saeta, o flecha; *nu tee 4haa*, el arco, o ballesta; *4habin / 4habih*, tirar con arco o flechar con ballesta; *4habil pocobal xebe4ambex xechee xe4am*, con mano armada fueron por ellos a los montes; *4hab // pocob*, armas.

Basseta (fol. 178) *chab*, el arco de tirar flechas, y de allí *ralchab*, hijo del arco y de flecha, y también *zimah* • (231v) *u chab Ɛih*, rayo del sol.

Tirado (fol. 23v) *uchuch 4heb* [corregido en el ms. en *4hab*], arco de tirar flecha • (41) *uchuch 4hab*, caja de saetas • (105) *4hab*, flecha • (174) *4hab*, saeta • (184) *quin 4habinic*, tirar saeta o flecha • (188v) *uchuch 4hab*, ballesta; *4habinel*, arquero.

Torresano (fol. 135) *4hab*, la saeta *[= 4ha]*.

Varea (fol. 277) *ru te 4ha*, arco o ballesta [< *val 4ha*, la flecha o saeta] • (318) *4ha*, arco o ballesta o la saeta; *rute 4ha*, el arco o la ballesta; *ral 4ha*, la saeta; *4habih*, tirar con arco.

Vico (n.d.a: fol. 260v) *4ha / 4hab*, saeta o flecha; *nu te 4ha*, el arco de la ballesta; *4habiƐaƐ*, la cometa; *4habih*, tirar, flechar.

CH'AKAT

Angel (fols. 203–203v) *4hacat*, el asiento de palo para sentarse; *tem 4hacat [. . .] 4hacat viah*, la cabecera, o almohada.

Basseta (fol. 162) *chacat*, asiento o almohada.

Saquic Calel (p. 311) *ch'acat*, almohada.

Tirado (fol. 16v) *4hacat viaj*, almohada • (106v) *rih 4hacat*, funda de almohada • (209v) *4hacat*, la almohada.

Varea (fol. 2) *4hacat*, banquillo • (318) *4hacat*, los banquillos que usan los Indios [. . .] lo que [se usa] por cabecera, almohada, ropa o banquillo, o palo o piedra; *4hacat*, el trono del Señorío, usan cuando ponen en Señorío en una banquilla de talla.

Vico (n.d.a: fol. 219) *xitam tem puakim 4hacat* [not translated: throne of turquoise and silver] • (258v) *4hacat*, el asiento de palo, o banquito, o silla, muy sahumada que usan los Indios, cuando hacen una cabeza del Pueblo, y en quiché cuando muere alguno de estas cabezas, avisan a Santa Cruz del Quiché y viene uno a dar la posesión a uno de los principales que ya ellos conocen por sus sobrenombres, y a esta silla llaman *4hacat tem*.

See also:

Varea (fol. 202) *4hacat* [= *moc*; *4hob*; chinamital], la parcialidad de cualquier cacique • (330) *4hacatah*, ser vencido.

Vico (n.d.a: fol. 201) *qui var qui 4hacatah*, ser vencido • (258v) *chi 4hacatih ta la*, ¡Siéntese Vd!: significa vencer, o quitar el poder (a alguien).

CH'AMIY

Angel (fol. 69v) *nu yaquem 4hamij*, llevar vara [> *yaquen*, llevar espada en la mano].

Basseta (fol. 179v) *chami*, vara o báculo.

Varea (fol. 321) *4hamey*, vara de Justicia o cualquier vara o bordón.

Vico (n.d.a: fol. 75v) *ah 4hameya*, alguaciles • (93) *nu yaquem espada nu yaquem 4hamey*, llevo levantada la vara • (260) *4hamiy*, la vara, o bordón, o lanza; *ah 4hamiy*, el alguacil.

CH'AYIK

Coto (1983: 329) *4hay*, majar con palo, piedra u otro instrumento, dando golpes.

CH'EKEN

Angel (fol. 208) *4hequen*, hormigas que salen y andan de noche, que se llaman zompopos, son grandes.

Varea (fol. 325) *4hequen*, las hormigas grandes o redondas.

Vico (n.d.a: fol. 262) *4hequem*, zompopos, o hormigas que salen de noche.

CH'UCH'UJ

Alonso (fol. 46v) *tin 4hu4huhiriçah ru vach*, bruñir papel.

Coto (1983: 25) *tin 4hu4huhiriçah ru vach*, alizar madera raspándola • (361) *4hu4huh + ih / vach*, cosa muelle, que está blanda al tacto, o lisa; *ti 4hu4huhir*, ponerse así la cosa; *tin 4hu4huhiriçah*, alisar o ablandar • (391) *4hu4huh + vach*, cuando cualquier género de paño es delgado y delicado al tacto • (543) *4hu4huh ru pam kul*, cuando la tela está delgada.

Tirado (fol. 4) *4hu4huhirisah 4,um*, ablandar cuero; *4hu4hujir*, ablandarse alguna cosa • (31v) *4hu4huj*, blanda cosa • (95) *4hu4huhirisan uvach* [regarding a polished, glazed ceramic vessel] • (96) *4hu4huhilah sanayb [sic]*, esmeril • (99v) *4hu4huj vach / rih*, estar algo lizo • (104v) *4hu4huhilah rizmal chih*, fina lana • (152v) *4hu4huhilah 4im*, paja suave • (206v) *4hu4huh*, cosa suave y blanda *[= bullulic]*.

Varea (fol. 330) *4hu4huh*, cosa blanda • (370) *ti 4hu4huhir ta ruvach* [not translated: to smooth two objects by rubbing them together. The author gives the example of bricks].

Vico (n.d.a: fol. 266) *4hu4huh*, blando, o liso; *4hu4huhilah qul*, manta blanda [< *4hu4huhiriçah*, ablandar algo, o ablandar cuero sobándolo].

Villacañas (fol. 64) *chuchuh*, alizada cosa; *chuchurizah*, alizar • (154) *chuchuh*, delicada persona.

ECHABEN

Basseta (fol. 184v) *ech*, lo que se posee; *echah*, poseer.

Tirado (fol. 22v) *echaj*, apropiarse para sí cualquier cosa.

Vico (n.d.a: fol. 71v) *ech*, en quiché es la simplicidad de los nombres de posesión [< *echah*, apropiarse algo] • (101v) *echah*, apropiar algo (cosa ajena).

EK'OW

Basseta (fol. 194) *ycouic*, pasar [e.g., *chicouna ucux chirech*, pasarásele primero la cólera]; *ycouisah*, hacer pasar a otro; *ycouibeh*, instrumento idem y también ver una cosa de paso.

Varea (fol. 38) *i4o*, pasar; *i4oviçah*, pasar a otro • (39) *i4ovibeh*, haber pasado por algún oficio o enfermedad; *i4ovibeh + vach*, aventajarse a otro mayor, o vistiéndose mejor, o hablar más que el haciéndose señor o mayor • (40) *i4ovibeh* [to pass (from one place to another); e.g., *tan tir i4ovibeh ronohel ama*Ɛ, *ahau*, obispo, provincial, oidor, anda visitando los pueblos]; *i4o + chupam*, pasar de parte a parte, traspasar algo.

Vico (n.d.a: fol. 105) *y4o*, pasar.

EL

Varea (fol. 18) *elebal*, por donde algo sale; *elic*, salida; *elebeh*, salirse afuera de lo que trata.

ELESAJ / ESAJ

Basseta (fol. 185v) *elezah*, sacar y librar; *elezanel // colonel*, salvador, libertador, redemptor.

Varea (fol. 18) *eleçah*, sacar *[= okotah]*; *eleçayh*, sacar de presto algo.

ET

Basseta (fol. 186) *et,* diminutivo [e.g., *xaet,* sólo un poco].
Coto (1983: 142) *xa 4aet,* de repente o de improviso.
Saquic Calel (p. 355) *xak c'ate',* de repente.
Tirado (fol. 91) *xaet,* en vano *[= xa loƐ].*
Varea (fol. 19) *et,* señal *[< etal]* • (240) *xa4aet / xaki4aet / 4aet,* de repente, o acaso o sin causa • (346) *4aet / xa4aet,* sin imaginarlo.
Vico (n.d.a: fol. 70) *et,* señal o en vano, o sin que, o para que [e.g., *xaet xin ruçuhuh,* en vano, o sin qué, o para qué me acusó]; *xa4ate et,* de repente [for this author, the root *et* can mean both "sign" and "measurement" (see *etal*)] • (117) *xa4aet,* de repente • (244) *4ate et,* de repente [e.g., *4ate et xul,* de repente vinó].
See also:
Zuñiga (in Miles 1957: 767) *xa et vinak,* man of little value [. . .] common people.

ETAK'AMARA

Angel (fol. 51v) *etan / etah,* medir, o trazar, o comparar • (93) *etah, meh4amah ru Ɛelem ru palemavan,* medir el anchor, y largor de la milpa.
Basseta (fol. 186) *etah,* medir, trazar [. . .] y con *caamah,* medir tierras.
Coto (1983: 477) *etabal che,* regla para señalar, como hace el carpintero o cantero y otros semejantes; *etabal 4am,* si es cordel; *ti u'etah,* significa señalar, reglar, o medir.
Tirado (fol. 139) *etam,* cosa medida; *su4ulic quin etanic,* medir derecho • (159) *etabal akan,* pie, medida común • (170v) *etabal chee,* regla de carpintero; *quin etanic,* reglar así.
Varea (fol. 19) *etah,* medir a palmos o con vara o palo, o con cuerda; *etah 4am,* medir (la tarea) / trazar (el vertido), midiéndolo con cuerda.
Vico (n.d.a: fol. 70) *etah,* medir, o trocar, o pesar, o comparar; *etax,* ser medido, significar, parecerse; *etabal,* medida [*et < et vachih,* discernir; *etam < etamchic,* lo señalado, o medido; *etamah,* conocer, saber] • (70v) *et 4amah,* ajustar el mecate.
See also:
Varea (fol. 199) *meh4amah,* medir la milpa a la larga, o a lo largo, extendiendo toda la cuerda, y después doblándola para medir lo ancho de la milpa.

ETAL

Angel (fol. 51v) *et,* señal.
Basseta (fol. 218) *retah,* denotar, significar.
Coto (1983: 477) *etabal che,* regla para señalar, como hace el carpintero o cantero y otros semejantes; *ti u'etah,* significa señalar, reglar, o medir • (479) *r'etal Ɛih,* reloj.
Tirado (fol. 54) *retal y4,* regla del mes • (75) *retal,* divisa, o insigna • (177) *etal / retal,* señal; *cancoh retal,* señalar, poner señal • (177v) *cancoh retal chiƐaƐ,* pongo señal en fuego.
Vico (n.d.a: fol. 70) *et,* señal o en vano; *et < etal* [e.g., *"at retal,"* dicen cuando uno ha de volver, y responde *"in rretal,"* yo seré la señal cierta que volveré]; *rumal retal,* por la señal.

ETZ'ABEJ

Coto (1983: 76) *ti u'e4,abeh / ti u'et4,anibeh,* burlarse de manos, retozando • (283) *etzan,* juego de muchachos que andan holgándose.

IKAJ

Coto (1983: 263) *ru vitul icahiel,* destral.
Vico (n.d.a: fol. 97) *ycah,* la hacha para cortar madera.

IKEM / EKEM

Coto (1983: 3) *iquem / equem*, adverbio [. . .] abajo de lugar • (45) *iquem / equem*, abajo; *r'equem v'ochoch*, abajo de mi casa.
Tirado (fol. 27v) *ikem // ajsik*, hacia abajo (esto es hacia la parte que da al Oriente [. . .]) hacia arriba (esto es, hacia el Occidente).
Torresano (fol. 34v) *riquen bey*, el camino de abajo.
Vico (n.d.a: fol. 101) *yquem*, abajo como de lugar, o cuesta.

ISM

Angel (fol. 78) *yzm*, los pelos, o las plumas de cualquiera ave, o la barba, o los pelos o la lana.
Varea (fol. 34) *izm*, cabello o pelo de cualquier cosa de lana o algodón [. . .] o las plumas de aves; *izmal* < *izmachi*, la barba.

JACH

Coto (1983: 38) *hach*, apartar con las manos la gente para hacer camino y pasar por medio, o apartar ramas o hierbas para poder pasar [. . .] apartar animales [. . .] apartar algo para otro.

JARIK

Angel (fol. 57v) *har*, envejecerse ropa • (70) *yaar* [> *ya*: agua en kaqchikel], hacerse agua, y derretirse como el metal en el fuego [≠ *har* en kaqchikel; *har* ≠ *haar* en k'iche'] • (70v) *yaar*, perderse del todo, acabarse • (90) *quiçach, quimayix, quiƐutux, mayh, Ɛutuh, yaar, chamux*, todos quieren decir acabar.
Anleo (fol. 41v) *ha*, el agua; *haar*, hacerse agua; *haariçar*, activo compulsivo, convertir algo en agua, o hacer que algo se haga agua.
Anonymous (fol. 4) *harizah*, ablandar cera o derretir algo.
Basseta (fol. 164) *atziac, haaric*, envejecerse la ropa • (187) *haaric*, derretirse como plomo y envejecerse la ropa, hacerse agua, fundir metal.
Coto (1983: 202) *ti har*, envejecerse la ropa, redes, cueros, petacas, la casa, la paja, etc. [≠ *yaar*: derretirse / fundir].
Saquic Calel (p. 320) *jar*, hacerse vieja una cosa.
Tirado (fol. 4) *haarisaj*, ablandarse o derretir algo • (65v) *haaric*, derretir (metal, cera, etc.) • (69) *cahaaric*, deshacerse la sal o la nieve • (91v) *xhar uatziak*, se envejeció la ropa; *har / Ɛelob*, envejecerse • (193v) *haarisabal puak*, crisol de fundir plata.
Vico (n.d.a: fol. 73v) *ha*, agua; *haar / haric*, se hace agua; *haah*, regar [≠ *har*: envejecer la ropa] • (94) *yaar* [< *ya*: agua, bebida en kaqchikel], hacerse agua como la sal o azúcar; *yaar* < *yaariçah*, fundir • (113) *xa ti har nu kul*, estoy cansado de gritar, de dar voces.

JETESAJ

Basseta (fol. 188v) *hetic*, llegar; *hetisah / hetesah*, hacer llegar [e.g., *het uloc*, acercarse; *het ubic*, desviarse] • (214v) *hetizah*, desviar *[= quibizah]*.
Tirado (fol. 16v) *hetisaj ru4*, allegar una cosa con otra • (73) *canhetizah ubic*, desviar de sí cualquiera cosa • (126) *canhetizah ru4*, juntar, o allegar una cosa con otra • (143v) *can hetisah vib apanok*, moverse, o retirarse hacia otra parte.
Vico (n.d.a: fol. 80) *tin heteçah nu 4ux*, prometer.

JIKIBA

Angel (fol. 61) *hiquiba*, confesar, o declarar; *hiquil*, derecho, o fiel; *hiquilic chahal*, fiel guardador, o cierto.

Basseta (fol. 189v) *hiquiba*, enderezar [. . .] derecho, sin perderse, sin dudar [and, added by another writer : "informar"].
Coto (1983: 137) *tin hiquiba*, declarar, informando la verdad *[= tin chohmiriçah]* • (186) *tin hiquiba*, enderezar [> *hic*, cosa derecha].
Saquic Calel (p. 321) *jic*, seguramente.
Tirado (fol. 85v) *canhiquiba nu4ux chuvach dios*, enderezar la intención a Dios • (122v) *mana hiquilic vinak tah*, persona inconstante.
Torresano (fol. 18) *hikil*, cosa derecha.
Varea (fol. 150) *hic*, derechamente, o derecho; *hiquic*, cortar derecho o parejo • (151) *hiquiba*, confesarse [. . .] certificar.
Vico (n.d.a: fol. 80v) *hiquiba*, lo derecho [. . .] confesar, declarar; *hiquic, hiquil, hiquiba*, enderezar.
Villacañas (fol. 128) *hiquiba nu cux*, confesarse • (147) *hiquil*, cierta cosa.

JIKIKEJ

Angel (fol. 60) *hic*, almohazar, o estirar ropa.
Coto (1983: 8) *tin hic*, acepillar • (131) *tin hic*, sobar con las manos en el vientre, piernas, etc. • (235) *tin hic*, flotar [*sic*, ¿"frotar"?] con la mano el cuerpo, estómago o otra parte del cuerpo • (406) *tin hic*, peinar [. . .] del mismo verbo usan para almohazar • (525) *tin hic*, sobar con la mano vientre, piernas, etc. [the idea of rubbing or massaging with large movements].
Tirado (fol. 167) *hic*, estirar.
Varea (fol. 154) *hic*, peinar, almohazar, sobar los pies o brazo, o barrer, cavar como quien rae las hierbas superficialmente no ahondando, raer trigo a grano que se mide.
Vico (n.d.a: fol. 80) *hic*, acepillar, o limpiar trigo o grana, o almohazar, o limpiar ropa • (83v) *hi4*, estirar, o entresacar • (90v) *hiquic ru vih*, desmelenado o baja la cabeza.
Villacañas (fol. 81) *hic // mes*, arrasar la medida.

JUSUK'

Basseta (fol. 192) *huzuc*, luego.
Tirado (fols. 15v, 122v) *huzu4 chanim*, al instante, por luego [. . .] luego, promptemente, incontinenti.

JUYUB

Alonso (fol. 207) *ah huyu ah taƐah*, provincial de una provincia.
Angel (fol. 67) *huyu*, las sierras, o montes, barrio, o lugar, o mata de hierbas; *nu huyubal nu taƐahal*, mi pueblo mi patria.
Anleo (fol. 46v) *xkah huyub xohukahibeh 4ut*, cayó el monte y nos cogió debajo (se pusó sobre nosotros).
Saquic Calel (p. 323) *juyub / chui juyub*, altiplano, montaña, campo (rural); *juyubal*, territorio.
Tirado (fol. 163) *hullub // taƐah*, provincia.
Varea (fol. 165) *huyu*, yerbas, y matas o monte o sierra, o serranía [. . .] significa pueblo; *nu huyubal*, mi pueblo; *ah ruvitak huyu*, personas serranas que viven en serranía, o personas bestiales *[= ah chicopilah vinak]*.
Vico (n.d.a: fol. 89) *huyu*, monte, o zacate, o la tierra (el quiché añade *-b*); *huyubal vinak*, gente montaraz, que vive en los montes.

KABKOJ

Angel (fol. 178) *ƐanƐoh*, cosa que está medio seca, o media amarilla.

Vico (n.d.a: fol. 17) *balboh / ƐanƐoh*, cosas que tienen diferentes colores, como duraznos.

KABRAQAN

Basseta (fol. 168) *cabracan*, temblor de tierra.

Varea (fol. 331) *cabarakan*, el temblor o terremoto [> *caba*, poner cantidad de tierra, maíz, cacao, etc., junta, amontonada; see D. Tedlock, 1985: 335–336].

Vico (n.d.a: fol. 27v) *cabrakan*, el temblor de tierra.

KANAB

Angel (fol. 25v) *cana*, la cautiva tomada en guerra o de otra suerte; *cana telechee.*

Basseta (fol. 171) *canab*, el despojo de la guerra; *canabih*, apresarlo; *canabih munib*, hacer esclavo.

Coto (1983: 80) *qui canon*, cazar animales; *tin canabah*, también cazar; *cana*, la caza que hay, y también significa cautivar; *cana*, la presa que se coge en guerra • (94) *cana // teleche*, cautivo y preso en guerra [. . .] a los que han sido cautivos, y después se avecindan y quedan libres, los llaman *he nimak achi* [≠ *munil*; *alabitz*; *4,ijl*, cautiverio o esclavitud como la de los negros].

Varea (fol. 333) *canabah*, hallar algo [. . .] ganar en la mercadería [. . .] cazar • (334) *cana // telechee*, cautivos ganados en la guerra [e.g., *xnucanabah xin telecheeh pa labal*].

Vico (n.d.a: fol. 31v) *cana // teleche*, cautivos • (183v) *canabih*, cautivar.

KAQ

Angel (fol. 31v) *cak hay*, cerros hechos a mano [> *hay*, casa (54v)].

Coto (1983: 120) *cak hay*, cuevas antiguas donde guardaban ídolos • (127–128) *cak hay*, unos cerrillos que solían hacer a mano para desde allí atalayar y ver lo que pasaba.

Varea (fol. 335) *cakhay*, montecillos redondos de piedra y tierra seca que hacían los antiguos *[= cubucak huyu].*

Vico (n.d.a: fol. 33v) *cakay*, cerro hecho a mano, o mogote.

KAWUJ

Coto (1983: 14) *vik // cauh*, adornar, componer o ataviar.

Tirado (fol. 10v) *cauunic*, aderezar o adornar algo.

Ximénez (1985: 167) *cauh*, componer, aliñar, arreglar; ataviarse.

KEJE

Basseta (fol. 188v) *he*, así, sí, afirmativo • (214) *quehe*, como [e.g., *chabana quehe ri*, hazlo como éste].

Tirado (fol. 25v) *quehe*, así • (73) *quehe vae*, como esto; *quehe uchi vach vae*, de esta manera, de esta forma • (83) *quehe panu4ux*, en mi juicio; en mi parecer • (104v) *quehe 4ut*, finalmente, por tanto pués, así mismo • (130v) *quehenaypu*, luego que . . . • (133v) *xavi quehe*, así también • (137) *quehe vae*, de esta manera, como esto • (149v) *utztah quehe*, ¡Ojalá! • (151v) *xavi quehe chic*, otro tanto • (161) *apa quehe vi*, ¿Por dónde? • (176) *quehe cubijh*, según dice.

Varea (fol. 337) *quere*, el modo y manera con que se piensa, dice o muestra o manifiesta alguna cosa.

KEM

Vico (n.d.a: fols. 96, 166) *ah quem*, mujer preñada.

KEWIJ

See: Ximénez (1985: 483) *queuo,* andar dando de codo.

KI'

Basseta (fol. 214v) *qui // matul,* ponzoña • (231v) *uquia,* bebida; *uqui cumatz,* la ponzoña de la culebra; *uqui,* ponzoña.
Coto (1983: 66) *iquim v4iya,* bebida de cacao con mucho chile • (426) *quiy,* ponzoña de víbora o otra culebra [en la pronunciación es menester cuidado que sea blanda y detenida un poco, a diferencia de *4iy,* por "mucho," y de *qui,* por "cosa dulce"].
Saquic Calel (p. 337) *qui',* dulce o sabroso [≠ *q'ui,* mucho].
Tirado (fol. 113v) *vu4ia,* cacao para beber.
Varea (fol. 338) *quii,* cosa dulce o sabrosa [. . .] significa la ponzoña [e.g., *ruquii cumatz 4anti*].
Vico (n.d.a: fol. 124) *4uiy,* ponzoña *[= matul]* • (167v) *quij // matul,* ponzoña • (211v) *u4ia,* cualquier bebida.
kinaq
Varea (fol. 339) *quinaƐ,* toda manera de frijoles o legumbres: *4ahlic,* las pintadas, *çaki-quinaƐ,* las blancas, *Ɛeka-quinaƐ,* las negras, *nimak quinaƐ,* los chinapopos, frijoles grandes.

KIRIREJ

Coto (1983: 143) *tin quir,* desanudar; *tin quir / tin quirila,* desabrochar • (145) *quir,* descargar al que va cargado *[= kaçah; too]* • (146) *quirir,* descostrarse (el barniz o encaladura en la pared, o yeso de las tablas, o la pintura del retablo) • (152) *ti quirir,* desmoronarse o deshacerse el pan, tamal, barro, cal [. . .] que no se pega bien.
Varea (fol. 233) *ta-solo ta-quira,* desenredar el hilo enmarañado [> *solo,* desenvolver (algo)] • (339) *quir,* desatar [. . .] desenvolver; *quirah,* arrojar cualquiera obra de barro, vidrio, jícaras, huevos para que se quiebren [. . .] sacudir polvo de algo; *quirir,* caer polvo o tierra de lo alto.
Vico (n.d.a: fol. 167v) *quir,* desatar, desenvolver, desanudar; *quirir,* caerse la fruta de los árboles, hojas o flores.
Ximénez (1985: 489) *quirir,* caerse, como fruta, flores, de los árboles; polvo.

KITZIJ

Angel (fol. 171v) *ki,* partícula que quiere decir cierto, o ciertamente *[= kitzih].*
Anleo (fol. 52v) *kitzih chi anim,* muy presto • (66v) *kitzih [= katzih],* cierto, ciertamente.
Anonymous (fol. 60) *kitzih tzih, kitzih u su4uliquil,* cierta y verdadera cosa.
Basseta (fol. 216) *quitzih,* adverbio, de verdad, ciertamente.
Tirado (fol. 53) *kitzih tzih,* cosa cierta • (59v) *kitzih,* certidumbre • (60v) *kitzih tzih canubijh chawe,* de verdad te lo digo • (148) *kitzih nu bij,* mi nombre proprio.
Torresano (fol. 31) *kitzih,* verdaderamente; *kitzihan,* verdaderamente con más afecto • (97v) *kitzih [. . .] vi* [assertion—e.g., *kitzih tzih xaban vi mac,* ciertamente que has pecado].
Varea (fol. 37) *ikitzih,* la verdad y la certidumbre.
Villacañas (fol. 145) *qui tzih tzih,* certificar.

KO

Tirado (fol. 105v) *covil // achihilal,* fortaleza de varón.
Torresano (fol. 40) *oh couh chic,* ya somos fuertes.
Varea (fol. 342) *cou,* cosa recia, fuerte, dura; *covin,* no ser pusilánime [. . .] tener valor, ánimo.
Vico (n.d.a: fol. 49v) *covin / covih,* esforzar la gente; *covirisah,* esforzar a otro.

KOLO

Torresano (fol. 33) *coloha*, ese debe de ser.

Varea (fol. 168) *colo mi xul*, quizás ha venido [a synonym for certain uses of *la*, partícula que se dice cuando se duda algo que ha sucedido, como si le preguntan a uno si ya vino el Padre: ¿*mi xul pe padre*? Response: *mi la xul / mi la ek xul / colo mi xul / mi xul cami*, puede ser que haya venido] • (341) *colo*, quizás.

Vico (n.d.a: fol. 51v) *colo*, quizás, aunque no se usa aquí.

KUBULIBAL

Coto (1983: 31) *tin cububa*, amontonar fruta, cacao, maíz [. . .] o, por el neutro, *ti cube*; *cubul*, montón así: *hu cubul, ca cubul, ox cubul* . . .

Torresano (fol. 132v) *cube*, sentarse.

Varea (fol. 342) *cubul*, cosa amontonada.

KUTAMIL

Basseta (fol. 177) *cutam*, tronco • (230v) *cavixal caƐutamil*, nuestro origen, Adam.

Coto (1983: 43) *cutam*, cuando el árbol está ya cortado [. . .] lo que queda con raíz en el suelo [. . .] se toma[n] por los ascendientes en la generación: *ka cutamil, ka xamalil, he nabey ka te, ka tata*. Tómase, también, por el cuerpo de la persona o animal • (552) *cutam*, tocón, que es el trozo del árbol cortado, lo que queda en la tierra con su raíz, y lo mismo de cualquiera otra mata o hierba, como lechuga, coles, etc.: *ru cutamil che, Ɛozm, ichah*, etc.—Si tiene retoños, llaman *vix*; *ru vixal che* • (559) *ka vixal, ka cutamil, ka nabey te, tata*, de los antepasados [. . .] nuestro tronco, nuestra raíz, fueron nuestros padres; *cutam*, en la persona, desde la cintura al cuello.

Varea (fol. 105) *cutam*, tronco que queda de árbol cortado [. . .] A sus padres llaman también los indios *nu vixal nu cutamil* [. . .] Dícenlo también de nuestros primeros padres Adan y Eva • (343) *cutam*, tronco de mata o de árbol, lo que queda después de cortado.

Vico (n.d.a: fol. 52v) *cutam*, tronco de un árbol; *vixal / cutamil / cupil*, origen.

KUXTABAL

Basseta (fol. 177v) *cuxtubal*, (en Rabinal) para acordarse, recuerdo.

K'AJOL

Angel (fol. 8) *al4ahol*, son los vasallos, o macehuales [. . .] vasallos por metáfora.

Tirado (fol. 108) *alaxik // 4aholaxic*, generación • (188v, 190v) *al // 4ahol*, vasallo / villano.

Torresano (fol. 39v) *yn 4ahol*, yo soy mozo.

Varea (fol. 346) *4ahol*, hijo o hijos varones [. . .] significa también el mancebo desde 13 hasta los 30 años, poco más o menos, aunque sea casado.

Vico (n.d.a: fol. 7v) *al 4ahol*, son los vasallos, o maceguales; *çakil al çakil 4ahol*, será el linaje humano • (41) *çakillal çak4ahol*, será el linaje humano; *kapasal al 4ahol*, vasallos por metáfora • (240) *4ahol*, hijo, o mancebo para casar, o sobrino; *4aholah*, engendrar varón.

K'AK'ALEN

Angel (fol. 192v) *4a4alih*, guardar, custodiar, espiar.

Basseta (fol. 168v) *cacalehic*, pastorear, guardar, espiar.

Coto (1983: 257) *tin 4a4alih*, guardar teniendo cuenta *[= chahih]* • (212) *tin 4a4alih*, espiar o acechar (esto es metaphorice, que no es con propiedad).

Tirado (fol. 97) *4a4alinel,* espia que asecha • (110) *quenuya soldados chu4a4alexic 4,ak 4oxtun,* guarnecer fortaleza con soldados.
Vico (n.d.a: fol. 138v) *4a4alih,* espiar, acechar (se entiende de algo).

K'ALAB

Basseta (fol. 170) *calab,* un palo en que atan la tela y la empiezan a tejer.
Varea (fol. 347) *4al,* atar algo por dos o tres partes, liar; *4alvach,* guirnalda que usan los Indios de un cerco de cuero o de rueda de cajeta adornada de plumas de *cakix,* guacamaya, o de *Ɛanan,* o de flores.
Vico (n.d.a: fol. 241) *4al,* atar [e.g., *xxim x4al,* fue atado]; *4al vach,* corona o guirnalda para la cabeza de rosas o de plumas para bailar.

K'AMO

Basseta (fol. 170v) *camo,* tomar y recibir.
Tirado (fol. 110v) *4amol bee,* guía; *can4am ubee pedro,* yo guío a Pedro.
Varea (fol. 348) *4am,* tomar, sacar, llevar, o traer llevando algo • (349) *4amovah,* agradecer, dar gracias.
Vico (n.d.a: fol. 231v) *4amo,* recibir, o ser tomado, o cobrar; *4amonel,* recibidor; *4amol bey,* ir delante; *4amol 4,iquin,* perro cazador.

K'AQOM

Angel (fol. 193) *4ak,* tirar con piedra o aflojar flecha, o herir.
Coto (1983: 48) *tin 4ak chi 4ha / qui 4akon,* asaetear; *4akonal,* asaeteador; *4akom,* asaeteado • (234) *4akol 4ha,* el flechero; *tin 4habih / tin 4ak r'al 4haa,* tirar flecha, o flechar • (306) *tin 4ak,* tirar la lanza [≠ *tin toƐ,* dar lanzada como quien da estocada]; *4akol,* lanzeador; *4akom,* lanzeado.
Curruchich Gómez and Coyote Tun (p. 47) *k'aqon,* tirar un objeto a distancia.
Tirado (fol. 21v) *4ak,* apedrear [. . .] tirar con piedra • (105) *quin4akan chichab,* flechar; *4akol chab,* flechero.
Varea (fol. 366) *4ak,* tirar con piedra o flecha.
Vico (n.d.a: fol. 246v) *4ak,* apedrear, o tirar con piedras, o con arco, flechar, o herir el sol reciamente, o lisonjear; *x4akatah,* flechado • (260v) *x4akayah san sebastian,* fue herido y flechado S[an] S[ebastián].
Villacañas (fol. 84) *caƐ chi cha,* asaltar [*sic,* "asaetear"?]; *Ɛacom,* asaeteado • (150) *caƐ chi abah,* dar pedrada.

K'AXK'OL

Tirado (fol. 156v) *rayil // 4ax4ol,* la Pasión de Jesucristo.
Torresano (fol. 135) *4ax4obiçah,* atormentar.

K'I

Saquic Calel (p. 337) *q'ui,* mucho [≠ *qui',* dulce o sabroso].
Tirado (fol. 144) *4iamul,* muchas veces.
Varea (fol. 354) *4iy,* mucho en número, o cosas líquidas; *4iyar,* crecer; *4iyarisah,* juntar, multiplicar, aumentar.
Vico (n.d.a: fol. 249) *4iy,* mucho.

K'IS

Basseta (fol. 216) *quizo,* acabar; *quizibal,* el fin.

Coto (1983: 224) *tin 4iz a Ɛih*, hacer estremecer a otro, amenazándole por algo de que le ha de matar, como para decir "no pararé hasta quitarte la vida."
Tirado (fol. 35v) *u4izbal*, cabo, o fin *[= utzam; utanalibal]*.
Varea (fol. 355) *4iz*, acabar, concluir; *x4iz ruƐih*, acabársele la ventura (al que es descubierto en su delito).
Vico (n.d.a: fol. 250) *4içon*, acabar, o concluir, o rematar.

K'O

Varea (fol. 356) *4ohe*, estar, vivir, morar.
Vico (n.d.a: fol. 64) *in4ohvi*, allí estoy • (250v) *4ohe*, vivir, o tener morada, o nacer • (251) *4oh*, está, y también quiere decir algunas veces, o alguna vez; *4ohlem*, la vida, o costumbre.

K'OJI'IK

Tirado (fol. 3v) *4oheic*, hábito, uso y costumbre [≠ *4oheical*, misterio] [. . .] La substancia de cualquier cosa, el semen del hombre, de la mujer y las partes ocultas del hombre y de la mujer.
Varea (fol. 357) *4ohlem*, la costumbre y condición, inclinación, natural, propriedad o maña [. . .] con la forma o falta natural con que nace cualquier cosa • (251) *4oh*, está, y también quiere decir algunas veces, o alguna vez; *4ohlem*, la vida, o costumbre.

K'OQOBAL / K'OQOBEN / K'OQON

Coto (1983: 45) *ti 4okon nu 4ux chire nu mac*, me arrepiento y duelo de mis pecados • (330) *tin 4okoh*, maldecir, echando maldición; *ru 4okobal mamaa, atita*, maldiciones de viejos; *ti 4okon mama, atit*, está maldiciendo el viejo o vieja.
Curruchich Gómez and Coyote Tun (p. 52) *k'oqob'ej*, lanzar un objeto.
Vico (n.d.a: fol. 254) *4okom*, *4okom nu 4ux*, me duele el corazón, o tener arrepentimiento, o mancilla; *4okiçah*, maltratar, o dar mala vida.
Ximénez (1985: 215) *coƐ*, desenclavar, tener mancilla, arrepentimiento; arrancar algo como pegajoso.

K'OT

Angel (fol. 197) *4otoh / 4otom / 4ot*, hacer molduría, escultura • (197v) *4oto*, cavar; *4oton ruchij / ruvach*, cosa escultada; *4otoh*, la cava, o la hoya • (198v–199) *4ot chijh*, preguntar por rodeos por sacar la verdad por saber las obras del próximo u otra cosa que no se publica [. . .] examinar, y sacar razones • (218) *4otobal*, escoplo.
Anonymous (fol. 60) *4otomuleu*, cimiento o sanja abierta.
Basseta (fol. 175) *coto*: entallar; *ahcot*, entallador [from another writer: *cotom vachibal*, imagen esculpida; *cotoh chirih tinamit*, cava de fortaleza].
Coto (1983: 77) *tin 4ot chijh*, buscar haciendo inquisición • (226) *4otol chi*, examinador; *4otbal chi*, examinación • (258) *4otom*, guarida para esconderse o defenderse, *4,ak 4oxtum, hul, çivan, 4otom*. Y deste género de guaridas usaban antiguamente para guarecerse de sus enemigos • (423) *4otom vleuh*, pozo seco y sin agua, como donde han sacado tierra para obra; *4otom ya*, pozo para sacar agua, como el de la Samaritana.
Tirado (fol. 7v) *can4ot upam abah / chee*, acanalar madera, o piedra • (8) *4oton ubeha*, acequia • (34v) *uchi 4otom haa*, brocal de pozo • (39) *4otom tem*, canal de madera • (40) *4otoh abah*, el acto de sacar piedra; *chi4otba*: cantera donde se sacan piedras • (43, 94) *4oton uleu*, tierra cavada; *4ot hul*, cavar haciendo hoyo • (43v) *4otom abah*, caja de piedra, o sepulcro • (68v) *can4ot caminak*, desenterrar muerto; *4oton pauleu*, desenterrada cosa • (88v) *uƐoton rib cumatz*, está enroscada la culebra • (89v) *4ot-*, entallar piedra, madera;

can4ot abah, cantear • (93) *can4ot uchijh*, examinar • (94v) *4otbal 4hi4h*, escoplo • (95v) *4ot-*, esculpir, cavar en duro como piedra, o madera [este verbo *4ot* es propiamente cavar] • (98v) *remelic 4otomhaa*, estanque de agua • (102) *4otom*, zanja para sembrar.
Varea (fol. 359) *4ot*, cavar, hacer hoyo [. . .] hacer sepultura.
Vico (n.d.a: fol. 252v) *4oton*, cavar; *ah 4ot*, entallador, o [el que] labra piedra o madera; *4otoh*, la cava • (253) *4otom ruchi ruvach*, ídolo.

K'OXAJ

Basseta (fol. 175v) *coxaj*, sencillo, o único.
Tirado (fols. 137v, 209v) *4oxah 4ul*, manta sencilla [≠ *laƐanic*, manta doble] • (177) *4oxah ba4,*, hilo sencillo.

K'OXOMA

Coto (1983: 212) *tin 4oxomah*, espiar o acechar de lejos • (350) *tin 4oxomah*, mirar contemplando o nivelando con la vista si va derecha la obra, edificio, o otra cosa [. . .] mirar de lejos, como para ver o oír lo que tratan otros [. . .] también, cuando de lejos van con la vista puesta a alguna parte, como a árbol, peña, cerro, etc., para salir a él, como los marineros que se gobiernan por el norte [. . .] este verbo *[4oxomah]* se compone de *4oxom*, que es la certificación que se hace con la vista de alguna cosa, como los exploradores que van a atalayar y contemplar las tierras y fuerzas de los contrarios, la disposición y gente que tienen [e.g., *x-rul toro hun vinak mukcheenel, nachanel, tan t'ul ru 4ama ru 4oxom tinamit, tan t'ul ru 4oxomah ka 4ohlem*, ha andado por aquí un espía, un observador, tomando cuenta del pueblo, ha venido a espiar cómo somos] • (372) *tin 4oxomah*, notar de lejos lo que otros hacen [e.g., *tan ko ru 4oxomah pe chi naht lae vinak*, nos está notando y mirando] • (487) *4oxom*, resolución o última palabra que se da, en lo que se trata, de lo que se ha de hacer o no.

K'OXTUN

Angel (fol. 198) *4oxtun*, fortaleza, o valiente; *ah 4,alam ah 4oxtun*.
Coto (1983: 126) *4,ak // 4oxtun*, cerca o muro de ciudad.
Tirado (fol. 93) *4,ak // 4axtun*, fortaleza • (110) *quenuya soldados chu4a4alexic 4,ak 4oxtun*, guarnecer fortaleza con soldados.
Varea (fol. 359) *4oxtun*, fortaleza, fuerte o baluarte, que había antiguamente donde estaba el Mayor Cacique con sus valientes soldados [. . .] Los Tzutuhiles llaman *4oxtun* a la cerca de pared de piedra seca, con que cercan sus milpas [. . .] las cercas de piedras secas de los corrales.
Vico (n.d.a: fol. 50) *coxtun*, castillo • (253v) *4oxtum*, fortaleza, o baluarte, o fuerte; *ah 4,alam ah 4oxtum*.
Villacañas (fol. 144) *coxtun*, cerca o muro; *tin caxtunih rih tinamit*, cercar el pueblo de muros.

K'UL

Varea (fol. 361) *4ul*, recibir [. . .] encontrar [. . .] tener conversación con otro [. . .] salir a ver o oír lo que dice o lo que quiere el que llega a la puerta; *4ulum*, estar juntas las tierras o casas.
Vico (n.d.a: fol. 255) *4ulun*, venir de nuevo, o parecerse, o acontecer de nuevo.
See also:
Varea (fol. 360) *4ulbat*, término o señal que divide los términos de pueblos o heredades o río o árbol o peña [. . .] y del camino que le cabe limpiar a cada pueblo • (361) *4ulhay*, vecino de casa y heredad *[vach 4ulhay vach 4ulbat]*.

Vico (n.d.a: fol. 254v) *4ulbat,* mojón de tierra, o términos • (255) *4ulhay,* mi vecino, con distinción que hay pared en medio o en frente, *vach 4ulbat, vach 4ulchi, vach 4ulha.*

K'UL U-WACH

Varea (fol. 361) *4ulvachih,* toparse con alguno o con algo; *4ulvach,* lo que acaso o por fortuna encuentro o hallo [≠ *4ululaah,* estar una cosa en frente de otra, o casas, montes, árboles, piedras].

Vico (n.d.a: fol. 254v) *4ulvachih,* toparse acaso con algo, participar algo.

LABAL

Alonso (fol. 129) *e ah labal e chay,* ejército [e.g., *e ah tinamit chay; e ah tzolola chay; e ah 4,utuhile chay; e ah rabinale chay*].

Angel (fol. 83) *labalin,* enemistar, o hacer guerra; *ah labal,* el soldado, o guerrero; *labal,* la guerra.

Basseta (fol. 175) *ahlabal,* perseguidor [. . .] el diablo, el enemigo *[= ah cotob; ahtza]* • (198v) *labalinel,* enemigo [from another writer: *labalih,* guerrear].

Tirado (fol. 8v) *covilah labalinel,* esforzado, guerrero • (21v) *canvaba vib chilabal,* apercebirse para guerra • (24) *labalibal 4hi4h,* armas • (29) *labal,* batalla, guerra; *labalij / labalinic,* batallar; *ahlabal,* guerrero • (31, 155) *mac labal,* pecados • (46) *labal,* combatir, pelear [= *tzaloh,* pelea] • (57v) *mac, labal,* culpa, pecado • (66) *canvelesah ulabalibal,* [yo] desarmo • (85) *labalin quib,* encontrarse peleando • (85v) *ah labal,* enemigo, guerrero • (95) *uchalahil ahlabal,* escuadrón de batalla • (102v) *qui4hobil e ah labal,* ejército de guerreros • (110) *quenuvik vinak chirech labal,* guarecer gente para la guerra; *labal,* guerra; *ah labal,* guerreador • (156) *labalinic,* pelea; *labalinel,* peleador.

Varea (fol. 104) *xvinakir xyacatah labal,* sea levantado guerra • (169) *labal,* el enemigo y contrario [e.g., *he kahlabal 4eche vinak*]; *labalih,* hacer guerra, pelear, reñir tanto que quieren venir a las manos • (169) *4hay // labal,* guerra, pelea, contrario, guerrero • (309) *ahlabal ahchay,* soldados [> *chay*: cierta piedra como navajas].

Vico (n.d.a: fol. 114) *labal,* la guerra *[= tzaloh].*

Villacañas (fol. 125) *labalih // Ɛaçah,* combatir o pelear.

LAQ'ANIK

Basseta (fol. 198v) *laƐo,* juntar.

Coto (1983: 394) *laƐe / laƐaba,* parear [. . .] vayan o estén dos cosas juntas.

Tirado (fols. 137v, 209v) *laƐanic 4ul,* manta doble [≠ *4oxah 4ul,* manta sencilla].

Varea (fol. 170) *laƐlot,* ir dos juntos • (170v) *laƐanic 4ul, laƐan ru vay, laƐan ru Ɛin,* ropa con dos hilos juntos, tela y urdimbre; *laƐaba,* dar o poner dos cosas juntas en alguna parte; *laƐaƐiyax,* andar a la par, juntos; *laƐeh,* dar, llevar, traer dos cosas juntas [≠ *lakam,* la bandera de guerra o el pendón].

Vico (n.d.a: fol. 114v) *laƐelaah,* ir unidos, o pareados • (115) *laƐe, laƐan, laƐaloh,* juntarse, unirse.

LOL

Angel (fol. 87) *lol,* grillo que canta.

Coto (1983: 150) *ti lolin ru pam,* que no hay más de grillos y chicharillas que cantan adentro [supports the idea that a house is abandoned or empty: *tolan hay*] • (256) *lol,* (grillos) verdes, cantadores [≠ *xil,* grillo, especie de cigarra que no tiene alitas, sino que salta] [. . .] Y cuando la noche está quieta y serena, que sólo se oye el chillido o canto de estos grillos, dicen: *ti lolin, ti xilan aƐa* • (523) *ti lolin chic,* cuando en el pueblo o casa hay enfermedad o hambre, y que las mujeres cesan de moler su pan, o cuando ha mucho que no se habita una casa, dicen: *tan t'oƐ lol, xil, rumal nima yabil*, esto es, "que los grillos y chicharillas están chillando en la casa por estar sola."

Varea (fol. 178) *lol*, cierta cigarra verde que está cantando toda la noche; *lolin*, significa haber gran silencio en casa o pueblo por enfermedad o hambre, que cesan las piedras de moler, o haber mucho tiempo que no habita una casa [e.g., *tan toc lol xil rumal nima yavabil*, entraron los grillos . . . ; *ti lolin chic ru cohol hay*, o *rumal vayhal*] • (242) *lol*, otro animalejo que canta de noche [its song is associated with a situation of hunger, of famine; e.g., *tan toƐ lol xil chupam chi vaihal*, haber tanta hambre].

Vico (n.d.a: fol. 118v) *lol*, el grillo • (119) *tilolin*, tener silencio, o sosegado.

LOLOJ

Coto (1983: 4) *ti lohe [= ti 4hu4hur]*, ablandarse mucho lo que se cuece al fuego, como carne, pescado, yerbas, etc. • (68) *lohan chic*, estar blanda una cosa de muy cocida *[< lohloh]*; *ti lohe*, ablandarse así.

Tirado (fol. 208) *sak loloh*, lo muy blanco en una ave.

Varea (fol. 178) *lohe*, ablandarse mucho lo que se cuece.

Vico (n.d.a: fol. 247v) *loloh ya*, agua cristalina.

LOLOXINAQ

Coto (1983: 425) *ti lo*, podrirse la ropa, el hilo, cordeles, que de podrida se rompe o corta; *looloxinak*: cuando son muchas cosas [. . .] y de éste usan cuando el papel se pudre o humedece • (495) *tin loo*, romperse de vieja, podrida, o hilo, papel, cuero, etc.; *loloxinak chic*, estar rota la cosa en muchas partes.

Varea (fol. 170) *lalot*, escoser mucho la llaga, picadura de víbora, o punzada de espina, o aguja, o herida, o chile fuerte [. . .] o los azotes *[= lemlot; ƐaƐaric]* • (178) *lo*, carcomarse pies o manos por andar con cal, lejía o ceniza o lodo; *loo*, quebrarse presto el hilo por mal hilado o podrido, o la seda, o estar tan vieja o rota, o la ropa o papel tan podrido que en asir del con poca fuerza sale el pedazo [< *loan*, ropa muy vieja y rota] • (305) *loloxinak*, andar muy pobremente vestido o viejo o roto.

Vico (n.d.a: fol. 114v) *lalot*, escocer, o quemar como hace el ajo en los ojos, o la mano que escuece • (118v) *loo*, dar comezón como hace la cal en las manos; *tilolot*, el frío, o dolor de comezón.

Ximénez (1985: 359) *lolot*, dar comezón como la cal.

LOT'OT'EJ

Angel (fol. 86) *tin lotheh*, llevar en las manos la criatura • (87v) *lotheh*, cercarse o tener en brazos.

Basseta (fol. 200) *loteh*, abrigar (y con *caluh*, abrazar, tener en brazos, llevar en palmas).

Coto (1983: 323) *tin lotteh*, llevar con tiento.

Tirado (fol. 187v) *lotih*, tener en los brazos, como en el bauptismo, que el padrino tiene al ahijado; o como se tiene a un enfermo descaecido.

Varea (fol. 179) *lotteh*, llevar o traer algo como tiento • (204) *lotteh*, recibir algo con la mano abierta [e.g., *ta-lotteh puvak, cacou, vay, pan aƐa*].

Vico (n.d.a: fol. 119v) *lote*, llevar en los brazos; *loteh*, secarse, o tener en los brazos.

LOTZ

Angel (fol. 88) *lotz 4u chix*, ser atenazado; *lotz 4uxlatal*, muerte; *tilotz*, punzar con lanzeta o con *chay* como acostumbran para enfermedad.

Basseta (fol. 200) *lotztum, xahol lotz tum* [from another writer: "un baile que así se llama"].

Coto (1983: 61) *lotz tun*, baile [. . .] que hacen tocando unas varas largas y huecas [. . .] A estas varas llaman *tun* (Por el señor obispo, don Agustín Ugarte [y Saravia], está prohibido este baile, fundado en un tratado que dél hizo el padre Antonio Prieto de Villegas, Comisario del Santo Oficio, hombre muy docto y muy gran lengua quiché, y que fue unos treinta años beneficiario de Matzatenango. Y aun pienso que por ordenanza del señor Visitador que está prohibido, como lo está por nuestras Constituciones, en el Capítulo celebrado el año de 1650, por Pascua del [E]spíritu Santo) • (508) *tin lotz*, cuando se pican en la frente, que es muy ordinario entre estos naturales, o en otra cualquiera parte donde tienen dolor, aunque sea en la boca del estómago o sobre el corazón; *lotzbal chay*, el instrumento con que sangran *[= toƐbal]*.

Tirado (fol. 97) *lotzovic // toƐovic*, espinar o punsar.

Varea (fol. 181) *lotz*, sangrar [. . .] o dar punzadas en la frente (con lanzeta o con *4hay*), sangría común y usada de Indios *[ti lotzo = ti toƐo]*; *lotz 4uch*, un baile de 4,utuhiles . . . [and also: *lotz*, yerbas acederas] • (284) *ta toƐo ta lotzo nu vi*, darse piquetes, uso de los Indios • (288) *lotz tun*, es un baile que usan con tres flautas [. . .] *tikaxah lotztun*.

Vico (n.d.a: fol. 120) *lotz 4uch*, atenacear [. . .] la tal muerte (atenaceado); *tilotz*, punzar o sangrarse de la frente por que les duelen y sanan.

MACH'MAL

Coto (1983: 544) *ti ma4han r'akan xocomil hab*, cuando la lluvia no cae derecha, sino que el aire la lleva de una a otra parte.

Varea (fol. 197) *ma4hah*, dar varazos, ramalazos o correazos que escuesen.

MAK

Angel (fol. 89) *mac*, el pecado [. . .] la voluntad.

Tirado (fol. 57v) *mac labal*, culpa, pecado • (155) *mac labal*, pecados.

Varea (fol. 190) *mac*, la intención o intento, el fin que os movió a hacer ésto [. . .] la obra de todo lo sobredicho.

MAKUJ

Varea (fol. 190) *macun*, hacer algún mal, pecar, tener culpa, ser culpado, delinquente, hablar mal; *macuh*, hacer algo de todo lo sobredicho, haber hecho o tener alguna culpa.

Vico (n.d.a: fol. 121v) *macun*, pecar [. . .] ofensar.

MATUL

Angel (fol. 91v) *matul*, ponzoña • (125v) *quij // matul*, ponzoña.

Basseta (fol. 201v) *matul*, unos aguacates pequeños [= *chutin oh*, aguacate pequeño]; *matul / qui*, la ponzoña.

Vico (n.d.a: fol. 124) *matul*, ponzoña *[= 4uiy]*.

Ximénez (1985: 377) *matul*, ponzoña, veneno.

MAYIJ

Angel (fol. 39v) *nuçip numayih*, mi dádiva, o mi ofrenda.

Anonymous (fol. 7v) *nimanic // mayihanic*, honorar, respetar, obedecer.

Basseta (fol. 201) *maih*, admira [≠ *maih*, negar, destruir, perder, aniquilar]; *maih, maihah*, ofrenda, ofrecer • (205v) *nima mayhabal*, un gran milagro *[= nima naval nima puz]*.

Tirado (fol. 7v) *nimanic // mayihanic*, respeto y obedencia • (11) *mayiha (+ -xel; -bal; -nel)*, admirable, admiración, el que se admira [. . .] adorar, adorable • (41v) *mayij toƐob*, caridad • (61v) *nusip // numayih*, dádiva, o don, del que da; *nucoch // numayih*, don,

del que recibe; *ahmayih*, dadivoso • (124v) *quinbe mayihanok*, voy a divertirme • (137v) *mayiha- (+ -xel; -nic; -h; -bal)*, maravilla; milagro.
Torresano (fol. 79v) *maihax*, cosa celebrada o reverenciada [< *maihan*, lo celebrado].
Varea (fol. 192) *maihah*, maravillarse, admirarse.
Vico (n.d.a: fol. 122v) *mayhah*, maravillarse, o admirarse, o engrandecer; *mayhanel*, admirador; *mayhaxel*, lo que se ha de admirar; *mayhabal*, milagro.

MAYIJ

Angel (fol. 90) *mayh*, acabar, o destruir; *quiçach, quimayix, quiƐutux, mayh, Ɛutuh, yaar, chamux*, todos quieren decir acabar.
Basseta (fol. 201) *maih*, negar, destruir, perder, aniquilar.
Coto (1983: 50) *tin maih*, asolar o destruir algo, como pueblo, milpa, etc.
Tirado (fol. 36v) *hupmayij kahok*, caer de rostro; *pacmayij kahok*, caer de espaldas • (157) *sachic // mayixik*, perdimiento y destruimiento.
Varea (fol. 192) *maih*, asolar, destruir, acabarse de perder o de morir la gente o milpa, cacahuatal *[= sach]*.
Vico (n.d.a: fols. 93v–94) *mayx [= yaar; chamur]*, acabarse del todo, perderse, no haber memoria [. . .] acabarse • (123) *maih*, asolar, perder la memoria de la tierra, o lugar, o gente, o negar *[= çach; yaar; chamur]*; *main*, tardarse; *mayx / Ɛutux*, destruir, aniquilarse, negar.

MEJ

Basseta (fol. 202) *meho*, inclinar la cabeza, humillarla o dar reverencia.
Coloch (pers. comm.) *ka-ø-mej-o ko lo ki-chi' ko lo ki-wach*, ellos se inclinan; *alawi la k-ø-ul qaj ko ki-mej-l-em*, allá donde vienen a prosternarse.
Varea (fol. 199) *meh*, por hacer reverencia, doblando el cuerpo.

MESESEJ

Angel (fol. 93v) *mezon*, barrer, o halagar a los niños, o a los gastos, traer las manos sobre sus cabezas.
Coto (1983: 44) *tin mez ru vi pahbal*, arrasar • (62–63) *tin mez*, barrer la casa, el patio, o limpiar camino, o desherbar las milpas o cacahuatales [. . . del verbo *tin mez* usan para decir que halagan pasando la mano por la cabeza [. . .] Esta acción suelen hacer cuando con cariño piden que hagan algo por ellos, particularmente los muchachos y mujeres. Y es muy común a todos, al enterrar un difunto, la mujer, hijos, o los más amigos y conocidos, en señal de sentimiento y del amor que le tenían, ir llegando a él y pasarle la mano dos o tres veces por la cabeza].
Curruchich Gómez and Coyote Tun (p. 61) *mesesej*, barrer con rapidez.
Tirado (fol. 111v) *canmes vui*, halagar, traer con la mano en la cabeza; *mezonel vuij*, halagador.
Varea (fol. 200) *mes*, barrer o limpiar caminos o milpa [. . .] halagar, pasándoles la mano por la cabeza o lomos [e.g., *ta-mesa ruvi a4ual*].
Vico (n.d.a: fol. 127) *mez*, barrer [. . .] halagar o traer a la mano sobre la cabeza [e.g., *chameza uvi a4al*, halaga esta criatura].

MOLAJ

Basseta (fol. 203) *molo / molih / moloba*, juntar, amontonar.
Tirado (fol. 7v) *molom / moloy*, gente acaudillada / acaudillador • (45) *molob patan*, coger y juntar los tributos; *mol-*, coger y juntar cosas esparcidas • (49v) *canmol, cancuch*

mayih vinak, junto y congrego (mucha) gente • (64v) *molonic,* demandar • (126v) *mol,* juntarse *[= popol; cuch].*
Torresano (fol. 113) *molah,* para contar diferencias de cosas *[humolah, camolah].*
Varea (fol. 203) *mol,* juntar cosas derramadas o distantes.
Vico (n.d.a: fol. 128v) *molah,* partícula para contar cosas, pláticas, o sermones; *mol,* acaudalar, o juntar.

MUJ

Alonso (fol. 231) *muh,* sombra contra el sol [. . .] que hacemos o hacen los árboles y también el cielo que llevan cuando andan las procesiones.
Angel (fol. 96v) *muh,* sombra o el palio para cubrir; *muhul xuvach cah,* anublar • (176v–177) *muh* [= *Ɛaalibal,* espaldar y sitial]; *qui4ohe chuxe amuh aƐaalibal,* estaré debajo de tu trono.
Basseta (fol. 204) *muh,* sombra [from another writer: "las madres del cacao"].
Coto (1983: 210) *muh [= Ɛalibal],* espaldar, o trono, asiento real; *oh 4oh xe a muh, xe a Ɛalibal,* estamos a tu orden / somos tus vasallos / estamos a tu amparo • (529) *muh,* sombra que hacen las cosas inanimadas, como la casa, árbol, piedra, etc.; *muh,* el quitasol o palio, o otra cosa que hace sombra; *ru muh muen* o *ticon,* sombra que ponen en los cacahuatales, que son unos árboles que siembran entre el cacao, que hacen sombra; *tan qui muhin,* gozar de sombra la persona o animal; *tin muhih,* hacer sombra a otro [. . .] en este sentido, se toma también por "amparar."
Curruchich Gómez and Coyote Tun (p. 62) *mujan,* refugiarse (del sol o de la luna).
Tirado (fol. 96) *muh // Ɛaalibal,* espaldar, o trono de Rey • (172) *muh Ɛaalibal quech santos,* retablo • (187) *muh / Ɛaalibal / muhun,* trono.
Varea (fol. 207) *muh,* sombra [. . .] significa palio [. . .] y el quitasol; *tan qui-muhin,* estoy a la sombra, o sesteando; *muh Ɛalibal,* el trono y el poder del Rey, y así estando sentado el Alcalde recién electo dándole la vara, dice un principal: *xcat-oc alcalde, at tamub, xcat-oc pa ru-muh, pa ru-Ɛalibal, dios rey, at ahauh chi at alcalde chic* [. . .] significa ampararse [e.g., *quin a-to at alcalde qui-4ohe ta cha-muhil*] [. . .] también llaman *muh* a los árboles que plantan a los cacahuatales para que les hagan sombra.
Vico (n.d.a: fol. 130v) *muh,* el palio o sombra; *muh Ɛalibal,* espaldar o trono de majestad • (228) *xe a muh xe a Ɛalibal oh 4o vi,* estamos debajo de tu amparo • (273) *muhan chee,* árbol muy sombrío *[= 4,uhan chee].*
Villacañas (fol. 70) *muhah che / muhibeh che,* ampararse detrás de algo contra el agua o el sol.

MUN

Angel (fol. 9) *alabitzil [= munil],* cautiverio • (96v) *mun,* el esclavo; *munil,* cautiverio, esclavitud.
Basseta (fol. 204) *mun,* esclavo (y *tzijh,* hacer esclavo); *munil tzijl,* esclavitud • (226) *mun // tzij,* esclavo.
Coto (1983: 94) *munil, alabitz, 4,ijl,* cautiverio o esclavitud como la de los negros [≠ *cana // teleche,* cautivo y preso en guerra].
Tirado (fol. 94) *mun // alabitz,* esclavo; *munil // alabitzil,* esclavonia • (114) *at umun ralabitz,* tu eres esclavo; *canmunih canvalabih vib,* hacerse uno mismo esclavo • (178) *mun alabitz,* siervo.
Vico (n.d.a: fol. 130) *mun,* el esclavo; *munil // 4,ijl,* cautiverio, trabajos afán.

MUQ

Basseta (fol. 203v) *muƐan*, sepultura; *muƐ*, sepultar, zambullir; *muƐu*, enterrar y encubrir en la tierra; *muƐuba*, esconderse y agacharse; *muƐutic*, encubrirse; *muƐcheeh*, acechar y encubrir.
Coloch (pers. comm.) *k-ø-in-muq-u*, voy a enterrarlo; *muq // pis*, enterrar, encubrir, sepultar; *ewam // muq*, enterrado, escondido [= refugee].
Vico (n.d.a: fol. 131v) *muk*, enterrar.

MUQUBAL

Angel (fol. 97v) *mukun / mukuh*, mirar.
Basseta (fol. 195v) *ylo // muƐuh*, ver • (203v) *muƐuh*, ver, mirar de lejos.
Coto (1983: 350) *qui mukun [= qui tzuun]*, mirar; mukubal, la vista, potencia, y [. . .] el lugar donde se mira algo.
Tirado (fol. 19v) *mukubal*, para ver • (39v) *xicoh chimukunic chiylonic*, me canse de mirar • (189) *mukunic / ylonic*, ver • (190v) *mukubal*, visión de los ojos [≠ *yloh pa varam*, visión en sueños].
Varea (fol. 208) *mukuh*, ver o mirar; *mukcheeh*, acechar, espiar.
Vico (n.d.a: fol. 131v) *mukuh*, mirar algo [. . .] mirar con atención, o de continuo • (132) *mukcheeh*, acechar; *ah muk*, la escucha del camino o el acechador; *muklechih*, divisar de lejos • (138v) *mukcheeh*, espiar, o acechar; *ah muk*, espía.

NABE

Curruchich Gómez and Coyote Tun (p. 64) *nabeyej*, adelantarse.
Tirado (fol. 10) *nabey*, adelantar, adelantamiento.

NIMABAL

Coloch (pers. comm.) *nimal* se dice de una comida especial, de fiesta.
Coto (1983: 230) *nimabal*, fe o creencia *[= oquibal / ikiquibal]*.
Tirado (fol. 161) *xaki caniman ri vino*, poner de cumplimiento vino (en la mesa).

NIMAL

Angel (fol. 103) *nimal*, grandeza, o mayoridad.
Tirado (fol. 109) *nimal*, grandeza en señorío.
Varea (fol. 220) *nimal*, hermano mayor del hombre, o hermana mayor de la mujer [. . .] también significa mayoría, o superioridad, grandeza.
Vico (n.d.a: fol. 139) *nim, nimal*, grandeza, o mayoridad, y se toma por la divinidad.
See also:
Coto (1983: 109) *nim*, el consuelo; *tin nimah*, consolar.

NIMANEL

Angel (fol. 102v) *nimah*, obedecer, honrar, tener en reverencia, o ensalzar alabando *[= nimabal]*; *nimanel*, el obediente.
Anleo (fol. 43v) *nim / nimah*, honrar a otro, o engrandecerlo [. . .] también significa obedecer a otro; *cat nu nimah*, yo te obedezco, esto es Yo te hago grande, Yo menor.
Anonymous (fol. 7v) *nimanic // mayihanic*, honrar, respetar, obedecer.
Basseta (fol. 162) *ahnim*, obediente [≠ *ah unum*, desobediente] • (206v) *nimah*, obedecer.
Tirado (fol. 7v) *nimanic*, acatar o tener respecto y obediencia • (70) *mana quin niman tah*, no obedezco; *mana nimanel tah*, desobediente • (122v) *mavinimanel*, inobediente • (149) *nima (+ -nic; -nel; -h)*, obedecer • (167v) *nimanel // Ɛahartizanel*, reverenciador • (192) *nimah*, servir una persona con servicio de criado [. . .] también significa obedecer.

Varea (fol. 219) *nimah*, obedecer, honrar, reverenciar [. . .] también significa no quedar saciado ni satisfecho en comer o beber por ser poco [e.g., *ma ni xu-nimah ru4ux vay*].
Vico (n.d.a: fol. 8v) *alan // niman*, obedecer.

NIMARISAJ

Angel (fol. 103v) *nimaric*, grandeza, o soberbia.
Tirado (fol. 178v) *nimarisabal*, soberbia; *quin4hau chinimal*, yo hablo con soberbia.
Vico (n.d.a: fol. 139) *nimar*, ensoberbecerse, ensalzarse; *nimariçah*, engrandecer, ensoberbecer; *nimariçabal*, soberbia.

OK

Varea (fol. 44) *oc*, entrar; *oquebal*, para decir "No me toca a mí, eso no está a mi cargo o cuenta, no tengo parte en eso" • (46) *oqueçah*, meter algo dentro de algo ; *oqueçayh*, meter con presteza y diligencia; *oquibeh*, entrar en alguna parte sin licencia, siendo casa de autoridad y respeto, o si entra a hurtar o a prender a alguno.

OKIKAM

Tirado (fol. 196v) *ma na roquican tah*, no es suficiente para lo que es menester.
Torresano (fol. 52) *roquic*, ser posible.
Varea (fol. 45) *oquic*, cosa justa y ajustada; *oquicam* [idea of appropriateness, of rightness, of accuracy—e.g., *mani roquicam tah quina 4hay ru vial mani nu mac*, no me puedes castigar justamente, porque no tengo culpa; *mani roquicam rochoch dios lae vinak mulanel chuvahay*, no cabe en la iglesia la gente que se amontonó afuera].

OKTISANEL

Basseta (fol. 207v) *octizan*, vestidura; *octizah*, hacer llorar • (229v) *vetizah [sic, ¿"uctizah"?]*, dar de beber [from another writer: *uctizanel*, el que da de beber].
Tirado (fol. 30) *octizanel*, bebedor *[= u4ianel]* • (62) *canvoctisah*, *canya ru4ia*, dar de beber a otro.

OPON

Coloch (pers. comm.) *ojala k-opon tan*, ¡Ojalá lleguen pronto!; *x-ø-opon-ik k-oj-tajin che la qa-wa*, él ha llegado mientras comíamos.
Varea (fol. 13) *apon*, para llegar uno a donde va.
Vico (n.d.a: fol. 11) *apon*, llegar [e.g., *quinapon panƐan*, llego (yo) a Guatemala].

OQOTAM

Basseta (fol. 207v) *ocotah*, dejar echar por ay, desterrar, seguir, y con el recíproco *uib*, correr.
Coto (1983: 143) *oƐotam chic*, desacompañado; *ti u'oƐotah*, desacompañar • (157) *oƐotah*, desterrar a alguno, echarlo del pueblo, de casa.
Curruchich Gómez and Coyote Tun (p. 67) *oqotaj*, perseguir.
Tirado (fol. 52) *oƐotam*, corrido; *cavokotah ubic*, correrlo de su poder • (66) *oƐotanic*, desacompañado, o desamparado, y aborrecido • (72v) *okotah*, desterrar • (78) *oƐotah ubic*, echar a otro.
Torresano (fol. 50v) *ve kitzih tivoƐotah can ivitzelal* [not translated: "if you truly abandon your sins (. . . God will forgive you)"] • (124v) *okotan*, desterrar; *okotax*, ser desterrado.
Varea (fol. 18) *okotah*, sacar, echar afuera *[= eleçah]*.

Vico (n.d.a: fol. 146v) *okotan / oƐotah*, desterrar, o despedir; *oƐotah*, dejar, desamparar, desacompañar, descasarse, o soltar *[< oƐotam, oƐotax, oƐotanel, oƐotaxel, oƐotabal, oƐotanem]*.
Villacañas (fol. 59) *ocotahel*, ahuyentar.

OQ'IK

Angel (fol. 109) *oƐ*, llorar, o bramar el toro, o tigre, o león, o balar las ovejas, o cantar los gallos, o gorjear las aves, o relinchar el caballo.
Basseta (fol. 209) *oqueh*, llorar y cantar el pájaro; *oquibal*, el llanto; *roquibal pich*, el canto de este pájaro.
Tirado (fol. 26v) *rokebal utiuj*, aullido el adive • (133) *oƐeh chisi4inic*, llorar a gritos.
Varea (fol. 52) *oƐ*, llorar [. . .] bramar, relinchar, rebusnar, cantar los gallos, y así los demás animales o aves; *oƐ + 4ux*, gran sentimiento, aflicción o tristeza; *oƐeh*, el llanto • (53) *oƐeh*, llorar por algo, o afligirse, entristecerse por algo; *oƐear*, estar o quedar triste, afligido o lloroso *[= biçor]*.
Vico (n.d.a: fol. 44) *nu çi4 voƐeh*, lloro o gemido • (147) *oƐeh*, llorar, bramar, tigre, león, etc.; *oƐebal*, el pesar, o llanto.

OYEW / OYOW

Alonso (fol. 46) *oyeuh*, hombre bravo *[= cak]*; *quinoyouar*, hacerse bravo *[= quincakar]*.
Angel (fol. 106v) *oyouar*, enojarse, o airarse [> *oyeuh*, el enojado]; *oyouariçah*, airar a otro • (107) *oyeuh*, el enojado *[= oyow]* • (179v) *nim ru ƐaƐal nu 4ux, nim royoual nu 4ux*, tengo grande rencor y enojo; *ƐaƐalah // oyeualah*, (hombre) fogoso y colérico.
Basseta (fol. 168v) *oyeual*, enojo, *caƐ // oyeu*, enojo • (208) *oyouariƐ*, enojarse; *oyoual*, enojo [from another writer: *oyoualah*, cruel].
Tirado (fol. 8) *quinoyovaric*, acelerarse en cólera, o enojo • (14) *chi oyoval*, airadamente • (45v) *oyoval*, cólera, o enfado; *oyovalaj achij*, colérico, airado • (68v) *cauelesah oyoval chu4ux*, desenojar a otro • (78v) *oyoval*, corage • (81v) *oyovaric // cakaric*, embravecerse • (86) *oyoval*, enfado • (88) *quinoyovaric*, me enojo • (106v) *oyeuh achih*, fuerte varón y muy esforzado • (107) *oyoval [= cakal]*, furia, o furor; *oyovarel*, furioso de enojo *[= cakarel]* • (122) *chi oyoval*, impacientemente • (149v) *4orroyoval usak vachibal nu4ux*, tengo odio • (163) *cantzur chi oyoval*, provocar a ira; *tzururic chioyoval*, provocación a ira • (172v) *oyovalah vinak*, persona rigorosa *[= ƐaƐalah vinak]*.
Varea (fol. 30) *camiquil oyoual*, odio mortal • (47) *oyeo*, persona colérica, brava y airada; *oyeval*, la ira, enojo, coraje; *oyevar*, enojarse, ser iracundo; *oyevariçah*, enojar a otro; *oyevaribeh*, enojarse con otro • (144) *oyouaribeh*, después que me enoje; *oyouariçala*, enojarse muchas veces.
Vico (n.d.a: fol. 144) *oyeuar*, enojarse; *oyeuh*, el enojo; *oyeuah*, airar *[= oyow]*.
Villacañas (fol. 84) *caƐ // oyeu*, áspero de condición.

PABAX

Coto (1983: 39) *pabaxic*, apercebimiento [. . .] o prevención *[= pixabaxic]*.
Varea (fol. 253) *paba*, alzar, poner derecho, arrimar, prevenir a otro para alguna cosa [. . .] poner en señorío u oficio o dignidad [e.g., *xipabax xinoc chuxe çamah vae alcaldeil vae 4,ibanic*]; paar, cosa que está parada y sin hacer nada.
Ximénez (1985: 140) *pab*, resguardarse, como debajo del árbol, por el aguacero; *paba*, enderezar, parar, arrimar, poner.

PAJ

Basseta (fol. 210) *maui xpahla pabe,* ¿no se cayó (o se lastimó) Vd en el camino? (muy usado); *pahic // zocotahic,* caer.

Tirado (fol. 186v) *pahic,* tropezar.

Varea (fol. 255) *pah,* verbo neutro, significa caer.

PAJTAJIK

Coloch (pers. comm.) *x-in-pajtajik,* yo fui engañado.

See also:

Coto (1983: 76) *pail,* burla; *tin paih / tin paibeh,* burlarse.

Varea (fol. 256) *paih,* burlar, chacotear con alguno [. . .] engañar.

PAQ'ABAL

Basseta (fol. 210) *paƐaba,* parar y arrimar; *pacalic,* parado, poner boca arriba [= *pacalic,* cuesta arriba]; *pacal vi,* cabeza arriba.

Coto (1983: 38) *tin pac,* apartar con las manos la gente para hacer camino y pasar en medio, o apartar ramas o yerbas para poder pasar; *pacbal,* apartamiento.

PEK

Vico (n.d.a: fol. 153v) *pec,* la cueva.

Saquic Calel (p. 335) *pec,* peñasco.

PEQ

Coto (1983: 80) *pek,* el pataxte (otro género de cacao).

Vico (n.d.a: fol. 29) *cacaou // pek,* el cacao / / pataxtes.

PERAJ

Angel (fols. 115v–116) *per,* partir desmenuzando como quien parte pan con las manos; *perah,* pedazo, o medio; *huperah,* un pliego o una hoja de papel.

Anleo (fol. 59v) *huperah, caperah . . . ,* para contar papel, pedazos de pan, de cajeta, tortillas, o mantas, o cosas que van tendidas unas sobre otras [. . .] Y también se entiende para reales, tostones, doblones, planchas de oro, o plata • (60v) *huperah,* un cuarto, o una hoja de papel; *caperah,* dos cuartos.

Coto (1983: 70) *hu per,* un bocado; *tin per,* partir.

Tirado (fol. 34v) *huperaj utiojil vakan,* un pedazo de la carne de mi pie • (175) *perah xahab,* sandalias de los indios • (209) *perah,* una manta con que crían niños que les sirven de cobija • (211) *huperah, caperah . . . ,* para contar tortillas, hojas de papel, y contar pedazos de pan, pedazos de ladrillos y adobes.

Torresano (fol. 36v) *ha ru perahil,* ¿Cuánto vale? • (113v) *perah,* para contar papel, hojas de libros, tortillas, mantas, o cosas que van tendidas unas sobre otras, o pedazos [. . .] *huperah, caperah,* etc.

Varea (fol. 260) *perah,* partícula para contar cosas anchas [. . .] sirve para contar las fresas tejidas o mantas sueltas; *per,* partir pan o fruta (en dos partes con la mano).

Vico (n.d.a: fol. 154v) *per,* partir, desmenuzado como pan; *perah,* pedazo; para contar papel, hojas de libro, tortillas, piernas de manta; *pere,* andar colgando como manta, o trapo; *pereba,* dar tendido en el suelo.

PICH / PIX

Angel (fol. 117v) *pichom Ɛoom 4ul,* manta labrada.

Coto (1983: 423) *tin pix*, hacer así estos plumages (para bailar), o otra obra de plumas, como abanicos, etc.; *ah pixola*, el oficial así; *tin pix*, cuando adornan las andas o algún altar con plumas o flores; *ah pixola [= ah Ɛo]*, a las mujeres que hacen huipiles labrados de plumas (derivados de los verbos *tin Ɛo* y *tin pich*. El primero, por "tejer con pluma o tuchumite, labrando el tejido"; el segundo, por "labrar con aguja." Y también usan del verbo *tin pix*; *vg. ta pixa izm ch'u vach nu pot*).
Varea (fol. 262) *pix*, coser plumas que llevan en la mano los que bailan [. . .] y de las que llevan sobre el cuerpo [. . .] coser y pegar abanicos de plumas; *ahpixola*, el que cose plumas o abanicos; dícenlo de las plumas de papagayo común, o de las grandes coloradas; a estas plumas llaman *4u4um*, *chiyom*, *4apibal ƐuƐ xahbal*; de las plumas que ponen en los huipiles dicen: *toc 4u4um chuchi pot*; y a las que hacen huipiles labrados llaman *ahƐola*, *ahpichola lae ixok hebel tibano pot*.
Vico (n.d.a: fol. 156) *pix [< pixo]*, hacer obra de plumas; *ah pixola [/ pixolay]*, los oficiales de esta obra.
Zuñiga (in Miles 1957: 768) *ah pix*, master feather worker, maker and keeper of feather dance garland.

PIS

Basseta (fol. 212) *pizo*, envolver.
Vico (n.d.a: fol. 157) *piz*, amortajar, envolver.

PIXAB

Angel (fol. 117) *pixaban / pixabah*, mandar, o apercebir, o encomendar, o dar licencia, o despedirse, o demandar licencia.
Basseta (fol. 211v) *pixab*, mandamientos.
Coto (1983: 193) *tin pixa / tin pixabah*, emplazar.
Curruchich Gómez and Coyote Tun (p. 72) *pixab'aj*, aconsejar en reuniones especiales como el caso de los discursos que se hacen en las bodas, bautizos, etc.
Saquic Calel (p. 335) *pixab*, consejo; but also: para siempre, ya nunca más.
Tirado (fol. 70v) *pixaaj*, despedirse • (128v) *pixab*, ley; *upixab amaƐ*, ley del pueblo • (137) *upixab tzih caminak vinak*, manda de testamento; *utzih upixab dios*, mandamiento de la ley de dios.
Varea (fol. 262) *pixa*, hacer plática mandando lo que se ha de hacer; *pixa / pixabah*, despedirse; *pixa*, el mandado o mandamiento; *pixabah*, mandar, apercebir [. . .] dar licencia [. . .] encomendar algo.
Vico (n.d.a: fol. 156) *pixa* [en k'iche': *pixab*], el mandamiento, o licencia; *pixabah*, mandar, percebir, encomendar, dar licencia; *pixabah*, despedirse.

POKOB

Angel (fol. 118v) *pocob*, la adarga, o rodela; *pocobah*, adargarse • (206) *4hab // pocob*, armas; *4habil pocobal xebe4ambex xechee xe4am*, con mano armada fueron por ellos a los montes.
Basseta (fol. 179v) *chanal pocob*, un Baile antiguo • (180) [from another writer: "gozo, alegría"] • (224) [regarding *chanal*, from another writer: *tun*, *chanal*, toda clase de música] • (212) *poƐob*, baile antiguo y el broquel.
Coto (1983: 401) *pocob*, pavés o rodela; *xahbal pocob*, las que hacen para bailar, unas rodelillas; *tin pocobah*, pavesarse o arodelarse [. . .] Yten, cuando con la mano hacen sombra a la vista para ver bien, poniendo la mano sobre las cejas.

Tirado (fol. 6) *pocobah*, abroquelarse • (10) *pocob*, adarga, rodela • (95) *pocob*, escudo, escudar [e.g., *canpocobah vub chinuƐab*, escudarse con las manos] • (110) *pocobah ib*, guarecerse con rodela.

Varea (fol. 263) *pocob*, el broquel o rodela; *pocobah*, abroquelarse [. . .] poner la mano sobre los ojos para ver algo que está lejos.

POQLAJ

Angel (fol. 121v) *pokilah*, el polvo [> *pok*, tierra blanca para juntar con la cal para encalar].

Basseta (fol. 212) *poƐlah*, un género de tierra, y dicen *nu poƐlahil*: mi miseria o desventura.

Tirado (fol. 82v) *poklah*, polvo.

Varea (fol. 264) *pok*, tierra blanca, para blanquear paredes, y junta con cal; *pokih*, enjalbegar; *poklah*, el polvo de la tierra, o cal.

Vico (n.d.a: fol. 161) *pok*, tierra blanca; *poklah*, el polvo.

POQ'OM

Coto (1983: 93, 98) *tin poƐ*, castrar colmenas *[= ti u'or cab]*; *poƐom chic*, colmena castrada *[= orom chic]*; *poƐonic*, castradura *[= oronic]* • (201) *tin poƐola*, entresacar.

Ximénez (1985: 65) *ah poƐon*, los de Chinautla.

PUCH

Torresano (fol. 134) *puch*, y (conjunción).

PWAQ

Basseta (fol. 162v) *zaqui puaƐ*, o, *canquaƐ [sic]*, tesoro • (171) *canapuaƐ*, oro, tesoro.

Coto (1983: 346) *4hi4h*, todo género de metal (excepto el oro y la plata que al uno llaman *Ɛana puvak* y, al otro, *çaki puvak*).

Tirado (fols. 29v, 151v) *Ɛanapuak*, oro [≠ *Ɛana4hi4h*, cobre (44v, 98); ≠ *raxa sakipuak*, estano, metal (98v)] • (94v) *sakipuak*, plata • (126) *ech Ɛanapuak*, joya de oro.

Varea (fol. 65) *ru yaal xit puvak*, el resplandor • (270) *puvakih*, platear algo [e.g., *puakim vae candelero*].

Vico (n.d.a: fol. 38) *çaki puak*, la plata; *Ɛanapuak*, el oro • (56) *ƐalƐa chachal puakim*, cuentas, o gargantillas, o manillas.

See also:

Zuñiga (in Miles 1957: 768) *ah xit ah puac*, lapidary, jeweler.

QAJIK

Angel (fol. 169v) *ka*, bajar, o descender [≠ *kah*, pedir prestado].

Basseta (fol. 169) *cahic*, tiene seis significaciones: 1/ caer de alto, 2/ con acusativo *vach* escarmentar, 3/ pedir prestado, 4/ parecer bien, 5/ consolar, 6/ quebrar palo o palabra.

Coloch (pers. comm.) *ya x-ø-qajik*, ha bajado (el sol); *k-ø-ul qaj ko ki-mej-l-em*, ellos vienen a prosternarse; *k-in-qajik*, yo bajo.

Curruchich Gómez and Coyote Tun (p. 75) *qa'*, bajar, apostar [≠ *qej*, prestar].

Varea (fol. 367) *ka*, partícula para decir haciabajo; *ka*, descender, bajar • (368) *kahom*, la bajada, o ida a tierras bajas; *kahibal*, instrumento para bajar, escalera; *kahibeh*, para decir el tiempo que ha que cayó uno enfermo [. . .] tener buena o mala suerte o ventura.

Vico (n.d.a: fol. 110v) *kah*, bajar, descender [e.g., *xkah kahok*, bajó bajando; *xkah kaha chi rih queh*, se bajó de la bestia].

QAJOM

Angel (fol. 45) *tin chaƐimah tin Ɛah,* alquilar • (170) *kahon,* pedir prestado.

Basseta (fol. 169) *cahic,* tiene seis significaciones: 1/ caer de alto, 2/ con acusativo vach escarmentar, 3/ pedir prestado, 4/ parecer bien, 5/ consolar, 6/ quebrar palo o palabra.

Coto (1983: 193) *tin kah,* en préstamo tomar algo; *kahom chic,* lo así tomado prestado.

Saquic Calel (p. 323) *kajom,* prestado.

Tirado (fol. 32) *xintzalih nu kahom,* ya volví lo que había prestado, y *kahon* es cosa alquilada; *nu kahon,* tengo prestado • (83) *quinkahanic,* emprestar; *kahom,* cosa emprestada; *kahanel,* emprestador; *kahanic,* emprestadura.

Varea (fol. 308) *chaƐimah // kah,* pedir prestado • (369) *kah,* pedir prestada cualquier cosa [. . .] pedir fiado *[< kahe, kahic].*

Vico (n.d.a: fol. 111) *kahom,* pedir prestado; *kahonel,* el prestador.

QASAJ

Coto (1983: 491) *tin kaçah a Ɛih,* aunque no lo usan en este sentido, significa "vencer a otro en la guerra."

Varea (fol. 368) *kasah,* echar algo hacia abajo [. . .] derribar y echar en el suelo • (369) *xukaçah nuƐih,* me ha vencido.

Vico (n.d.a: fol. 110v) *kaçan,* bajar algo; *kaçabal ya,* la pila del bautismo en quiché; *kaçan,* triunfar [e.g., *xukaçah huyutaƐah,* triunfó, venció] • (111) *kaçan quihuyu tinamit,* ganar pueblo o ciudad; *in kaçay çivan tinamit,* (yo soy) el conquistador; *xkaçan ruƐih ralaxic,* venció • (113v) *maquitah kaçar ruchuƐa ri achi,* es invencible.

QATZ / QATZIJ

Anleo (fol. 66v) *katzih [= kitzih],* cierto, ciertamente.

Varea (fol. 369) *ki,* partícula para rogar algo con eficacia y encarecimiento, cierta y verdaderamente y sin falta [. . .] y para preguntar lo cierto y verdadero de algo [. . .] [y] para decir lo más cercano • (370) *kitzih,* cosa cierta y verdadera, o cierta y verdaderamente [. . .] sin falta y verdaderamente, sin duda; dícese por gran afirmación.

Vico (n.d.a: fol. 111v) *ka,* adverbio: ciertamente, o cierto.

QIBISAJ

Basseta (fol. 214v) *quibizah,* desviar *[= hetizah]*; *quibisah ubic,* apartar o desviar allá.

See also:

Coto (1983: 8) *kibuh + pe,* acercar; *kibuh + apon,* apartar.

Varea (fol. 370) *kibuh,* acercar o desviar algo, aventándolo o dándole empellón; *kibuh,* añadiéndole *pe* significa generalmente acercar cualquier cosa; añadiéndole *apon* significa apartarla.

Q'ALAJISAJ

Alonso (fol. 207) *qui Ɛalahisan,* publicar lo que no se sabe [≠ *Ɛalah çakil / etamabal chic,* publicar cosa sabida de muchos].

Anleo (fol. 20) *Ɛalahiçah,* declarar • (67) *Ɛalah,* claro, claramente.

Basseta (fol. 170) *calah,* clara cosa, manifiesta, pública; *calahobisah,* declarar, descubrir • (194v) *yebala nu tzih,* hoc est *mahabi xnucalahisah* [not translated: "I promise not to reveal"] • (230) [from another writer: *c'ul nu calahizah,* vengo a declarar . . .].

Coto (1983: 10) *tin Ɛalahiçah ru chohmil,* aclarar la verdad de algo *[= tin chohmiriçah]* • (137) *tin Ɛalahiçah,* declarar lo dificultuoso • (146) *tin Ɛalahiçah,* descubrir (el secreto) • (490) *tin Ɛalahiçah,* revelar algo, como el secreto, o lo que está escondido • (523) *tin Ɛalahiçah,* significar.

Curruchich Gómez and Coyote Tun (p. 77) *q'alajin*, despejar dudas • (78) *q'alajirisaj*, explicar lo que no está claro.
Tirado (fol. 20v) *Ɛalahisaj*, aparecerse, manifestarse [like Jesus Christ who appeared before the Apostles following his resurrection] *[= 4ut]* • (63v) *Ɛalahisa-*, declarar, o pronunciar algo • (67v) *Ɛalahisa-*, descubrir • (123) *canbijh can Ɛalahisah chirech justicia*, (yo) informo a la justicia • (137) *Ɛalahisa-*, manifestar *[= 4utun]* • (157) *Ɛalahizah chuvach padre*, confesar ante el Padre • (161) *xax chiƐalahin vi*, por fin se ha de descubrir • (172) *Ɛalahisah*, revelar.
Torresano (fol. 30v) *calah chic a mac*, tu culpa es patente; *calah vachil xabijh*, dijístelo en público.
Varea (fol. 225) *mani Ɛalah avach pa Ɛekum*, (¿Quién eres?) no te conozco a escuras • (374) *Ɛalah*, cosa que se ve claramente [. . .] cosa sabida y notoria; *Ɛalahisah*, publicar lo secreto.
Vico (n.d.a: fol. 125v) *ma ki pa Ɛalah vachil ri*, ¿no fue eso público? • (228) *Ɛalahiçah*, declarar, manifestar; *Ɛalah vachil*, públicamente y muy claro.

Q'ALEL

Angel (fol. 119v) *Ɛalel ah pop*, el señor del petate, principal • (176v) *Ɛalel ahpop*, cacique, señor.
Basseta (fol. 170) *calel achi*, capitán.
Tirado (fol. 35v) *Ɛalel ahpop / Ɛalel ahau*, cacique Señor Principal • (40v) *uƐaal achij*, capitán *[= rahpop achij; 4amolbe; cahpop achihab]*.
Varea (fol. 373) *Ɛalel*, cierto cacique [e.g., *Ɛalel ahpop juan*].
Vico (n.d.a: fol. 4) *Ɛalel ahau*, gran señor • (227v) *Ɛalel ah pop*, cacique o señor; *Ɛalel ya*, buboso.

Q'ALIBAL

Angel (fols. 176v–177) *muh [= Ɛaalibal]*, espaldar y sitial; *qui4ohe chuxe amuh aƐaalibal*, estaré debajo de tu trono.
Coto (1983: 50) *Ɛalibal*, verbal de *ti Ɛae*, por estar grave, como recostado de espaldas; *muh Ɛalibal*, asiento principal donde sólo se sientan los señores, obispo, gobernador, etc.
Tirado (fol. 96) *muh // Ɛaalibal*, espaldar, o trono de Rey • (172) *muh Ɛaalibal quech santos*, retablo • (187) *muh // Ɛaalibal // muhun*, trono.
Vico (n.d.a: fol. 130v) *muh // Ɛalibal*, espaldar o trono de majestad • (228) *xe a muh xe a Ɛalibal oh 4o vi*, estamos debajo de tu amparo; *Ɛalibal*, espaldar de los caciques y señores de otro tiempo.

Q'ALQ'AB

Angel (fol. 180) *ƐalƐa 4ual yamanic*, joyas.
Coto (1983: 283) *chuncu ƐalƐa*, brazaletes [≠ *yacapulul*, o *raxon*, pieza de oro que estaba asida a las narices; *oquinak ru te cacao xavi puvak*, joya colgada del labio bajo; *ru vuam puvak*, o *r'abahim puvak he4el ch'u kul ahau*, cuentas de oro, o otro metal, colgadas a los pechos; *ru Ɛop*, zarcillos; *ru nap Ɛa*, los anillos; *ru chachal ru kul*, gargantillas al cuello; *ru chachal ru Ɛa*, brazaletes o manillas].
Guzmán (p. 21) *chuncu // ƐalƐa*, las manillas; *ƐalƐa // chuncu*, joyas.
Vico (n.d.a: fol. 56) *ƐalƐa chachal puakim*, cuentas, o gargantillas, o manillas • (227v) *ƐalƐa // chuncu*, joyas; *ƐalƐa puakim 4,ak*, joyas; *ƐalƐa*, manillas; *xin ƐalƐabah uij*, adornarse con ellas.
Ximénez (1985: 151) *4alƐab*, joyas y manillas.

Q'AM

Angel (fol. 177v) *Ɛaam*, escalera, o puente.
Basseta (fol. 170v) *cam*, la puente [≠ *caam*, soga, cordel, mecate, o puente].
Saquic Calel (p. 323) *k'a'am*, escalera [≠ *k'a'm*, puente].
Tirado (fol. 161) *Ɛaam*, puente.
Varea (fol. 374) *Ɛam*, puente, y la escalera de los Indios, que es un palo solo, hechos escaloncillos en él.
Vico (n.d.a: fol. 228v) *Ɛam*, escalera o puente.

Q'ANBOL

Anleo (fol. 54) *Ɛaboloboh*, cosa muy amarilla, como frutas, flores.
Coto (1983: 29) *ti Ɛa bole*, ponerse amarillas las frutas [. . .] toda fruta que madura y sazona, aunque no tenga el color amarillo; *Ɛa boloboh*, participio.

Q'AQ'

Coto (1983: 328) *ƐaƐal tepeval*, magestad; *ƐaƐ tepeuh pedro*, es grande, magestuoso Pedro.
Varea (fol. 249) [en la entrada *xtecoc yamanic / kokol xtecoc*, piedras preciosas, el autor anota: ya no se usan sino *4ual, ƐaƐal, tepeval*] • (377) *nim ru ƐaƐal ru tepeual dios*, rey, gran Majestad y Señorío.
Vico (n.d.a: fol. 231) *ƐaƐal, tepeual*, magestad y fogosidad [e.g., *xoh ru ƐaƐariçah xoh ru tepeuriçah can kanimahaual dios*, nos ensalzó Dios (. . . cuando se hizó hombre)]; *ƐaƐ*, fuego, lumbre; *ƐaƐalah achi*, hombre animoso • (231v) *ƐaƐal 4ual yamanic*, joyas.
Villacañas (fol. 66) *nima ƐaƐal tepeual*, alteza o grandeza.
See also:
Zuñiga (in Miles 1957: 767) *nu kak nu tepeu*, your majesty, greatness, highness; *yah kak yah tepeu*, man of such greatness, adored almost as a god (*kak tepeu* could well be translated hot majesty. This is also one of the old terms for god; it has the meaning of inaccessability, in addition).

Q'IN

Varea (fol. 383) *Ɛin*, urdir la tela; *Ɛinobal*, el telar; *ru Ɛin*, el hilo que se urde.
Vico (n.d.a: fol. 235) *Ɛin*, urdir tela; *ru Ɛin*, se llaman las vueltas que da el chiquihuïte entre tejido.

Q'OJOM

Angel (fol. 183v) *Ɛohom*, el tambor, o instrumento; *Ɛohoman*, tañer atabal, o instrumento.
Coloch (pers. comm.) *q'ohom*, instrumento de música en general, pero designa más específicamente el gran tambor cilíndrico de madera con parches de piel.
Coto (1983: 52) *Ɛohom*, atambor o atabal [. . .] y así llaman también un palo hueco que tocan con dos palillos; *tin Ɛohomah / qui Ɛohoman*, tocar así el atambor, o tepanaguaste, que llama el mexicano.
Curruchich Gómez and Coyote Tun (p. 82) *q'ojomaj*, ejecutar (música en un instrumento).
Tirado (fol. 53) *Ɛohomaxic*, tocar (música) • (123v) *Ɛohom*, instrumento músico [. . .] la caja, el parche de guerra • (180) *Ɛuzilah Ɛohomabal*, música suave.
Torresano (fol. 13) *ah Ɛohom*, músico.
Varea (fol. 384) *Ɛohom*, el tambor de tepunavaz.
Vico (n.d.a: fol. 236) *Ɛohom*, el atambor, o atabal; *Ɛohoman* (absoluto de *Ɛohomah*), tañer atabal.
Villacañas (fol. 139) *castilan Ɛohom*, vihuela • (147) *cohom*, citara.

Q'OSIBAL

Angel (fols. 184v–185) *Ɛoçin / Ɛoçih,* maltratar golpeando con palo, o tañer atabal o apuñetearse; *Ɛoçih + çi4,* pregonar, o dar gritos o alaridos con la mano dando en la boca; *Ɛoçih quij,* pelear como dos gallos.

Coto (1983: 203) *chi Ɛoçibal ixim,* era donde trillan el maíz [. . .] donde lo golpean.

Saquic Calel (p. 325) *k'osibal,* aporreador.

Tirado (fol. 39) *paƐosibal 4hy4h,* campanario; *Ɛosiy 4hi4h,* campanero que las tañe • (134) *Ɛosibal chee,* mazo para mazar *[= vonibal chee]* • (174) *Ɛosih,* sacudir algodón bariándolo; *Ɛosin bot,* algodón sacudido • (181) *canƐosih guitarra,* tañer guitarra • (184) *can Ɛosih uchij ha,* yo toco a la puerta; *naohin canƐosih uchij ha,* yo toco ligeramente a la puerta • (192v) *cuƐocih rijb ri ha chuvach tak abah,* se golpea el agua contra las piedras [. . .] aporrearse, golpearse.

Varea (fol. 385) *Ɛosih,* dar golpes tañendo campana o tambor, o aporrear algodón u otra cosa.

Vico (n.d.a: fol. 208) *que luluben que Ɛoçin qui chih,* dar alaridos • (236v) *Ɛoçin,* tañer atabal, o campana, o golpear, o apuñetear, dar de palo; *tin Ɛoçih nu chij ulululu,* dar alaridos como dan los indios dando con la mano en la boca.

Villacañas (fol. 76) *coçih chiche,* aporrear.

Q'UMAR

Varea (fol. 385) *Ɛumar,* madera, ropa o paja podrida o molida de vieja.

Vico (n.d.a: fol. 237) *Ɛumar,* podrirse la madera.

Q'UQ'

Angel (fol. 186v) *ƐuƐ // raxon,* pájaro verde.

Basseta (fol. 176) *cuƐ,* la pluma verde y el pájaro que la cría [= *cuƐ,* la ardilla]; *Ɛuc // raxon,* plumas verdes y azules.

Coto (1983: 171) *nu ƐuƐ nu raxon,* a la hija doncella (es vocablo de que usan de amor, de estima, como "mi presea, mi joya") • (401) *ƐuƐ,* pájaro que estiman mucho, y sus plumas, y a la cosa preciosa, llaman así. Y, cuando dan la hija para casamiento, encareciendo que dan la prenda de más estima, dicen: *x-tin ya nu meal, nu ƐuƐ, chauichin,* "te entrego mi hija, mi pluma de quetzal" • (423) *ƐuƐ,* plumas, unas largas y verdes con que bailan; *xahbal ƐuƐ,* plumeros o plumajes que los indios hacen de estas plumas para bailar *[= ikanih ƐuƐ].*

Saquic Calel (p. 325) *k'uk',* quetzal (pájaro).

Tirado (fol. 96) *raxon ƐuƐ abah,* esmeralda, piedra preciosa • (155) *ƐuƐ patan,* pecho, o tributo • (189v) *raxa ƐuƐ,* pluma verde, rica • (200) *maƐuƐ,* el pájaro quetzal.

Varea (fol. 387) *ƐuƐ,* plumas verdes largas con que bailan, y por la doncella; *nuƐuƐ nuraxon xtinya chave re numeal xti4ule avu4in.* Y por el tributo: *nuƐuƐ nupatan.*

Vico (n.d.a: fol. 238) *ƐuƐ,* las plumas verdes para bailar.

Q'UTIJ

Angel (fol. 90) *quiçah, quimayix, quiƐutux, mayh, Ɛutuh, yaar, chamux,* todos quieren decir acabar.

Vico (n.d.a: fol. 237v) *Ɛutuh,* asolar, destruir [*mayh tantiƐutux qui mayx qui chamur,* destruirse, asolarse].

RAX

Angel (fols. 128v, 178) *Ɛanal // raxal*, riquezas.

Anleo (fol. 43v) *Ɛanal, raxal*, gloria; *koh Ɛanaric, koh raxaric*, seremos gloriosos y bien aventurados en la gloria; *raxih* [activo de *rax*], significa comer fruta verde, por sazonar, o yerbas comestibles • (49v) *raxa*, agua fría • (54v) *rax*, cosa verde, o húmeda, o color cardenalado.

Basseta (fol. 217) *rax*, verde o húmedo de mojado; *raxaƐual / zaquiƐual*, piedras preciosas; *raxcat*, sacrificio antiguo de animales vivos • (217v) *raxteu*, fríos y calenturas, enfermedad; *raxvinaquil*, sanidad; *raxvinac*, sano.

Tirado (fol. 9) *raxvinak*, alentado, no estar enfermo • (30v) *uƐanal urraxal vach uleu*, bienes de fortuna • (38) *raxteu*, calentura con frío *[= teuh 4atan]* • (67v) *errayij urraxal uƐinomal vuach uleu*, deseadores de bienes temporales • (141) *raxcab*, miel blanca de abejas • (172v) *raxƐab*, rocío que cae del cielo • (175) *raxvinakil*, salud; *yaal raxvinakil*, saludable, cosa que da salud • (189v) *raxa ƐuƐ*, pluma verde, rica • (190) *quin raxaric*, verdecerse; *raxaric*, verdura.

Varea (fol. 185) *rax*, cosa verde, cosa azul [. . .] fruta no madura [. . .] o carne que no está bien cocida o asada *[= mani saom]*; *raxar*, teñirse algo de verde o azul; *raxal // Ɛanal*, riquezas afortunadas • (374) *Ɛanal // raxal*, abundancia de bienes y riquezas.

Vico (n.d.a: fol. 94v) *u Ɛanal // u raxal*, sus riquezas • (170v) *rax*, verde o azul, o color verde, o fruta por madurar, o carne no cocida • (171v) *raxvinak*, hombre sano, o mujer; *raxƐab*, el rocío de la noche.

RAXON

Basseta (fol. 176) *raxom*, pluma azul y el pájaro • (217v) *raxom*, un pájaro azul celeste muy hermoso.

Coto (1983: 283) *raxon*, pieza de oro que estaba asida a las narices *[= yacapulul]*.

Tirado (fol. 96) *raxon ƐuƐ abah*, esmeralda, piedra preciosa • (127v) *ahay 4ual, yamanic, raxon*, lapidario de piedras preciosas • (200) *raxon*, pájaro del pecho musgo, y las alas azules.

Varea (fol. 186) *raxom*, pájaros azules.

Vico (n.d.a: fols. 60v, 254v) *4ual raçon*, (esmeralda) que hay en Santa María de Jesús en el río, Visita de Xelahuh • (95v, 254v) *4ual raxon*, tesoro • (170v) *raxon*, pajaritos verdes o sus plumas, para hacer ciriales, o penachos, o guirnaldas.

RAYIJ / RAYIL

Basseta (fol. 216v) *raybal*, codicia, deseo; *rail // caxcol*, el dolor.

Tirado (fol. 44) *rayi-*, codicia • (50) *rayi-*, lo deseado, desear • (57) *urrayixic uvach ulewal*, codicia de las cosas temporales.

Varea (fol. 184) *raih*, desear, codiciar; *rainic* o *raibal*, el deseo.

Vico (n.d.a: fol. 169v) *rain, raih*, desear, codiciar; *raih, raibal*, la codicia • (184) *rail*, ser uno muy pobre, y no tener que comer ni beber, ni con que mercar lo.

RIQO

Basseta (fol. 218v) *riƐo*, alcanzar, coger, y según el P[adr]e Damian: extender [. . .] hallar.

Vico (n.d.a: fol. 98v) *ri4*, alcanzar o coger en pecado.

SA

Angel (fol. 33) *çaanuvach*, salir galán, estrenarse, o estrenarse de nuevo; *bi tuçaa nu vach tan yn avilim*, ¿quién soy yo para que me tengas tanta cuenta?; *nak tuça auach*, ¿qué soy?

Basseta (fol. 235v) *za*, secar al sol [≠ *zaa*, ven acá . . .] • (236v) *zaom*, frito en sartén; *zaovach*, estrenado [e.g., *maha chiçavuach*, no usado, *zaom chic cuubal chic*, cosa usada pero nueva]; *zao*, asar, estrenar algo.

Coto (1983: 224) *tin ça ru vach*, estrenar alguna cosa que se pone (vestido, sombrero, etc.); *çaom chic ru vach*, cosa ya estrenada • (257) *çaom chic ru vach*, el huipil que es ya usado • (317) *kina* + *ça* + *vach*, lograr [de] alguna cosa [. . .] lograrse algo [e.g., *kin x-in ça ru vach nu kahom ri ƐuƐ*, he logrado lo que he alquilado] • (383) *tin ça chi muh*, orear, poner aire • (511) *ti ça / ti çao*, secarse algo al sol, id est, que de propósito lo sacan para este efecto [e.g., *ti çao ch'u va Ɛih / ch'u va ƐaƐ / chi muh*, secar al sol / al fuego / al aire]; *çaom chic*, cosa así seca; *ti çao*, también significa asar al fuego o horno • (543) *ça*, secar / exponer al sol [e.g., Y si acaso tiñen el hilo de algún color [. . .] y allí lo ponen y, en tomando tinte, lo sacan al sol y dicen: *ti li4 o ti ri4 ka mu pa mubal che, chiri ti ça vi ch'u va Ɛih*, "estírese el hilo en los palos para que se seque al sol." Tienen por abusión que, si estando el hilo al sol, o cuando lo están tiñiendo, pasa alguna mujer preñada y lo mira, que pierde el color. Y así si lo advierten, la llaman, y que pase la mano por sobre el hilo. Y, con eso, dicen que vuelve a tomar el color que había perdido].

Curruchich Gómez and Coyote Tun (p. 87) *sa'*, asar / asolear.

Tirado (fol. 102) *saa uvach ri atziak*, estrenar ropa • (151) *cansaa pa caƐik*, orear, poner al aire a secar • (156) *saol 4,uum*, pelleja que los asolea.

Varea (fol. 225) *sa*, asar o secar; *sa* + *vach*, estrenar.

Vico (n.d.a: fol. 35) *ça*, asar, o secar; *tiçanuvach*, por salir galán, mostrarse de nuevo; *taçana*, mira, o atiende; *çaom*, oír, o atender; *nak tuça avach*, ¿quién te festeja?

Villacañas (fols. 84–85) *ça chua quih*, asolear como cacao o chile; *ça*, asar en asador; *çaom*, cosa asada • (130) *sah* + *uach*, consumir *[= mayh + uach]*.

SACHIK

Angel (fol. 90) *quiçach, quimayix, quiƐutux, mayh, Ɛutuh, yaar, chamux*, todos quieren decir acabar.

Coloch (pers. comm.) *k-in-sach-ik*, estoy perdido, extraviado [statement].

Vico (n.d.a: fols. 29, 55v) *çach*, perdonar, borrar.

SAMAJEL

Tirado (fol. 80v) *samahel taƐoon / takoon*, embajador; *takon zamahel*, enviado • (128v *usamahel s[an]to padre uvuj uholom s[an]ta yglesia*, legado del Papa • (139v) *samahel // takon*, mensajero • (178) *zamahel // takon*, siervo, criado que sirve.

Torresano (fol. 11) *ronohel vinak xe be pa çamah*, todos fueron al trabajo • (49v) *qui çamah*, sus oficios • (50) *chu çamahixic chu 4uxlaxic dios*, en servicio de Dios • (73) *mi xul çamahel*, vinó el mensajero.

Vico (n.d.a: fol. 195) *ru çamahel xibalbay* [así se nombran el *tucur* y el *xo4h* (aves que andan de noche)].

SAQIL (AL K'AJOL)

Santo Domingo (fol. 5) *çacquil al çacquil cahol*, ser del linaje humano; *Ɛampatal al cahol*, vasallos por metáfora.

Varea (fol. 226) *sak*, lo claro, y tierra clara sin arboleda; *ni4ahsak*, el mundo.

Vico (n.d.a: fol. 7v) *çakil al çakil 4ahol*, el linaje humano • (41) *çakillal çak4ahol*, será el linaje humano; *kapasal al 4ahol*, vasallos por metáfora.

SAQKAB

Basseta (fol. 225) *tzahƐab*, tizate • (236) *zaƐcab*, el tizate, con que hilan huntándose los dedos y lo comen [from another writer: *zakcabih*, barnizar].

Coto (1983: 62) *çakcab*, barniz blanco como albayalde, que es un género de tierra que el mexicano llama Tizate [= *titil*; *Ɛan abah*, barniz, uno como margarita con que antiguamente se solían enbarnizar los rostros] • (549) *çak cab*, tierra blanca, o tizate, que llaman, de que usan las mujeres para hilar su algodón.

Saquic Calel (p. 341) *sakcab*, tizate / piece of gypsum used by weavers to dry the fingers.

Tirado (fol. 184) *sakcab*, tizate.

Varea (fol. 227) *sakcab*, una tierra blanca con que hilan las mujeres. Otra tierra blanca para enjalbegar; *sakcab*, barniz blanco de pintores.

Vico (n.d.a: fol. 38v) *çakcabij*, embarnizar algo.

See also:

Coto (1983: 99) Antiguamente, cuando eran puestos los caciques en sus señoríos, tenían ciertos barnizes con que se ungían y embijaban, y a éstos llamaban: *titil, Ɛana abah, caka vleu*.

SIK'IJ

Angel (fol. 40) *çiquin [/ çi4in]*, dar voces, o gritos, o llorar; *çi4*, la voz.

Coto (1983: 94) *qui çi4in*, clamar, dar voces; *çi4*, clamor, alarido de guerra.

Tirado (fol. 43v) *si4-*, clamar, dar voces • (62) *ci4ih*, dar voces para llamar a alguno • (161v) *si4inic*, pregón; *si4ih*, pregonar.

Torresano (fol. 133) *çi4ih*, llamar.

Varea (fol. 10) *ah çi4*, el pregonero, o el que grita.

Vico (n.d.a: fol. 44) *çi4in / çi4ih*, dar voces, llamar o llorar; *nu çi4 voƐeh*, lloro o gemido; *çi4*, la voz.

SILIBISAJ

Basseta (fol. 237v) *zilizah u vach*, bambalear; *ziltzotiƐ*, temblar las carnes *[= coycotiƐ; birbotiƐ; tuhtubiƐ]*; *zilobiƐ, zolo [sic, ¿zilo?]*, dar bueltas y de ay debanar [. . .] menearse y se toma por temblar [from another writer: *zilic*, víbora].

Coloch (pers. comm.) *x-ø-ki-silib-i-sa-j*, ellos lo movieron.

Coto (1983: 281) *tin çiloh / tin çiloniçah / tin çilobiçah*, hurgar • (342) *qui çilon*, menearse alguna cosa, o persona, animal; *tin çiloh, tin çilobiçah*, activos.

Torresano (fol. 133) *çilob*, menearse.

Vico (n.d.a: fol. 43) *çil*, mercar algo, bullir, menear • (280v) *tzilatza*, menear continuamente.

Ximénez (1985: 647) *ziloh*, menear, bullir.

SILILIK

Angel (fol. 39) *tiçilil tibahah rupa vino*, ser el vino muy fuerte.

Coto (1983: 189) *ti çilil*, enfriarse mucho el cuerpo por haberse mojado, o por el mucho frío, o porque lo está el suelo • (239) *ti çilil chi ya*, fresca agua, muy fría *[= ti bahah]* • (240) *ti çilil chi teu chi nu 4ux*, cuando en el estómago sienten gran frío.

Vico (n.d.a: fol. 43) *tiçilil ti bahah ru pan vino*, ser dulce el vino.

Ximénez (1985: 647) *zilil*, enfriarse el agua; *ziliza*, enfriar, menear; *zilih*, menear; *ziloh*, menear, bullir.

See also:

García Hernández et al. (p. 28) *ca-silowic*, está ebrio, está medio bolo.

SIMAJ

Basseta (fol. 178) *chab*, el arco de tirar flechas y de allí *ralchab*, hijo del arco y de flecha, y también *zimah*.
Tirado (fol. 163v) *simaah utzaam*, punta aguda.
Vico (n.d.a: fol. 43) *çimah che*, estaca.

SK'AQIN

Anleo (fol. 42v) *x4akin chic carah*, poco le falta • (48v) *x4akin*, poco; *x4akin chic*, poco más • (49v) *z4akin*, poco, o pequeño; *z4akin chic*, otro poco más.
Basseta (fol. 162) *zcaquin chic carah*, más es menester • (237) *zcaquin*, poco; *zcata*Ɛ, plu[ral] [from another writer: poca cosa repartida; *zquin*, un poco].
Tirado (fol. 15) *utzchic z4akin*, algún tanto está mejor • (62v) *z4akin*, poquita cosa *[= hubi*Ɛ*]* • (63) *z4akinachina 4atena*, de aquí a un poco [> *4atena*, después] • (99) *xa s4akin nuxol ru4*, poca distancia hay de mí con él / a él • (131) *z4akin*, un poco; *xa z4akin*, sólo un poco • (160) *z4akin chuxe ucamic*, poco antes que muriera • (188) *z4akin chic*, un poco más; *z4akin mavi*, un poco menos.
Vico (n.d.a: fol. 74v) *z4akin*, un poco; *z4akin chic*, un poco más; *z4itak*, un poco.

SOCH

Angel (fol. 41) *çoch*, la sonaja que traen los indios cuando bailan • (41v) *çochah*, sonajear.
Basseta (fol. 238) *zoch*, una jicarita con piedras dentro con que tocan [from another writer: *zoch* ó *zochoch*, la cascabel víbora].
Coto (1983: 93) *çoch*, el cascabel que la víbora tiene en la punta de la cola. Cuando lo suena y menea, dicen: *tu çeloh ru çoch*. Tienen los indios unas jicarillas o calabazillas con muchos agujerillos y un palillo en medio, de donde le cogen, y echen dentro unos granillos o piedrezuelas con que, en meneándolas, suenan mucho, y les sirven para bailar y para acallar a las criaturas. A éstos llaman también *çoch*, por la similitud que el sonido tiene al de la víbora. De aquí el verbo *tin çochah*: usar de éstos, sonándolos [≠ *4al akan*: cascabel que se ponen en los pies para bailar] • (212) *ru çoch castilan ixim*, espiga de trigo • (530) *çoch*, un género de sonajas que tienen los indios [. . .] y hacen acallar a los niños con ella; *ti çochan*, sonar.
Saquic Calel (p. 342) *soch*, chinchín / gourd rattles.
Tirado (fol. 179v) *soch 4hi4h*, sonajas.
Varea (fol. 234) *sochoh*, la víbora de cascabeles, y una calabacilla horadada, y con granos dentro que la van sonando los bailadores, y a esta calabacilla le llaman *soch*; *soch*, los cascabeles de la víbora, y la dicha calabacilla, y la usan para acallar los niños [e.g., *tan tiqui-sochah qui-soch xahol*].
Vico (n.d.a: fol. 46) *çoch*, sonaje, con que baylan, o cosa de la víbora.
Ximénez (1985: 651) *zoch*, el acacaste con que bailan; cascabeles de víbora.

SOKOTAJ

Angel (fols. 40–40v) *çocotah*, lastimarse; *tin çoc chuvah uleu*, yo lo tiendo en el suelo.
Basseta (fol. 238) *zo*Ɛ*otah*, *zo*Ɛ*otahic*, herirse, etc. y lo oiras cuando dan la bienvenida: *ma vi xzo*Ɛ*otahla pabe paho*Ɛ, ¿no se lastimó Vd en el camino?
Coto (1983: 448) *tin çoc*, punzar *[= tin to*Ɛ*]*.
Saquic Calel (p. 342) *soc*, lastimar; *socotajic*, herida.
Tirado (fol. 131v) *soconic*, llagar hiriendo; *socotahinakil*, llaga, lastimadura • (136v) *zo*Ɛ*otahic*, mancha o mancilla; *xso*Ɛ*otah ri saki 4ul*, se manchó el paño blanco • (137) *canso*Ɛ*o*, manchar, o mancillar • (177v) *retal socotahinakil*, señal de herida.

Varea (fol. 174) *ru lemahal socotahinak,* la cicatriz o señal que queda después de sana la herida, llaga o quemadura • (232) *soc,* extender petate o manteles o ropa de cama [. . .] emparejar la tierra donde hay hoyos y altos y bajos; *soc,* herir con alguna cosa; *soc // toƐ,* punzar.
Vico (n.d.a: fol. 44v) *çok,* herir [e.g., *xçocotah rakan*].
Villacañas (fol. 157) *çocotahinac,* descalabrado.

SOLKOPIJ

Basseta (fol. 226v) *tzoƐopih* [sic], soltar, dejar • (227) *tzolcomih,* volver [from another writer: *tzolcopih, idem*].
Coto (1983: 72) *tin çolcopih,* volver lo de arriba abajo, o de una a otra parte *[= tzol-Ɛomih].*
Varea (fol. 255) *tzolƐomih / çolcopih / pachƐomih,* volver una cosa de una parte a otra, o lo de abajo arriba [. . .] volver la cabeza adonde tenía la cola • (297) *çolcopih / tzolƐomih / pizcolih,* volver una cosa de arriba abajo, lo de dentro afuera, lo de delante atrás.
See also:
Varea (fol. 233) *sol,* ir haciendo una madeja grande, rodeándola a dos palos distantes para después poder bien debanar el algodón hilado y teñido; *ta-solo ta-quira,* desenredar el hilo enmarañado; *solo,* desenvolver (algo) • (250) *x4opih / x4opin,* soltarse [. . .] dejar.

SUK'ULIK

Anonymous (fol. 60) *kitzih u su4uliquil,* cierta y verdadera cosa.
Basseta (fol. 238v) *zuƐ,* ir derecho a una parte sin extraviarse; *zuculic,* adv[erbi]o de verdad; *zuƐuba,* enderezar o poner derecho; *zuƐmaih,* declarar.
Saquic Calel (p. 343) *suc' / suc'ulic,* recto, derecho; *suc'maj,* enderezar.
Tirado (fol. 27) *4o su4ulic,* haber razón; *usuculil,* la verdad • (62) *canchol usu4uliquil,* doy cuenta, o razón de algo • (65) *chisu4ulic,* derechamente; *su4ul quinbinic,* (yo) camino derecho • (85v) *su4mayi-,* enderezar • (95) *su4ulic 4,ib,* escritura verdadera • (123) *mavi chisu4ulic,* injustamente • (124) *su4ul quinbe,* (yo) voy derecho • (139) *su4ulic quin etanic,* medir derecho • (163) *huzu4 chanim,* promptamente • (178) *maui suculic,* siniestra cosa • (190) *su4uliquil,* verdad.
Vico (n.d.a: fol. 55) *çu4ulic,* la verdad [> *çu4e / çu4ul* (65)].

SU'

Coto (1983: 234) *çubak,* otro género de flautilla, que tocan con los tamboriles, que es de carrizo *[= ah].*
Varea (fol. 234) *suybak,* flauta grande que tañen cuando bailan, juntamente con los tamboriles.

TA / TO

Basseta (fol. 220) *tao,* oír, entender lo que se le dice.
Coloch (pers. comm.) *x-ø-in-to,* lo he oído; *x-ø-u-ta ri re,* él lo ha oído; *ri ka jinta(j) ka-ø-ki-to,* ellos no oyen nada.
Vico (n.d.a: fol. 177v) *ta,* oír algo.

TAJ

Villacañas (fol. 10) *tah,* optativo [. . .] ¡Ojalá!

TAJINIK

Basseta (fol. 220) *tahinic*, estar actualmente en algo [e.g., *mapa quintahinic*, por ventura no estoy actualmente en ello].

Coloch (pers. comm.) *sa la ka-ø-tajin-ik x-ø-u-'anik*, ¿qué es lo que está haciendo?; *x-ø-oponik k-oj-tajin che la qa-wa*, él llegó mientras estabamos comiendo.

Vico (n.d.a: fol. 61) *tahin*, significa actualidad cuando se hace algo aquí en quiché.

TANABA

Angel (fol. 132v) *tanaba [> tane]*, cesar de hacer algo.

Basseta (fol. 220) *tanaba*, cesar la obra.

Tirado (fol. 35v) *utanalibal*, cabo, o fin *[= utzam; u4izbal]* • (60v) *cantanaba ubanic*, ceso de hacerlo; *tanal chic*, tanalem, cesación.

Vico (n.d.a: fol. 179v) *tane*, cesar de hacer algo, o concluir.

TAPICH'OLOL

Angel (fol. 133) *tapi4holol*, un pájaro pequeño que canta bien como ruiseñor.

Basseta (fol. 209) *roquibal pich*, el canto de este pájaro • (220v) *tapichol*, un pajarito.

Tirado (fol. 200) *tipicholol*, pájaro pequeño de muy celebre canto • (201v) *tapicholol*, el curruchiche.

Varea (fol. 274) *tapi4holol*, un pájaro que canta bien; curruchich.

Vico (n.d.a: fol. 157) *pi4h*, un pájaro que tienen agüero los Indios con él, que encantando, que lo oyen, es fuerza que les ha de suceder algo • (180) *tapi4holol*, un pájaro que canta como ruiseñor.

TAQAN

Basseta (fol. 219v) *taƐo*, enviar mensaje.

Saquic Calel (p. 344) *tak*, enviar; *takom*, enviado.

Tirado (fol. 70v) *tak-*, despachar • (80v) *samahel taƐoon / takoon*, embajador; *takon zamahel*, enviado • (178) *zamahel / takon*, siervo, criado que sirve.

Torresano (fol. 81) *tak* [< *takom*, mensajero].

Varea (fol. 275) *tak*, enviar a mandados a alguno; *takon*, el que hace los mandados [. . .] enviar a llamar a alguno.

Vico (n.d.a: fol. 182) *tak*, enviar, o ir a llamar.

TAQ'AJ

Alonso (fol. 207) *ah huyu ah taƐah*, provincial de una provincia.

Tirado (fol. 16v) *taƐarisaj*, allanar • (163) *hullub // taƐah*, provincia • (173v) *tacah*, sábana o valle.

Vico (n.d.a: fol. 182v) *taƐah*, la costa, o llano.

TARIJ

Basseta (fol. 220v) *tarih*, arrojar de una mano a otra.

Coto (1983: 359) *tin tarih*, dar mojinetes o puñadas • (448) *tin tarih*, dar puñadas (cerrado el puño).

Tirado (fol. 195v) *tarih*, golpear la puerta al abrirla o cerrarla.

Varea (fol. 275) *tarih*, dar golpe en cosa que hace ruido; *tarata*, golpear como está dando golpes en puerta o tambor, tepunaguaste; o hacer ruido cualquiera obra de barro o silla que menean, estando juntos y dándose una con otra.

Vico (n.d.a: fol. 179v) *tar*, golpearse la puerta • (180v) *xin tarih xe re chi nu Ɛa*, le dí debajo de los dientes con mi mano • (191v) *tarih*, arrojar.

TE

Torresano (fol. 133) *tee*, la madre [in Cakchiquel and in Tzutujil; *chuch* in Quiché].
Varea (fol. 277) *te*, la madre natural de uno, o la hermana de mi madre, mi tía [. . .] dicen los hombres a todas las mujeres casadas, en cortesía; *ru te 4ha*, arco o ballesta.
Vico (n.d.a: fol. 185) *tee*, la madre o tía • (260v) *nu te 4ha*, el arco de la ballesta.
See also:
Coto (1983: 80) *ru te*, a las madres del cacao, que es lo que sale de las primeras mazorcas, y es cacao grande y crecido.

TELEB

Varea (fol. 278) *teleh*, llevar o traer algo en el hombro o sobre la cabeza; *telebal caminak*, la tabla en que cargan los difuntos; *telebal santos*, las andas.
Vico (n.d.a: fol. 183) *tele*, llevar al hombro; *teleb*, el hombro.

TELECHE

Angel (fol. 135) *telecheen*, cautivar [. . .] el cautivo.
Coto (1983: 94) *cana // teleche*, cautivo y preso en guerra [. . .] a los que han sido cautivos, y después se avecindan y quedan libres, los llaman *he nimak achi* [≠ *munil*; *alabitz*; *4,ijl*, cautiverio o esclavitud como la de los negros]; *tin telecheeh*, para decir que fuerzan a mujer, o roban niño o doncella, etc.
Varea (fol. 278) *telecheeh*, luchar [. . .] y derribar a mujer para pecar o forcejando y tirándole de la mano, sacarla de lo público y meterla en lugar secreto; *telecheeh*, cautivar o maniatar a los vencidos en guerra; *nu cana nu teleche*, mi caza; *cana // teleche*, cautivo ganado en guerra // en caza.
Vico (n.d.a: fol. 31v) *cana // teleche*, cautivos • (183) *xtelecheex*, fue cautivo [e.g., *xtelecheex hun ahauh rey pa labal tok xlabalin*, fue cautivo un Rey en la guerra cuando pelearon]; *teleche*, el cautivo *[= cana / canab]*.

TEM

Angel (fol. 135) *tem*, la viga, o madre para sostener, o asiento.
Basseta (fol. 162) *ahauaribal tem*, asiento de Magestad o grandeza • (221) *tem*, viga, cuartón, y asiento [e.g., *hun nima xoƐohauaribal tem*, un asiento de Reina]; *temah*, tomar asiento; *ahauaribal tem*, asiento de Rey.
Saquic Calel (p. 344) *tem*, banquito.
Tirado (fol. 81v) *cohon*, *utemal ha*, casa enmaderada; *cancoh tem chuiha*, enmaderar casa • (186, 190v) *tem*, vigas.
Varea (fol. 278) *tem // 4hacat*, trono de señorío.
Vico (n.d.a: fols. 183v–184) *tem*, la viga para sustentar, o asiento; *tem 4hacat*, el asiento, el trono [. . .] un banquillo que les daban y en el se sentaban en señal que los hacían cabezas de calpul, que era de grande autoridad y cuidado que los sahumaban [e.g., *tin temah tin 4hacatih tem 4hacat*, tomar la cabecera en el banquete, o convite; *lal temtoninak ha*, está Vmd lleno de riquezas de cacao, de algodón, etc.] • (219) *xitam tem puakim 4hacat* [not translated : throne of turquoise and silver].

TIJ

Angel (fol. 137) *tih*, probar algo, aplacarse, en juego o en borrachez, o experimentar.
Coto (1983: 445) *ta tiha na tijh*, prueba la comida; *tih*, es muy usado para cualquiera cosa que se intenta hacer de compra, pleito, pretención, etc.
Torresano (fol. 45v) *tihoh*, castigar.

Varea (fol. 281) *tih*, convidar a comer o beber [. . .] probar, gustar algo [como desafiarse a pleitar].

TINAMIT

Basseta (fol. 221v) *tinamit ama*Ɛ, pueblo o ciudad.
Siméon (p. 473) *tenamitl*, muro, barrera, fortificación de ciudad.
Tirado (fol. 36) *hutak remaj, hutak tzobah chitinamit*, cada provincia • (46) *chirih tinamit, chuvach tinamit*, comarca del pueblo; *chirih tinamit ahilanvi*, comarcano • (167v) *yohol tinamit*, revolvedor de pueblo.

TINTOT

Basseta (fol. 221v) *tinouic*, palpitar el corazón de miedo *[= cohouic]*.
Coto (1983: 224–225) *tin tinih / tin tinita v'akan*, hacer estruendo o ruido con los pies, o con golpes; *ti tinitot*, sonar así el ruido o estruendo; *ti tinin r'akan*, estruendo o ruido de pasos; *ti tinin*, estruendo o ruido que hace el volcán de fuego *[= hinin; birbot]* • (530) *ti tino vi / ti biro vi ru chi vleuh*, tierra que suena por estar hueca; *ti tinin / tibirbot ru chi cak i*Ɛ, sonar el viento o norte.
Curruchich Gómez and Coyote Tun (p. 96) *tiniloh*, caminar pesadamente haciendo ruido con los pies; *tinito'*, caerse un objeto pesado.
Tirado (fol. 102v) *catinin*, hacer estruendo • (114v) *catinin rakan*, hacer ruido con los pies • (167) *tininem*, ruido *[= tararem]* • (173) *catinin ca*Ɛ*ik*, el aire hace ruido • (187) *catinin vinak*, hace ruido la gente (un tropel de gente).
Varea (fol. 282) *tinin*, tronar [. . .] andar con mucho ruido, pisando fuertemente, dando grandes patadas que se oyen de lejos como el que va apriesa *[= tino; biro ; birbot; nicnot]*.
Vico (n.d.a: fol. 187) *tinitot rakan*, hacer ruido con los pies [≠ *tinin / tiltot*, tronar] • (190) *tintin*, retumbo de la campana.

TOPONOWOTZ'

Varea (fol. 275) *tarih / tarata*, golpear como está dando golpes en puerta o tambor, tepunaguaste • (278) *tepunavaz*, el toncontín, o el tun o palo hueco que tocan los Indios [e.g., *tu*Ɛ*oçih tepunavaz*] • (384) Ɛ*ohom*, el tambor de tepunavaz.
Vico (n.d.a: fol. 184) *tepenauaz*, el tamboril de palo hueco [e.g., *que*Ɛ*oçin tepenauaz quecubakin*, y cuando tienen ellos sus días buenos que llaman *utzilah* Ɛ*ih*, lo tocan a media noche y con ésto se sabe en todo en Pueblo, y en particular en Samaya*Ɛ*, los días de los *cholol* Ɛ*ih*].

TOQ'OBAXINAQ

Basseta (fol. 222v) *to*Ɛ*o*, punzar, herir punzando; *to*Ɛ*ob cavach*, pobres de nosotros; *to*Ɛ*obal*, el instrumento con que se agujerea la cosa o barrena, o punzón *[= vorobal]* [from another writer: *to*Ɛ*obaxinak uvach*, cuitado, desdichado].
García Hernández et al. (p. 147) *tok'ob u wach*, expresión de lástima por alguna desgracia sufrida por otra persona.
Varea (fol. 181) *ti to*Ɛ*o [= ti lotzo]*, sangrar [. . .] o dar punzadas en la frente (con lanzeta o con *4hay*), sangría común y usada de Indios • (284) *to*Ɛ, punzar, o jurgar o dar con la punta de algún palo, caña, cuchillo, dar puñalada, estocada; *ta to*Ɛ*o ta lotzo nuvi*, darse piquetes, uso de los Indios; *ahto*Ɛ*ola*, el sangrador • (355) *to*Ɛ*bal* [= *4ix 4hay*, una punta o lancetilla de piedra con que pican y sangran en la frente].
Vico (n.d.a: fol. 84v) *to*Ɛ*ob nu vach*, pobre de mí, miserable • (192) *to*Ɛ, cortar, herir, dar de punta; *to*Ɛ*e*, dar de punta; *to*Ɛ*olibeh*, enfadar; *to*Ɛ*oliben*, enfadador por cobrar

deudas, o dar prisa a las obras, o dar a hacer muchas cosas • (192v) *ah toƐob*, los que sangran; *titoƐ Ɛabah / titoƐ nuƐa*, me sangré; *toƐbal Ɛabah*, lanceta [= *4ixchay*]; *toƐol Ɛabah*, sangrador; *toƐoh*, apuntalar; *toƐ / [w]or*, herir / agujerear • (193) *tok'ob + vach*, pobre, desdichado, amacillado; *toƐobiçah + vach*, tener misericordia, socorrer • (234) *ah Ɛih ah toƐol*, adivinador [= *ah Ɛih ah cun*].

TUN

Angel (fol. 145v) *qui xaho tun*, bailo (el) tun.

Basseta (fol. 224) *tun*, trompeta [from another writer: *tun, chanal*, toda clase de música].

Coto (1983: 541) *tin tunah*, tañer trompetas [. . .] de *tun*, que es la trompeta [. . .] también suelen decir *tin xupuh trompeta*, que es soplar la trompeta • (559–560) *tun*, así llaman unas varas largas de que antiguamente hacían unas trompetas: *tzoloh tun*; *ah tun*, el trompetero; *tin tunah*, tocar así estas trompetas.

Tirado (fol. 123v) *tun*, el clarín y las trompetas • (186v, 187) *tum*, trompeta; *ah tum / tunanel*, trompetero.

Torresano (fol. 13) *ah tum*, trompetero.

Varea (fol. 288) *lotz tun*, es un baile que usan con tres flautas; *tikaxah lotztun*.

Vico (n.d.a: fol. 196) *tun*, las calabazas como trompetas que tañen; rayo del sol.

Villacañas (fol. 106) *tun*, bocina; *ah tun*, bocinero.

TUXARIK

Basseta (fol. 224v) *tux* [from another writer: retoñar, echar ramas [. . .] florecer]; *tuxlel*, retoño de los árboles.

Saquic Calel (p. 349) *tux*, retoño; *tuxan*, retoñar.

Tirado (fol. 155) *utux tiquil uvij tuu*, pezón de teta; *utux tiquil uxe manzano*, pezón de fruta • (167v) *catux ri chee*, reverdece el árbol [= *carraxavic*] • (172) *quetux chee*, retoñan los árboles.

Vico (n.d.a: fols. 63v, 75, 276) *nu tux nu haleb*, mi descendencia [> *haleb*, figura, réplica] • (197v) *tux*, pepita de algodón [. . .] y, en quiché, descendencia.

T'ILILIK

Basseta (fol. 221v) *tililic*, hacer ruido, gritar o dar muchas voces.

Coto (1983: 210) *tin til*, espantar los pájaros u otros animalejos en las milpas, guardándolas y dando gritos.

See also:

Angel (fol. 134) *tiltot*, tronar.

Tirado (fol. 131) *til-*, lucir, resplandecer • (168v) *catiltotic*, relucir • (186) *catiltotic*, trasluciente.

Varea (fols. 187, 282) *tiltot* [= *reprot; rimrot; yayot*], resplandecer la plata, el oro, relámpago o rayo.

Vico (n.d.a: fol. 187v) *tiltot*, tronar, y por cosavisos, o resplandecer; *titiltot ti be*, como la hormiga que lleva algo blanqueando; *mayh catiltot uchi uvach*, relumbrar mucho.

T'IRIRIK

Coto (1983: 199) *ti cu ttire / cu ttirittoh*, entumecerse pie o mano, o dar calambre, o adormecerse • (290) *cu tiritoh chic*, estar así con muchísimo frío; *x-cu tire nu Ɛa*, estar yerto de frío.

Ximénez (1985: 537) *tirir*, estar unas cosas muy frías; *tiritic*, acalambrado, insensible; *tiritoh*, miembro encogido.

TZAL

Basseta (fol. 224v) *tza*, la guerra; *tza // labal*, la guerra, enemistad.
Coto (1983: 99) *que tzalo quij*, combatir unos con otros • (258) *tin tzal*, guerrear [= *tin labalih; ti 4ulelaah*]; *tzalol / tzalonel / ah tzal*, el guerreador • (407) *tin tzal*, pelear [. . .] y así, cuando hacen algún baile, que pelean haciendo los Moros, dicen: *ti qui tzal quij, ti qui labalih quij, he xahol*.
Tirado (fol. 46) *tzaloh*, pelea.
Varea (fol. 292) *tzal*, hacer guerra o batalla, o cuando bailan la historia de Golias o Moros; *tzal // labalih*, hacer guerra o batalla [e.g., *tiqui-tzal qui tiqui-labalih qui, que tzalo qui xahol*].
Vico (n.d.a: fol. 114) *tzaloh*, la guerra [= *labal*] • (273v) *tzal*, hacer guerra, o dar batalla, o pelear; *tzal // 4ulelaah*, batallar; *tzaloh*, batalla.

TZALAJ

Angel (fol. 219v) *tzalan*, cuesta abajo; *tzalan chic Ɛih*, hacer días pequeños que son por el mes de noviembre, diciembre y enero.
Saquic Calel (p. 347) *tsalan, tsalanic*, de lado.
Tirado (fol. 57v) *tzalanic huyub*, cuesta de lado • (127) *utzalatziquil huyub*, ladera de cuesta; *tzalaba*, ladear; *tzalanic*, de lado.
Torresano (fol. 18v) *tzalan*, cosa ladeada.
Varea (fol. 292) *tzale*, estar recostado de lado, ladearse; *tzalaba*, poner de lado, ladear otra cosa.

TZAQ

Angel (fol. 219) *tzakon*, acabar, o dar fin [. . .] abortar • (220v) *tzak*, alanzar, o arrojar; *tzak bix*, levantar el canto.
Varea (fol. 293) *tzak*, arrojar • (294) *tzakon*, acabar de hacer algo.

TZARAJMAQ

Tirado (fol. 97v) *tzarah mak*, piedra esponja.

TZELEJ

Basseta (fol. 225v) *tzalih, tzaleh*, acto de volver; *tzelehic*, volverse.
Saquic Calel (p. 347) *tsalij*, regresar, devolver; *tsalij ulok*, regresar aquí.

TZIJ

Saquic Calel (p. 348) *tsij*, palabra, cuento, verdad, discurso; *tsijoj*, contar, narrar; *tsijon*, hablar; *tsijoxic*, cuento, leyenda.
Torresano (fol. 53) *ru tzih dios*, la ley de Dios.
Varea (fol. 179) *loƐolah tzih tu biih*, hablar bien, honesta, comedida, y honradamente.
Vico (n.d.a: fol. 277v) *tzih*, palabra, o precepto; *utzihoxic*, noticia; *tzihol*, plática o memoria del tiempo.

TZU

Tirado (fol. 141v) *tzu // muqu // il*, mirar.
Vico (n.d.a: fol. 279v) *tzuun*, mirar, acatar.

TZUKUJ

Vico (n.d.a: fol. 32) *tzucuh*, buscar, adquirir, granjear, contratar [e.g., *ca nu tzucuh nu 4azlibal*, (yo) busco mi remedio] • (55) *çucuh*, buscar; *canutzucuh*, te busco aquí • (273) *4,u4uh*, buscar algo, adquirir, granjear, o contratar.

TZUQBAL

Coto (1983: 38, 538) *tin tzuk*, sustentar, dando de comer; *tzukbal*, el sustento.
Varea (fol. 10) *ah tzukula*, los que proveen de lo necesario para la comida de los religiosos que viven entre los indios • (299) *tzuk*, mantener dando sustento a personas o animales que están en tu cargo; *tzukbal*, ración.
Vico (n.d.a: fol. 279v) *tzuk*, sustentar, alimentar, servir, o tributar; *tzukbal*, sustento.

TZURUTYAJ

Basseta (fol. 227v) *tzuru*, puscar a cólera, torear [from another writer: *tzurtzu*, el vahido en Rabinal].
Saquic Calel (p. 349) *tsuric / tsurun / tsurunic*, desafiar; *tsurunel*, provocador, coqueador, persona que provoca.
Tirado (fol. 126) *e4,anem tzurbal vacax*, juego de toros • (163) *cantzur chi oyoval*, provocar a ira; *tzururic chioyoval*, provocación a ira • (185) *tzuruh vacax*, torear toros • (193v) *can tzuru*, yo coqueo.
Vico (n.d.a: fol. 55) *çur*, coquear, torear; *ta tzurutza ri vacax*, torear • (279v) *tzur [< tzurutza]*, coquear o atorear (vacas).

TZ'AJTZ'AT

Coto (1983: 17) *ti tzah*, agotarse o embeberse el agua o otro licor en la tierra o vasija, o agotarse el río o pozo • (343) *ti tzah*, menguarse cosa líquida en la vacija, o menguarse el río o laguna • (346) *ti tzah*, mermarse el peso o medida, si es de cosa líquida, vino, aceite, etc.
Varea (fol. 292) *tzah*, agotarse o menguarse, o embeberse o secarse en agua en donde está [e.g., *mixtzah nutiohil mixibakir*, me he secado y enflaquecido].
Ximénez (1985: 555) *tzah*, agotar, menguarse el agua; *tzahih*, dar de bofetadas; sonar, hacer ruido; tener gran sed; consumirse presto [. . .] el agua.
See also:
Basseta (fol. 225) *tzahih*, dar bofetada o palmada [< *tzahtza*, frecuentativo, dar palmadas o patear]; *tzahtza nu cab*, hacer ruido con las manos dando palmadas.
Varea (fol. 300) *4,ahih*, dar palmada en algo, o bofetón; *4,ahah*, tronar [. . .] dar gran traquido como cuando cae rayo [. . .] significa pisar muy recio que suena cuando anda; *ti4,ahah he xahab chi cakan*, ir haciendo gran ruido con los pies.
Vico (n.d.a: fol. 274) *tzahtza*, llamar golpeando con continuación o dando palmadas.
Villacañas (fol. 83) *tzahtza*, arrullar (el niño).
Ximénez (1985: 555) *tzahtza*, dar golpes en los hombros.

TZ'APIL

Angel (fols. 213–213v) *4,ape*, ser preso.
Coto (1983: 3) *tin 4,apih*, abajar alguna cosa, cubriéndola u abrigándola • (126) *tin 4,apih nu ticom chi 4,ak*, cercar la heredad de pared • (127) *tin 4,apih*, cerrar generalmente [. . .] este verbo se forma de *4,ap* que es cerradura o instrumento para cerrar, o cosa que se cierra; *tin 4,apih*, cerrar o tapar algún agujero a piedra y lodo; *tin 4,apih nu Ɛa*, cerrar el puño, la mano • (181–182) *tin 4,apih*, encerrar algo poniéndolo a recaudo o guardándolo, pan, maíz, etc.; *4,apim + ih*, encerrado y recogido en [una] celda.

Tirado (fol. 181) *4,api-*, tapar.
Torresano (fol. 82v) *4,ape* [< *4,apal*, el que está encerrado].
Varea (fol. 300) *4,ape*, encerrar algo en alguna parte; *4,apih*, cerrar, encarcelar, cobijar, cubrir, encubrir, tapar • (301) *4,apihƐih*, (días) que suelen caer en Cuaresma en los cuales los Indios que se recogen todos los animales monteses [i.e., *oon, tap, iboy, ak*].
Vico (n.d.a: fol. 211) *4,apiƐih*, [. . .] que monta de cinco días con que ajustaban el año de trescientos y sesenta días • (268) *4,apih*, encerrar, o encarcelar, o cubilar, o cubrir, o tapar; *4,apiƐih*, los cinco días sueltos, o intercalares que hacen fin del año: 360 días y el *4,apiƐih* que son cinco hacen 365; 18 meses a veinte días cada mes que es según cuentan los indios el año.

TZ'AQ

Angel (fol. 214) *4,ak*, obra de cantería o de albanería.
Basseta (fol. 224v) *tzaƐ*, edificio • (225) *tzaƐo / bito*, formar cosas de barro.
Coto (1983: 126) *4,ak // 4oxtum*, cerca o muro de ciudad.
Tirado (fol. 93) *4,ak // 4axtun*, fortaleza • (110) *quenuya soldados chu4a4alexic 4,ak 4oxtun*, guarnecer fortaleza con soldados.
Varea (fol. 301) *4,ak*, hacer ladrillos; *ah4,ak*, el albañil.
Vico (n.d.a: fol. 74v) *nima hay // nima 4,ak*, la torre de Babel • (268v) *4,ak*, obra; *ah 4,ak*, albañil, o cantero; *ti 4,akax 4uxtum* [not translated : to erect a citadel] • (269) *4,ak*, formar [e.g., *x4,akatah xbittitah vinak rumal dios*, fue formada la gente por Dios].

TZ'AQAT

Basseta (fol. 225) [from another writer: *tzakal*, casta o linaje; *tzacatahic*, engendrar, generación]; *tzacat*, completo; *tzacatiƐ*, perfeccionado así; *tzaƐatisah*, ajustar o perfeccionar.
Curruchich Gómez and Coyote Tun (p. 105) *tz'aqatisaj*, agregar.
Tirado (fol. 35) *tzakat*, cabal, lo que viene justo • (58) *tzakat*, cumplida • (124) *ohtzakat cohbe*, vamos todos juntos.
Varea (fol. 301) *4,akat*, cumplir, acabar [. . .] cosa cumplida, cabal; *4,akat // chinamital*, parcialidad • (302) *4,akat molah ruvach*, de todos géneros o muchas cosas distintas.
Vico (n.d.a: fol. 63v) *ru 4,akat ru chinamital*, los de mi linaje • (269) *x4,akatah xbittitah vinak rumal dios*, fue formada la gente por Dios • (275v) *tzakat / 4,akat*, cumplir [e.g., *mix4,akat nu Ɛih*, ya se cumplieron mis días]; *tzakatiçah*, cumplir algo; *tzakatah*, cumplir el número de los que faltan; *4,akat // chinamital*, (los) parientes y conocidos; *tzakat // molah*, muchas maneras, o diversas cosas.
Villacañas (fol. 121) *tzacat // chinamital*, casta o linaje.

TZ'U'UM

Tirado (fol. 4) *4hu4huhirisah 4,um*, ablandar cuero; *4hu4huhirisam 4,um*, cuero ablandado • (52) *4,um ximbal*, correa de cuero.
Torresano (fol. 44) *4,um*, azotes.
Varea (fol. 19) *4,um*, cuerda *[= 4am]* • (305) *4,um*, todo cuero o pellejo de persona o animal.
Vico (n.d.a: fol. 272v) *4,um*, pellejo, o cuero arrugado, o las tetas de la mujer (en quiché es *tub*); *ru yal 4,um*, la leche.

TZ'ULEY U-JI'

Coto (1983: 5) *tin 4,uleh*, abrazados están, o dormir debajo de una manta • (47) *tin 4,uleh*, arroparse [. . .] [cuando] el marido y mujer duermen juntos debajo de una manta; *4,ulebal*, la manta o frezada que así les sirve; *4,uley richin*, el que así arropa.

Varea (fol. 305) *4,uleh,* dormir dos debajo de una ropa [. . .] estar juntos y abrazados y mezclados los pies.
Ximénez (1985: 579) *tzul,* dormir juntos, abrazados, empernados.

UL

Tirado (fol. 27) *ul,* avenida de agua, o desrumbadero.
Varea (fol. 54) *ul,* pedazo de tierra o de algún monte que se derrumba en tiempo de aguas [. . .] cierta enfermedad de las milpas que se les secan todas las hojas [. . .] avenida de río; *uluvu,* desrumbarse gran parte del monte; *ulatah,* desrumbarse monte o edificio.
Vico (n.d.a: fol. 207v) *ul,* avenida de agua; *telel ul, tantel ya y ul,* dicen al anublo de los sembrados.

ULEW

Varea (fol. 55) *uleuh,* la tierra; *vuleu,* mis tierras y heredades; *oh uleu oh 4habak ri oh vinak,* somos terrenos formados de tierra; *vuleval nu 4habakil / nu tiohil,* mi cuerpo • (56) *ulevar,* volverse tierra.
Vico (n.d.a: fol. 188v) *titil Ɛana abah xak caka uleuh,* colores con que eran puestos en señorío, como eran puestos en señorío como ungidos [. . .] *ah titil, ah Ɛana abah çak, ah caka uleuh.*

UMAL

Anleo (fol. 66v) *xa rumal,* por cuanto y así.
Torresano (fol. 83) *ym camel rumal pedro,* yo tengo de ser muerto por Pedro.
Varea (fol. 56) *umal,* causa, o culpa, o por mí o por otro • (124) *bi rumal,* ¿A qué propósito o razón? (vituperando o riñiendo al que hizó algo mal hecho).
Vico (n.d.a: fol. 19v) *bi ruma,* ¿porqué es eso, por qué razón o causa? • (271v) *nakipa rumal xina4,ubu,* ¿porqué me engañaste?

UTIW

Angel (fol. 155) *utiuh,* lobos, adives, coyotes.
Tirado (fol. 10v) *utiuh / utiu,* adive • (26v) *rokebal utiuj,* aullido el adive • (130) *utiuh,* lobo o loba, adive.
Varea (fol. 58) *utiu,* coyotes.

UTUY

Basseta (fol. 231v) *utuy,* un animal a manera de liebre que se come.
Coto (1983: 327) *vtuy,* animalejo llamado *vtuy.*
Guzmán (p. 32) *utuy,* cotuza.
Varea (fol. 58) *utuy,* animalejo que se come.
Ximénez (1985: 601) *utuy,* un animalejo llamado cotuza.

UXLANIK

Varea (fols. 59, 60) *uxlan,* descansar [. . .] estar sin hacer nada y no trabajar.

WAJAJIK

Basseta (fol. 228v) *vahanic,* el ruido de los árboles o cosa semejante; *vahahem,* ruido.
See also:
Coto (1983: 498) *vahin,* ruido de chorro de agua, como de fuente, o como cuando mean los caballos • (499) *ti vain,* cuando hay voces que riñen y hablan muchos juntos.
Varea (fol. 106) *vohoh,* sonar hojas secas por darles el viento, o menearla, o pisarlas.

WAJIM

Varea (fol. 88) *vaim,* la comida [. . .] la boda o banquete.

WARABAL

Coto (1983: 283) *hun varabal,* jornada, camino de un día.

Varea (fol. 97) *varabal,* el lugar donde se duerme [. . .] hacer noche y dormir en un pueblo.

WARAM

Basseta (fol. 229) *varah,* velar algo.

Tirado (fol. 35) *cayustaj nu holom rumal varam,* cabecea mi cabeza por el sueño.

Varea (fol. 97) *varah,* velar a enfermo [. . .] o velar y guardar el camino si hay ladrones o quieren prender el ausente.

WE

Coto (1983: 521) *vue,* si, condicional [. . .] si, dudoso, o si acaso; *vueta,* si por ventura; *vueta quere,* si fuere así; *vue bala / vueta bala,* si en algún lugar o alguna parte.

Varea (fol. 98) *ve,* palabra para otorgar o conceder algo [. . .] significa: si acaso, si sucediere [. . .] dudar de lo que dicen; *ve ta,* y si por ventura, o si, si acaso.

WINAQ

Angel (fol. 26) *cavinak,* cuarenta.

Anleo (fol. 12v) *vinak,* este nombre [. . .] [es] copulativo indeclinable; solo se declina con numerales, v.g. *oxib vinak,* tres personas [. . .] tiene diversas significaciones y ambiguas • (62) *huvinak, cavinak . . . ,* para contar meses al modo de los Indios que son de veinte en veinte días.

Tirado (fol. 36) *hutak le chivinak,* cada edad de gente, cada siglo; *hutak vinak,* cada mes a la cuenta de los naturales • (158) *vinak,* persona; *vinakil,* personalmente • (189) *uvinak hunab,* veinte años.

Torresano (fol. 41) *in xax vinak chic tok xatul,* yo había sido sano cuando tu viniste.

Varea (fol. 103) *vinak 4u,* ídolo de ellos [los indios] que formaban de la ceniza de sus buenos caciques.

Vico (n.d.a: fol. 139v) *nimak vinak,* Principal, o anciano que entiende en los pleitos o casamientos • (205) *vinak,* persona hombre o mujer; *vinakir,* criarse, o nacer, o concebirse; *vinakiriçah,* salir al coz • (205v) *vinak 4u,* ídolo hecho de los polvos quemados de los pasados; *vinak 4uin / 4uih,* hacerlos semejantes ídolos, y fabricarlos • (206) *vinak,* gente [. . .] autoridad; *ma qui xa nu vinak tzih,* no es por mi autoridad; *nima vinak,* principal • (266v) *balamilah tak vinak,* los bárbaros.

WINAQIL

Angel (fol. 151v) *vinakil* [e.g., *çachinak ru vinakil nu xiquin,* perdí el oído]; *nima vinak,* principal; *nima vinakil 4ovi,* está en gran puesto.

Basseta (fol. 230v) [from another writer: *nima vinakil,* nobleza].

Tirado (fol. 158) *vinak,* persona; *vinakil,* personalmente.

Varea (fol. 103) *nu vinakil,* no significa [mi] persona –no hay en esta lengua palabra para decir mi persona o tu persona– sino para decir "gente de mi pueblo o chinamital" • (104) *ru vinakil ya,* es el Diablo que habla en río, fuente o charcos, y los espanta; *ru vinakil huyu,* el diablo que les habla encima o dentro del monte, son abusiones que tienen.

Vico (n.d.a: fol. 205v) *ru vinakil ya,* un género de agua; *ru vinakil huyub,* un género de tierra o montes.

WIQ

Angel (fol. 152v) *vikital chi4al, vikital chi4hi4h,* adornado, o compuesto o armado [. . .] emponerse, o armarse.
Basseta (fol. 230) *viƐo,* componer, aderezar [> *viƐ,* añadir].
Saquic Calel (p. 354) *wik,* adornar, añadir.
Tirado (fol. 10v) *vikonic,* aderezar o adornar algo • (20) *vik-,* añadir • (47v) *vik-,* componer, adornar alguna cosa *[= cavu-]* • (92) *viko,* engerir; *vikon che,* palo injerto • (110) *quenuvik vinak chirech labal,* guarecer gente para la guerra • (210) *vik-,* cosa bien vestida.
Varea (fol. 101) *vik,* acrecentar o añadir algo [. . .] adornar y componer la casa, iglesia o altares para fiestas [. . .] revestirse los Ministros del altar [. . .] engalanarse o componerse como en los días festivos [. . .] adornarse [. . .] ponerse en las puntas de los pies para alcanzar algo • (102) *vikitah,* hacerse rico el que antes era pobre, o el que anda compuesto, antes desnudo y pobre.
Vico (n.d.a: fol. 207) *vikital chi4hi4h,* armado, compuesto; *tinvik vij,* componerse, armarse.

WIT

Angel (fol. 152) *vit,* la encina [. . .] cabo de hacha.
Varea (fol. 105) *vit,* cierta cavassa; *ru vital icah,* el cabo de la hacha.
Vico (n.d.a: fol. 206) *vit,* la encina; *ru vital ycah,* el cabo de la hacha.

WIXAL

Basseta (fol. 230v) *cavixal caƐutamil,* nuestro origen, principio [. . .] Adam.
Coto (1983: 461) *viix,* las raíces todas que salen de un árbol o mata, así las que están debajo de tierra como en la superficie • (552) *cutam,* tocón, que es el trozo del árbol cortado, lo que queda en la tierra con su raíz, y lo mismo de cualquiera otra mata o hierba, como lechuga, coles, etc.: *ru cutamil che, Ɛozm, ichah,* etc. [. . .] Si tiene retoños, llaman *vix; ru vixal che* • (559) *ka vixal, ka cutamil, ka nabey te, tata,* de los antepasados [. . .] nuestro tronco, nuestra raíz, fueron nuestros padres.
Varea (fol. 105) *vix,* la raíz de todo árbol [. . .] A sus padres llaman también los indios *nu vixal nu cutamil* [. . .] Dícenlo también de nuestros primeros padres Adan y Eva.
Vico (n.d.a: fol. 206) *vixal,* el tronco del árbol.

WOROM

Angel (fol. 107v) *oro; tiuoro,* hacer agujero, corromper virgen, horadar.
Basseta (fol. 222v) *vorobal / toƐobal,* el instrumento con que se agujerea la cosa o barrena, o punzón • (232) *voro,* barrenar, sodomitar; *vorom uxe,* abierto el tal; *cac vorom,* nuevamente abierto; *vorel [= orel],* agujero.
Coto (1983: 93) *ti u'or cab,* castrar colmenas; *orom,* colmena castrada; *oronel,* castrador; *oronic,* castradura así *[= tin poƐ; poƐom; poƐol cab; poƐonic]* • (98) *orocom r'ochoch ru 4ohlibal cab,* colmena que se cría en los huecos de los árboles *[= orocom ru pa che]* • (277) *qu'in oro,* horadar, hacer agujero en algo; *ti u'or,* activo; *orom [= orotahinak],* cosa horadada [≠ *t'i4o*: hacer horado o agujero que pase de una parte a otra].
Tirado (fol. 28v) *vor,* barrenar, taladrear • (119v) *quinvoronic / canvoro,* horadar; *canƐaxah uvoric,* horadar, y pasar de la otra parte [. . .] traspasa el agujerear; *voron / vorom,* horadado • (181) *vorbal,* taladro.
Varea (fol. 48) *or* [< *orahel,* agujero]; *oral,* cosa agujereada.
Vico (n.d.a: fol. 144v) *or,* horador, barrenador; *orotahinak ruƐarakan,* llagado de pies y manos (llagas de Jesucristo); *orol,* el agujero; *oroh ru pam,* cosa que tiene muchos agujeros.
Villacañas (fol. 58) *rorel,* agujeros o llagas de Christo.

XAJ

Angel (fol. 160) *xaho,* bailar; *xahbeh,* con que se baila, sea máscara, vestido, o el dinero que se ofrece.
Coto (1983: 60) *qui xaho,* bailar o danzar.
Torresano (fol. 125) *xah,* bailar.
Varea (fol. 238) *xah,* bailar al son de algo [. . .] o representar bailando alguna invención; *nima xahoh,* el baile común de muchas plumas; *xaho,* bailar; también andar contoneándose con brío y garbo: menear la cola, halagando el perro [...]; estar encrespado el pavo y arrastrar las alas por el suelo cuando enamora a la pava.
Vico (n.d.a: fol. 215) *xaho,* bailar; *xaholbey,* andar callejeando • (215v) *xahbeh,* bailar algo, como bailan, con máscaras o penacho.

XAJAB

Angel (fols. 159v–160) *xahab,* suela, o zapatos, u otro calzado; *xahabin,* las suelas que son usadas.
Varea (fol. 238) *xahab,* todo calzado, zapatos, sacles, alpargatas.
Vico (n.d.a: fol. 215) *xahab,* suelas, o zapatos, o otro calzado.

XAKAK

Coto (1983: 6) *xacaba,* abrir las piernas, o despernancarse estando parado.
Ximénez (1985: 605) *xac,* abrir las piernas [. . .] abrir como piernas, tijeras, compás.

XAMBE

Angel (fol. 160) *xambey,* después, o el trasero después de los otros; *xambey chic,* y más después.
Basseta (fol. 232v) *xambe,* detrás, o último.
Tirado (fol. 14v) *chixambeyal canok,* a la postre • (124) *ynxanbe canok,* voy postrero *[≠ quin nabeyahic]* • (161v) *xanbecanok,* postrero, trasero; *xanbeahic,* postrimería.
Varea (fol. 239) *xambey,* el que va o viene atrás [. . .] significa después; *xambeyah,* hacer algo tarde o después de otro.
Vico (n.d.a: fol. 215v) *xambey,* después, o detrás de los otros.

XAQI

Coto (1983: 489) *xa / xaki,* partícula restrictiva [. . .]: mas, empero, sino que.
Tirado (fol. 8v) *xaki 4ateet,* accidentalmente, de repente • (63) *xaki,* de balde o graciosamente.
Torresano (fol. 29v) *xaki,* solamente.

XAWI

Tirado (fol. 74) *xavi,* y [e.g., *Ɛih xavi aƐab,* día y noche].
Vico (n.d.a: fol. 216) *xavi, xaviquehe, xavi4ut,* el mismo, de la misma manera.

XAX

Torresano (fol. 40v) *xax in vi,* yo había sido (preterito plus quam perfecto) • (41) *in xax vinak chic tok xatul,* yo había sido sano cuando tu viniste.
Varea (fol. 239) *xax . . . vi,* da a entender que es fuerza, o por su naturaleza, o por costumbre la cosa que se hace.

XERE

Varea (fol. 241) *xere,* mas, o empero.

XIL

Angel (fol. 162) *xil*, grillo que canta de noche; *retal aƐa.*
Basseta (fol. 233v) *xil // lal*, género de grillos que cantan de noche.
Coto (1983: 256) *xil*, grillo, especie de cigarra que no tiene alitas, sino que salta [≠ *lol*, grillos verdes, cantadores] [. . .] Y cuando la noche está quieta y serena, que sólo se oye el chillido o canto de estos grillos, dicen: *ti lolin, ti xilan aƐa.*
Varea (fol. 242) *xiil*, un animalejo como grillo, que canta mucho de noche [*xil // lol*: idea of hunger, of famine; e.g., *tan toƐ lol xil chupam chi vaihal*, haber tanta hambre].
Vico (n.d.a: fol. 218v) *xil*, grillo que canta de noche.

XIMILIK

Anonymous (fol. 60) *ximbal upam queh*, cincha de bestia.
Basseta (fol. 233v) *xim*, atar; *ximilic*, atado [from another writer: *ximobalha*, cárcel; *ximilic*, encerrado; *ximbal*, atadura].
Saquic Calel (p. 356) *ximbal*, cosa con la cual se amarra.
Tirado (fol. 41) *ximobalha*, cárcel • (52) *4,um ximbal*, correa de cuero • (83v) *canxim chi4ama 4hi4h*, encadenar • (177v) *xim + pam*, ceñir.
Torresano (fol. 82v) *xime* [< *ximel*, el que está atado].
Varea (fol. 243) *xim*, atar [. . .] prender [. . .] ceñirse [. . .] envolver algo en el pañuelo [. . .] liar la petaca o carga de leña.
Vico (n.d.a: fols. 107, 218v) *xim*, atar, enlazar, prender, ceñir *[= yut].*

XIRXOTILEB

Angel (fol. 162v) *xirixot*, cantar el grillo.
Tirado (fol. 39v) *caxirixot xir*, canta el grillo, o cigarra.
Varea (fol. 243) *xirixot*, silbarle a uno las narices por tenerlas tapadas del romadizo.
Vico (n.d.a: fol. 219) *xiri, xiril, xirixak*, cantar los grillos, o cigarras.
Ximénez (1985: 619) *xir*, cantar como grillo o cigarra; *xirixot*, cantar grillo o cigarra.
See also:
Ximénez (1985: 617) *xihxot*, estar tambaleando de miedo.

XIT

Angel (fol. 163) *xit*, piedras verdes como turquesadas; *ahxit*, oficial de estas piedras.
Basseta (fol. 162v) *al, xit, yamanic*, piedras preciosas *[= coƐ; xtecoc]* • (234) *xit*, piedra preciosa de muchos colores [from another writer: *xit*, turquesa]; *xitah*, pintar de colores; *xitamha*, casa pintada de muchos colores.
Coto (1983: 283) *xit, 4ual, yamanic, xtekok*, piedras que tenían por preciosas, con que se adornaban.
Varea (fol. 65) *ru yaal xit puvak*, el resplandor • (243) *xit*, piedra verde como turquesa; *ah xit ah puvak*, llaman ahora al que dora, platea y pinta retablos o imágenes.
Vico (n.d.a: fol. 219) *xit*, piedras verdes como turquesas; *ah xit*, oficial de ellas [from another writer: *tultecatl*].
See also:
Zuñiga (in Miles 1957: 768) *ah xit ah puac*, lapidary, jeweler.

XMUT

Coloch (pers. comm.) *u-xmut kaj wara*, aquí está el ombligo del mundo; *u-xmut kaj u-xmut ulew*, el ombligo del cielo el ombligo de la tierra (i.e., Rabinal).

XOQ'OJAW

Tirado (fol. 174v) *ka xoƐohaval*, nuestra señora • (177v) *yxokohavab*, señoras; *xoƐohau*, señora.
Torresano (fol. 134v) *yxokohavab*, las Señoras.
Varea (fol. 245) *xoƐohau*, señora, mujer de señor, cacique o Alcalde. No se usa ya sino en la Sierra y en Tzololya. *XoƐohau* dicen en toda lengua a la mujer o muchacha que tiene las bubas de la tierra, porque se están mano sobre mano sin hacer nada porque no pueden.
Vico (n.d.a: fol. 220v) *xoƐohauah*, la señora, o princesa.

XTAPAKAL / XTAKAPAL

Alonso (fol. 143v) *castilan xtacapal*, haba.
Coto (1983: 240) *xtacapal*, frijoles [. . .] colorados • (268) *castilan xtacapal*, haba *[= castilan quinaƐ]*.

XTAPYAK

Vico (n.d.a: fol. 225) [from another writer: *xtapiyac*, zapatos, en la lengua antigua de Rabinal].

XTEKOQIB

Angel (fol. 167) *xtecoc*, piedra preciosa • (178v) *kokol xtecoc*, piedra preciosa.
Basseta (fol. 162v) *coƐ, xtecoc*, piedras preciosas *[= al; xit; yamanic]* • (234v) *xtecoƐ*, piedra preciosa, vide *coƐ*, etc.
Coto (1983: 283) *xtekok, 4ual, yamanic, xit*, piedras que tenían por preciosas, con que se adornaban.
Varea (fol. 249) *xtecoc yamanic / kokol xtecoc*, piedras preciosas, ya no se usan sino *4ual, ƐaƐal, tepeval*.
Vico (n.d.a: fol. 60v) *yamanic xte4o4*, piedra preciosa como diamante, o esmeralda • (223) *xtecoc*, piedra preciosa *[= kokol xtecoc; yamanic 4ual]* • (254v) *4ual yamanic 4ubul chactic*, riquezas [> *4ubul chactic*, cosa hecha de plumas]; *4ual abah tah kokol xtecoc yamanic*, piedras preciosas.

XUK

Angel (fol. 166) *xucul*, el hincado; *xu4ulem*, el acto de hincarse.
Torresano (fol. 95v) *xuque* [< *xuqui*, el que está de rodillas]; *xuquxuh*, los que están de rodillas.
Varea (fol. 246) *xuque*, arrodillarse; *xuculibeh*, dar ofrenda a Dios • (247) *xuc*, humillar el cuerpo.
Vico (n.d.a: fol. 221) *xuque*, hincarse de rodilla • (222) *xucun*, andar a gatas.

XUKUTAL

Anleo (fol. 49) *chu xu4ut*, en el rincón [≠ *chuxiquin*, en la esquina].
Basseta (fol. 184) *chuxucut ha*, en el rincón de la casa • (235) *xuƐut*, rincón.
See also:
Angel (fol. 166v) *xucul*, lado derecho o izquierdo.
Tirado (fol. 131) *u xu4ut*, lado.
Vico (n.d.a: fols. 68v, 222) *chucaxu4ut*, a los dos lados.

YA

Varea (fol. 65) *ya*, dar, poner algo en alguna parte o arrimarlo; *yao*, la ofrenda • (66) *ya*, por rendirse o dejarse coger, o por caer en lazo.

YAK

Angel (fol. 69v) *yaquen,* llevar espada en la mano; *nu yaquem 4hamij,* llevar vara.
Basseta (fol. 192v) *yaco,* vencer, levantar algo del suelo, menospreciar, pisar y convidar, resgatar • (193v) *yaqueh,* llevar algo en la mano.
Tirado (fol. 129) *yacom,* levantado; *yac // valah,* levantar.
Varea (fols. 56, 69) *yacatah,* levantarse (de la cama) • (67) *yac,* alzar y poner a recaudo algo • (68) *yac,* hacer, edificar casas; *yac,* incitar a uno • (69) *yaqueh,* llevar vara larga o espada, o tenerla en la mano, o llevar lata o leño grueso y largo al hombro • (166) *ti birbot chi ƐaƐ mix yacatah nah tibe chi cah,* alzarse gran llama con gran ruido.
Vico (n.d.a: fol. 92) *ca nu yac uleuh chivakan,* piso la tierra con (mis) pies • (92v) *yacatah,* levantarse • (93) *yacaba,* levantar alguna buena costumbre; *yaqueh,* llevar algo levantado [e.g., *nu yaquem espada nu yaquem 4hamey,* llevo levantada la vara] • (95v) *yaqueh,* llevar en la mano como bordón o vara, o llevar en la boca los perros, o gatos a sus hijos.

YAK

Basseta (fol. 192v) *yaƐ,* zorra que es la que se come las gallinas.
Ximénez (1985: 297) *yac,* el gato de monte.

YAKALEM

Coto (1983: 455) *yacal,* sosegada.
Ximénez (1985: 297) *yacal,* hacer bonanza.

YAKI

Angel (fol. 72) *yaqui vinak,* toda persona extranjera que habla la lengua mexicana, o los Mexicanos.
Basseta (fol. 193v) *yaqui ixoc,* mujer ladina.
Tirado (fol. 127) *yaqui vinak,* persona ladina.
Torresano (fol. 13) *yaqui,* mexicano.
Varea (fol. 72) *yaqui vinak,* persona mexicana; *yaqui chiin,* hablar en mexicano *[≠ caslan chiin].*
Vico (n.d.a: fol. 95v) *yaqui,* toda gente extranjera que habla lengua mexicana, y los mismos mexicanos.
See also:
Varea (fol. 67) *yac,* mercadear, tratar en mercadería; mercar aquí y ir a vender por ay.
Vico (n.d.a: fol. 92) *yac* [classifier: *huyac,* una parte; *huyac chic,* otro género de gente].

YAMANIK

Angel (fol. 71v) *yamanic,* piedra preciosa [. . .] *4ual yamanic* • (180) *ƐalƐa 4ual yamanic,* joyas.
Basseta (fol. 162v) *al, xit, yamanic,* piedras preciosas *[= coƐ; xtecoc].*
Coto (1983: 283) *yamanic, 4ual, xtekok, xit,* piedras que tenían por preciosas, con que se adornaban.
Tirado (fol. 127v) *ahay 4ual, 4ual, yamanic, raxon,* lapidario de piedras preciosas.
Varea (fol. 71) *yamanic,* joyas antiguas *[4ual yamanic; xtecoc; chiquirin puvak; chachalim puvak].*
Vico (n.d.a: fols. 60v, 95v) *yamanic xte4o4,* piedra preciosa como diamante, o esmeralda • (223) *yamanic 4ual,* piedra preciosa • (254v) *4ual yamanic 4ubul chactic,* riquezas [> *4ubul chactic,* cosa hecha de plumas]; *4ual abah tah kokol xtecoc yamanic,* piedras preciosas.

YEBAL

Basseta (fol. 194v) *yeba*, dar.

Coto (1983: 19) *tin yeeh*, aguijar, darse prisa o correr *[= quin an; tin covih]* • (439) *tin yeeh*, dar prisa para que se haga algo; *yeebal*, la prisa *[= paƐaƐebal; toƐolibebal]*; *ti yeeh nu tzih*, cuando uno habla de prisa en lo que pide o cuenta.

Varea (fol. 73) *yeeh*, dar prisa a que uno haga algo; *yeeyic*, el porfiado que no obedece a los que le aconsejan lo que le está bien, sino que lleva adelante su intento, como si uno se quiere [ir] a otro chinamital, y le aconseja el Alc[alde] o su amigo que no lo haga, y el porfiado de hacerlo.

Vico (n.d.a: fol. 97) *yeeh*, dar prisa; *yeebal* [= Quiche' *chichuƐabah*, darse prisa, forzar].

YIQ'IK

Coto (1983: 420) *tin yeƐ*, pisar con los pies *[= tin palibeh]*.

Varea (fols. 73, 74) *yeƐ*, pisar.

YO'PIJIK

Basseta (fol. 196) *yopihic*, acercarse.

Vico (n.d.a: fol. 100v) *ulic // yopehic*, la venida.

YUSK'UPIJ

Coto (1983: 143) *tin yuzƐupih*, desatar, soltando cavalgadura o otro animal *[= ti u'izƐopih; tin quir]* • (161) *tin yuzƐupih*, cuando dejan el pleito y no lo siguen más *[= ti u'izƐopih; ti u'oƐotah]* • (529) *tin yuzƐupih*, soltar de la mano, dejar lo que en ella tiene uno [≠ *tin quir*, soltar desatando].

Curruchich Gómez and Coyote Tun (p. 32) *isq'opij*, liberar.

Varea (fol. 84) *yuzƐupih*, dejar el pleito, no seguirlo [. . .] o desatar el atado, o sacar de prisiones [. . .] o soltar bestia atada.

Vico (n.d.a: fol. 108) *yuspih*, dejar, soltar.

Ximénez (1985: 333) *yutzcupih*, sacar de prisiones, dejar el pleito, desatar; *yuspih*, dejar, soltar.

YUT'UT'

Coto (1983: 51) *yut*, atar bocas de talega, costal, flores en ramillete, atar por los pies animales o aves [. . .] atar de pies y manos a alguno; *yuttutahic*, atadura.

Curruchich Gómez and Coyote Tun (p. 119) *yut*, amarrar.

Varea (fol. 82) *yut*, atar bocas de talegas, sacos, matates, pies del delincuente o del difunto o de aves, carneros, para llevarlos de una parte a otra, o el pie del manojo de flores [. . .] o atar dinero o cacao o cosa tal en pañuelo. Usan de este verbo por amenazar que lo han de castigar atado • (83) *yuteh*, llevar algún dinero, cacao, o cosa tal atado en paño, o cabo de ayate, o en el huipil; *yute*, guardar cosa atada sin desatarlo.

Vico (n.d.a: fol. 107) *yut*, juntar, atar, por ensenar en el seno, o enaldar, o manosear flores, atarlas en uno *[= xim]*; *ta yutu a puak*, guardas dinero en paño.

YUXTAJ

Coto (1983: 79) *yuxuxiyax*, estar o andar cabizcaído.

Tirado (fol. 35) *cayustaj nu holom rumal varam*, cabecea mi cabeza por el sueño.

Varea (fol. 83) *yuxba*, caérsele la cara o bajar la cabeza al que le piden algo que no gusta, como si le dicen si se quiere casar con tal persona, o que pague la deuda, o si quiere trabajar, o ir conmigo de camino; *yuxpih*, está ya convaleciente el enfermo.

Vico (n.d.a: fol. 107v) *yux4ut varam*, cabecear de sueño • (108) *yux*, cabecear.

Ximénez (1985: 333) *yux*, cabecear otorgando; *yuxba*, hacer gestos con los ojos; ponerse delante del que come para que le de algo.

References

Acuña, René

1975 *Introducción al estudio del Rabinal Achí*. Mexico: Centro de Estudios Mayas, Instituto de Investigaciones Filológicas, Universidad Nacional Autónoma de México.

1978 *Farsas y representaciones escénicas de los Mayas antiguos*. Mexico: Centro de Estudios Mayas, Instituto de Investigaciones Filológicas, Universidad Nacional Autónoma de México.

1982 *Rabinal Ači apu Oljantaj: Dramska prikazanja naroda maja i inka*, translated by Ljubomir Ristanovič. Krusevač: Bagdala.

1983 "El Popol Vuh, Vico y la Theologia Indorum." In *Nuevas perspectivas sobre el Popol Vuh*, edited by Robert M. Carmack and Francisco Morales Santos, pp. 1–16. Guatemala: Editorial Piedra Santa.

Akkeren, Ruud van

1988 "Interpretación etnológica del drama Rabinal Achí de Guatemala." *Folklore americano* 45: 99–127. Mexico.

Alcina Franch, José

1957 *Floresta literaria de la América indígena*. Madrid: Aguilar.

1968 *Poesía americana precolombina*. Madrid: Prensa Española.

Alonso, Juan

n.d. Vocabulario en lengua castellana y guatemalteca, que se llama cak chi quel chi [17th century]. Manuscript in the Bibliothèque nationale, Paris [anonymous copy attributed to J. Alonso].

Álvarez, Cristina

1980 *Diccionario etnolingüístico del idioma maya yucateco colonial, I: Mundo físico.* Mexico: Centro de Estudios Mayas, Instituto de Investigaciones Filológicas, Universidad Nacional Autónoma de México.

1984 *Diccionario etnolingüístico del idioma maya yucateco colonial, II: Aprovechamiento de los recursos naturales.* Mexico: Centro de Estudios Mayas, Instituto de Investigaciones Filológicas, Universidad Nacional Autónoma de México.

Álvarez Aguilar, Silvia

1986 "Un nuevo enfoque del Rabinal Achí: Estudio etnográfico y etnológico." *Revista de la Universidad de San Carlos* 1: 65–72. Guatemala.

Angel [Fray]

n.d. Bocabulario de la lengua cakchiquel [17th century]. Manuscript in the Bibliothèque nationale, Paris [transcribed from Vico, n.d.a].

Anleo, Bartholomé

n.d. Arte de la lengua 4iché [18th century]. Manuscript in the Bibliothèque nationale, Paris [copy dated 1744, signed by Antonio Ramírez de Utrilla].

Anonymous

n.d. Vocabulario en lengua quiché y castellana [17th century]. Manuscript in the Bibliothèque nationale, Collección Angrand 9, Paris.

Arias-Larretta, Abraham

1968 *Literaturas aborígenes de América. Azteca, Incaica, Maya-Quiché.* Buenos Aires: Edición Interamericana [1st ed. 1951].

Arnauld, Marie-Charlotte

1993 "Los territorios políticos de las cuencas de Salamá, Rabinal y Cubulco en el Postclásico (Baja Verapaz, Guatemala)." In *Representaciones del espacio político en las tierras altas de Guatemala,* edited by Alain Breton et al., pp. 43–109. Cuadernos de Estudios Guatemaltecos 2. Guatemala: Centro Francés de Estudios Mexicanos y Centroamericanos.

Arnauld, Marie-Charlotte, and Alain Breton

1993 "Tzamaneb: Enfoques pluridisciplinarios sobre el Postclásico maya en los Altos de Guatemala." In *Perspectivas Antropológicas en el Mundo Maya,* edited by María-Josefa Iglesias Ponce de León and Francescc Ligorred Perramon, pp. 285–308. Madrid: Sociedad Española de Estudios Mayas and Instituto de Cooperación Iberoamericana.

Arnauld, Marie-Charlotte, and Dominique Michelet

1991 "Les migrations postclassiques au Michoacán et au Guatemala." In *Vingt Études sur le Mexique et le Guatemala, réunies à la mémoire de Nicole Percheron,* edited by Alain Breton, Jean-Pierre Berthe, and Sylvie Lecoin, pp. 67–92. Toulouse: Presses Universitaires du Mirail.

Ballantine Irving, Thomas

1985 "Warrior of Rabinal: The Ballet of the Sacred Drum (with Ballet Music)." In *The Maya's Own Words,* part 3, pp. 79–96. Culver City: Labyrinthos.

Barrera Vásquez, Alfredo, ed.

1980 *Diccionario maya Cordemex.* Mérida: Ediciones Cordemex.

Basseta, Domingo de

1698 Vocabulario español quiché y quiché español. Manuscript in the Bibliothèque nationale, Paris.

Baudez, Claude-François, and Pierre Becquelin

1984 *Les Mayas*. Paris: Gallimard.

Baudissonne, Luis, ed.

1944 *Rabinal Achí*. Buenos Aires: Nova.

Baudot, Georges

1976 *Les lettres précolombiennes*. Toulouse: Édouard Privat.

Becquelin, Pierre

1969 *Archéologie de la région de Nebaj (Guatemala)*. Mémoires 2. Paris: Institut d'Ethnologie.

1970 "Histoire et acculturation chez les indiens Ixil du Guatemala." *Journal de la Société des Américanistes* 59: 7–26. Paris.

Becquelin Monod, Aurore

1979 "Examen de quelques paires sémantiques dans les dialogues rituels des Tzeltal de Bachajon (langue maya du Chiapas)." *Journal de la Société des Américanistes* 66: 235–263. Paris.

1986 "Le sang et le corps, ou le blanc et le noir? Contribution à l'étude du parallélisme dans la tradition orale des Maya." *Journal de la Société des Américanistes* 72: 7–31. Paris.

Bertrand, Michel

1991 "Une fondation à double inconnue: Réflexions autour de la naissance de San Pablo Rabinal." In *Vingt Études sur le Mexique et le Guatemala, réunies à la mémoire de Nicole Percheron*, edited by Alain Breton, Jean-Pierre Berthe, and Sylvie Lecoin, pp. 337–347. Toulouse: Presses Universitaires du Mirail.

Bourdé, Guy, and Hervé Martin

1983 *Les écoles historiques*. Paris: Éditions du Seuil.

Brasseur de Bourbourg, Charles Étienne

1855 [Carta de Brasseur de Bourbourg a Ephraïm G. Squier, 7 de agosto de 1855], *The Athenaeum*, no. 1467 (December 8, 1855), pp. 1435–1436. London.

1861–68 *Collection de documents dans les langues indigènes, pour servir à l'étude de l'histoire et de la philologie de l'Amérique ancienne . . .*, 4 vols. Paris: Arthus Bertrand [and Auguste Durand].

1862a "Grammaire de la langue quiché." In *Collection de documents dans les langues indigènes . . .*, vol. 2, part 1. Paris: Arthus Bertrand.

1862b "Rabinal-Achi ou le drame-ballet du Tun." In *Collection de documents dans les langues indigènes . . .*, vol. 2, part 2. Paris: Arthus Bertrand.

1864 "Relation des choses de Yucatan de Diego de Landa." In *Collection de documents dans les langues indigènes . . .*, vol. 3. Paris: Arthus Bertrand and Auguste Durand.

1871 *Bibliothèque mexico-guatémalienne: Précédée d'un coup d'œil sur les études américaines dans leurs rapports avec les études classiques et suivie du tableau par ordre alphabétique des ouvrages de linguistique américaine contenus dans le même volume, rédigée et mise en ordre d'après les documents de sa collection américaine*. Paris: Adrien Maisonneuve.

1940 "Dos cartas inéditas del Abate Brasseur de Bourbourg, dirigidas al Doctor José Mariano Padilla, fechadas en Rabinal el 23 de mayo y 3 de junio de 1855." *Anales de la Sociedad de Geografía e Historia* 16(4): 298–303. Guatemala.

1945 "Antigüedades guatemaltecas: Tres cartas del abate Brasseur de Bourbourg." *Anales de la Sociedad de Geografía e Historia* 20(1): 7–17. Guatemala.

1946 "De Guatemala a Rabinal: Episodio de un viaje en la América del Centro en los años de 1855 y 1856." *Anales de la Sociedad de Geografía e Historia* 21(2): 157-170. Guatemala [1st ed. 1859. *Revue européenne* 146–74, 275–301. Paris].

Bray, Warwick

1977 "Maya Metalwork and Its External Connections." In *Social Process in Maya Prehistory*, edited by Norman Hammond, pp. 365–403. New York: Academic Press.

Breton, Alain

1982 "'Le Christ s'est arrêté à Rabinal . . .': Voyages légendaires et espace sacré des Quiché-Achí." *Cahiers de la RCP 500* 4: 141–169. Paris: Centre National de la Recherche Scientifique and Institut d'Ethnologie.

1989 "El 'complejo ajaw' y el 'complejo mam': Actores rituales y héroes míticos entre los Quiché-Achí de Rabinal (Baja Verapaz, Guatemala)." In *Memorias del II Coloquio Internacional de Mayistas (Campeche, 17–22 de agosto de 1987)*, pp. 17–27. Mexico: Centro de Estudios Mayas, Instituto de Investigaciones Filológicas, Universidad Nacional Autónoma de México.

1991 "Un besoin infini d'ancêtres." In *Mayas: La passion des ancêtres, le désir de durer*, edited by Alain Breton and Jacques Arnauld, pp. 150–158. Paris: Éditions Autrement.

1993 "Territorio, alianzas y guerra en el 'Rabinal Achi': La continuación de un mito, un viraje decisivo de la historia." In *Representaciones del espacio político en las tierras altas de Guatemala*, edited by Alain Breton et al., pp. 29–41. Cuadernos de Estudios Guatemaltecos 2. Guatemala: Centro Francés de Estudios Mexicanos y Centroamericanos.

1994 "Les figures du guerrier et du roi dans le 'Rabinal Achi': Une version maya du couple *celeritas/gravitas*." In *Mille ans de civilisations mésoaméricaines: Des Aztèques aux Mayas: Volume d'hommage à Jacques Soustelle*, edited by Jacqueline de Durand-Forest and Georges Baudot, vol. 2, pp. 143–164. Paris: L'Harmattan.

2001 "Algunas observaciones acerca del calendario ritual y el sistema de los 'cargadores del año' en Nebaj." In *Arqueología de la región de Nebaj (Guatemala)*, Pierre Becquelin, Alain Breton, and Véronique Gervais, pp. 219–231. Cuadernos de Estudios Guatemaltecos 5. Guatemala: Centro Francés de Estudios Mexicanos y Centroamericanos.

1999 *Rabinal Achi: Un drama dinástico maya del siglo XV*. Guatemala: Centro Francés de Estudios Mexicanos y Centroamericanos.

Breton, Alain, Charlotte Arnauld, Alain Ichon, François Lartigue, and Yvon Le Bot

1993 *Representaciones del espacio político en las tierras altas de Guatemala*. Cuadernos de Estudios Guatemaltecos 2. Guatemala: Centro Francés de Estudios Mexicanos y Centroamericanos.

Breton, Alain, and Jacques Arnauld, eds.

1994 *Mayas: La pasión por los antepasados, el deseo de perdurar*. Mexico: Editorial Grijalbo [1st ed. 1991. Paris: Éditions Autrement].

Brunhouse, Robert L.

1973 *In Search of the Mayas*. Albuquerque: University of New Mexico Press.

Campbell, Lyle

1983 "Préstamos lingüísticos en el Popol Vuh." In *Nuevas perspectivas sobre el Popol Vuh*, edited by Robert M. Carmack and Francisco Morales Santos, pp. 81–86. Guatemala: Editorial Piedra Santa.

Carmack, Robert M.

1968 "Toltec Influences on the Postclassic Culture History of Highland Guatemala." In *Archaeological Studies of Middle America*, Middle American Research Institute, Publication 26, pp. 42–92. New Orleans: Tulane University.

1973 *Quichean Civilization: The Ethnohistoric, Ethnographic, and Archaeological Sources*. Berkeley: University of California Press.

1976 "La estratificación quicheana prehispánica." In *Estratificación social en la Mesoamérica prehispánica*, edited by Pedro Carrasco and Johanna Broda, pp. 245–277. Mexico: Secretaría de Educación Pública and Centro de Investigaciones Superiores, Instituto Nacional de Antropología e Historia.

1979 *Evolución del reino quiché*. Guatemala: Editorial Piedra Santa.

1981 *The Quiché Mayas of Utatlán: The Evolution of a Highland Guatemala Kingdom*. Norman: University of Oklahoma Press.

Carmack, Robert M., ed.

1988 *Harvest of Violence: The Maya Indians and the Guatemalan Crisis*. Norman: University of Oklahoma Press.

Carmack, Robert M., John W. Fox, and Russell E. Stewart

1975 *La formación del reino quiché*. Publicación especial 7. Guatemala: Instituto de Antropología e Historia.

Carmack, Robert M., and James L. Mondloch, eds.

1983 *El Título de Totonicapán*. Fuentes para el Estudio de la Cultura Maya 3. Mexico: Centro de Estudios Mayas, Instituto de Investigaciones Filológicas, Universidad Nacional Autónoma de México.

Chávez, Adrián Inés

1979 *Pop Wuj*. Mexico: Ediciones de la Casa Chata.

1990 *Pop Wuh, le livre des événements*, translated by Anny Amberni. Paris: NRF-Gallimard.

Chinchilla Aguilar, Ernesto

1951 "La danza del tum-teleche o loj-tum." *Antropología e Historia de Guatemala* 3(2): 17–20.

Cid Pérez, José, and Dolores Martí de Cid

1964 *Teatro indio precolombino*. Ávila: Aguilar.

Cook, Garrett

1983 "Mitos de Momostenango comparados con el Popol Vuh." In *Nuevas perspectivas sobre el Popol Vuh*, edited by Robert M. Carmack and Francisco Morales Santos, pp. 135–161. Guatemala: Editorial Piedra Santa.

Coto, Thomás de

n.d. *Vocabulario de la lengua cakchiquel y guatemalteca* [ca. 1690]. Manuscript in the American Philosophical Society Library, Philadelphia.

1983 *[Thesavrvs verborvm]. Vocabulario de la lengua cakchiquel v[el] guatemalteca, nueuamente hecho y recopilado con summo estudio, trauajo y erudición*. Edited by René Acuña. Mexico: Instituto de Investigaciones Filológicas, Universidad Nacional Autónoma de México.

Crespo M., Mario

1968 Algunos títulos indígenas del Archivo General del Gobierno de Guatemala. MA thesis, Universidad de San Carlos de Guatemala.

Curruchich Gómez, María-Luisa, and Serapio Coyote Tun

n.d. "Diccionario de verbos." Unpublished manuscript. Guatemala.

Dain, Alphonse

1975 *Les manuscrits*. Paris: Les Belles Lettres [1st ed. 1949].

Davies, Claude Nigel

1977 *The Toltecs: Until the Fall of Tula*. Norman: University of Oklahoma Press.

De León, Luis Z.

1985 *Carcha': Una misión en Guatemala entre los Kekchíes de Alta Verapaz*. Historia de las Misiones Salesianas 1. Torino: Centro de Estudios de las Misiones Salesianas.

DesRuisseaux, Pierre, and Daisy Amaya

1987 *Popol Vuh: Le livre des événements: Bible américaine des Mayas-Quichés*. Montréal, VLB Éditeur; Pantin, Le Castor Astral [French adaptation from Chávez 1979].

Edmonson, Munro S.

1965 *Quiché-English Dictionary*. Middle American Research Institute, Publication 30. New Orleans: Tulane University.

1971a *The Book of Counsel: The Popol Vuh of the Quiché Maya of Guatemala*. Middle American Research Institute, Publication 35. New Orleans: Tulane University.

1971b "Historia de las tierras altas mayas según los documentos indígenas." In *Desarrollo cultural de los Mayas*, edited by Evon Z. Vogt and Alberto Ruz Lhuillier, pp. 273–302. Mexico: Centro de Estudios Mayas, Instituto de Investigaciones Filológicas, Universidad Nacional Autónoma de México [1st ed. 1964].

1973 "Semantic Universals and Particulars in Quiche." In *Meaning in Mayan Languages: Ethnolinguistic Studies*, edited by Munro S. Edmonson, pp. 235–246. The Hague: Mouton.

1985 "Quiche Literature." In *Supplement to the Handbook of Middle American Indians, 3: Literatures*, edited by Munro S. Edmonson, pp. 107–132. Austin: University of Texas Press.

Englekirk, John E.

1957 "El teatro folklórico hispanoamericano." *Folklore Americas* 17(1): 1–33. Coral Gables.

Escalante Arce, Pedro Antonio

1989 *Brasseur de Bourbourg: Esbozo biográfico*. San Salvador: Pedro A. Escalante Arce.

Estrada, Juan de, and Fernando de Niebla

1982 "Relación de Zapotitlán (1579)." In *Relaciones geográficas del siglo XVI: Guatemala*. Edited by René Acuña, pp. 15–61. Etnohistoria, serie Antropológica 45.

Mexico: Instituto de Investigaciones Antropológicas, Universidad Nacional Autónoma de México.

Faurie, Valérie, trans.
1991 *Popol Vuh: Le Livre des Indiens Mayas Quichés*. Paris: Albin Michel [French adaptation from Recinos 1947].

Fought, John
1985 "Cyclical Patterns in Chorti (Mayan) Literature." In *Supplement to the Handbook of Middle American Indians, 3: Literatures*, edited by Munro S. Edmonson, pp. 133–146. Austin: University of Texas Press.

Fox, John W.
1978 *Quiche Conquest: Centralism and Regionalism in Highland Guatemalan State Development*. Albuquerque: University of Mexico Press.
1987 *Maya Postclassic State Formation: Segmentary Lineage Migration in Advancing Frontiers*. Cambridge: Cambridge University Press.

Freidel, David A.
1985 "New Light on the Dark Age: A Summary of Major Themes." In *The Lowland Maya Postclassic*, edited by Arden F. Chase and Prudence M. Rice, pp. 285–309. Austin: University of Texas Press.

Fuentes y Guzmán, Francisco Antonio
1932–33 *Recordación florida: Discurso historial y demostración material, militar y política del Reyno de Guatemala* [ca. 1690]. Biblioteca Goathemala 6–8. Guatemala: Sociedad de Geografía e Historia de Guatemala.

Galinier, Jacques
1990 *La mitad del mundo: Cuerpo y cosmos en los rituales otomíes*. Mexico: Universidad Nacional Autónoma de México, Centro Francés de Estudios Mexicanos y Centroamericanos and Instituto Nacional Indigenista.

Garapon, Antoine
1985 *L'âne portant des reliques: Essai sur le rituel judiciaire*. Paris: Éditions du Centurion.

Garavito, Julián
1968 "Rabinal Achi." *Europe* 473: 63–65. Paris.

García Hernández, Abraham, Santiago Yac Sam, and David Henne Pontious, eds.
1980 *Diccionario quiché-español*. Guatemala: Instituto Lingüístico de Verano.

Garza, Mercedes de la
1989 "Los alucinógenos en la religión maya." *Memorias del II Coloquio Internacional de Mayistas (Campeche, 17–22 de agosto de 1987)*, pp. 1399–1409. Mexico: Centro de Estudios Mayas, Instituto de Investigaciones Filológicas, Universidad Nacional Autónoma de México.

Gillin, John
1952 "Ethos and Cultural Aspects of Personality." In *Heritage of Conquest: The Ethnology of Middle America*, edited by Sol Tax, pp. 193–222. Glencoe: Viking Fund Seminar on Middle American Ethnology.

Gossen, Gary H.
1974 *Chamulas in the World of the Sun: Time and Space in a Maya Oral Tradition*. Cambridge, Mass.: Harvard University Press.

Guzmán, Pantaleón de

1984 *Compendio de nombres en lengua cakchiquel* [1704]. Edited by René Acuña. Gramáticas y diccionarios 1. Mexico: Instituto de Investigaciones Filológicas, Universidad Nacional Autónoma de México.

Hanks, William F.

1989 "Elements of Maya Style." In *Word and Image in Maya Culture: Explorations in Language, Writing, and Representation*, edited by William F. Hanks and Don S. Rice, pp. 92–111. Salt Lake City: University of Utah Press.

1992 "Intertextualité de l'espace au Yucatán." *L'Homme: Revue Française d'Anthropologie* 122–124(2–4): 53–74. Paris: École des Hautes Études en Sciences Sociales.

Henríquez Ureña, Pedro

1936 "El teatro de la América española en la época colonial." *Cuadernos de cultura teatral* 3: 9–50. Buenos Aires.

Hill, Robert M., II, and John Monaghan

1987 *Continuities in Highland Maya Social Organization: Ethnohistory in Sacapulas, Guatemala.* Philadelphia: University of Pennsylvania Press.

Himelblau, Jack J.

1989 *Quiche Worlds in Creation: The Popol Vuh as a Narrative Work of Art.* Culver City: Labyrinthos.

Ichon, Alain

1982 "Identification de quelques sites protohistoriques dans la région de Rabinal et Cubulco." *Cahiers de la RCP 500* 4: 55–77. Paris: Centre National de la Recherche Scientifique and Institut d'Ethnologie.

Ichon, Alain, Denise Douzant-Rosenfeld, and Pierre Usselmann

1988 *La vallée moyenne du Chixoy (Guatemala), 6: Occupation préhispanique et problèmes actuels.* Paris: Centre National de la Recherche Scientifique and Institut d'Ethnologie.

Jakobson, Roman

1963 *Essais de linguistique générale,* 1: *Les fondations du langage.* Paris: Les Éditions de Minuit.

Kozinska Frybes, Joanna

1985 "El mundo de las representaciones precolombinas." MA thesis, University of Varsovia.

Kubler, George

1989 "Brasseur de Bourbourg: Americanista." In *Memorias del II Coloquio Internacional de Mayistas (Campeche, 17–22 de agosto de 1987)*, pp. 1119–1124. Mexico: Centro de Estudios Mayas, Instituto de Investigaciones Filológicas, Universidad Nacional Autónoma de México.

Kuhn, Thomas S.

1962 *The Structure of Scientific Revolutions.* Chicago: University of Chicago Press.

L'abeille, l'homme, le miel et la cire

1981 *Catalogue de l'exposition du Musée national des arts et traditions populaires (23 octobre 1981–19 avril 1982).* Paris: Ministère de la Culture, Éditions de la Réunion des Musées Nationaux.

Landa, Diego de
1978 *Relación de las cosas de Yucatán*. Mexico: Editorial Porrúa.

Le Bot, Yvon
1992 *La guerre en terre maya: Communauté, violence et modernité au Guatemala*. Paris: Éditions Karthala.

Le Clézio, Jean-Marie Gustave
1976 *Les prophéties du Chilam Balam*. Paris: NRF-Gallimard.

Leinaweaver, Richard E.
1968 "Rabinal Achi: Commentary and English Translation." *Latin American Theater Review* 1(2): 3–53. University of Kansas, Center of Latin American Studies [English version from Monterde 1955].

Lincoln, J. Steward
1942 "The Maya Calendar of the Ixil of Guatemala." *Contributions to American Anthropology and History* 38: 98–128. Washington, D.C.
1945 *An Ethnological Study on the Ixil Indians of the Guatemala Highlands*. Microfilm Collection of Manuscripts on Middle American Cultural Anthropology 1. Chicago: University of Chicago Library.

Lovell, William George
1985 *Conquest and Survival in Colonial Guatemala: A Historical Geography of the Cuchumatán Highlands, 1500–1821*. Kingston: McGill-Queen's University Press.

Mace, Carroll Edward
1967a "New Information about Dance-Dramas of Rabinal and Rabinal-Achí." *Xavier University Studies* 6(1): 1–19. New Orleans.
1967b "Nueva y más reciente información sobre los bailes-drama de Rabinal y del descubrimiento del Rabinal-Achí." *Antropología e Historia de Guatemala* 19: 20–37 [revised Spanish version from Mace 1967a].
1970 *Two Spanish-Quiché Dance-Dramas of Rabinal*. Tulane Studies in Romance Languages and Literature 3. New Orleans: Tulane University.
1973 "Charles Étienne Brasseur de Bourbourg, 1814–1874." In *Handbook of Middle American Indians, 13: Guide to Ethnohistorical Sources*, edited by Howard F. Cline and John B. Glass, part 2, pp. 298–325. Austin: University of Texas Press.
1981 "Algunos apuntes sobre los bailes de Guatemala y de Rabinal." *Mesoamérica* 2: 83–136. Antigua Guatemala and South Woodstock.

Martínez, Marcos
n.d. Arte de la lengua utlateca o kiche, vulgarmente llamado el Arte de Totonicapan [17th century]. Manuscript in the Bibliothèque nationale, Paris.

Miles, Suzanna W.
1957 "The Sixteenth-Century Pokom-Maya: A Documentary Analysis of Social Structure and Archaeological Setting." *Transactions of American Philosophical Society* 47(4): 735–781. Philadelphia.

Montalbán, Leonardo
1929 "Rabinal Achí." In *Historia de la literatura de la América central*, 2 vols. San Salvador: Talleres tipográficos del Ministerio de Instrucción Pública.
1945 "Rabinal Achí." *Revue de l'Institut français d'Amérique latine* 2: 115–140. Mexico [reprint from Montalbán 1929].

Monterde, Francisco

1955 *Teatro indígena prehispánico (Rabinal Achí)*. Biblioteca del Estudiante Universitario 71. Mexico: Universidad Nacional Autónoma de México [revised version from Raynaud and Cardoza y Aragón 1953].

1963 "Rabinal-Achí: Drama-ballet maya-quiché." *Cuadernos de Bellas Artes* 4(12): 73–92 and 5(1): 69–84. Mexico [reprint from Monterde 1955].

1980 "Rabinal Achí." In *Literatura maya*, edited by Mercedes de la Garza et al., 291–341. Biblioteca Ayacucho 57. Barcelona: Editorial Galaxis [reprint from Monterde 1955].

Neuenswander, Helen

1986 *Dualism: A Linguistic and Cultural Phenomenon among the Cubulco Achi (Mayan)*. Ethnology Series 1. Guatemala: Instituto Lingüístico de Verano.

Norman, William M.

1983 "Paralelismo gramatical en el lenguaje ritual quiché." In *Nuevas perspectivas sobre el Popol Vuh*, edited by Robert M. Carmack and Francisco Morales Santos, pp. 109–121. Guatemala: Editorial Piedra Santa.

Oakes, Maud

1973 *The Two Crosses of Todos Santos: Survivals of Mayan Religious Ritual*. Princeton, N.J., Princeton University Press [1st ed. 1951].

Omont, Henri

1925 *Catalogue des manuscrits américains de la Bibliothèque nationale*. Paris: Librairie ancienne Honoré Champion, Édouard Champion.

Orellana, Sandra Lee

1984 *The Tzutujil Mayas: Continuity and Change, 1250–1630*. Norman: University of Oklahoma Press.

Padial Guerchoux, Anita Louise, and A. Manuel Vázquez-Bigi

1991 *Quiché Vinak: Tragedia: Nueva versión española y estudio histórico-literario del llamado "Rabinal-Achí."* Colección Popular 446. Mexico: Fondo de Cultura Económica.

Palm, Walter

1961 *Der Mann von Rabinal, oder Der Tod des Gefangenen, Tanzspiel der Maya-Quiché*. Frankfurt: Suhrkamp Verlag [German version from Monterde 1955, with an introduction and epilogue].

Percheron, Nicole

1982 "Essai ethnohistorique sur l'occupation de la Baja Verapaz au Postclassique (XIIe-XVIe siècle)." *Cahiers de la RCP 500* 4: 9–54. Paris: Centre National de la Recherche Scientifique and Institut d'Ethnologie.

Péret, Benjamin

1955 *Livre de Chilam Balam de Chumayel*. Paris: Denoël.

1989 *Anthologie des mythes, légendes et contes populaires d'Amérique*. Paris: Albin Michel [1st ed. 1960].

Piel, Jean

1989 *Sajcabajá. Muerte y resurrección de un pueblo de Guatemala, 1500–1970*. Mexico and Guatemala: Centro Francés de Estudios Mexicanos y Centroamericanos and Seminario de Integración Social Guatemalteca.

Pinart, Alphonse-Louis

1883 *Catalogue des livres rares et précieux, manuscrits et imprimés, principalement sur l'Amérique et sur les langues du monde entier.* Paris: Librairie Veuve Adolphe Labitte.

Pruner-Bey, Franz

1863 "Rapport sur l'ouvrage de M. Brasseur de Bourbourg: Grammaire de la langue quiché et vocabulaire: Drame quiché 'Rabinal Achi,' musique de Guatemala (Paris, 1862)," *Bulletin de la Société d'anthropologie* 4: 8–17. Paris.

Ramos Elorduy de Conconi, Julieta

1982 *Los insectos como fuente de proteínas en el futuro.* Mexico: Editorial Limusa.

Raynaud, Georges

1980 *Le Popol Vuh: Les dieux, les héros et les hommes de l'ancien Guatémala, d'après le Livre du Conseil.* Paris: Librairie d'Amérique et d'Orient, Adrien Maisonneuve [1st ed. 1925. Paris: Ernest Leroux].

Raynaud, Georges, and Luis Cardoza y Aragón

1929–30 "Rabinal-Achí: El Varón de Rabinal: Ballet-Drama de los Indios Quichés de Guatemala (con la música indígena)." *Anales de la Sociedad de Geografía e Historia* 6(1): 45–51, (2): 197–201, (3): 347–370, (4): 381–391. Guatemala.

1953 *Rabinal-Achí: El Varón de Rabinal: Ballet-Drama de los Indios Quichés de Guatemala (con la música indígena).* Biblioteca Popular "20 de octubre" 43. Guatemala: Ministerio de Educación Pública [reprint from Raynaud and Cardoza y Aragón 1929–1930].

1972 *Rabinal-Achí: El Varón de Rabinal: Ballet-Drama de los Indios Quichés de Guatemala (con la música indígena).* Sepan Cuantos . . . 219. Mexico: Editorial Porrúa [idem].

Recinos, Adrián

1947 *El Popol Vuh: Las antiguas historias del Quiché.* Mexico: Fondo de Cultura Económica.

1980 *Memorial de Sololá, Anales de los Cakchiqueles: Título de los Señores de Totonicapán,* translated from Quiché by Dionisio José Chonay. Guatemala: Instituto de Antropología e Historia and Editorial Piedra Santa [1st ed. 1950].

1984 *Crónicas indígenas de Guatemala.* Guatemala: Academia de Geografía e Historia [1st ed. 1957].

Recinos, Adrián, and Delia Goetz

1974 *The Annals of the Cakchiquels: Title of the Lords of Totonicapán,* translated from Quiché by Dionisio José Chonay. Norman: University of Oklahoma Press [1st ed. 1953].

Recinos, Adrián, Delia Goetz, and Sylvanus G. Morley

1977 *Popol Vuh: The Sacred Book of the Ancient Quiché Maya.* Norman: University of Oklahoma Press [1st ed. 1950].

Ridder, Robert J.M. de

1989 *The Poetic Popol Vuh: An Anthropological Study.* Utrecht: Rijksuniversiteit.

Rodríguez Rouanet, Francisco

1962 "Notas sobre una representación actual del Rabinal Achí o Baile del Tun." *Guatemala indígena* 2(1): 45–56. Guatemala.

Sacor Quiché, Hugo Fidel, Silvia Álvarez Aguilar, and Enrique Anleu Díaz

1991 *Rabinal Achi o Danza del Tun*. Cuadernos de Investigación 1-90. Guatemala: Universidad de San Carlos, Dirección General de Investigación.

Santo Domingo, Tomás de

1693 Vocabulario de las lenguas cakchiquel y castellana. Manuscript in the Bibliothèque nationale, Paris.

Saquic Calel, Felipe Rosalío

1989 *Idioma quiché/Quiché Language*. Guatemala: Editorial Piedra Santa.

Schele, Linda, and David A. Freidel

1990 *A Forest of Kings: The Untold Story of the Ancient Maya*. New York: Quill, William Morrow.

Shaw, Mary, ed.

1972 *Según nuestros antepasados: Textos folklóricos de Guatemala y Honduras*. Guatemala: Instituto Lingüístico de Verano.

Siméon, Rémi

1986 *Diccionario de la lengua nahuatl o mexicana.* Mexico: Siglo XXI [1st ed. 1885, Paris: Imprimerie nationale].

Smith, A. Ledyard

1955 *Archaeological Reconnaissance in Central Guatemala*. Publication 108. Washington, D.C.: Carnegie Institution of Washington.

Sodi Morales, Demetrio

1964 *La literatura de los Mayas*. Mexico: Editorial Joaquín Mortiz.

Soustelle, Jacques

1979 *L'Univers des Aztèques*. Paris: Hermann.

Tedlock, Barbara

1991 *Time and the Highland Maya*. Albuquerque: University of New Mexico Press [1st ed. 1982].

Tedlock, Dennis

1983a *The Spoken Word and the Work of Interpretation*. Philadelphia: University of Pennsylvania Press.

1983b "Las formas del verbo quiché." In *Nuevas perspectivas sobre el Popol Vuh*, edited by Robert M. Carmack and Francisco Morales Santos, pp. 123-132. Guatemala: Editorial Piedra Santa.

Tedlock, Dennis, ed.

1985 *Popol Vuh: The Mayan Book of the Dawn of Life*. New York, Simon & Schuster.

Teletor, Celso Narciso

1945 "Bailes que representan los indígenas en la Baja Verapaz." *Anales de la Sociedad de Geografía e Historia* 20(1): 51-52. Guatemala.

1955 *Apuntes para una monografía de Rabinal (B. V.) y algo de nuestro folklore*. Guatemala: Editorial del Ministerio de Educación Pública.

Termer, Franz

1957 *Etnología y etnografía de Guatemala*. Guatemala: Seminario de Integración Social Guatemalteca.

Tirado, Fermín Joseph

1787 Vocabulario de lengua kiche. Manuscript in the Tozzer Library, Peabody Museum of Archaeology and Ethnology, Harvard University, Cambridge Mass. [copy of a more ancient and anonymous document].

Toledo Palomo, Ricardo

1965 "Los bailes del tum en los siglos XVI y XVII." *Folklore de Guatemala* 1: 61–67. Guatemala.

Torresano, Estevan

1754 Arte de lengua kakchikel. Manuscript in the Bibliothèque nationale, Paris.

Tovilla, Martín Al[f]onso

1960 *Relación histórica descriptiva de las provincias de la Verapaz y de la del Manché del Reino de Guatemala* [1635]. Edited by France V. Scholes and Eleanor B. Adams. Guatemala: Editorial Universitaria, Universidad de San Carlos.

Townsend, Paul G.

1980 *Ritual Rhetoric from Cotzal*. Guatemala: Instituto Lingüístico de Verano.

Varea, Francisco de

n.d. Calepino en lengua cakchiquel [ca. 1620]. Manuscript in the American Philosophical Society Library, Philadelphia [copy dated 1699, signed by Francisco Cerón].

Vázquez, Francisco

1937–44 *Crónica de la provincia del Santísimo Nombre de Jesús de Guatemala de la orden de nuestro seráfico padre San Francisco* [1714–1717], 4 vols. Biblioteca Goathemala 14–17. Guatemala: Sociedad de Geografía e Historia de Guatemala.

Vico, Domingo de

n.d.a Vocabulario de la lengua cakchiquel, con advertencia de los vocablos de las lenguas quiché y tzutohil [16th century]. Manuscript in the Bibliothèque nationale, Paris [anonymous copy from the 17th century].

n.d.b Arte de la lengua qiche ó utlatecat, seguido del modo de bien vivir, en la misma lengua [16th century]. Manuscript in the Bibliothèque nationale, Paris [anonymous copy from the 18th century].

Villacañas, Benito de

n.d. Arte y vocabulario de la lengua cakchiquel [ca. 1692]. Microfilm in the University Museum Library, University of Pennsylvania, Philadelphia.

Villacorta Calderón, José Antonio

1942 "Rabinal Achí, pieza escénica de los antiguos quichés de Rabinal." *Anales de la Sociedad de Geografía e Historia* 17(5): 352–375. Guatemala.

Yurchenco, Henrietta

1978 *Music of the Maya-Quichés of Guatemala: The Rabinal Achi and Baile de las Canastas*. Album no. FE 4226. New York: Folkways Records.

1986 "El baile de las canastas y otras sobrevivencias del teatro prehispánico maya-quiché." *Anales de la Academia de Geografía e Historia de Guatemala* 60: 75–87. Guatemala.

Ximénez, Francisco

1926 *Escolios a las historias del origen de los indios de esta provincia de Guatemala*. San Salvador: Ediciones de la Biblioteca Nacional.

1929–31 *Historia de la provincia de San Vicente de Chiapa y Guatemala de la Orden de predicadores* [ca. 1715–1720], 3 vols. Biblioteca Goathemala, 1–3. Guatemala: Sociedad de Geografía e Historia de Guatemala.

1975 *Historia de la provincia de San Vicente de Chiapa y Guatemala de la Orden de predicadores*, 4 vols. Guatemala: Ministerio de Educación.

1985 *Primera parte del Tesoro de las lenguas cakchiquel, quiché y zutuhil, en que las dichas lenguas se traducen a la nuestra, española* [ca. 1710]. Edited by Carmelo Sáenz de Santa María. Guatemala: Academia de Geografía e Historia de Guatemala.

1993 *Arte de las tres lenguas kaqchikel, k'iche' y tz'utujil* [ca. 1710–1715]. Edited by Rosa Helena Chinchilla Mazariegos. Biblioteca Goathemala 31. Guatemala: Academia de Geografía e Historia de Guatemala.

Index

Page numbers in italics indicate illustrations.

Absence: of a narrator, 5; as a structural characteristic of the warrior, 150(n74), 183(n141), 287, 290, 302, 303, 306
Academia de las Lenguas Mayas, 51
Achi Ajaw, 299(n17), 313
Achij Mun Ixoq Mun (character), 27, 31(n53), 33–34, 125(n7), 293(n11). *See also* Slaves
Acropolis, of Kajyub, 29(n46)
Actor, 5, 27, 34, 292–293, 295
Adoption, 300, 302
Age, 138(n48), 145(n60); advancement in, 300; opposed to youth, 300; privilege of, 29, 299
Agouti *(Dacyprocta punctata)*, 143(n56)
Agriculture: in opposition with hunting, 302, 315; in relation to the calendar, 38
Ah Pop, 296
Aj Kejay, 301(n19)
Ajaw, 29, 34, 35, 37, 38, 124(n2), 125(n3), 143(n57), 169(n114), 254(n214), 297–300. *See also* King; Lords
Ajaw Teken Toj Teken Tijax (character), 36–38
Ajkejay, 21, 23. *See also* Aj Kejay
Alcaldes, 295
Allegiance, act of, 26
Alliance: matrimonial, 32, 33(n57), 221(n193), 306, 308, 315; political, 22, 26, 142, 292
Alta Verapaz, *8*, 32, 133(n32), 185(n146)
Altar, 284; in Catholic church, 299(n17); pre-Hispanic, 39(n74), 283
Alvarado, Pedro de, 38(n68), 277(n230), 302(n21)
Ambiguity: as a rhetorical figure, 46, 293; of the relationships, 42, 300
American wolf. *See* Coyote
Analepsis, 142(n53)
Anales de los Cakchiqueles, 2, 3, 7(n13), 19, 21, 23, 38(n72), 41(n80), 292, 312, 316
Anales de los Xahil, 7(n13)
Ancestors, 35, 129(n17), 299, 301, 313, 314; food of, 144(n59), 314; living conditions of, 21; migration of, 32, 299; relations with the living, 127(n12), 169(n114); respect to, 29; speech of, 49
Animals, 142–143(n56), 144, 219(n187), 301, 312, 313; hunted, 311
Ant tree (*Platymiscium*), 256(n216)
Antigua, *20*, 135(n25)
Antonomasia, as a rhetoric figure, 33(n58)

Ants, 311, 313. *See also* Animals; Bees; Flies; Insect; *Zompopo*
Apiculture, techniques of, 311, 312(n27). *See also* Bees; Hives
Apidae, 154(n59). *See also* Apiculture; Bees; Hives
Apu Ollantay, 7(n11)
Aq'ab, 23. *See also* Kawinal
Archaeological site, 22, 23, 27, 30, 38, 139, 176, 195(n158), 282, 283, 286(n4), 313(n29)
Archaeology, 19, 40, 167(n107), 177(n129), 313(n29)
Archaism, in language, 2, 220
Archivo General de Centroamérica (Guatemala), 284, 296
Arms, 31; coat of, 39; to carry in, 299, 303; and legs, 168
Arrow, 39(n74), 128(n15), 154(n86), 172(n120). *See also* Weapons
Atalaya, 41(n78)
Atitlán, 38(n70). *See also* Lake Atitlán; *Memorial de Tecpán-Atitlán*; Santiago Atitlán
Atlantic coast, 19. *See also* Gulf
Attack, 309; against the Quiché, 41(n6), 297; against the Rabinaleb, 24, 42, 288, 289(n6), 305, 310
Author, of the *Rabinal Achi*, 4, 5
Authority: indigenous conception of, 241(n207); of the king, 6, 241(n207), 297, 298, 300, 302; of the Quiché, 27, 41, 279, 287, 302, 306, 310; Spanish Catholic, 3; of the village, 266(n225)
Ax, 235(n205), 312(n27). *See also* Hatchet; Weapons
Aztec, 5, 22, 37, 150(n75), 277(n230), 299(n17)

Baja Verapaz, *8*, 22
Bakaj, 21. *See also* Wuqamaq'
Balam Ajaw Balam K'iche' (character), 26, 35–36, 41, 297, 307
Balam Akap (Quiché ruler), 23
Balam Kej (dance), 5(n7)
Balam K'itze' (Quiché ruler), 23, 35
Balamwak, 281, 284, 289, 290
Ballgame, 32(nn54, 56)
Barrios, 191(n155)
Bath, 284. *See also* Steam bath
Battle, 4, 21, 133(n32), 157(n93), 307
Bean (*Phaseolus*), 316; types of, 147(n69), 178, 305
Bees, 39, 144, 312(n27), 313–314; hunting of, 194(n157), 301, 311, 313. *See also* Ants; Flies; Hives; Insect
Belej Tz'aq Belej K'oxtun, 282
Belejeb Moqoj Belejeb Chumay, 280, 282, 302(n22)
Beleju, 25
Bibliothèque nationale (Paris), 1, 12, 50, 319
Bird, 31, 39, 276(nn229, 230), 277(n231). *See also* Feather
Bleeding, 135(n38); for prophylactic purposes, 157(n93); ritual before battle, 4, 287, 305. *See also* Battle; Drum; Trumpet
Bone, carved out, 132(n28). *See also* Skull
Border, 25, 42, 133(n32), 155(n89), 288, 296, 303; control and defense of, 22, 24, 41(n78), 224(n197), 295; disputed, 314; reinforcement of, 289
Boundaries, 166(n105), 295, 296, 303
Bow. *See* Arrow
Bracelet, 31, 132(n28)
Breadnut tree (*Brossimum*), 194(n158), 312(n27)
Brother, 26, 142(n53), 202(n166), 297, 306; in-arms, 292; in-law, 33(n57)

Cacao (*Theobroma*), 150(nn75–77), 167(n109), 305, 306, 307(n25)
Cahabón (river), 32
Cajcoj, 25. *See also Título Cajcoj*
Cakchiquel (group), 19, 21, 22, 23, 30(n48), 31, 41, 128(n15), 220(n191), 283, 297, 301, 302(n21); as allied to the Quiché, 24; capital of, 195(n158); conflicts with the Quiché, 4
Cakchiquel (language), 1(n1), 37, 39(n73), 50, 145(n61), 212(n176), 220(n191), 221(n194)
Calendar, 75; as origin of name, 28, 124(n1); in relation with agriculture, 38; ritual and divinatory (260 days), 29, 304; solar (365 days), 37
Canillá, *20,* 282
Cannibalism, 146(n66). *See also* Food; Sacrifice; Sacrificial victims
Canopy, 166(n106), 209(n172). *See also* Throne
Capital (town), *20, 286;* of the Cakchiquel, 194–195(n158) (*see also* Iximché); of the Poq'omab, 23, 312 (*see also* Chwitinamit; Kaqjay; Pakaqja); of the Quiché, 19, 21, 38–41, 188(n141), 287, 303, 306, 310 (*see also* Q'umarkaj; Utatlán); of the Rabinaleb, 19, 21, 24, 25, 27, 30, 280, 286(n4), 291, 303, 305 (*see also* Kajyub; Tzamaneb). *See also* City

Captive, 26, 28, 133(n34), 134(n36), 261(n222). *See also* Capture; Prisoner
Capture, 26, 27, 273(n228), 279, 290(n7), 291, 296, 305, 310, 315
Cardinal points, 170(n115), 296
Castration: of the hives, 311–313. *See also* Hives
Cave, 313
Center, 170(n115), 181(n138); ceremonial, 22, 117(n129); as domain of the king, 298, 303; village, 191(n155); of the world, 35, 304. *See also* Navel
Ceremony, 3, 49; of investiture, 128; to solicit rain, 283; to Xipe Totec, 37
Chajoma (group), 30(n48). *See also Título Chajoma*
Chajul, *20,* 28, 36, 45, 125(n2), 132(n26)
Chak (Mayan god), 30
Chakach, 220(n191)
Chakachib Tzamanib, 29–30, 35, 307. *See also* Tzamaneb
Chapel, 283
Charamiyex (dance), 5(n7)
Chatinibal, 281, 284, 286(n4), 289, 303. *See also* Bath; Kidnapping
Chiapas, 35(n62)
Chiché, 282, *286*
Chichen Itzá, 19
Chichicastenango, *20,* 21, 282
Chichimeca, 299(n17), 302
Chi Kabraqan, *286.* *See also* Chi Nim Che'
Chikaqyuq'. *See* Kajyub; Kaqyuq' Tzilik Kakoqonik Tepekanik
Chi K'arkaraxaj. *See* Balamwak
Chi K'otom, 280, 282, 287
Chi Kunu. *See* Balamwak
Chilam Balam, 2
Children, 9, 10, 18, 35, 127(n12), 143(n57), 153(n82), 172(n120), 279, 280, 288–289, 290, 291, 297, 298, 301(n18), 303, 305–306, 308–310, 316. *See also* Vassals
Chinautla, *20,* 25, 312
Chi Nim Che', 280, 282, 284
Chi Pixab, 21, 24
Chi Q'osibal Taq'aj Tulul. *See* Balamwak
Chi Rok'obaya Tz'ikin, 280, 282, 305
Chisalin, 41(n78)
Chisaliya, 280, 283, *285,* 291, 303
Chismachi. *See* Pismachi
Chi Tikram. *See* Chi K'otom
Chi Tintot Wi Poqlaj. *See* Balamwak
Chitukan, 282, *285*
Chiwiloy, 22
Chixoy (river), 19, *20,* 21, 22
Cholochik Jyub Cholochik Chaj, 280, 282
Cholochik Tz'aq Chun. *See* Chi Rok'obaya Tz'ikin
Chontalpa, 19
Choreography, 4, 5, 6, 18(n29)
Chorti, 42(n82), 45(n85)
Chronology, 25, 48, 50, 256, 288
Chuacus (sierra), *8,* 21, 23, 24
Chuaq'enum, 282
Chuwila. *See* Chichicastenango
Chwamonte', 284
Chwirok'bal, *281,* 282
Chwitinamit, *20,* 21, 25(n40), *285,* 313
Citadel. *See* Fortress
City, 39–41, 191(n155), 194(n158), 291
Classic period, 22, 33(n57), 316
Clothing, 26, 33(n58), 145(n61)
Clouds, 29, 133(n34), 167(n109), 186(n148), 296, 305. *See also* Cold; Danger; Desolation
Cobán, *20,* 31(n53), 32, 33, 313. *See also* Alta Verapaz; K'ekchi
Codex Padilla, 7(n13)
Cofradías, 49, 220(n191)
Cold, 155(n89), 167(n109), 219(n186), 296, 303, 305
Coloch Garniga, José-León: family of, 18; as friend and informant, 13, 18, 29, 32, 39, 49
Colonial period, 3, 4, 25, 34, 157(n93), 194(n157), 312(n27). *See also* Spanish Colony
Colors, 31, 168(n113), 219(n187)
Commemoration, 6, 279
Conflict: between king and warrior, 302; on the possession of the *Rabinal Achi,* 18; between Rabinaleb and Poq'omab, 48, 300, 305, 313(n29), 314; between Rabinaleb and Quiché, 19–22, 27–28, 35, 280, 287, 292, 300, 314
Conquest, 21, 155(n89), 157(n93), 171(n118), 176(n127), 290, 292, 302–303, 314–315; of the basin of Rabinal, 23, 24, 25, 133(n32), 180(n138), 280, 291; of the Ixil region, 36(n66); Spanish, 4, 5, 10, 13(n25), 22, 36(n66), 38(n70), 312(n27)
Corn, 305, 314
Corn tree. *See* Breadnut tree (*Brossimum*)
Corners, of the world, 170(n115), 181(n138), 297, 304, 309. *See also* Cardinal points
Corpus Christi, 28(n46)
Council, 21, 41, 306. *See also* Authority, of the Quiché
Coyote *(Canis),* 142(n56), 301, 309

Crickets, 146(n64). *See also* Desolation; Destruction
Crown of Spain, 2
Cuatrillo, 51
Cubulco, 4, *20*, 21, 22, 23, 133(n32), 185(n145), *281*, 282, 283, 284, 286, 289(n6), 295(n13), 313
Cuchumatanes (Sierra), *8*, 21, 36(n66), 124(n2)
Cunen, *20*, 36(n66), 125(n2), 132(n26)

Dais, of feathers, 299. *See also* Canopy; Throne
Dance, 31, 156–157(n93), 221(n193); before battles, 4; before sacrifice, 261(n222); of *Quiché Vinak*, 4; of *Rabinal Achi*, 5, 6, 13, 15, 18, 27, 33, 34, 35, 130(n21), 235, 283, 295, 301, 303; of the Tun, 3, 14 (*see also Xajoj Tun*); war/warrior, 3, 4, 133(n32)
Danger, 167(n109), 296, 303
Darkness, 302, 313, 314
Datura stramonium, 218(n185)
Dawn, 21, 29(n46), 35, 176(n128)
Day, 127(n13), 173(n121), 176(n128), 302, 306, 309, 314; associated to birth, 132(n31), 301; calendrical, 29(n45), 37, 181(n138), 304 (*see also* Calendar); Rabinal as original place of, 35(n63)
Death, 26, 276–277(nn230, 231), 300, 302, 307, 315
Defeat, 133(n34), 171(n118), 174(n123), 234(n203), 244(n210), 276(n230), 302(n22), 309
Defense. *See* Border
Deixis, 5, 151(n77)
Desolation, 133(n34), 146(n64). *See also* Destruction
Destiny, 234(n203), 300, 304
Destruction, 281, 289, 291
Dialogue, 27, 53, 130(n21), 142(n53), 171(n118), 228(n200), 288, 295; accompanying dances, 5(n7); constructing the story, 19, 47; loss of, 48; overlapping, 2, 46, 53; pieces of, 259(n219), 292–293; uselessness of, 293(n12)
Diegesis, 27, 142(n54)
Dignitary, 5, 38(n68), 277(n231), 309
Dignity, 298
Directions. *See* Cardinal points; Corners
Discourse, 5, 43, 53, 295, 317(n30); direct, 46, 53, 293; formal and ritual, 42(n81), 44, 170(n115), 237(n206); modern, 171(n115); overlapping, 293 (*see also* Dialogue); reported, 46, 48, 53
Diviners. *See* Healers
Divinity, 28, 304; affiliation to, 28; of rain, 30. *See also* God
Drink, 26, 218(n185), 219(n188), 221(n194), 287, 314. *See also* Food
Drum, 132(n26); of the bleeding, 287, 305; slit, 3(n3), 256(n216); with stretched skins, 256(n216). *See also* Bleeding; Music; Musical instruments; Trumpet
Duality, 30, 299

E' (Quiché ruler), 23–24
Eagle, 34; warrior, 27, 34, 259(n219), 293(n11)
Earth, 43, 170(n115), 284, 293(n11), 295, 297, 309. *See also* Navel
East, 155(n89), 171(n116), 224(n197), 309
Eating, 138(n47), 144(n59), 219(n188), 310, 314. *See also* Drink; Food
Ekempek, 280, 282, 313
Emerald. *See* Stone, precious
Enemy, 28, 292, 293(n12), 297, 310. *See also* Brother
Epi-Toltec, 19, 24, 41. *See also* Toltec
Eponymy, between ruler and place, 41, 151(n78), 176(n126), 298(n15)
Estancias. See Barrios
Ethnohistoriography, 301, 317
Ethnonym, 28, 30(n48), 293, 311–312
Etymology, 28, 30, 283, 311; folk, 28, 176(n128)
Expedition, 4, 42, 289, 303, 310

Father, 10, 13, 19, 21, 26, 31(n52), 35, 287, 297, 300; terminology for, 169(n114), 254(n214); without, 133(n34)
Feast, of Saint Paul and Saint Sebastian, 6
Feather, 31, 221(n193), 231(n201), 276(n230), 298(n16), 305; object of tribute, 167(n109); throne and dais of, 166(n106), 299; workers and artisans, 167(n108), 306. *See also* Jewels; Paraphernalia; Quetzal
Female, 31; male and, 33–34
Fertility, 37; of land, 27, 179(n136), 303, 305
Fight, 34, 133(n32), 154(n86), 194(n157), 294, 307. *See also* Battle; War; Warrior
Flies, 311, 313, 314; of honey, 144(n59), 195(n158), 305, 309–311. *See also* Bees; Hives; Honey; Insect
Flight, of the Uxab Poq'omab, 25(n41), 280, 288, 307, 311, 313, 315
Food, 26, 144(n59), 145(n63), 168(n112), 219(n190), 305, 306, 308–310, 313–314; for the god, 138(n47); for the king, 303, 305, 313. *See also* Eating

Fortress, 24, 40, 43, 139(n49), 145(n63), 151(nn77–78), 177(n129), 308–310; as military garrison, 291; as opposed to ravines, 167(n109); in ruins, 186(n109), 290; residence of the king and lords, 26, 41, 129(n18), 155(n89), 298–299. *See also* Center

García Peláez, Francisco de Paula, 7
Gathering: in relation with hunting, 225(n198), 301(n18), 302(n20), 303, 309, 311–312, 314. *See also* Bees; Hunting
Gems. *See* Stone, precious
Generation, 143, 168–169(n114), 300; dynastic, 21, 36
Genre, 34; literary, 3, 4, 5, 46, 317; the trial as specific, 316
Gnats. *See* Ants; Bees; Flies; Insect
God, 21; food for, 138(n47), 310 (*see also* Food); offering to, 316; of the Quiché, 28, 310; sun, 277(n230). *See also* Divinity
Gómez, Félix, 29(n45)
Governor, 41, 288. *See also* King; Lords
Grandchildren, 168(n114). *See also* Children
Grandfather, 10, 13, 29(n47), 169(n114). *See also* Father; Grandchildren
Gravity. *See* Authority, indigenous conception of
Gulf: Atlantic coast of the, 19; of Mexico, 24

Hamlet, in relation to village, 185(n145), 289. *See also* Settlement pattern
Hatchet, 132(n26), 295. *See also* Ax; Weapons
Healers, 29(n45), 284
Hero, 297
Historia Quiché de don Juan de Torres, 3, 144(n59), 166(n105), 301, 313
Hives, 144(n59), 311–313. *See also* Apiculture; Bees; Honey
Honey, 144–145(n59), 194(n157), 195(n158), 218(n185), 301, 305, 309–310, 311–313. *See also* Apiculture; Bees; Hives
House: of castration, 313; deserted, 146(n64); as lineage, 301(n19); long or great, 40(n77), 41; toll, 41
Hubris, 299
Huehuetenango, *20,* 21
Hummingbird, 218(n185), 277(n230)
Hunahpu, 32(n54)
Hunting, 27, 134(n36), 194(n157), 225(n198), 273(n228), 276(n229), 296, 301, 302, 303, 308–311, 313–315. *See also* Bees; Honey; Predator and prey

Ikomak'i, 21, 23. *See also* Wuqamaq'
Ilocab, 41(n78)
Immobility: of the king, 213, 299, 313. *See also* Mobility, of the warrior
Inca, 7(n11)
Independence, political and territorial, 23, 36(n66), 300, 302, 314, 316
Insect, 144–145(n59), 218, 313–314. *See also* Ants; Bees; Flies; Gnats; Hives
Insignia, of power, 31, 266(n225), 297. *See also* Paraphernalia
Investiture, of the king, 21, 128(n15)
Itzamna (Mayan god), 30
Ixil (group), 36(n66), 125(n2). *See also* Chajul; Nebaj
Ixil (language), 42(n82), 45(n85)
Iximché, *20,* 22, 194(n58). *See also* Cakchiquel; Capital (town)
Ixtink'urun, 180(n138), 280, 283, *286,* 291, 303, 304

Jade. *See* Stone, precious
Jaguar, 143(n56), 212(n178), 309; king, 36. *See also* Eagle
Jakawitz, 21, 35, 41
Jewels, 229. *See also* Stone, precious
Job Toj (character). *See* King
Journey, 295, 316; ancestral, 299(n17); of Job Toj, 299; of K'iche' Achi, 280, 282, 287, 303–304; of Rabinal Achi, 280, 283–284, 285, 289–290; of time in space, 181(n138). *See also* Traveling
Joyabaj, *20,* 21, 185(n146), 282, 284, 286, 287, 289
Justice, and marriage as functions of the king, 29, 299

Kajyub, *20,* 27, 48, 151(n77), 177(n129), 181(n138), 195(n158), 282, *285, 286,* 288, 291–292, 296, 301, 303, 305, 315; and Chwitinamit (Nim Poq'om), 21, 24, 25(n40), 313; as a definitive capital, 280, 291; as a military garrison, 291; and Pakaqja, 313; and Saqkijel, 25(n40); and Tzamaneb, 25, 290–291, 298(n15), 314, 316; and Utatlán-Q'umarkaj, 19, 286, 287, 306. *See also* Fortress
K'amba, 41, 283, *285, 286,* 304; conquered by K'iche' Achi, 180(n138), 280, 289, 291, 303; controlled by the Rabinaleb, 279, 288, 305
Kaqixajay. *See* Ikomak'i
Kaqjay, 23
Kaqyuq' Tzilik Kakoqonik Tepekanik, 26, 150(n77), 291(n8). *See also* Kajyub

Kaweq (Quiché lineage), 22, 28, 30, 35, 41
Kawinal, *20,* 23
Kawuq (Rabinal lineage), 29–30, 307
Kebatzunja, 21. *See also* Wuqamaq'
K'ekchi (group), 31(n53), 32, 33(n57), 34(n61)
K'ekchi (language), 1, 32(nn54, 56), 212(n178)
K'ibaja, 21. *See also* Wuqamaq'
K'iche' Winaq (dance). *See Quiché Vinak*
K'iche' Achi (character). *See* Rebel; Warrior
Kidnapping: of Job Toj, 213(n179), 279, 281, 284, 290, 291, 299; of Rabinaleb, 26, 290(n7); of the "white children," 279, 280, 288, 289, 291, 310
King: corporal characteristic of, 128(n15) (*see also* Perforation); figure of, 297–300; and the fortress, 26, 139(n49), 213(n181); initiatives of, 41, 299; as master of the rain and sacrifice, 38, 41; as a mediator, 26, 293; and the warriors, 46, 279, 280, 290, 291–292, 300–302, 303, 316
Kingdom: Quiché, 19, 21; of Uspantán, 36(n66). *See also* Royalty
Kinship, 35, 169(n114). *See also* Brother; Father; Grandfather; Grandchildren
K'iq'ab (Quiché ruler), 21–22, 23, 24, 25, 30, 38
K'isintun, 180(nn137, 138), 280, 283, *285, 286,* 291, 303, 304
K'okaib (Quiché ruler). *See* E'
K'otuja (Quiché ruler), 21
K'uluwach Abaj, 280, 284
Kumatza (river), 283
Kunen. *See* Cunen

La Parra, Francisco de, 15, 51
Ladinos, 124(n2)
Lake Atitlán, *20,* 21, 283
Lancet, 156(n93). *See also* Bleeding
Landa, Diego de, 13(n25), 312(n27)
Lanquín, *20,* 32(n54)
Lime, 162(n97), 188(n152), 281. *See also* Prison
Lineage, 21, 22, 35, 139; ancestral, 129(n17); dynastic or royal, 2, 133, 143. *See also* House
Liquors. *See* Drink
Loj Tum (dance), 3
López, Nicolás, 8, 10, 11
Lords: and the fortress, 41; and vassals, 35. *Ses also* Ajaw; King
Los Cimientos-Patzaj, 30, 286(n4)
Los Encuentros, 23(n35)
Lotzo Tun Lotzo Q'ojom (dance), 4
Lowlands, 32–33

Macehuales. *See* Vassals
Mahuk'utaj (Quiché ruler), 23
Male, 28, 33, 34, 294
Mam, 145(n60). *See also* Ancestors; Grandfather; Grandchildren
Marimba, 256(n216)
Marking: of the land, 155(n88); a territory, 166(n105), 176(nn125, 127), 303, 304. *See also* Measure
Mask, 34(n61), 49
Mayan languages, 29, 35(n62), 42(n82), 144(n59), 212(n178), 218(n185)
Mayan literature, 2, 7, 42
Measure, 188(n151); of territory and lands, 166(n105), 176(n125), 303; unit of, 150(n75)
Memorial de Tecpán-Atitlán, 7(n13)
Memory, 13, 29, 127(n12), 166(n105)
Mendoza, Bonifacia, 312(n27)
Messenger, 151(n77), 154(n85), 287, 306–307, 308
Metal, 166–167(n107), 305
Metamorphosis: into a bird, 276(n230); into insects, 277(n231), 288, 313
Mexica. *See* Aztec
Migration, 25, 302, 315, 317; ancestral, 32(n55), 166(n105), 299(n17), 301, 313; different phases of, 19, 23, 24, 292; of insects, 311, 313; as myth, 313–314; as a source of legitimacy, 19. *See also* Ancestors
Mimesis. *See* Diegesis
Missionaries. *See* Spanish missionaries
Mobility, of the warrior, 295. *See also* Immobility, of the king
Momostenango, 4, *20,* 295(n13), 304(n24)
Moqotz'u'um, 280, 283, 290
Motagua (river), *8, 20,* 21, 283
Mother, 154(n86), 220(n191); as a title, 31. *See also* Queen
Mukwits Pilocab, 41(n78)
Music, 6, 18(n29), 47, 260(n220), 261(n222)
Musical instruments, 18, 49(n94). *See also* Drum; Trumpet
Myth: and history, 301, 317; of creation of Rabinal, 29(n46), 35(n63), 299(n17), 313; of creation of Tres Cruces, 289(n6), 316; of migration, 314; of Momostenango, 285(n13). *See also Yegua Achi*; *Yew Achi*

Nacxit, 128(n15)
Nahua, 124(n2). *See also* Nahuatl
Nahuatl, 33(n58), 37, 38, 132(n30), 212(n178), 218(n185), 221(n194), 256(n216)
Navel, of the sky and the earth, 171(n118), 181(n138), 291, 298, 304, 305, 306, 308. *See also* Center
Nebaj, *20,* 304(n24)
Nijaib (Quiché lineage), 30
Nim ja. See House
Nim Poq'om. *See* Chwitinamit
Nimpokom, 23, 24. *See also* Chwitinamit
Noble, 38, 221(n193); as opposed to common folk and vassals, 35, 143(n57), 301(n18), 316. *See also* Lords

Ojob Toj. *See* Job Toj
Onomastic, 1(n1), 27, 30(n48)
Oral tradition, 4, 13, 25(n41), 49, 179(n136), 289(n6), 295(n13), 312, 313, 314, 316
Oronik Kaqjay, 312–313
Ox Tun (dance), 3

Pa Amaq'a. *See* Zacualpa
Paca *(Coelogenys)*, 212(n178)
Pachalib, 282
Pacific coast, 21
Pacing. *See* Measure
Padilla, José Mariano, 7, 9
Pakaqja, 23, *285,* 313(n29)
Palace, 215(n182), 280. *See also* Fortress
Pamaq'a. *See* Zacualpa
Pan Ch'alib, 280, 282, *286*
Pan K'aqil, 279, 280, 284, 289, 310
Pan Tz'ajaxaq, 280, 282, *286*
Panajache'el, 280, 283, 290
Panimaché, 282
Pank'aqil, *281, 286. See also* Pan K'aqil
Pantzuy, 133(n32)
Papel del origen de los señores, 22–24
Paradigm, 280, 301, 314–315, 317
Parallelism, 2, 42–46, 53
Paraphernalia, 31–33; of power, 298. *See also* Insignia
Paraweno. *See* Chi Nim Che'
Passion of Jesus Christ, 168(n111)
Pataxte. See Cacao
Patronym, 30(n48), 311
Patzaktzuy, 23
Patzka: as ancestors, 299(n17), 313; dance, 5(n7)
Peace, 300, 314; recommendations of, 37, 249(n211), 279, 287, 306
Pérez Manuscript: and Brasseur's edition, 15–18, 47–49; facsimile of, 55–122
Pérez, Manuel, 15, 16, 18, 47–49, 51, 131(n24), 137(n46)
Perforation, 128(n15). *See also* Investiture
Periphery, as domain of the warrior, 303. *See also* Cold; Danger
Piercing, 133(n31), 211(n177). *See also* Perforation
Pismachi, 21, 38
Pokom, 22, 312
Popol Vuh, 2, 3, 12(n22), 19, 23(n36), 28, 32(nn54, 56), 35, 38(n69), 41(n80), 170(n115), 292, 314, 316
Poq'omam (group), 312(n28)
Poq'omchi' (group), 312(n28)
Postclassic period, 34, 40, 177(n129)
Prayer, Christian, 208(n170). *See also* Ritual speech
Preclassic period, 22
Predator and prey, 311, 313, 315
Princess (character), another name for "Mother of the Quetzal and the Green Feathers," 31, 298(n16)
Principal, 29, 295, 297, 298, 299, 310
Prison, 281, 289
Prisoner, as food, 138(n47), 146(n66), 168(n112), 310. *See also* Cannibalism; Captive; Capture; Sacrifice
Projectiles, 128(n15), 172(n120). *See also* Arrow; Spear
Prolepsis, 142(n53)
Pueblo Viejo-Chichaj, *20,* 30(n48)
Pueblo Viejo-Chixoy, 23, 36(n66)

Q'anajal. *See* Ekempek
Quanimaché, 295
Qubulahay. *See* Ikomak'i
Queen, 27, 34, 209(n171), 213(n179), 220(n191), 251(n212)
Quetzal *(Pharomachrus mocinno)*, 31, 32. *See also* Bird; Feather
Quetzaltenango, *20,* 21
Quiché (department), *8,* 38
Quiché Vinak (dance), 3, 4, 295, 297
Quiché-Achi (language), 12, 52
Q'umarkaj, 19, *20,* 21–22, 38–41, 286. *See also* Q'umarmachi; Utatlán
Q'umarmachi, 300, 306, 307(n25). *See also* Q'umarkaj; Utatlán
Q'uq'umatz (Quiché ruler), 21

Rabinal, *8, 20, 285, 286;* Acuña and Mace in, 14–15; ancient royalty in, 19, 27, 30,

33, 34, 291; archaeological investigations in, 22–23; basin of, 21–22, 24, 35, 42, 133(n32), 176(n128), 280, 283, 286, 288–290, 312; Brasseur in, 7, 9–11; dances of pre-Hispanic origin in, 5(n7); field research in, 48–49; kinship and marriage in, 35, 129(n17), 169(n114), 221(n193); municipality of, 18(n31); patronal feast of, 6; Quiché dialect of, 9, 12, 28; Ximénez in, 310
Rabinal Achi (character). *See* Warrior
Rabinalá, 282
Rabinaleb (group). *See* Kajyub; Rabinal; Tzamaneb
Rain: ancient Mayan divinities of, 30; associated with Job Toj, 124(n1); associated with the name Toj, 29(n46), 37–38, 41; ceremonies for, 29(n46), 283; and mountains, 184(n143)
Ravines, and the fortress, 167(n109), 191(n155)
Raxaj, 254
Raxchich, 23
Rebel, K'iche' Achi as, 300, 302. *See also* Chichimeca
Rebellion, of the Rabinaleb against the Quiché, 25, 37. *See also* Conflict
Relación de Zapotitlán, 22
Relación Tzutujil, 3
Relation des choses de Yucatan, 13(n25)
Repetition, 2, 42, 43, 45, 46. *See also* Discourse, reported; Parallelism
Representation: ancient indigenous system of, 2, 39, 299, 302, 310, 313, 317; of the *Rabinal Achi,* 5–6, 279, 301, 303; of sacrificial dances, 3
Resguardo, 41(n78)
Revolt, against K'iq'ab, 22
Rhetoric, 2, 12, 42, 45–46, 167(n107), 293
Ritual speech, 6, 42(n81), 44, 49, 127(n12), 170(n115)
Rituals. *See* Bleeding; Calendar; Dance; Dialogue; Discourse; Ritual speech; Sacrifice
Rotzjayib, 21. *See also* Wuqamaq'
Royalty, 19, 291, 302, 316; and war, 38
Ruins. *See* Desolation
Ruler. *See* King

Sacapulas, *20,* 21, 189(n152)
Sacred bundles, 299(n17)
Sacrifice, 38, 302; of a captive, 261(n222); Christian figure of, 6; clandestine practice of, 38(n70); founding, 299(n17), 301; and fertility, 37; of a man of high rank, 250(n212), 310; and tributes, 38. *See also* Cannibalism; Food; Sacrificial victims; *Temalacatl; Tzompantli*
Sacrificial victims, 168(n112), 310–311
Saint Paul: celebration of, 6; patron saint of Rabinal, 10. *See also* San Pablo
Saint Sebastian, celebration of, 6
San Agustín Acasaguastlán, *20,* 283
San Andrés Sajcabajá, *20,* 32(n55), 295
San Andrés Semetabaj, 296
San Carlos University of Guatemala, 18(n29)
San Cristóbal Verapaz, *20,* 185(n146), 312(n28)
San José Poaquil, *20,* 30(n48)
San Juan Comalapa, *20,* 30(n48)
San Martín Jilotepeque, *20,* 30(n48)
San Miguel Chicaj, *20,* 29(n45), 133(n32)
San Pablo (patron of Rabinal), 289(n6). *See also* Saint Paul
San Pedro Carchá, *20,* 32–33, 221(n193). *See also* Alta Verapaz; K'ekchi
San Sebastián Lemoa, *20,* 282
Sandals, 179(n136), 295, 303. *See also* Clothing
Santa Cruz del Quiché, *20,* 38, 282, *286*
Santa Rosa Chujuyub, *20,* 21
Santiago (patron of Cubulco), 284, 289(n6)
Santiago Atitlán, 132(n25)
Santísimo Sacramento del Altar, 29(n46), 299(n17). *See also* Achi Ajaw
Sapota tree (*Lucuma mammosa*), 284
Saq Tz'ikin, *281,* 282
Saqkijel, 177(n129), 180(n138), 280, 283, *285, 286,* 291, 303, 305; and Kajyub, 25(n40)
Scepter, 297. *See also* Insignia
Semuc Champey, 32(n54)
Servants. *See* Slaves
Settlement pattern, 191(n155)
Shield, 154(n86), 295. *See also* Weapons
Sic, Julian, 284
Sight: control through, 40(n77), 40–41, 255(n215)
Sis, Bartolo, 8–11, 13–17, 48, 126(nn10, 11), 131(n24)
Skull, 10, 39(n74), 287. *See also* Bone
Skunk, 142(n56)
Sky. *See* Earth; Navel
Slaves, 28, 33–34, 126(n9), 143(n57), 293
Son. *See* Children; Vassals
Sovereign. *See* Authority; Fortress; King
Space: of the action in the *Rabinal Achi,* 281–286; of the fortress, 186(n148); representa-

tions of, 302; and time, 181(n138), 304 (*see* Calendar)
Spanish (language), 51, 129(n19), 319
Spanish Colony, 39(n74), 283(n3)
Spanish Conquest, 4, 5, 10, 13(n25), 22, 36(n66), 38(n70), 312(n27)
Spanish missionaries, 4, 208(n170); Dominicans, 133(n32)
Spear, 128(n15), 267(n225). *See also* Weapons
Speech. *See* Dialogue; Discourse; Ritual speech
Squash (*Cucurbita*), 153(n83), 305, 306
Squier, Ephraïm, 9
Squirrel, 276(n229)
Steam bath, 145
Stick: of the backstrap loom, 219(n189); oneself with a tip or lancet, 156(n93); as a weapon, 132(n25), 266(n225)
Stone: as boundary mark, 296, 303; powder of, 132(n30); precious, 31, 125(n6), 132(n28), 266(n225) (*see* Feather); pumice, 145(n63); as a weapon, 172(n120)
Subjects. *See* Children; Vassals
Subsistence. *See* Food; Hunting
Sun, 10, 34, 167(n109), 299(n17). *See also* *Ajaw*; Day; Uitzilopochtli

Tecpán, *20*, 195(n158), 295, 297(n14)
Tecum Uman, 38(n68), 277(n230)
Temalacatl, 39(n74)
Tepescuintle. *See* Paca
Teponauaztli, 256(n216)
Tezulutlán, 133(n32)
Throne, 166(n106), 297, 299. *See also* Canopy; Dais
Tierra de guerra, 133(n32)
Tijax, as name of a day, 29. *See also* Ajaw Teken Toj Teken Tijax
Tinientes, 49
Título Cajcoj, 3, 25
Título Chajoma, 3, 30(n48)
Título C'oyoi, 3, 23(n36), 36, 133(n32)
Título de los Indios de Santa Clara La Laguna, 3
Título de los Señores de Totonicapán, 2, 3, 19, 23(n36), 32(n55), 41(n79), 292, 314
Título Nijaib III, 3
Títulos Xpantzay, 3, 138(n47)
Todos Santos Cuchumatán, *20*, 304(n24)
Toj. *See* Ajaw Teken Toj Teken Tijax
Tojil (Quiché god), 28, 38(n71)
Toltec, 19, 34, 132(n26). *See also* Epi-Toltec
Toponymy, 27, 32(n54), 40, 282–284
Totonicapán, *20*, 21. *See also* *Título de los Señores de Totonicapán*
Town. *See* Capital (town); City
Transition, from Tzamaneb to Kajyub, 291
Transmission, of the *Rabinal Achi*, 7, 10, 13, 17
Traveling, as a structural characteristic of the warrior, 295, 299, 303–304, 308–309. *See also* Journey
Tree, 35, 129(n17). *See also* Ant tree; Breadnut tree; Sapota tree
Tres Cruces, *281*, 282–284, *286*, 288–290, 295(n13). *See also* Tzamaneb
Tresillo, 15, 51, 312
Tribute, 22, 290, 295(n13); articles of, 31, 150(n75), 167(n109), 298. *See also* Cacao; Feather
Trompetas Tum (dance), 3
Trumpet, 3(n3), 156(n93), 180(n137), 287, 305. *See also* Bleeding; Drum; Music; Musical instruments
Tuhal. *See* Sacapulas
Tula, 19(n32), 33(n57), 39(n76)
Tum Teleche (dance), 3, 4, 261(n222),
Tun dance. *See* Dance: of the Tun
Tzacol Pitol (Quiché god), 24
Tzahachac, 282. *See also* Pan Tz'ajachaq
Tzam Ja, 280, 284, 290
Tzam Q'am Karcha, 31–32. *See also* San Pedro Carchá
Tzamaneb, *20*, *281*, *286*, 287; archaeological identification of, 30; destruction of, 291; as first capital of the Rabinaleb, 21, 24, 30, 313; and Kajyub, 25, 290–292, 298, 314, 316; and regional toponymy, 283, 286, 303; and the Uxab-Poq'omab, 42, 48. *See also* Tres Cruces
Tz'aq Poq'om. *See* Chwitinamit
Tzeltal, 35(n62), 42(n82), 212(n178)
Tz'iquin (Quiché ruler). *See* E'
Tzompantli, 39(n74)
Tzotzil. *See* Tzeltal
Tzutujil (group), 19, 21
Tzutujil (language), 220(n191)

U Chuch Q'uq' u Chuch Raxon (character), 31
Uitzilopochtli, 277(n230)
Uleutum (dance), 3
Underworld. *See* Xibalbá
UNESCO, 18(n31)
Uspantán, *20*, 36(n66), 311
Usumacinta (river), 19, 32(n55)
Utatlán, 23, 25, 36(n66), 282, 287, 289. *See also* Q'umarkaj; Q'umarmachi
Uxa, 24

Vassals, 23, 30. *See also* Children
Velación de la máscaras, 49
Verse: in the *Rabinal Achi,* 13, 43; rhythm of, 12; parallel, 43–45, 53
Victims. *See* Sacrificial victims
Violence, in Rabinal (1979–1985), 49
Virility. *See* Warrior

War, 22, 132(n25), 287, 311, 315, 316; for capture, 134(n35), 138(n47), 146(n66), 168(n112), 296, 310; chief, 30; dances, 4, 133(n32); holy, 310–311; and peace, 314; and royalty, 38. *See also* Battle; Conflict; Expedition; Fight; Sacrificial victims; Warrior
Warrior, 4, 10, 19, 30, 34, 39, 221; characteristics of, 130(n22), 183(n141), 276(n229), 291(n8); dances, 3–4; defeated, 276–277(nn230, 231); domain of, 303; figure of, 292–297, 308; as a hunter and kidnapper, 289(n6), 291, 310–311, 313; and king, 291–292, 297, 299–302, 307, 316. *See also* Eagle; Garrison; Jaguar
Wasps, 314. *See also* Bees; Insect
Weapons, 26, 132(nn25, 30), 155(n86), 263(n223), 295, 296. *See also* Arrow; Ax; Bow; Shield; Spear
Weasel, 142(n56)
Weaving, 132(n29), 219(n190)
West. *See* East
White sapote (*Casimiroa edulis*), 283
Wildcat. *See* Agouti
Wind. *See* Cold; Danger
Wishes, 196(n159); final, 251(n212)
Woman, 35, 143(n57), 168(n114), 220(n191); K'ekchi, 31–34, 221(n193). *See also* Alliance, matrimonial; Kinship; Queen
World, 35, 39, 43, 170(n115), 181(n138), 187(n150), 295, 304. *See also* Center; Corners; Navel
Wuqamaq' (group), 21, 133(n32)

Xajoj Tun (dance), 3, 9(n14), 10, 14
Xbalanqué. *See* Hunahpu
Xeknup, *281,* 284
Xibalbá, 32(n54)
Ximbaja, 180(n138), 280, 283, *285, 286,* 303
Xol Chaqaj, 280, 282, *286,* 287
Xolchiaqaj, 282. *See also* Xol Chaqaj
Xolop, Esteban, 13, 15, 18, 29(n45), 47, 49(nn93, 94)
Xolop, Eugenio, 16(n27), 18(n30), 48(n92)
Xolop, María, 18, 49
Xoq'ojaw (character), 34, 209(n171), 213(n179). *See also Ajaw;* Queen
Xoyabaj, 30. *See also* Joyabaj

Yaki, 28, 36, 45, 124–125(n2), 132(n26). *See also* Chajul; Cunen
Yegua Achi, 4, 295(n13)
Yew Achi, 4, 289(n6), 295(n13), 316
Yucatán, 19, 21, 312(n27). *See also Relation des choses de Yucatan*
Yucatecan Maya, 2, 13(n25), 218(n185)

Zacquila, 295
Zacualpa, *20,* 185(n146), 284, *286,* 289
Ziz, Bartolo. *See* Sis, Bartolo
Zompopo, 163(n101), 301. *See also* Ants